For my old friends
Simon Manclark, Chris Bellia and
Penny Fuller

Contents

Figures

Tables

Foreword

In less than thirty years the study of football has been transformed from a marginal curiosity – the preserve of journalists, fans and antiquarians – to an area of major academic interest. In part, this is a reflection of the transformation in sports history in general, in part, a reflection of the changing patterns of history itself. What, not too long ago, seemed unimportant and even frivolous has become a subject of major intellectual scrutiny. In the process, the sheer volume of print devoted to each and every aspect of the game of football (in all its forms) is staggering. Recent bibliographies of football and sports history are themselves voluminous. The reasons for this remarkable shift are not hard to find.

First, football itself has come to occupy a central position in contemporary popular culture, driven forward by major global commercial pressures, and spread into all corners of the world by ubiquitous televised coverage. A game which was once located primarily in its European and South American heartlands is now avidly followed the world over. Second, the rise of the modern game raises perplexing questions about recent changes in cultural and economic patterns, which have attracted a range of scholars in the arts and social sciences. Football has, in brief, become a focus for major interdisciplinary scholarly work. There has, in addition, been an erosion of the intellectual (but more especially the academic) barriers which once kept the study of football (and other sports at arm's length). Old intellectual prejudices have simply collapsed under pressure from a new historiography, and all that within a generation. In part, this has been a result of the changes in higher education, and the redefining of academic studies. What once seemed too popular, too vulgar even, is now viewed as central and attractive.

What has been equally striking in the recent writing about football has been the ability of younger scholars to find something new to say about what seemed a clear and undisputed subject. It was sometimes hard to imagine what more could be said about the game – its history and sociology – which had not already been discussed. Of course, the continuing interest in the game is also a function of a new generation of scholars feeling unhappy with, and not persuaded by, the work of their predecessors. This is, of course, a familiar pattern in other areas of historical research. The book which follows, however, has claims to be more important than merely disagreeing with earlier writers in the field. Adrian Harvey's study is a fundamental and revisionary reappraisal of the widely accepted knowledge of the early history of football in Britain. It challenges much of what we accept about the way football emerged.

First, it is a major study rooted in imaginative and painstaking research in materials which others have barely touched. The wide range of data which the author assembles to support his arguments will, in itself, prove invaluable for subsequent scholars in the field. More important however is the way Harvey takes the basic assumptions of earlier historians, and subjects them to critical scrutiny. Harvey does that by testing those assumptions against detailed historical evidence. Where once we had persuasive generalisations, Harvey offers us specific argument, rooted in painstaking research. The end result is a challenge to prevailing academic orthodoxy. Indeed this book provides a series of interrelated challenges to some of the most widely accepted views about popular culture in the nineteenth century, disputing for example assumptions about public school influence, and about the nature of plebeian football. It is, in sum, a book of major importance which will set a new agenda for all historians interested in the history of the people's game.

James Walvin
Professor of History
University of York

Series editors' foreword

There are many untold football stories.[1] This is an important one, and it will be followed shortly in the series Sport in the Global Society by two more untold stories: *Soccer's Missing Men: Schoolmasters and the Spread of Association Football*[2] and *A Social History of Indian Football.*[3]

Some will consider that the title of this original study suggests more than it delivers and indeed an exegesis of the hitherto undisclosed early moments of modern football in all its varied forms and variant locations in one volume is an impossibly gargantuan task. However, a firm step backwards onto British fields rather than a bold step forward onto foreign fields allows a proper appreciation of this contribution to the history of the game, albeit regional rather than global.

Metaphorically it is a journey on a stop and start district line train rather than a non-stop mainline express and thus opens up new vistas to the traveller more accustomed to well-frequented routes.

New opinions, John Locke once wrote sententiously, tend to be suspected and usually opposed, without any reason other than the fact that they are not already commonplace.[4] As far as we are concerned, Locke, in this case, is well wide of the mark. We are more than content to press the merits of this igneous football 'incendium'.

Nevertheless, it remains the case that for a good part of its first one hundred years and certainly well back into the late nineteenth century, football, especially association football, was much more than just a British game. And it is a truism today to state that for many in the modern global village the game has become much more than a game. In view of its contemporary political, economic and cultural importance the historical roots of the game demand careful exhumation.

Reconstruction of this now massively mass sport has been too frequently a past conceit that has depended too much on a too prevalent assertion that modern football had its origins on the expensive and extensive playing fields of the nineteenth-century public schools.[5] There has been a corresponding inclination to narrowly locate the matrix of modern football in the English public school. There is an exigent need for historians to probe the cliché and to dig for other roots of the game in popular culture at home and abroad. Harvey is doing this for Britain; others are doing it elsewhere.[6]

In an imperial and post-imperial setting, for example, attention is now firmly focused as much on the frequently purposeful assimilation by the indigene as the often well-meaning dissemination of the imperialist. Due to a (happy)[7] accident of history much of modern sport owes its earliest origins,[8] but not its later evolution, to the late nineteenth-century Anglo-Saxon imperialist. But even in imperial South Asia, for example, soccer was the early tool for the assertion of a distinctive South Asian identity, the expression of a defiant nationalism and a source of anti-imperial bonding. Until now subsequent post-imperial indigenisation has been largely an untold story.

Modern football is an offspring now claimed by the entire world; England gave it birth; early in its first hundred years it was already a multi-cultural child. Thus, the history of modern football is the history of cultures. Harvey attempts in one cultural setting to weave the microcosmic into the macrocosmic; future global attempts will reveal further cultural variations associated with football within the global village and produce illustrations of the subtle relations between them. Sometime ago, James Walvin suggested that more emphasis needed to be placed on local studies without losing sight of the broader context,[9] and added that general structures, of course, had their place but they needed to be subjected, and inevitably would be subjected, to the qualifications of specific and local peculiarities.[10] Harvey has proved Walvin right. Others are hard on his heels.

J. A. Mangan and Boria Majumdar
Swanage and Calcutta
November 2004

Notes

1 One to appear in the future, for example, will be an untold story entitled *The Making of Association Football: A Sociological History of the Peoples' Game* by Eric Dunning and Graham Curry. It also deals in part with the early origins of modern football from a new perspective. It is in preparation.
2 Colm Hickey and J. A. Mangan, *Soccer's Missing Men: Schoolteachers and the Spread of Association Football*, forthcoming as a Special Number of *Soccer and Society* and as a planned Spin Off volume in the series Sport in the Global Society.
3 Boria Majumdar and Kausik Bandopadhyay, *A Social History of Indian Football*, forthcoming as a Special Number of *Soccer and Society* and as a planned Spin Off volume in the series Sport in the Global Society.
4 *The Oxford Book of Quotations* (Oxford: OUP, 1996, Fourth Edition) p. 424.
5 See chapter 4 of J. A. Mangan's *Athleticism in the Victorian and Edwardian Public School: The Emergence and Consolidation of an Educational Ideology* (London: Cass, 2000, New Edition) for a discussion of the extent and expense of a sample of public school playing fields.
6 Majumdar and Bandopadhyay are a topical example. See note 3.
7 In view of the state of modern association football, especially in Britain, some may well consider the use of the term infelicitous.
8 For imperial illustrations, see J. A. Mangan, *The Games Ethic and Imperialism: Aspects of the Diffusion of an Ideal* (London: Cass, 1998).
9 James Walvin, 'Sport, Social History and the Historian', *The British Journal of Sports History*, 1:1 (1984) p. 10.
10 Ibid.

Preface

The roots of this book stemmed from a reference that I chanced upon in an issue from 1841 of the Victorian newspaper *Bell's Life in London*. I was interested in Victorian chess and as *Bell's* contained one of the earliest and most informative chess columns from the period, it was a natural source for me to consult. However, the fragment that caught my eye, tucked away at the very bottom of the chess column, had nothing to do with the 'royal game' – as chess's advocates were inclined to title it, but rather to what would later become known as 'the beautiful game' – football. I was surprised to see such a reference because I knew that according to the established history of football by the 1840s the old 'mob' game of football had long since become extinct and the new, modern, codified, variety had yet to be transplanted from the public schools to the wider population. However, the teams that I had just uncovered had certainly nothing to do with the privileged confines of the public schools, for they were servants who worked in Edinburgh's hotels. Clearly, such people did not fit into the established histories of football. Where, then, did these players belong? From that time forth I began to look for references to football in early Victorian newspapers and while they were by no means copious it was quite clear that the established view of the game required some modification. The product of my research formed the core of my MA dissertation in Victorian Studies at Birkbeck College in 1990, a work that was examined by Professor Roy Foster and Professor Asa Briggs. At that stage I was still inclined to accept many aspects of the established history of football, particularly the role of the public schools in the creation of the modern game. In 1991, after an examination of the archives of one of the earliest football clubs, Sheffield, I began to realise that the role of the public schools in the creation of modern football had been severely exaggerated. Since then I have expanded my research and the product of my findings can be found in this book.

Preface

Acknowledgements

While this book is almost entirely the product of my own research (on the occasions when I am indebted to the work of others such facts are gratefully acknowledged). I owe the following people thanks for making material available to me: David Barber (Football Association Library), Rex King (Rugby Football Union Library). Both these gentlemen were kind enough to help me decipher difficult words and I am especially grateful to the former for his kindness and patience which enabled me to present the enclosed photographs from the FA minute book. I am particularly grateful to Professor Eric Dunning and Dr Kenneth Sheard for being so sporting as to give me permission to reproduce a table from their book, *Barbarians, Gentlemen and Players*, even though they were aware that my views were critical of those that they adhered to. I am indebted to the co-operation of the staff of the following libraries: Bodleian Library, British Library, British Newspaper Library (notably Robin Dansie), Ewart Library Dumfries, Sheffield City Archives, Stirling Central Library. The archivists of the following public schools were very helpful: S. A. Wheeler (Charterhouse), P. Hatfield (Eton), A. Hawkyard (Harrow), J. Field (Westminster), S. Bailey and R. Custance (Winchester). The only public school that did not reply to my letters was Rugby. While undertaking my DPhil at Nuffield College, Oxford University, I discussed some of the themes that were later to appear in this book with my supervisor John Stevenson and my College supervisor John Goldthorpe. As for the text itself, I am very grateful to Nancy Brownlow whose suggestions improved it considerably. I would like to record my gratitude to the following people who were involved in the publication of this book: Samantha Grant, Vicky Johnson, Kate Manson, Jon Manley, Allison Scott, S. Swarnalatha, Antony Vincent, Professor James Walvin, Pat Wemyss and Professor Gareth Williams. I am also grateful for the assistance rendered by many other people, such as Geoff Hare, Val Hubbard of Leicester University, William Bell and Regina Drabble of Sheffield council, Piers Morgan and Laura Steadman of the Rugby Football Union, Robert Hendley and Derrick Harvey, the staff of three of my local libraries: Grahame Park, Kingsbury and Mollison Way, who enabled me to contact various people and organisations via email. I am especially grateful to Robert Hendley who was kind enough to take a great deal of trouble in photographing extracts from the FA minute books and advising me on the best way of presenting illustrations. I would like to thank the

British Library for granting me permission to publish the illustrations within the book and the Football Association for permitting me to publish photographs of their minute book for 1863.

On a personal level I would like to tender my thanks to the staff in the Dryden ward of Northwick Park Hospital, the place to which I was admitted for treatment in March 2002. At the time I was unable to walk and largely oblivious to what was going on around me. I was diagnosed with multiple sclerosis but made a most remarkable recovery, being discharged after a mere two-and-a-half weeks in hospital. I am in no doubt at all that this was due in no small measure to the kindness and care of the staff. Additionally, of course, the strong support of my family facilitated this recovery. Essentially speaking, this book is due to the kindness of the hospital staff and my family, without whom I would have been in no state to write it. Of course, I still have some problems but realise that things could have been much worse and tender my thanks accordingly.

Introduction

Waiting for kick-off

Both the varieties of football that originally hailed from Britain, the Rugby and Association games, have probably never been as popular as they are now. The association game, or soccer as it has become generally known, is now almost globally popular and judging by the last few World Cups, before long a team from Asia, Africa or North America will go on to win the trophy. Rugby's progress has been less dramatic but the game is becoming increasingly international and is surely destined to continue to expand. Of course, periodically it is likely that both varieties of football will be afflicted by problems stemming from a downturn in the world economy and difficulties generated by financial mismanagement. Collectively, however, their future appears bright. Peculiarly enough, despite this very little is known about the origins of modern football and many questions relating to its growth and development remain unanswered.

Football is a very old game, especially in Britain. Why, then, did it not become a major commercial sport until the final quarter of the nineteenth century? By then, many other sports in Britain, notably horse racing, cricket and boxing, had long been major commercial enterprises, consisting of hugely popular contests involving professional competitors and watched by thousands of spectators. Why, then, was football so slow in developing into a major commercial industry? Indeed, given this, why did football develop into a commercial industry at all? The explanation offered by the early historians of the game was that football only became popular because boys from public schools took the rough, wild and undisciplined game that had existed for hundreds of years in the wider community and codified it. These new laws transformed football into a popular game by making it accessible to a mass public. Such is the established picture of the origins of modern football.

Yet was any of this true? Football certainly became codified in the latter half of the nineteenth century. Indeed, it became so codified that it split into two games, rugby and soccer, whose relationship was often uneasy at best. But who actually created these football games? Who turned them into commercial sports? In the case of the rugby game, the rules hailed from the public school that gave its name to the sport, though as we shall see other forces did much to transform aspects of the code. While the rules of soccer have always been credited to the public schools, in actual fact they sprang from many sources and were modified significantly. One of the major sources of these transformations was the football culture that emerged in Sheffield during the 1850s. With regard to football as a commercial sport, in the final quarter of the nineteenth century there was a significant divergence between rugby and soccer, especially over the issue of professionalism. The effect of professionalism on the rugby game was dramatic. In 1895 those adhering to attitudes stemming from the public schools opposed professionalism and this led to the rugby code splitting into two rival camps. By contrast, the commercial dimension of soccer emerged more steadily and was accommodated by those who stemmed from public school backgrounds, many of whom went on to perform vital roles, notably as administrators.

The following book is an attempt to provide the real story of the evolution of both major football codes: rugby and soccer. Much of the story has never been previously told, not least because most of the early historians of the game, almost all of whom were former public school boys, had little or no interest in events outside the confines of such privileged walls. This study attempts to redress the balance by using contemporary sources to uncover the real truth of the first hundred years of modern football.

The book consists of the following chapters. In Chapter 1, we consider the football that was conducted on Shrove Tuesday, a variant that was often rough and wild and popularly regarded as the earliest variety of the game. In Chapters 2 and 3 we consider more regularly occurring contests, first those conducted in public schools and then in the wider community. Chapter 4 details the earliest modern football culture, that of Sheffield, a place that can plausibly be regarded as inventing modern soccer. Chapters 5, 6 and 7 are concerned with the growth of football in the rest of the country, especially the emergence of administrative bodies such as the Football Association (FA) and the Rugby Football Union (RFU). In Chapter 8 we survey the growth of league and cup competitions and the strain that the increasing commercial element placed upon the administrative structure.

1 What football was not

The history of Shrove-football

Almost everyone who has the least knowledge of football has a very clear idea of what the game looked like in the pre-industrial era. The picture that they will present is extremely graphic, and features a large indistinguishable mob wrestling for the ball. Such a contest is 'a free-for-all', without rules, contested by unlimited numbers who are able to deploy every ounce of their strength and guile in an effort to drive the ball into their opponents' goal.[1] Predominantly, the game occurs on annual holidays, particularly Shrove Tuesday, and is regarded as descending from an ancient popular custom. Reports of such events are very well known and for many people this represents the only form of football that was practised in the period previous to the dissemination of the codified variety that was created in the English public schools of the nineteenth century.

Although the above view is very common, it is erroneous, and this book is *not* about Shrove-football. While the mêlées that we know as Shrove-football certainly did occur – indeed, they *still* do occur in a few places – football is a much older game than the Shrove-variety, and for at least 300 years matches have been occurring between teams made up of equal numbers of players, often consisting of fewer than ten people on each side.[2] While such games attracted altogether less attention than the picturesque conflicts that occurred on Shrove Tuesday, they were probably far more common than those annual struggles. It is these games, contested by even numbers on each side and regulated by rules, that form the bulk of the subject matter in this book, and as the author will argue, such games can plausibly be seen as the ancestors of the varieties of football, both association and rugby, that became so popular in the latter part of the nineteenth century and are such large commercial industries today.

Given the above preamble the reader might expect this opening chapter to come to an abrupt end. However, while the Shrove-game has little to contribute to the evolution of the rules of football, it is of considerable relevance to an issue that is intimately related to the game's history, namely, the attitude of the authorities towards popular recreation, and it is this subject that forms the substance of Chapter 1. This chapter will examine three related issues. First, we shall consider an influential thesis which maintains that between 1750 and 1850 the scope of attacks on popular sports was so severe that by 1850 the recreational world of the labouring population was a vacuum. Having accomplished this we will then turn to an assessment as to whether Shrove-football was enjoying growth or suffering decline during the nineteenth century. Finally, we will consider the varying fortunes of Shrove-games in order to gain an insight into the forces that were influencing popular recreational culture during the nineteenth century. It is now time to turn to the first part of our study, an examination of the view that popular recreations suffered a severe attack during the period 1750–1850.

The fate of popular recreations between 1750 and 1850

Many historians have claimed that in the years between 1750 and 1850 the recreational activities of the lower orders declined sharply, due largely to the increased application of commercial expertise, in both agriculture and industry. Broadly speaking, they claim that these developments affected the working population in five ways. In the first place, the local gentry, who had often sponsored the labouring population's sports and games, were discouraged from doing so by critics, many of whom were motivated by strong Evangelical religious beliefs, who highlighted the immorality and disorder that stemmed from such recreations. This removed much of the upper-class patronage and protection of the lower orders' sport. Second, concern over the disruption caused to commerce by the recreational practices of the lower orders prompted mercantile interests to introduce legislation to curb such activities and an efficient body to enforce these laws. The application of such legislation eliminated many recreations by rendering them illegal. Third, the practice of enclosures, whereby common land was seized and agriculture rationalised, meant that many of the population were forced to leave the countryside, where there was an abundance of potential areas in which they could pursue recreation, and move to the newly expanding cities, in which there was very little open space. Fourth, the working hours of the labouring population increased substantially, particularly for those who left the land and found employment in factories, thus depriving them of time in which they could pursue recreation. Finally, the general standard of living, in terms of the capacity of wages to purchase food and accommodation, fell, thus resulting in a decline in both the disposable income and the health and energy of the labouring population.[3] Cumulatively, according to Malcolmson, these developments meant that during the first half of the nineteenth century the newly urbanised labouring population confronted a recreational 'vacuum' that would only be replaced in the years after 1850.[4] As he says: 'Much of the rural past had to be set aside, and most of the migrants discovered that the expanding urban centres had, as yet, only an extremely restricted recreational culture to put in its place'.[5] The recreational vacuum that had been created by the steady erosion of the sports that were available to the labouring classes was eventually filled by the widespread dissemination of sports that had been refined by the upper and middle classes in public schools, most notably football. Whereas the popular sports, typified by Shrove-football, had been governed by few, if any, rules, the new versions of the games were carefully regulated by codes of law, as with the rugby and association versions of football. In addition to this, these newly codified sports were eventually transformed into commercial industries based upon the revenue generated by spectators. As Harrison writes: 'the problem of leisure in an industrial society was solved through codifying sporting rules, which saved both time and space: through catering for spectator sports, which facilitated vicarious athleticism'.[6] In essence, the anarchical struggles of the Shrove-game, in which anyone could participate, were replaced by the carefully regulated football match where the experience of the vast majority was limited to spectating. Most historians maintain that it took some time for this commercial sporting industry to develop, the general consensus being that it appeared in the 1870s and 1880s.[7]

Having set out the above argument and the five assumptions that underpin it, we must now assess whether such a thesis is supported by the evidence. We begin by considering the first contention, the extent to which criticism dissuaded the gentry from supporting and sponsoring popular recreations, and the significance of such a withdrawal of patronage. An examination of the evidence indicates that the gentry were largely uninfluenced by criticism of their support of popular recreations. More importantly, from at least the 1790s other more commercially oriented sponsors, most notably publicans, had been creating and organising sport for the labouring classes and as a consequence of this, the role of the gentry in promoting such activities for the lower orders experienced a natural decline.[8] With reference to the second assumption of the thesis, that the appearance of a series of new laws on the statute resulted in popular recreations being declared illegal and consequently suppressed, it is noticeable that until at least the 1830s there is almost no evidence of this. Indeed, many activities, including blood sports such as prizefighting and bull-baiting, remained quite legal for much of this period.[9] The general attitude of the law towards recreations can be summed up by the statement of the foremost Scottish justice:

> assemblages for purposes no wise illegal, though sometimes contrary to morals, as foot-ball, racing, cock-fighting etc, when the purposes of the meeting are not public disturbances or the accomplishment of any violent and illegal objects, do not fall under 'the offense of mobbing and rioting'.[10]

Additionally, a significant factor in discouraging the authorities from intervening against popular recreations was the lack of an efficient police force. The Metropolitan police was established as the model for an efficient force in 1829 but local authorities were slow to adopt their practices and it was not until 1857 that they were introduced nationally.[11] In consequence of this, although the law gradually changed, with various acts being introduced, notably those attacking cruel sports in 1835 and 1849, their impact was often diluted by the attitude and resources of local authorities, facts which ensured that many nominally illegal activities persisted. In view of this, it appears that the effect of legislation on popular sports has been substantially overrated. The third point made by advocates of the view that popular recreations were being eroded during the first half of the nineteenth century relates to the impact of enclosures and the migration of the population from rural to urban areas. This, they contend, deprived the lower orders of the space in which to play. Chronologically, the thesis is undermined by the fact that the structure of the English village was transformed long before 1700, by which time 75 per cent of all land enclosures had occurred.[12] In essence, the most drastic changes had long preceded 1700. As for the newly urbanised population, some efforts were being made to provide them with recreational areas. While the bill creating public walks stated that 'no athletic games or sports be permitted', provision was to be made for playgrounds 'suitable for gymnastic exercises', with only boxing, wrestling and animal baiting being excluded.[13] However, in large measure, the efforts to promote recreational areas by both government and local authorities were limited in their impact and while the effect of the migration of the population from rural to urban areas was probably considerably less than envisaged by scholars such as Malcolmson, it is clear that recreational space was a problem in some urban areas.[14] The fourth assumption of those advocating a decline in the recreational opportunities of the labouring population emphasises the effect of the increased working hours of factory employees as compared to agricultural labourers. It seems likely, however, that this has been severely exaggerated, for while the evidence is often fairly sketchy, it appears that there was little difference between the hours worked by industrial and agricultural workers.[15] Additionally, substantial evidence exists to demonstrate that many old work routines persisted within urban industrial areas, and that the hours worked in factories rose neither dramatically nor steadily.[16] As for the final point, the decline in the standard of living of the labouring population between 1750 and 1850, although limited information means that historians depend on 'controlled conjectures rather than very firm evidence', there is a general consensus that after 1830 the standard of living of the lower orders improved, though the picture for the preceding decades is mixed.[17]

As we can see from the above there is little to support the contention that changes in the social and economic circumstances of the labouring population led to a decline in their access to recreations in the period between 1750 and 1850.[18] Having accomplished this, we must now consider the second part of the chapter, an examination of the fate of Shrove-football during this period.

Shrove-football in the nineteenth century

The prevailing view amongst historians is that Shrove-football suffered a significant decline during the nineteenth century and this is often presented as embodying industrial societies' erosion of traditional popular culture.[19] Magoun, the foremost researcher into Shrove-football is in no doubt concerning the reasons behind the game's decline and writes:

> decline in Shrove Tuesday football seems to have been due in large measure to its official suppression as leading to breach of the peace; also its play on public highways often led to an intolerable interference with the increasing road traffic of the later nineteenth century.[20]

Malcolmson expands this view considerably, detailing the pressure, in terms of both laws and criticism, that was brought to bear against Shrove-football and more informally organised versions of the game.[21] Unquestionably, laws were deployed against football at both national and local levels. An example of the former was a bill in 1831 that specified that anyone who should 'play at football, tennis, fives, cricket or any other games upon any highway or on the sides thereof' would be fined forty shillings.[22] Local authorities also discouraged the game, as in 1801, when the magistrates at Fulwood (Preston) ordered the constables and church wardens to prosecute anyone indulging in the 'common practice of leaping, playing at football, quoits, bowls and many other unlawful games' on Sunday, with offenders being fined three shillings and four pence or placed in the stocks for three hours.[23] Likewise, there are many examples of critics endeavouring to undermine the game by presenting counter attractions. An example of this occurred on Maudlin Sunday in August 1820, when local Primitive Methodists attempted to undermine the rowdy annual football match between the Yorkshire villages of Preston and Hedon, by holding a camp meeting on a nearby hill, consisting of preaching, prayer, tea drinking and gentler recreations, such as the singing of hymns.[24] As the nineteenth century progressed, the enemies of Shrove-football in a number of places in Britain endeavoured to suppress the game entirely by deploying the newly established police force against it, most notably at Richmond in 1840. While, as we shall see, such examples could be easily multiplied, it is a long way from establishing that there was a generalised attack on Shrove-football, let alone that the game suffered a general decline in the nineteenth century. Indeed, as Tables 1.1–1.3 demonstrate, Shrove-football expanded during the period.

Table 1.1 lists the venues in which Shrove and other festival football games were held from 1533, when the first mention of such a game occurs, through to 1799. Throughout this entire period such games are only found at twenty venues. As can be seen, the number of games increases as the centuries progress, there being over four times as many in the eighteenth century as there were in the sixteenth. To an extent, of course, this might simply be a reflection of the amount of available source material, but given the comparative copiousness of the chronicles from the sixteenth century it appears unlikely that this would explain the disparity entirely.

At first sight, Table 1.2, which lists the Shrove-games that were subjected to official pressure, appears to substantiate dramatically the views of those scholars who maintain that popular recreations, typified by traditional football, suffered an intense attack during the nineteenth century. Of the eleven games listed, eight were suppressed and three forced to move. However, such figures should not be dealt with in isolation. Table 1.3 lists every Shrove-game that was not subjected to decisive attack by either local or national officials during the nineteenth century. Indeed, only three of them encountered any official pressure whatsoever, and in no case was this successful. Of the thirty-five games in Table 1.3, eighteen died of natural causes between 1800 and 1879 and a further six did likewise between 1880 and 1900, while the games that were practised in

Table 1.1 The venues of festival football games, both Shrove and other varieties previous to 1800[a]

Venue	*Sixteenth century*	*Seventeenth century*	*Eighteenth century*
Alnwick (1788)			x
Ashbourne (1683)		x	x
Bristol (1660)		x	
Bromfield (1799)			x
Chester (1533–40)	x		
Corfe Castle (1551–1887)	x	x	x
Derby (1746–1846)			x
Devonshire (1785)			x
Duns (1724)			x
Glasgow (1573–1609)	x	x	
Hawick (1760)			x
Inveresk (1795)			x
Jedburgh (1704)			x
Kingston-upon-Thames (1790)			x
Kirkmichael (1795)			x
London (1642)		x	
Oxford (1622–23)		x	
Seascale (1770)			x
Shrewsbury (1601–03)		x	
Workington (1797)			x
Total venues per century	03	07	14

Notes

a F. Magoun, *History of Football: From the Beginnings to 1871*, pp. 101–2. It may well be that additions need to be made to this list. For instance, judging by a report of a Shrove-match at Sedgefield in *The Sporting Magazine* February 1802, p. 348, the game there may well stem from the eighteenth century. However, the author has been unable to uncover earlier references. The Easter game at Workington is not mentioned by Magoun but is referred to in *N&Q* 10th series vol. 1 (January–June 1904) pp. 194, 230, where it was first mentioned in 1797 and as possibly continuing into the twentieth century. See also *The Sporting Magazine* May 1802, p. 114. An annual match was conducted on Christmas Day at Kirkham but aside from the fact that it appears to have died out by 1874 we have no information on the dates when it was extant. In consequence of this it has been excluded from the study. H. Fishwick, *The History of the Parish of Kirkham in the County of Lancaster* (Rochdale: Cheetham Society, 1874) p. 206.

x The presence of a game during the century.

eleven locations during the nineteenth century survived into the twentieth.[25] Cumulatively, throughout the nineteenth century Shrove-football was played at forty-six locations. Not only is this three times as many as in the eighteenth century, but double that of the entire period 1533–1799. Put in these terms, far from suffering a drastic decline, Shrove-football enjoyed a general growth during the nineteenth century. However, we must not overlook the effect of official pressure, which resulted in eleven of the forty-six Shrove-games, that is almost 25 per cent, being either suppressed or moved. These figures become still more significant when we limit our study to those Shrove-games that were active between 1800 and 1873. During that period there were a total of twenty-six that

Table 1.2 A list of the games that either disappeared or moved due to attack between 1800 and 1900[a]

Year	*Initial location of game*	*Moved to*	*Moved to*
1820–29	Beverley (1825 s.)	Alnwick (1828)	
1840–49	Richmond (1840 s.)	Twickenham (1840)	Derby (1846 s.)
	Leicester (1847 s.)		
1850–59	East Mousley (1857 s.)		
1860–69	Ashbourne (1862)	Hampton (1864 s.)	Kingston-upon-Thames (1866 s.)
1870–79	Hampton Wick (1873 s.)		

Notes

If the game was suppressed it has an s. All others had their locations moved.

a F. Magoun, *History of Football: From the Beginnings to 1871*, pp. 102–3. R. Storch, 'The policeman as domestic missionary: urban discipline and popular culture in Northern England 1850–80', *Journal of Social History* 9:4 (1976) p. 492.

Table 1.3 A list of the decades in which traditional football games ended without being subjected to pressure[a]

1800–09	South Cardiganshire (1800s)		
1810–19	Bushey Park (1815)	Teddington (1815)	
1820–29	Wigtown (1826)		
1830–39	South Wales (1830s)	Scone (1835)	Atherstone (1839)
1840–49	Hawick (1842)		
1850–59	Camptown (1857)	Newport Pagnall (1858)	Laxton (1850s)
1860–69	Epsom (1862)	Melrose (1866)	Rothbury (1867)
	Thames Ditton (1867)		
1870–79	Stoneyhurst (1870s)	Kirkham (1874)	Whitby (1876)
1880–1900	Scarborough (1886)	Chester-le-Street (1887)	Corfe Castle (1887)
	Ilderton (1889)	Duns (1896)	Dorking (1897)
After 1900	Fumuckirk	Jedburgh	Kirkwall
	Keighley	Pembrokeshire	Sedgefield
	Skipton	Whitehaven	Wooler
	Workington	Yetholm	

Note

a *Bell's Life in London* 17 February 1839. *Edinburgh Evening News* 19 February 1910. H. Hutchinson, 'Evolution of games at ball', *Blackwoods* vol. 153 (1893) pp. 758–9. J. Lowerson and J. Myerscough, *Time to Spare in Victorian England* (London: Harvester Press, 1972) p. 119. F. Magoun, *History of Football: From the Beginnings to 1871*, pp. 101–2. *Midland Sporting Chronicle and National Register of Sports*, 25 February 1853. *Yorkshire Post*, 19 February 1896.

were not subjected to decisive attack: Atherstone, Bushey Park, Camptown, Corfe Castle, Dorking, Duns, Epsom, Hawick, Jedburgh, Laxton, Melrose, Newport Pagnall, Rothbury, Scarborough, Scone, Sedgefield, Skipton, South Cardiganshire, South Wales, Stoneyhurst, Teddington, Thames Ditton, Whitehaven, Wigtown, Wooler, Workington. Seen in this light, the eleven games that were decisively affected by official pressure become considerably more important, for they amount to almost a third of the thirty-seven games that were held on Shrove Tuesday throughout Britain. Obviously, this shows that the experience of Shrove-games differed profoundly during the nineteenth century and in the third and final part of the chapter we will examine the reasons behind this.

The factors which influenced Shrove-football games during the nineteenth century

In this, the third and final part of the chapter, we will consider the key elements that determined the fate of an area's Shrove-game. This study will consist of three sections. In the first section we will provide an overview of the diversity of Shrove-games. Section two will involve a detailed consideration of three Shrove-games, those at Derby, Kingston-upon-Thames and Ashbourne. Finally, in section three, we will provide a broad examination of the various factors that determined the fate of a Shrove-game.

Diversity of Shrove-games

We begin with our first section, an examination of the diversity of Shrove-games. Although it was once believed that Shrove-football was a survival from a pagan celebration, Magoun has established that the game was of far more recent invention, appearing over 200 years after the first mention of ordinary football.[26] As to the individual Shrove-games themselves, in the nineteenth century only two, Corfe Castle (started 1551) and Ashbourne (1683), could truthfully claim a lineage exceeding 100 years, the rest being of far more recent origin. Naturally, this did not prevent their supporters from claiming a great antiquity for their particular game. In this, they were very similar to many other forms of recreation, it being very common for publicans to sanction the sports that they were initiating as commercial speculations as being 'ancient'. In 1815, for instance, the publicans at Birch village (Lancashire) invented an 'ancient festival' of sports and recreations.[27] By 1846 publicans at Stalybridge insisted that an effort by their rivals from Ashton to sponsor sporting events on the local green was 'an infringement of our ancient rights'.[28] Shrove-football afforded many examples of games possessing a spurious antiquity, two notable cases being Kingston-upon-Thames and Sedgefield. At Kingston-upon-Thames, despite claims to the contrary, the Shrove-football was *not* mentioned in old accounts of the area. Similarly, there was nothing to support the contention that the Sedgefield game was initiated by a charter from the local church in 1027.[29] Of course, many Shrove-games had no pretensions to antiquity, being simply spontaneous affairs, as with the match between two companies of the South Durham Militia that occurred on the frozen surface of the river Tees in 1855, or the game in 1830 between two players at Bridge-end.[30]

The image that we have of Shrove and other traditional football games is an extremely violent one, in which long-hostile groups are given the opportunity to vent their hatreds. There are many examples of this. For instance, the football at Whitehaven, 'a game without rules', between the miners and the shipwrights, was largely a violent struggle conducted in the river.[31] In Scotland, adversarial groups squared up to one another annually. The Ettrick-Yarrow match often spilt over into a severe quarrel, that was only quieted when the ball was cut up.[32] This malignity seems to have flowed to the surface despite the most careful preparations. In December 1835 the two 50-men teams representing Scone and Perth, led respectively by Lord Stormont and the local provost, trained hard and conducted the contest on a well-marked pitch supervised by an umpire and two judges. However, the match had to be abandoned when a dispute prompted the immense crowd to invade the pitch, during which fracas Lord Stormont was hit by a stone.[33] The Welsh were also vulnerable to such hatreds, the annual Christmas Day match between the parishes of Llandyssal and Llanwenog was a curious fusion of feud and feast, in which individual street battles were periodically punctuated by pauses for refreshment.[34]

Despite all this, however, predominantly speaking most games appear to have been comparatively good natured. The football matches held to celebrate New Year's Day at Wigtown in 1826 featured:

> the parties marched two and two with drums beating and colours flying, to the Town-house, where copious libations of the mountain dew made them all 'unco happy', and as there was no scarcity on the field, it was little to be wondered at that so many of their spouses were to be seen arming them home tack and tack.[35]

This was not untypical of the mood of many such events, which often appear good humoured rather than violent. At least one Shrove-match, that at Derby, was the focus of skill and strategy rather than violence, it evidently being very rare for disputes over cheating to occur.[36] Indeed, this contrasted with the boys' game at Derby that was played on Ash Wednesday where 'disputes are more common than in the men's game', a fact which meant that grown-ups from both sides 'attend to see that fair play is done'.[37] The Selkirk–Yarrow match of 1815 was watched by a crowd numbering 2,000 and despite a 'rough and animated contest' was full of good sportsmanship.[38]

As we can see from the above, Shrove-games were often of comparatively recent invention, and the levels of violence within them varied substantially. While some games ventilated the hostility between rival groups, others resembled celebratory festivals, and a few fused elements of both impulses. The key element about Shrove-games was their diversity, a point that we will now expand in this, the second section of this part of our study, when we take a detailed look at three Shrove-games, those at Derby, Kingston-upon-Thames and Ashbourne. Let us commence with the first that suffered suppression, Derby.

Derby

The Shrove-game at Derby had adjusted itself to accommodate the increased urban development of the town, and in order to minimise the disruption that the event caused had been changed from foot-ball to hug-ball, which commentators contrasted with the more expansive game practised at Kingston-upon-Thames.[39] In 1830 an observer described the Derby game as drawing support from all ranks, particularly tradesmen, while noting that 'even the magistracy and clergy take part'.[40] However, shortly after this Derby's football began to attract criticism for the lawless behaviour that it gave rise to.[41] This criticism embraced a wide social spectrum and amongst the earliest and fiercest denunciations were those stemming from the local trade union magazine, *The Pioneer*, which condemned the Shrove-football as 'barbarous recklessness', and urged that the union deploy its power to destroy the game. In 1834 the union endeavoured to create a rival attraction to the Shrove-football by organising a procession to a four-acre field where over a thousand people were entertained with hymns and speeches and then fed.[42] Eleven years later, in 1845, another predominantly working-class group, The Derby Temperance Society, sought to either suppress or undermine the Shrove-game, and in alliance with the local bourgeoisie of silk and lace manufacturers, lawyers, clergy, and most prominent of all, tradesmen and shopkeepers, presented 'an address to the mayor on suppressing the football'.[43] The Temperance Society, like the trade unionists of 1834, set up a festival to rival the Shrove-game, consisting of a number of entertainments, including refreshments, dancing and music. This festival attracted about 500 people, including some who had formerly been prominent participants in the Shrove-game, facts which indicate that a large number of those attending were from the lower orders.[44]

The petition urging the suppression of the annual Shrove-football match that was presented to the mayor of Derby in 1845 met with his support, but in addition to banning the game he endeavoured to provide alternative recreations for the local inhabitants by offering prizes for football and other games that were to be held on an open space. Unfortunately, when a few players did pursue the Shrove-game in the town centre, this contravened the terms that those subscribing to the alternative sports had insisted upon, leading to the intended recreations being cancelled. Inevitably, this led to a great deal of disappointment amongst those who had abstained from the Shrove-game, prompting a severely contested Shrove-game on Ash Wednesday.[45]

The following year, in 1846, the mayor decided to use the police and special constables to prevent the Shrove-game, while providing the newly reestablished horse-race meeting as an alternative entertainment for the lower orders.[46] In a conference with 'several old players', who surrendered the Shrove-ball to him, the mayor promised to use his influence with the manufacturers to obtain a day's holiday for the workers, as well as promoting a subscription that would provide a railway trip on Shrove Tuesday. As it was, thousands descended on the marketplace and tried to play football. The police and special constables proved inadequate to deal with such a crowd and a near-riot ensued in which the mayor was struck by a brickbat. Inevitably, the dragoons were deployed and a number of arrests made, offenders being bound over and fined £20. On the following day there was further trouble and a number of additional arrests were made. Shortly afterwards, 178 people, virtually all of who were from the middle ranks, signed a petition thanking the mayor for suppressing the football. After this the Shrove-game in Derby gradually faded away.[47]

As we have already seen, the opponents of the Shrove-football in 1845 stemmed from all social ranks, including a large number from the lower orders. The game's supporters were from similarly varied backgrounds. Some, it appears, were influential citizens.[48] A large number of people who belonged to the machinery of law and order, namely, the enrolled pensioners, 'participated warmly in the game', prompting the mayor of Derby to request that the central authorities provide him with cavalry to enable him to put the football down because he could not trust the pensioners.[49] Additionally, an examination of the 1850 edition of *Slater's Directory* reveals that at least ten of the twenty people who were prosecuted as being supporters of football stemmed from commerce and trade. The breakdown of the thirteen defendants whose occupations could be established was as follows: three shopkeepers, three publicans, two butchers, a coal dealer, bricklayer, silk thrower, beerseller and one man who was either a grocer or a glover.[50] Predominantly, however, it seems likely that many of those who participated in the football were just ordinary working men.

The most ambitious attempt to identify those who supported football stems from Delves, who maintains that for a variety of reasons the Shrove-game at Derby in 1845 was used by the local working class, especially the framework-knitters, as 'a vehicle for social protest'.[51] Since their defeat by the manufacturers in a bitter strike in 1833–34 the framework-knitters had suffered from the steady erosion of their wages and Delves believes that they tried to use the Shrove-game to accomplish three goals. In the first place, 'the game was probably also seen as the guardian of the two-day holiday' and, at a time when 'the weakness of labour threatened leisure time', a way of preserving this.[52] Second, the framework-knitters used the holiday offered by the Shrovetide-game to gather and project a union that would protect them from further depredations by their employers. Finally, given that by 1845 many of the manufacturers who had been such bitter opponents of the framework-knitters during the strike were now on the town council 'the game might have offered a good opportunity to wipe off old scores'.[53]

While it is quite possible that Delves might be correct in this, there is no indication that the trade-union movement ever articulated such a case. As has already been mentioned, in the 1830s the union was bitterly opposed to football, and it is certainly the case that in 1846 the Chartist paper, *The Northern Star*, supported the suppression of Derby's Shrove-game.[54] By Ash Wednesday and possibly even Shrove Tuesday 1846, the chief supporters of football were largely 'women and grown-up lads' rather than mill-workers, who appear, according to the statements of a factory owner who was working as a special constable, to have attended work as usual.[55] This evidence suggests that the dispute over football had become almost a generational matter, crystallised by a special constable providing bail for a defendant: the offender was his son.[56]

Delves remarks, somewhat paradoxically, that: 'the conflict over Derby football is most meaningfully to be understood in class terms. But class attitudes and alignments were complex and changed over time'.[57] The strongest evidence indicating the class-based nature of opinion on Shrove-football stems from a detailed examination of the petition commending the mayor's suppression of the game in 1846. While a very large number of occupations are listed (Table 1.4), when analysed according to Armstrong's framework of social hierarchy, the vast bulk of the 178 petitioners stems from classes II and III (Table 1.5) and can clearly be classified as middle ranking. Naturally, it is debatable how representative such a sample is of public opinion, for it may be that many of the lower orders who were opposed to

Table 1.4 The occupational breakdown of supporters for the suppression of Shrove-football at Derby in 1846

Occupation	*1921*	*1951*	*Total individuals*
Attorney	1	1	6
Baker	3	3	3
Basket maker	2	3	1
Book seller	2	3	5
Boot and shoe warehouse	2	3	1
Boot maker	2	3	8
Brass founder	3	3	1
Brazier	4	4	1
Bricklayer	3	3	1
Butcher	2	3	4
Cabinet maker	3	3	3
Carver	3	3	1
Chemist	2	3	9
Clerk	2	3	1
Confectioner	2	3	3
Cooper	3	3	1
Corn factor	2	2	1
Corn institution	2	2	1
Doctor/surgeon	1		9
Draper	2	3	7
Engineer	3	3	1
Fire office agent	2	2	2
Firms			9
Furniture broker	2	2	2
Gentleman	1	1	1
Greengrocer	2	3	12
Hairdresser	3	3	4
Harness maker	2	3	1
Hatter	3	3	1
Hosier	2	3	2
Iron founder	3	3	1
Iron master	2	3	1
Iron merchant	2	2	1
Iron master	2	3	3
Jeweller	2	3	1
Joiner	2	3	4
Lace dealer	2	3	1
Landscape painter	2	3	2
Life office agent	2	2	1
Marble mason	2	3	2

Table 1.4 Continued

Occupation	*1921*	*1951*	*Total individuals*
Merchant	2	3	1
Miller	2	3	1
Office agent	2	2	1
Optician	3	3	1
Paper maker	3	3	1
Plumber	3	3	2
Post office agent	2	2	1
Printer	2	3	2
Publican	2	3	4
Rag dealer	5	5	1
Railway wagon builder	3	3	1
Saddler	2	3	1
Seed crusher	3	3	1
Shop keeper	3	3	1
Silk manufacturer	1	1	3
Silk thrower	3	3	2
Stone mason	3	3	2
Superintendent registrar	2	2	1
Tailor	3		4
Timber merchant	3	3	1
Watchmaker	2	3	2
Workhouse official	2	2	1

Table 1.5 Overview of the social ranks of the petitioners at Derby in 1846 as established by Armstrong from the 1921 and 1951 census

	Social classes	*Occupations*	*Individuals*
1921	I	04	19
	II	35	91
	III	20	33
	IV	01	01
	V	01	01
Total		61	145
1951	I	03	10
	II	09	11
	III	45	109
	IV	01	01
	V	01	01
Total		59	132

the Shrove-game were never asked to sign the petition, but the document suggests that those individuals who were from trade and commerce who were prosecuted on behalf of the Shrove-game were not representative of the general sentiment of their occupation. The same might also be true for those members of the lower orders who attended the rival attractions offered by the Temperance Movement, though the comparatively large numbers involved, some 500 or so, makes this less compelling. We will probably never know the attitude of the trade union movement in Derby towards Shrove-football in the 1840s, but it seems likely that by 1846 much of the protest was not the product of organised labour but other, more peripheral groups, described as 'women and grown up lads'.

The memorial opposing the Shrove-football at Derby was a petition from local citizens that appeared on page 1 of *Derby Mercury* 18 March 1846, thanking the mayor and the magistrates for suppressing the Shrove-game. It contained the names of 178 people. The information on the occupations of 141 petitioners was gathered from *Slater's Directory* for Derby (1850), there being no mention of 37. In 12 cases two different occupations could plausibly be apportioned to a particular name and this accounts for the disparity between the number of individuals and occupations. The information on the social classification is from W. Armstrong's article 'The use of information about occupations', in E. Wrigley (ed.) *Nineteenth Century Society* (Cambridge: CUP, 1972) pp. 215–23. Armstrong applied the social classifications from the 1921 and 1951 census to material from the York enumerators' books of 1841 and sets forth the hierarchies in descending order with the top class classified as 1, and the lowest 5. In two occupations, doctors and tailor, there is no classification provided for the 1951 categories and they are consequently ignored in Table 1.5. Similarly, the memorial listed nine firms, which are excluded from both the 1921 and 1951 categories.

Kingston-upon-Thames

The second venue for Shrove-football that we shall examine in this section of our study is Kingston-upon-Thames. The history of the Shrove-football at Kingston-upon-Thames was utterly different to that of Derby. From its very inception, in the late eighteenth century, the Shrove-football at Kingston-upon-Thames had enjoyed very widespread support, including the gentry, tradesmen and the labouring classes.[58] This persisted, and as late as 1858 the town council was almost unanimous in its support for the game, a view that was doubtless strengthened by a petition from 132 local tradesmen in favour of football.[59] Unlike Derby, where, as we have seen, trade and commerce appear to have been predominantly hostile to the game, Kingston's trade seems to have benefited from it, doubtless due to the expenditure lavished by residents and visitors during such a festival.[60] By the 1860s, the extent of traffic and commerce was such that it was decided to prevent the sport being played on the public thoroughfare, a suitable recreational ground having been provided by the corporation as an alternative venue.[61] In order to pre-empt trouble, the police dominated the town centre, but most of those who endeavoured to play there were women, children and youths, and the protest was curbed with comparatively little conflict.[62] The following year there was an attempt by lads, boys and a few unemployed labourers to stage a procession and then play in the marketplace, but this was soon curbed, only three arrests being made. Interestingly, football was not supported by the respectable mechanics, 'who are supposed to traditionally regard it as their public holiday'.[63] In this, it reminds us of the football at Derby in 1846, where the game appears to have been restricted largely to more marginal groups.

Ashbourne

The third venue of Shrove-football in this section of our study is Ashbourne. The Shrove-game at Ashbourne was so popular that it became the subject of a song that was performed in a local theatre on 26 February 1821. Until 1858, when a clergyman made an unsuccessful attempt to have it suppressed, Shrove-football effectively enjoyed unanimous support amongst all ranks.[64] Two years later, the newly installed rural police attempted to disperse the 500 or so footballers, thus creating a great deal of trouble. This resulted in over sixty arrests being made, with 'many of the most respectable inhabitants of the town' being summoned before the magistrates. In response to this a defence committee was established, and over £60 subscribed towards it.[65] The following year there were further prosecutions, and the moral standing of the police was substantially compromised when it transpired that no townsman had complained about the game and that the football's suppression was entirely on the initiative of the newly established police force.[66] A total of twenty-six defendants were fined, eighteen of whom had to pay a shilling, while the chief offender was charged two pounds. From that time forth football was transferred to the outskirts of the town, in accordance with an agreement between the authorities and the game's supporters.[67] At first things went well but in 1878 a player was drowned in a stream, prompting the authorities to attempt to ban the game the following year. Events came to a head in 1880, when there was a great deal of trouble. In 1881 a further agreement was made and from then on football was well supported.[68]

The games at Derby, Kingston-upon-Thames and Ashbourne highlight how diverse the experience of Shrove-football could be. At Derby, football enjoyed some support amongst the upper and middle class but was generally disapproved of by them, because it interfered with public order and commerce, a fact that caused its demise. By contrast, at Kingston-upon-Thames commerce favoured the Shrove-game which was regarded as increasing rather than restricting business. It was only when this situation changed, some twenty years after that of Derby, that a decision was made to transfer the game elsewhere. The attitude of the upper class in the three locations also varied. At Derby, they appear to have been largely hostile to Shrove-football, though keen on other sorts of recreations, notably horse-race meetings. The latter sport caused trouble with some members of the council who were staunch Evangelicals. By contrast, Kingston's council was almost unanimous in its support for football, the sole dissenting voice being the lone member with Evangelical beliefs. At Ashbourne, most of the leading figures of the area were firm supporters of football and bitter opponents of attempts to suppress it. Unlike at Derby and Kingston-upon-Thames, where the police acted in response to local requests to suppress the game, at Ashbourne the police initiated action themselves, in flat opposition to influential local opinion.

Having considered the fate of three Shrove-football games, it is time to broaden our discussion to assess the factors that determined the fate of Shrove-games in Britain, the third section of this part of our study.

The survival of Shrove-games generally depended upon a complicated equation involving a number of variables. The most fundamental of these was the relative strength between the forces of authority (generally the police) and the footballers. The ideal situation from the point of view of the authorities was to confront a Shrove-game that had limited support. These could be easily suppressed, as at East Mousley in 1857, where the game was extinguished by fining the sole defendant a shilling.[69] The second best situation for the police was to enjoy significant support from the local community. At Richmond, Shrove-football was banned by the police after complaints by some of the principal inhabitants but was not easily suppressed because it had a significant following, and the resulting struggle led to a number of police being injured and a few arrests being made.[70] However, while popular sympathy was desirable, as we saw at Ashbourne, the crucial point was the strength of the police. At Ashbourne, although the police lacked any popular support, by displaying sufficient determination they were able to enforce their will and compel the Shrove-game's supporters to transfer it elsewhere. The reason why they were able to do this was because the Ashbourne footballers were comparatively law-abiding. By contrast, at Duns (1835) and Dorking (1839) attempts at suppressing the local Shrove-games failed because of the determined opposition they encountered.[71] More significantly still, in 1881 the police at Nuneaton were 'roughly handled' when they tried to prevent hundreds of labourers kicking balls through the street on Shrove Tuesday and were consequently unable to prevent the game.[72]

While such victories were rare, they also tended to be unnecessary, because Shrove-football was often able to ensure its survival against all but the most determined attack by maintaining good relations with influential opinion within the community. As we have seen, this was the case at Ashbourne and Kingston-upon-Thames, and assisted its survival at Dorking, where although protests against the holding of the Shrove match in the main street commenced in 1839, the support that the custom enjoyed amongst the influential was such that it persisted. Indeed, *The Southern Weekly News* reported in 1888 that despite heavy snow large numbers of players participated.[73] Shrove-games were sometimes firmly embedded into the established social hierarchy: at Sedgefield, for instance, the sport was very popular with all classes, the parish clerk being carried shoulder high at the end of the contest.[74] In a number of instances the local Shrove-game received very sympathetic treatment from the judiciary. At Twickenham, when the footballers acceded to the justice's instruction that they should move the Shrove-game from the streets to a nearby field, the judiciary contributed half a crown to the game's fund.[75] At Derby, the magistrate gave the ringleaders of football some very lenient sentences, prompting the mayor to complain to the secretary of state.[76]

In large measure the survival of a Shrove-game depended on its luck. If its location was such that it could attract commerce to the area, as with the game at

Kingston-upon-Thames, it was assured of significant support.[77] Similarly, the existence of a sympathetic patron could be very important. The best example of this is the Alnwick game, which was played in the streets until 1828. At that point the authorities insisted that it caused too much disruption, so it was transferred to a nearby field. Throughout the entire period the game enjoyed the support and sponsorship of the duke of Northumberland, who in addition to providing prizes and refreshments paid for any damages that were incurred.[78] The Alnwick game is illustrative of what is probably the most important factor in the survival of any Shrove-game, flexibility. As urban society expanded and the pace of commerce accelerated it was vital that Shrove-games accommodated themselves to these new realities, reinventing themselves in a different location. This appears to have happened quite often and in 1864 Shrove-football was being reintroduced into London, hundreds playing in the annual Shrove-game at Battersea Park.[79]

Having surveyed the evidence we can see that there is very little to support the idea that between 1750 and 1850 the recreational opportunities of the labouring population suffered a decline. To an extent this is reflected in the occurrence of Shrove-football, which tends to increase during the period. However, despite this general growth, Shrove-football suffered a number of significant attacks, particularly between 1825 and 1873, which demonstrates both the increasing desire and capacity for both local and national authorities to intervene in the regulation of recreational culture. The relative experience of the various Shrove-games emphasised their diversity, with survival often depending on a variety of factors, not least their capacity to adapt flexibly to changes in circumstances. Having said this, however, it is now almost time to leave Shrove-football but before we go let us return to Derby on Shrove Tuesday 1856. Although the Shrove-football that once caused so much anarchy in the town centre has long been extinct,

> here and there might be seen a knot of lads outside the town keeping up the old custom of football, although this amusement has become by degrees beautifully less, till it has well nigh been discontinued.[80]

One wonders what sort of game they were playing. Perhaps it was related to an annual match that was recorded in the area as occurring between the parishes of Littleover and Mickleover, who played 'kick-ball', with twenty players on each side?[81] In large measure, the future of football might well have rested with the descendants of such games, which were to eventually blossom into the varieties that we know today as rugby and association. Of course, all that lay in the future, and it is now time for us to turn our attention to a far more privileged group than the lads who were enjoying a few hours' holiday from Derby's factories: the boys and masters of Britain's elite educational institutions, the public schools and Cambridge and Oxford universities.

2 Entertaining the social elite

Football in the public schools and universities 1555–1863

In 1802 a commentator observed approvingly that football, cricket, fencing and military exercises are 'improving youthful exercises' present at all large schools.[1] From this it can be seen that by the early nineteenth century the virtues of sport were appreciated in many of the major schools of England. Such admiration would certainly have accorded with the sentiments of some of those who had founded the great schools, notably Wykeham and John Lyon, who held sport in high esteem.[2] However, during the first half of the nineteenth century such feelings were far from universal, and in 1834 the headmasters of Eton (Dr Hawtrey) and Shrewsbury (Samuel Butler) were united in their complaints about the pressure exerted upon them by the parents of pupils, who constantly demanded an increase in the amount of sport at their respective schools.[3]

For a variety of reasons, not least the increase in the number of pupils, headmasters were largely powerless in curbing the practice of sport at public schools.[4] The basic element of discipline within schools was the prefect-fagging system, in which the older boys were permitted free -rein in the day-to-day running of the institution. Fundamentally, the low ratio of teachers to pupils meant that even if they had wanted to, most masters would have been wary of interfering with the rights of the prefects for fear of causing trouble, if not rebellion.[5] As a consequence of this, the older boys, principally the prefects, had a great deal of latitude and often organised sports, which all but the most determined masters were largely powerless to prevent. Additionally, influential groups that were ancillary to the schools, primarily parents and former pupils, promoted sports avidly. It was the enthusiasm of these groups, allied to the boys themselves, that fostered the various sports in schools. While to begin with many masters were apathetic, if not hostile towards sport, and the extent of their promotion of recreations rarely transcended the provision of playing fields, by the 1850s this attitude had been largely replaced by more respectful views. Sport, which had once been tolerated for a mixture of fear and apathy, came to be regarded as fostering many healthy moral and physical virtues, as well as encouraging discipline. Thus, headmasters took a growing interest in the provision of healthy recreational activities and began to employ masters purely for their ability in games.[6] By 1860 athletics was well organised in most schools, with the importance of sport accelerating in almost every foundation during the rest of the century.

This growth in the official provision of sport in public schools was rapid and within the space of twenty years schools had gone from having occasional 'hare and hounds'

Figure 2.1 A picture of the Oxbridge rugby match from 1880. Taken from *The Illustrated Sporting and Dramatic News* 6 March 1880, p. 600.

UNIVERSITY OF EDINBURGH FOOT BALL CLUB.

MR EDITOR: Having recently chronicled in your valuable pages a match, or rather a game, for it proved no match at all, between this rapidly rising club and the 93d Highlanders, when the former were beaten, although, I believe, very honourably, in consequence of having to play with the men, whereas it was originally understood to be with the officers, perhaps you will be kind enough to insert the following particulars of a match between the Scotch and English members composing this club:—The match played on Saturday week was for some days previous agreed upon, and looked forward to with great interest by both parties, and although public opinion was in favour of the English, yet from the names selected on the opposite party, well known to the club as among their best players, it was impossible to imagine which side would ultimately win. It was agreed that the most games out of five should decide the match, but at five o'clock, should the games not be finished, then the umpires should give it in favour of the side which had won most games. 24 members composed each side, distinguished on the Scotch side by a green badge, and on the English by a red. About two o'clock, all preliminaries having been settled, the game commenced, and both parties went to work in right good earnest. For a long time, from the intense exertions of both sides, it appeared that they were as equally matched as could be, but from the English sides having left their goals undefended, a lucky hit placed the first game to the credit of the Scotch party. A few minutes being allowed for getting breath, the ball was played off, and each party now exerted themselves to the utmost. The English having learnt experience, covered their goals, and, after a short struggle, the second game was won by Mr Jones, on the English side, in a very clever manner. The excitement now rose to its highest pitch; nearly 500 people had collected on the Links, who, in the most unpardonable and selfish manner, crowded over the ground so that the goals and players were perfectly unrecognizable. The third game was, after a hard struggle and warm dispute, gained by Mr Frost on the English side. The last game was fought long and hard, and as the time (five o'clock) drew near, after having been in the hands of the Scotch several times, the game turned in favour of the English, who worked like Britons, and at a few minutes to five, had brought the ball to within a few yards of the goal, when another kick would have won it but for a Scotchman, who took the ball off the ground, and claimed a free kick, resisting every effort made to take the ball from him. The umpire, who saw the circumstance, immediately disallowed the claim, which, however, was poor satisfaction, after losing the chance of the game. The game proceeded, and the English party strained every nerve, and would doubtless have won, had not the umpires' "time's up" settled the game. The English party having won two games out of three by five o'clock, according to agreement the umpires decided that the English side had won. Among those that distinguished themselves on the English side were Messrs Russell, Broadbent, Gobbould, Aldridge, Frost, Jones, and Cousens; while on the Scotch the names of Nasmyth, Smyth, Currie, Frazer, Dickson, Bone, and Christison are the most conspicuous. Great credit is due to both the umpires (Messrs Paterson and Wilson) for the impartiality of their decisions, when party spirit ran so high. Sincerely hoping you will be able to find space in your valuable journal for this long and tedious yarn, you will oblige, Mr Editor,

ONE OF ENGLAND'S RISING GENERATION, AND AN ADMIRER OF HER SPORTS.

Figure 2.2 Letter from *Bell's Life in London* 29 March 1851, p. 7 describing what might be classified as the very first England–Scotland football match. It is clear that they are playing the type of football game that was very popular in Britain, particularly Scotland, until at least the 1850s. The game contains the first recorded instance of cheating at football, a player diving on the ball and incorrectly claiming a 'fair catch' in order to prevent the other side from scoring. See p. 85.

runs to full sports meetings. In 1845 Eton's annual steeplechase commenced, followed by those at Cheltenham and Harrow in 1853, Rugby (1856), Winchester (1857), Westminster and Charterhouse (1861).[7] Sports meetings also enjoyed a rapid growth at the universities. The first such regular event commenced at Oxford in 1850, with a meeting at Exeter College.[8] This was followed by meetings at the following colleges: Balliol, Pembroke, Wadham and Worcester (all 1856), Oriel (1857), Merton (1857) and Christchurch (1859). By 1861 separate college meetings were general at Oxford and from 1860 an Oxford University Sports meeting was held, open to all undergraduates. In the various Cambridge colleges regular organised sports meetings developed somewhat later than at Oxford, but in 1857 Cambridge University Sports meeting was founded.[9] By 1861 all public schools and universities were holding annual sports meetings.[10] An idea of the growth experienced in organised football activity at the various public schools can be obtained from the following Tables 2.1–2.3.

Table 2.1 Organised football matches at Eton and Harrow 1840–50

	1840	*1841*	*1842*	*1843*	*1844*	*1845*	*1846*	*1847*	*1848*	*1849*	*1850*
Eton	02	02	02	01	01	02	01	01	04	10	05
Harrow			01						01		

Table 2.2 Organised football matches at nine public schools 1851–58

Schools	*1851*	*1852*	*1853*	*1854*	*1855*	*1856*	*1857*	*1858*
Cheltenham		01	01					
Eton	23	17	35	23	31	27	28	32
Harrow		03	06	11	05	04	10	10
Marlborough	01	01	03	10	04	03	03	05
Rossall								01
Rugby		05	06	03	10	06	04	04
Shrewsbury			04	01	01	05	03	02
Westminster	03		04			14	09	08
Winchester	02		02		08	04	03	10

Table 2.3 Organised football matches at public schools 1859–67

Schools	*1859*	*1860*	*1861*	*1862*	*1863*	*1864*	*1865*	*1866*	*1867*
Brighton	03	05	06	11	10	02	08	02	06
Cheltenham	03	06	05	06	08	02	08	11	09
Clifton						06	04	03	07
Eton	49	20	23	31	11	07	02	19	13
Haileybury								01	11
Harrow	11	11	13	08	17	10	09	02	04
Lancing	01	01	01		01	01			01
Marlborough	05	04	06	08	08	04	05	04	09
Radley	05	03				04		06	10
Rossall	02			01		05	10	12	13
Rugby	06	01	06	09	10	07	11	11	12
Sherborne					01	01			
Shrewsbury	07	02	06	07	10	13	10	02	08
Tonbridge	03			01					
Uppingham			04	03	07	08	05		06
Wellington								09	08
Westminster	09	07	08	12	09	07	03	08	09
Winchester	14	08	02	08	11	08	11	10	11

These tables are based almost entirely upon the reports that appeared in newspapers and are not necessarily a comprehensive record of organised football activity at any foundation.

It must be said, however, that by no means everyone would have regarded such a development as a good thing. In 1848 a commentator named Bain complained about the limited nature of higher education in Britain and observed that the only development permitted to 'great natural gifts of eye and hand, was in the extra-academical occupations of boating, cricket or horsemanship'. Bain considered this to be a frivolous waste and regretted that it was a 'pity they cannot apply their gifts to feeling a pulse or guiding a scalpel'.[11] This criticism reminds us of the first specific reference that we have to football from an elite institution. In 1555 the authorities of St John's College, Oxford University, forbade the game. Football was off to a bad start. Let us now see how it got on.

The following chapter consists of four sections. The first examines football at the various public schools in the years up to 1863. The second section is devoted to football at Cambridge and Oxford Universities. In the third section we consider the interactions between various elite institutions, in terms of both playing matches and creating joint codes. The fourth section assesses the impact that the football of the elite institutions had on the wider society.

The public schools

In this, the first section of the chapter, we consider football at the following public schools; Charterhouse, Eton, Harrow, Marlborough, Rugby, Shrewsbury, Westminster and Winchester. This is followed by a section dealing with football at minor public schools. We conclude with an overview of public school football. We begin with football at Charterhouse.

Charterhouse School

Until 1821 the only playground available at Charterhouse was known as 'Green', and consisted of 330 square feet of very uneven ground that was 'full of holes, and quite unfit for the playing of games'.[12] As a consequence of this, the only games that seem to have been played were hoop racing and football in cloisters, the latter game being unique to Charterhouse. The cloisters were a long, brick, barrel-vaulted arcade that were about ten feet wide with buttresses on one side separating windows that opened on to Green. At either end of the arcade there were doors and these constituted the goals. A former player recorded that

> When the game was played by a limited number of players, six or nine a side, it was a really fine game. But when a big game was ordered, such as Gownboys v School, in which all fags had to block the respective goals and the mass of players filled the arcade, it was a very poor game indeed, consisting of a series of 'squashes' or dead blocks, in which the ball was entirely lost to sight, and a mass of humanity surged and heaved senselessly, often for

> as much as half an hour at a time. But whether played by many or by few, the game was unavoidably rough.[13]

In 1821 the green was levelled, expanded and improved. The result of this was to produce two greens, 'Upper Green' and 'Under Green'.[14] From that time onwards, an association-type game (i.e. one played predominantly with the feet) gradually evolved, albeit one in which a considerable amount of handling was permitted.

From March 1853 reports of matches at Charterhouse began to appear in the sporting press, commencing with a game between the Oppidians and the Gown Boys. In 1856 Charterhouse were visited by St Bartholomew's Hospital, and by 1860 the Dingly Dell Club were regular opponents of the School, continuing to visit until 1864. Curiously enough, these matches precede the establishment of the first football eleven at Charterhouse, which was organised in October 1862 and played upon Under Green. The Club drew up printed rules for the game and these included a declaration that 'if any disagreement arise concerning the above rules, or any clause therein contained, the matter shall stand over for discussion until the conclusion of the game in which the players are then engaged'.

Many of the teams who visited Charterhouse were pickup elevens, often assembled by an old Carthusian. While most of the games occurred outside, on at least one occasion, on 5 November 1862 when Mr Cardale's team, who called themselves 'The Grand Amalgamated Mediocrities', visited, the weather was so bad that the match was conducted in 'cloisters'.[15] During 1862 Charterhouse won one, drew two, lost three in 'foreign matches', describing their results as 'tolerably satisfactory because the 'eleven is in its infancy'.[16]

As can be seen, Charterhouse was vigorous in its interaction with outsiders. This activity continued in 1863, where a number of external teams visited, notably Crusaders, St Bartholomew's Hospital, Tonbridge Wells School and Civil Service. The last team appear to have included a number of old Carthusians. Charterhouse had a very positive outlook towards contact with the wider world and it is noticeable that Hartshore, the captain of Charterhouse team, was the only person at the first couple of meetings of the Football Association (FA) who was currently attending a public school.

Eton college

The first mentions of football at Eton were in 1747 and 1766.[17] However, the School's archives have no reference to football until the latter half of the nineteenth century.[18] By the 1820s it was well established that hockey and football were Eton's winter games, while cricket and rowing were the recreations of the summer.[19] The two main varieties of football that were found at Eton were the field game and the wall game, though there were other additional types, distinctive to particular colleges.[20] Until at least the 1820s the field game was regarded as quite inferior to the wall game and was played chiefly by the minor clubs of the College.[21]

The various football games at Eton were regulated by numerous laws, a former pupil complaining about the 'interminable multiplicity of rules about sneaking, picking up, throwing, rolling in straight, etc.'.[22] Teams in the field game were made up of eleven players on each side, consisting of eight forwards and three behinds, playing on a pitch that was 120 yards long and 80 yards wide. The aim was to get to any part of the opponents' goal line, with three points being awarded for a goal (i.e. forcing the ball between the goal posts, which were 12 feet by 6 feet, with a slender cross bar) and a point for a rouge (scored by touching the ball after it has crossed the opponent's goal line on either side of the goal posts, or kicking the ball over the goal line while being charged).[23] The ball was about half the size of that used in association and could not be passed forward. As a consequence of this the attackers advanced in a solid phalanx.[24] A key element of the field game was the bully, a type of scrimmage that could be violent.[25] In 1827 G. W. Lyttleton remembered the robust nature of the football he played at Eton, recording that he 'seldom saw much of the ball but frequently saw and felt the nailed shoes of my adversaries'.[26] The rules of the field game were committed to writing in 1847.[27] It is unclear when players of the field game began dressing for football. Green claimed that from the 1840s boys used their gowns as a convenient wrap in their journeys to and from the field. By contrast, Wayte maintained that the football eleven had no distinctive dress until 1860.[28]

The wall game was simply the field game played in a narrow space.[29] It appears that this area diminished as time progressed, for until at least 1820 the wall game was played on a much wider strip of ground and bore a strong resemblance to the field game.[30] By the 1830s the wall game's pitch had shrunk dramatically. Whereas the pitch used for the field game was eighty yards wide, that of the wall game was just five or six yards wide, bounded on one side by a wall that stretched for one hundred yards and then made a right angle.[31] The goals were very small and the confined nature of the playing area meant that players had to wear special protective gear. It appears that games were very physically demanding and thus limited to an hour.[32]

It is difficult assessing how violent the wall game was. A player from the 1820s recorded that:

> But upon the whole, we think that fewer are seen hobbling back from the distant hockey fields, than from the less remote scene of foot-ball playing; and that many enter without fear into a 'bully' at hockey, who would dread the more dense 'rouge' at football.[33]

However, 'An Old Colleger' defended the wall game against charges that it was brutal and declared that the only injuries that player's suffered were wounded shins and that these were rarely noticed because player's were absorbed in the excitement of the game. Those players who were concerned would use book covers to pad and bandage their legs and shins. Generally, however, 'An Old Colleger' regarded this as unnecessary and noted that despite being in the thick of every rouge, and wearing thin trousers, cotton stockings and 'low walking shoes', Captain Wyndham of the Life Guards only ever had his shins injured.[34] While this might be so, by the 1840s matches could be quite violent and on at least one occasion a player had a leg broken.[35]

The date of the origin of the wall game is not known but it cannot have been earlier than 1717. By 1811 the wall game was well established and until the 1820s was practically the only football game at Eton, though there were 'occasional trifling games in the open'.[36] The main club was the upper club and consisted of about forty players, all from the upper forms, who would regularly play the wall game, with eighteen to twenty players on each side.[37] The chief match was that between the Collegers and the Oppidians, which commenced from at least the 1820s. From the very first it had the reputation of being the fiercest of all the matches, but there was no real harm caused until 1827, when a major fight developed. This conflagration led to the fixture being banned for some years, though by at least 1837 it had recommenced.[38] These annual matches were absurdly unbalanced numerically, some seventy Collegers taking on 200 or so Oppidians. In an effort to mitigate this it was suggested at one stage that four masters be allowed to play on the Collegers side, but this came to nothing.[39]

The rules of the wall game were obviously well established by at least the 1820s and it is noticeable that it was not until 1845 that referees or umpires were used to supervise that most combustible of fixtures the Collegers–Oppidians match.[40] Two years later, when Powell became the superintendent of the wall, he began to keep records of that event.[41] In 1849 the first formal set of rules was drawn up and printed for the game, on the sole authority of the senior keeper, F. E. Stacey.[42] A year later, the headmaster threatened to ban the wall game because of the way members of the sixth form had abused their power.[43] Gradually, the wall game became more organised and by 1860 the wall eleven began wearing specific colours. [44]

With regard to press attention, coverage of Eton's football commenced in *Bell's Life in London* on 27 November 1840, presumably based upon a letter from a pupil or an old boy.[45] However, matches based upon the house and other forms of division were occurring at Eton long before this. From 1848 there was a vast increase in the amount of football activity in both the wall and the field games, football having become the principal sport of the school, drawing very large crowds.[46] While most games continued to be played purely between teams of Eton schoolboys, from 1851 a number of visiting sides began to appear, particularly old Etonians from Oxford, and from 1852 teams of Old Etonian officers.[47] In 1857 Eton hosted a very prestigious fixture, when teams of old Etonians, representing Oxford and Cambridge respectively, played a Varsity match, with the Prince of Wales being amongst the spectators.[48]

Until the 1840s there was little official encouragement of football at Eton, though the school did provide a field in which the game could be played.[49] Football was officially countenanced for the first time in season 1841–42, when it was found to be of great use in ensuring that the pupils remained within bounds.[50] As was earlier mentioned, in the 1830s Dr Hawtrey, Eton's headmaster, had been very critical of the emphasis placed on sport by many of the parents of his school's pupils. However, such was the extent of his conversion that when it was rumoured, in November 1842, that a mild form of scarlet fever had broken out at the school because of the boys playing football at that time of year, Dr Hawtrey insisted on football continuing and issued the following letter to the press:

> The manly game of football continues to be played at Eton as it always has been played, and I have received no intimation from any person capable of forming an opinion that it was any other than beneficial to the health of the scholars.[51]

As has already been noted, from 1848 there was a substantial increase in the amount of football played in the College. Such a growth in the level of activity would have inevitably prompted an increase in the amount of disputes involving rules and this was probably the reason for the first attempt of formal codification of football laws that occurred in 1849. Clearly, the official organisation of football was increasing towards the end of the 1840s, and while we do not know when it was decided to create tournaments for football, from at least 1850 the term 'Cocks of College' was used to describe the house that had proved triumphant over the others. In 1860 an annual cup was awarded for this, 'The Wayte Cup'.[52]

Harrow School

In the 1820s the masters at Harrow did encourage sports, the chief activities being cricket, racquets and football.[53] In terms of publicity, reports of Harrow's football began to appear in the press from 1842.[54] However, the major promotion of sports commenced with the accession of C. J. Vaughan, a former pupil of Thomas Arnold, to the headship (1845–59). Vaughan used prefects rather than masters to try and inspire boys into playing sport and encouraged the fifth and sixth form pupils at Harrow to set up the Philathletic Club to regulate and organise their games. Vaughan was influential in developing the intellectual rationale for athletic games, stressing their role in moral education.[55]

Reports from newspapers show that from at least the 1840s annual tournaments were being held to establish the champion house at football.[56] The matches conducted between the competing houses varied substantially, one in 1848 being quite violent, while another from 1853 was conducted with great sportsmanship. On that particular occasion, although there was no regular umpire one of the teams sportingly disallowed a goal that they had scored although it seemed to be quite fair.[57] It is tempting to relate such behaviour to the formation of the Philathletic Club, which was founded in 1853, and became the chief lawmaking authority of Harrow football.[58] While the bulk of games that the Club organised were house matches, during the 1850s teams of old Harrovians began to visit from Oxford in 1857 and Cambridge in 1859.[59] Additionally, commencing in 1859 various pickup teams, assembled by old Harrovians, played at the School. From 1860 an annual match was staged between Harrow and old Harrovians from Trinity College, Cambridge.[60] The first truly external match at Harrow occurred in 1862, when Harrow played the Dingly Dell Club, using Harrow's code.[61] While Harrow were not particularly active in their contact with outsiders, the Philathlete Club did at least reply to the FA in 1863.[62]

The rules of Harrow's football can be summarised as follows. Teams consisted of eleven players, two backs, five center forwards, two right wing, two left wing, there being no goalkeeper.[63] The ball was larger than the association ball and shaped like a church hassock, with rounded ends and sides. In the Harrow game goals were called 'bases' and marked with high poles, a 'base' being scored when the ball passed between the poles at whatever height.[64] As with many public school games, the offside law was very strict, preventing players from touching the ball if they were in front of it. This situation meant that the onus was on following behind the player who was dribbling the ball. A fair catch could be claimed if the ball was caught before it had bounced and the player called 'Yards'. This would entitle him to run three yards and make an unchallenged kick. It was very common for goals to have been scored by this method, the technique being to turn round and give a gentle kick to a follow-up player who would then catch the ball and claim a free kick.[65] While it was forbidden to hold, trip or push an opponent, charging was legitimate.[66] There were no punishments for the infringement of rules but the umpire had the power to send players off and award goals as penalties.

Marlborough College

In 1851 Marlborough's disciplinary problems culminated in a rebellion by the pupils and this forced the authorities to adopt a new approach in the administration of the College. From that year onwards the school appears to have taken sport, especially football, very seriously and it is noticeable that from November 1851 they began sending reports to newspapers about College football.[67] In August 1852 Cotton became headmaster of Marlborough and used school games to foster a new master–boy relationship, through which he could curb the disciplinary problems of the school. In addition to reforming the prefect system by enlarging their functions, Cotton used sport in two significant ways. First, he employed younger staff who were interested in sport. Second, regular games were organised that would break down the unofficial system of 'tribes' (groups of boys).

The staff Cotton employed were younger and significantly more interested in sport than those of the past, and were typified by a clergyman, Fowler, who in 1855 scored for the fifth form in their match against the school.[68] Marlborough's football rules were based upon those of Rugby School and the College's staff, in addition to trying to enforce a stricter application of this code, sought to graft on some of Rugby's skills.[69] Generally this was accomplished by a mixture of carrot and stick, involving the awarding of prizes and the expression of criticism.[70] This interest meant that the masters 'altogether reformed our football, turning it from a private farce to a great school institution'.[71] With regard to the problem of 'tribes', in order to split these groupings up matches were played between the various houses, alphabetical divisions, north vs south, and other permutations.

While many of these ideas were not new, their use having been expanding previous to the 1850s, Cotton did a considerable amount to systematise this philosophy. Ironically, Cotton did not play games and regarded them as a necessary evil that could assist the establishment of order into the school.[72] It is unclear how Cotton's ideas concerning the use of sport to foster closer ties between boys and masters were spread because Cotton did not publicise them in print and few of his staff worked in other schools.[73]

Rugby School

In the early nineteenth century the two favourite sports at Rugby were fishing and running.[74] Football appears to have attained popularity somewhat later, presumably related to the fact that by 1816 the School authorities had provided the boys with a plot of eight acres in which to play.[75] Unfortunately there are no contemporary accounts of football during this period, and the only record that we have appeared in 1876, written by Bloxham, who had been a pupil at Rugby in the first quarter of the nineteenth century. According to Bloxham, until the 1820s the school football was quite simple and largely excluded the use of the hands. Indeed, 'no one was allowed to run with the ball in his grip towards the opposite goal'. Additionally, 'there was no special uniform for football'.[76] Bloxham claimed that it was the illegal activity of a schoolboy, William Webb Ellis, that led to the introduction of the practice of carrying the ball in the hands in Rugby's version of football.[77]

In 1895 Rugby School assembled a committee to examine Bloxham's evidence. However, despite being unable to adduce a single person who had either witnessed or knew someone who had witnessed Ellis's exploit, they endorsed Bloxham's account. The committee concluded that in 1820 handling was absent from Rugby's football but at some time between 1820 and 1830 the innovation of running carrying the ball was introduced, in all probability by Ellis. The innovation was regarded as of dubious legality but between 1830 and 1840 it obtained customary status and was duly legalised by the Big-side levee of 1841 and finally by the rules of 1846.[78] As need hardly be said, the various statements of the committee do not accord with the evidence that was presented before them, which failed to sustain any part of the account that Bloxham had provided concerning the alleged exploit of Ellis. Naturally, this means that the Ellis story, though charming, has little to add to the origins of Rugby's football game.[79]

The first clear idea that we have of football at Rugby School comes from the period when Thomas Arnold was headmaster, 1828–41. As headmaster of Rugby School Arnold endeavoured to reform the institution by placing greater emphasis on order and personal morality. Arnold believed that childhood was a selfish, ignorant state and that boys needed to be taught to suppress their egotism, which he endeavoured to accomplish by a range of initiatives.[80] According to Dunning and Sheard one of the chief tools that Arnold used in an effort to reform the behaviour of pupils at Rugby was sport and they claim that he 'adhered to an emergent educational ideology which laid stress on the "character forming" properties of team games'.[81] For Dunning and Sheard there were two key elements in this, for they write that Arnold's 'principal *direct* [their italics] contribution to the development of football lay in his prohibition of field sports and mild encouragement of team games'.[82] Dunning and Sheard maintain that Arnold regarded the sons of aristocrats as causing disciplinary problems within the school and therefore made a conscious decision to refuse to admit them. Additionally, they maintain that Arnold attacked the recreations that were most identified with the sons of aristocrats, field sports.[83] By removing the disruptive influence of aristocrats and curbing the disciplinary problems resulting from field sports, Arnold instilled order into the School. The creation of an ordered and disciplined environment helped to foster team games, thus enabling the boys to develop their version of football, which included a number of distinctive elements such as H-shaped goals, the use of an oval ball, and the creation of informal assemblies during which rules were decided.[84] Cumulatively, Dunning and Sheard claim that 'following Arnold's reforms, the game of rugby football began to become more complex, distinct and "civilised", i.e. that it began to undergo a process of modernisation'.[85] One significant manifestation of this was that 'handling began to be emphasised at the expense of kicking'.[86]

While the idea that the development of organised sport at Rugby owed a significant debt to the reforms instituted by Thomas Arnold is potentially seductive, it is largely contradicted by the evidence. To begin with, despite the fact that Arnold wrote copiously on education, nowhere does he ever mention sport having a role in education! Indeed, while Arnold approved of healthy, lawful, recreation he did little to sponsor it.[87] Significantly enough, *Tom Brown's School Days*, the text that has done most to foster the idea of Arnold's interest in the educational virtues of sport, provides glaring evidence of how little importance he attached to sport, for it is noticeable that he is not even present at the sporting highlight of the year, the big end of term cricket match, having departed for his holidays![88] One of the early reviewers of *Tom Brown's School Days* stated that there was no indication that Arnold ever regarded athletics as having a key role to play in education and that he was not a 'patron saint of athleticism'. 'His letters may refer to Rugby's amusements, but they give no proof that he took the sort of view of them which is taken by Tom Brown. On the contrary, the exuberant animal spirits of the boys filled him with a sort of sorrow'.[89] Thus, although Arnold has sometimes been presented as promoting the idea that sport had a vital role in the moral education of boys, there is no evidence for this, and the ideology was created by a number of others, notably Vaughan, Cotton, Thring, Walford and Almond.[90]

Dunning and Sheard argue that Arnold opposed the admission of the sons of aristocrats to Rugby.[91] However, an examination of the evidence demonstrates that during Arnold's tenure (1828–41) Rugby became *more*, not less aristocratic, as Table 2.4 shows. As can be seen, in both absolute and percentage terms, the number of pupils admitted whose parents were titled increased during the decade that Arnold was in charge, that is 1831–40, by comparison with the earlier period (1821–30). Dunning and Sheard maintain that 'Arnold's opposition to the aristocracy…caused him…to wage war on hunting, shooting, fishing and other aspects of the traditional aristocratic-gentry life-style'.[92] Given that nowhere does Arnold make such a statement, this is simply the assumption of the authors. Fundamentally, all Arnold appears to have been doing was to outlaw these sports because they resulted in pupils straying out of bounds and causing trouble for the surrounding farmers. This was precisely the same policy as that pursued at Eton, a school that no one has ever accused of being anti-aristocratic, whose masters began, in 1841, to 'countenance' football because it 'contributed to keeping the students within bounds'.[93]

Table 2.4 Comparison of the admission of pupils from aristocratic families at Eton, Harrow and Rugby 1821–40

School	*Years*	*Titled*	*Total*	*%*	*Years*	*Titled*	*Total*	*%*	*% dif*
Eton	1821–30	283	1,397	20.25	1831–40	232	1,296	17.96	−2.3
Harrow	1821–30	107	592	18.07	1831–40	117	575	20.34	+2.3
Rugby	1821–30	24	520	4.61	1831–40	59	888	6.64	+2.03

Source: T. Bamford 'public Schools and social class, 1801–1850' *British Journal of Sociology* xii (1961) p. 225.

Note

Columns 2–5 deal with the decade 1821–30 and detail the number of pupils whose parents were titled and the total number of students. Column 5 represents the amount of titled pupils as a percentage of the overall intake. Columns 6–9 do likewise for the period 1831–40. Column 10 compares the percentages of pupils admitted whose parents were titled and represents this as either a +, if the figure for the latter decade exceeds that of the former, or − if the earlier period exceeds that of the latter.

As we have seen, there is no convincing evidence of Arnold supporting an educational ideology based upon the use of games, nor of his opposing the admission of the sons of aristocrats. Having established this, let us now consider what we know about the football played at Rugby during Arnold's tenure as headmaster. Given that we know so little about the football played at Rugby previous to Arnold's arrival, there is no real way of establishing the extent to which it changed under his headship. It is certainly the case that of the fifteen witnesses who appeared before the Rugby committee in 1895 only one claimed that substantial changes occurred in the rules during Arnold's tenure as headmaster (see Table 2.5). Of course, given the age of the witnesses and the fact that they were providing evidence on events that occurred over fifty years previously, such testimony must be treated with profound caution, but it certainly indicates that there is no reason for believing that the rules of Rugby's football underwent change during Arnold's tenure as headmaster.

While the statements upon which Table 2.5 was based need to be treated with caution, we posses two other sources that were almost contemporary with Thomas Arnold's period as headmaster. The first of these was Tom Hughes's book *Tom Brown's School Days*, while the second was from another old boy, Newmarch, who, however, appears to have spent little time at the School and was regarded by some later writers as being an unreliable source.[94] Let us look at what these writers have to say about Rugby's football during Arnold's reign as headmaster (1828–41).

Hughes's account of football in *Tom Brown's School Days* appears to be a game that was played largely with the feet. However, it was legal to run holding the ball providing that you had caught it before it had bounced more than once, as the following quote makes clear:

> no need to call though, the School-house captain of quarters has caught it on the bound, dodges the foremost schoolboys, who are heading the rush, and sends it back with a good drop-kick well into the enemy's country.[95]

Table 2.5 Opinions of the witnesses examined by the Rugby Committee in 1895 on whether the game changed during the headmastership of Thomas Arnold 1828–41

Name	*Years when first played*	*Permanent*	*Change*
Harris, T.	1828	yes	
Allen	1830	yes	
Deane	1830	yes	
Fowler	1830	yes	
Lyon, J.	1830	yes	
Nevill	1830	yes	
Birch	1831	yes	
Garratt	1831	yes	
Arbuthnot	1832	yes	
Gibbs	1832	yes	
Harris, J.	1832	yes	
Cunningham	1833	yes	
Hughes	1834		yes
Lyon, E.	1834	yes	
Benn	1835	yes	

Source: A. J. Lawrence *The Origins of Rugby Football. Report of the Sub Committee of the Old Rugbeian Society* (Rugby 1897) pp. 12–26.

Note
This table was derived by examining the statements that the various witnesses gave the Rugby committee concerning their memories of the football played at Rugby during the period when they were pupils. The second column lists the year when the student believes he commenced playing football and the third and fourth columns detail the extent to which the game changed during his time there. If the student believes that the practice of running carrying the ball having caught it before it had bounced twice was legal at the time when he first commenced playing a yes is recorded in the third column indicating that no substantial change occurred in the rules of the Rugby game during Arnold's tenure. If, on the other hand, the practice of running holding the ball was illegal when the student first began playing football but changed during Arnold's reign a yes is recorded in the fourth column.

Curiously, in his evidence before the committee of 1895 Tom Hughes stated that in 1834 running holding the ball was effectively forbidden and while it gradually became more prevalent, particularly in the season 1838–39, it was not until season 1841–42 that running carrying the ball was made lawful (providing that the ball had bounced no more than once).[96] If this is correct, the game described in *Tom Brown's School Days* must be from the end of Arnold's tenure, for there are no protests against those player's who ran carrying the ball.

Newmarch has nothing to add to this aspect of the rules, but does provide evidence, albeit somewhat garbled, on the dress that players used for football, indicating that the only distinctive uniform for football was the wearing of white trousers, as the following quotes show:

> the first indications of a match at football are the prevalence of white trousers at calling-over, even in Winter time.[97]

> divesture of jackets, braces and other impediments to a free use of limbs, and also hats.[98]

Writing in 1848, he compares the modern day dress with that of Arnold's time and states:

> Considerable improvement has taken place within the last few years, in the appearance of a match, not only from the great increase in the number of boys, but also in the use of peculiar dress, consisting of velvet caps and jerseys.[99]

Tom Hughes specifically tells us that the closest approximation to football dress that the boys had was white trousers.[100] However, a third source, Arbuthnot, indicates that during Arnold's time the boys wore velvet caps for football. On 29 October 1839 the Queen visited Rugby and requested to see a game of football, whereupon 'the players hung up their waistcoats and coats on palings and played, arrayed in white trousers, belts and velvet caps'.[101] While it is clear that players did adopt a uniform for this particular football match, it seems likely, as Macrory suggests, that this was in no sense typical. On the contrary, the boys were simply putting on a show, 'regardless of their best dress', in response to the queen's request to see a game of football.[102] From all this it appears that during Arnold's time white trousers were the only part of a players clothing that were distinctively linked to football. As for the three innovations that Dunning and Sheard identify as occurring during this period, the H-shaped goals, oval shaped ball and the holding of assemblies during which rules were decided, while Hughes provides a picture of the H-shaped goals, nowhere is there a mention of the other two elements.

As such, the above accounts, from Hughes, Newmarch and Arbuthnot, are effectively all the information that we have concerning football at Rugby during the period when Arnold was headmaster. By contrast, the evidence flows far more copiously and reliably when dealing with the game during the time of Arnold's successor, Tait (headmaster at Rugby from 1842 to 1852). During Tait's period we have two excellent sources on the football at Rugby School. First, there are the printed rule books that appeared in 1845, 1846 and 1847. Second, we have a verbatim account of a specific match that occurred on 26 September 1846, that was written by Thomas Arnold's son, W. D. Arnold, as an 'attempt to record the feelings, expressions, and circumstances, which attended the first introduction of football for the year, and the still more glorious epoch, the first day of the sixth match'.[103] This account was an attempt to provide a precise mimetic representation of the match that was played on 26 September 1846 and was written by someone who was a keen spectator of games at the School, and whose presence was recorded at a number of later fixtures, notably in October 1853.[104] Arnold's account is far clearer than that of Hughes, and is evidently based upon the same rules, as the following quotes demonstrate.

The game that W. D. Arnold describes is one in which players run holding the ball:

> Already has the leader of the Sixth side, the captain of hare and hounds, got the ball under his arm, and who may hope to stop him?[105]

However, they can only run with the ball if they catch it before it has bounced twice.

> one, adroit, active, cunning, has caught it on the bound, with slippery wiles evades countless adversaries, and with one successful drop sends it over the heads of the advancing party.[106]

> just as the ball is within one hundred yards of goal it is caught by some stalwart champion of the twenty, put under his arm and suddenly 'Maul him!' 'Well done!' 'Go it!' re-echoes from three hundred lungs.[107]

When tackled, however, these players did not relinquish the ball, but clutched on:

> Then comes the tug of war. The hapless and too adventurous hero who first grasped the ball, and he who first dared to stay his advance by his rough embrace, locked in each other's arms, the foundation of a pyramid of human flesh, giving vent to screams, yells and groans unutterable.[108]

In addition to the picture offered by W. D. Arnold, we have a number of other sources and from these we can see that during the period when Tait was headmaster Rugby's football became significantly more advanced and organised than during Arnold's time. This manifested itself in five ways: (1) the creation of a printed code, (2) increased attention to house matches, (3) the creation of informal meetings to discuss matters, (4) the employment of specific dress for football, (5) the use of the oval shaped ball. Let us now discuss these.

1 While it is clear that Rugby's rules for football had long been known by the pupils, and were presumably available in written form, in 1845 a decision was taken to print them, with revised versions appearing in 1846 and 1847. The most likely reason for this was the increase in the amount and variety of football matches played at the school and a consequent rise in disputes. Such an interpretation certainly accords with the following preamble that preceded the rules that were published in 1846:

> The following set of rules is to be regarded as a set of decisions on certain disputed points, than as containing all the Laws of the Game, which are too well known to render any explanation necessary to Rugbeians.[109]

Obviously, such laws were not designed for outsiders, but rather to preserve the game for Rugbeians. This is amplified by comments from Newmarch on rule 18 of the laws of football that the School established on 7 September 1846, which he declared to be 'decidedly an innovation'. Newmarch continued:

> If the book of rules is intended to preserve the game from degenerating, we think it due to Rugbeians of former days, that the laws which they established be adhered to by their successors.[110]

2 The question of whether football at Rugby enjoyed a significant growth during Tait's period is not easy to resolve. While there is considerable evidence that more attention was being paid to the game by the boys, typified by the existence of internal records of the house matches, notably *School House Fasti*, which only commence in 1842, other indicators undermine this somewhat.[111] While the records that the schoolboys kept list every champion house from 1842, they also suggest that during Tait's reign as headmaster there were only three years, 1842, 1846 and 1850, when house matches were held.[112] It is unclear why such fixtures were absent in the other years, but presumably different matches were being played.

3 With regard to informal meetings during which discussion takes place, W. D. Arnold left us a vivid account of this in his report of the levee of Big-side that occurred in September 1846.[113]

4 During Tait's period as headmaster, and in stark contrast to the picture presented by Hughes, the players wore specific uniforms for football, particularly different coloured caps to designate their house.[114] The impact of these uniforms is described vividly:

> The big school is now filled, a glistening array of whites, soon to lose their dazzling hue; fellows who are coming out in caps for the first time vainly trying to hide the blushing velvet in their hats.[115]

Players wore these caps throughout the game and Arnold observed that 'stray caps are picked up and restored'.[116] Newmarch noted the change in uniforms as compared to the era when Thomas Arnold was headmaster.

> These vanities have, as far as we could judge from a match at which we were present a few months ago, now gone out, leaving, however, the many-coloured caps and jerseys to contrast with white trousers.[117]

5 While there is no mention of the oval ball in W. D. Arnold's account, we know that by 1851 the ball was certainly in use, because the firm that manufactured it won medals at both the 1851 and 1862 Exhibitions for their achievement.[118]

A thorough examination of the evidence reveals that there is little reason for crediting the reforms instituted by Thomas Arnold with the appearance of a codified Rugby football. On the contrary, the key developments occurred under Arnold's successor, Tait.[119] While the codification that occurred under Tait was significant to the development of Rugby's football, the game seems to have experienced its most pronounced growth under Tait's successors. In 1853 the games committee was created, and new groupings collected for matches, such as 'Dissyllables vs School', an experiment that was described as 'good'.[120] By 1855 old Rugbeians were extensively involved in matches, notably the Sixth Form vs School, in which they played on both sides.[121] While there were occasional bad accidents, such as a player suffering a broken leg, predominantly the standard of football at the School was extremely high, and observers particularly praised the players for putting the ball down when tackled, thus avoiding mauls.[122] The attitude of Temple (headmaster from 1857 to 1869) towards football was probably typical of Rugby's headmasters, inasmuch as he took a keen interest in the game but did not promote it.[123]

As we have seen, Rugby's printed code was not designed for outsiders, and certainly was not an attempt to disseminate their game. Indeed, there is no evidence that Rugby made any attempt to publicise its football.[124] Rugby was one of the last of the major schools to start submitting reports of their football to the press and did so because: 'Having often seen football matches at Eton in your paper, allow me to send you one from "the football" school, Rugby.'[125] The writer, Francis Tongue described himself as an old Rugbeian who lives nearby and watches the matches.[126] Unfortunately he did not last long, an attack of the gout preventing him from attending, thus making him rely on reports that were provided by a friend.[127] It was not until 1866 that the 'head of School' began submitting reports to the press, and even notices that were sent on Rugby's football to such august chronicles as *The Times* were private initiatives.[128] In essence, Rugby seems to have been largely uninterested in its public profile and made no organised effort to promote itself despite the interest that *Tom Brown's School Days* had stimulated.

Shrewsbury School

Between 1827 and 1830 the footballers at Shrewsbury School confronted the sustained opposition of the headmaster, Samuel Butler, who banned his pupils from playing the game and was aided in this by the Reverend Arthur Willis, who rode around on his chestnut pony uncovering illegal play.[129] Gradually Butler's opposition was worn down and he was forced to relent, even to the point of allowing the boys to play football on one of the School's cricket fields.[130] When Kennedy succeeded Butler football became a fully accepted part of the School's recreational culture, though paradoxically this removed some of its appeal, the very covertness of the activity during Butler's time having given it a fascination that its legal manifestation could not match.[131] However, by season 1846–47 football had regained its popularity and plenty of pupils made use of the playing field that Kennedy had provided them with. Soon, indeed, pupils had no choice but to enjoy the game, for all those who boarded at the school were compelled to play football three times a week unless they were excused on medical grounds.[132]

The first reports of football from Shrewsbury School to the national press commenced in 1853 and from that time forth there is a very detailed record of the game there.[133] While predominantly matches were between houses, there were a variety of internal divisions, including those relating to the alphabet, picked sides and such like, some of which were contested between teams that were not numerically equal. The games were usually competitive but conducted fairly, though on occasion there are references to there being 'many walking wounded'.[134] By the 1860s the School's houses fielded first and second elevens representing their various age groups, who competed together on a league system for a silver bowl. There were four categories: senior, middle, junior, junior house.[135] During the period there was little contact with external sides, though three matches did take place between 1861 and 1863. In 1861 some friends of old Salopians, some of whom were former pupils from Charterhouse and Harrow, who had played football with them on Cambridge's Parker's Piece, made up an eleven to take on Shrewsbury School.[136] A year later a large crowd watched a match between Shrewsbury School and Shropshire, the latter team including many captains and reverends, most of who were old Salopians.[137] In 1863 the same sides met again.[138] When the FA was formed in 1863 Shrewsbury wrote to them and enrolled as members.[139]

The earliest extant copy of Shrewsbury's football, which was known as Douling, is from 1855. Shrewsbury's football was for unlimited numbers, though preferably for 12-a-side, and the objective was to score two goals. As there were no crossbars in Shrewsbury's game a goal could be kicked at any height. Handling was completely forbidden except for a straight catch, that is catching the ball before it bounced, for which the player was allowed a free kick. After 1864 this became the only time it was legal to handle the ball, with those offenders who broke this rule having a free kick awarded against them.[140] The offside law was severe and dictated that there was to be 'no standing wilfully between the ball and the opponents goal'. Naturally, such a law encouraged dribbling.[141] The rules of Shrewsbury were in no sense comprehensive, for although they did not forbid hacking, in practice it was not allowed.[142]

Westminster School

In 1710 a game of football was recorded as having been played on the green at Westminster School.[143] It seems likely that the practice persisted and by the 1840s football was being played on the green 'with no ulterior motive beyond amusement'.[144] As the following shows, it was a fairly simple game:

> The width between the two goals was the whole length of the Green, and the goals were imaginary lines at either end, a few yards in advance of the railings – lines recognised, but as truly imaginary as the equator… There were an indefinite number of goal-keepers, perhaps eight or ten, for the distance between goals was short, and the breadth of the goals comparatively great, a 'goal' would otherwise be too easily obtained. The rules were very simple. Sides were chosen from all the boys in the Green. Holding and throwing were not allowed, but the scrummages were sufficiently hot, and a 'rally' by the iron railings became sometimes agonising if not dangerous.[145]

Figure 2.3 An early example of artists appreciating the 'fun' of playing rugby. Taken from *The Illustrated Sporting and Dramatic News* 27 November 1880, p. 249.

Another source gives a quite different view of the game from this period, claiming that until 1851 football at Westminster contained many similarities with the game at Rugby School, including running carrying the ball and punching the ball with the fist. However, this was abolished and after 1851 the only legal way of handling the ball was to make a fair catch, which allowed a player to take two or three paces and then take a half-volley (not a punt).[146]

While it is difficult reconciling these two accounts, it is certainly obvious that a significant change occurred in football at Westminster in 1851. In November of that year the first reports of football were submitted from the School to the national sporting press, and simultaneously with this, the School's *Town Boy Ledger* details the football activity of the pupils.[147] From then on these two sources, often simultaneously, record a wide variety of games in the school, including a range of permutations, such as tall vs short, Queen's Scholars vs Town Boys and such like. In 1856 the School's football eleven were listed in a newspaper and from 1857 it was common for a variety of pickup teams to visit, as well as the occasional club, such as Dingly Dell.[148] Amongst the most intriguing clashes was the match at Vincent Square in 1859 between old and present Harrovians vs Westminster. The rules in this match presented considerable difficulties because 'the game of each is so different'.[149] In the early 1860s Westminster played various external opponents, such as Dingly Dell, Eton, Haileybury, Harrow. and Charterhouse.[150]

Winchester College

In 1825 matches were played at Winchester College with twenty-five players on each side. The game was very tough, and described as 'one, long maul'. Winchester's ball was heavier than that used in association football and as dribbling was forbidden one of the main objectives of the game was to charge down the opponent's shots, which must have often been a very painful business.[151] The Winchester goals were 27 yards away, and were simply a line cut in the earth, there being no cross bar (though no goal could be kicked above five yards high).[152] Winchester's football was regarded as the hardest and hardiest of the public school games, though there were evidently few injuries. The sheer physical pain of playing probably prevented its adoption at University.[153] Nonetheless, Winchester's football game was probably the model for the field game at Eton.[154] The rules of the Winchester game were not printed until 1863.[155]

Winchester's football was badly organised until at least 1839, with matches only being arranged the evening before.[156] By contrast with this, the prefects were tyrannically efficient in their treatment of juniors, insisting that they stand, often shivering, for more than an hour merely to kick the ball back if it went out of play.[157] By the 1850s football had become better organised.[158] The bulk of matches were internal, based upon various divisions such as Collegers vs Commoners, first six vs next twenty two, various houses, long vs short, light hair vs dark hair.[159] By 1858 teams were distinguishing themselves with different colour jerseys; red jerseys vs blue jerseys.[160] In 1859 Winchester played their first match against a team of officers from the garrison, all of whom appear to have been former Wykehamists.[161] The College's first matches against outsiders occurred in 1859, taking on Harrow and later Radley.[162]

Minor public schools

The initiative for submitting reports on football activity at the various minor public schools appears to have stemmed largely from pupils and former pupils. The first of such reports came from Cheltenham College in 1852, followed by Tonbridge (1857), Rossall (1858), Brighton College and Radley (1859), with Uppingham's appearing in 1861.[163] Predominantly, sporting facilities were quite rudimentary until at least the 1850s, games being conducted on gravel pitches at Mill Hill and Tonbridge schools.[164] By the 1860s masters were beginning to take a more prominent role in sports, especially Thring of Uppingham. As the decade wore on masters, such as Mr Brindberg of Cheltenham College, took the field with the boys.[165]

It appears that many minor public schools used rules that were related to the game at Rugby School. The word *related* must be emphasised, for in many cases the schools appear to have been reasonably catholic, incorporating elements from a variety of games, such as Eton's rouge and Rugby's drop-kicks. A number of examples of this appear during the 1850s and 1860s, notably Radley, Brighton College, Cheltenham College and Tonbridge.[166] The most intriguing set of rules was those of Haileybury. In 1840 Arbuthnot, a Rugby pupil, moved schools to Haileybury. Upon arriving, he worked to undermine the existing football game of the school, which was based on that of Harrow, and to replace it with a modified version of the rules used at Rugby School. The resulting code was almost entirely that of Rugby School's except that running carrying the ball was abolished.[167] While the Haileybury code had been created by a committee of boys, the rules used at Lancing and Uppingham owed much to the masters there. In 1856, Lancing College created its own code of football, which had teams of 12-a-side, and the game was regarded as a means of fostering teamwork.[168] Thring of Uppingham was a mass of ideas concerning football rules and during the early 1860s penned many letters, articles and books on the subject.

Broadly speaking the internal football matches of a school were divided into two types. The first were regular, specific, divisions, most commonly house matches. By contrast, the second were more transient and arbitrary selections, relating to hair colour, surnames and such like.[169] Almost all of the various minor public schools had matches of both types.[170] A number of institutions, notably, Cheltenham College and Radley, expanded the variety of their internal football somewhat by staging annual matches between old and present players.

During this period there was very little contact between minor public schools and outsiders. The one significant exception to this was Radley. In 1859, a team of Wykehamists from Oxford visited Radley and played a half-hour match.[171] During the same year Radley played teams from University and Brasenose colleges, Oxford. The following year Wykehamists from Oxford visited Radley and used both Radley's rules and ball.[172] In November 1860, Brighton and Lancing Colleges contested what seems to have been the first match between minor public schools. 1860 was also the year when Cheltenham College assembled a team from the nearby town, whom they then played using the College's rules. The following year Brighton College followed suit, assembling a team from surrounding schools. It appears that such ventures were not successful, largely because the outsiders had difficulties understanding the codes of the minor public school's football. The most significant interaction between a minor public school and outsiders during the period was the relationship between Uppingham School, primarily their master, Thring, and the FA. Uppingham joined the FA but did not send a delegate. Thring himself corresponded copiously with the London-based organisation.[173]

An overview of public school football

At most foundations during this period it was the boys rather than the masters who promoted and organised football. Predominantly speaking, until the 1840s the various school authorities did little more than provide fields in which the boys could play and their chief concern seems to have been to prevent their charges from making a nuisance of themselves during their leisure time. As we have seen, there is no evidence that Rugby's headmaster, Arnold, promoted sport and the crucial changes in that School's football occurred under Arnold's successor, Tait, during which period the game appears to have become significantly more organised. It must be emphasised that these changes, which included the creation of the first printed code of rules, were the initiative of the boys themselves and unrelated to any official volition. During the 1840s a number of public schools, notably Eton and Shrewsbury, began to adopt a more positive attitude towards the boys' football, but it was not until the onset of the 1850s that headmasters such as Vaughan and Cotton began to actively promote sport by employing masters who would participate in the boys' games at their respective schools of Harrow and Marlborough.

School football was based upon house matches, though other forms of division were sometimes used. As the period progressed there were an increasing amount of internal tournaments, some of which were supervised by the masters. However, the bulk of the various public school football clubs were created via the initiative of the boys. Predominantly, such external matches as they had were restricted to fixtures against teams of old boys who were returning to their former school. Only two of the schools, Charterhouse and Westminster, had much contact with outsiders, playing matches against other public schools, pickup teams, teams of old boys and such like. Socially, there appears to have been very little contact with those who were not from public school and no attempt to disseminate their football game into the wider community. Football at the various public schools remained very insular, with boys retaining the distinctive aspects of their game, typified by their various rules and occasionally embodied by highly idiosyncratic games, notably Charterhouse's 'Cloisters' and Eton's 'wall game'. Similarly, almost every public school appeared to use a different type of ball, ranging from Harrow's flat cheese-shaped object through to the weighty bulk beloved by Wykehamists. Cumulatively, such games did not lend themselves to contact with outsiders and while it would be erroneous to claim that footballers at the various schools remained completely separate, effectively speaking very little interaction occurred.

University football

While, as we shall see in chapter three, footballers at a number of Scottish universities were very active, for the purposes of this chapter the term university simply means the elite institutions of Cambridge and Oxford. The vast bulk of the intake of both universities stemmed from public schools and thus, potentially, the presence of so many footballers from different foundations provided an excellent opportunity for them to interact.

Cambridge

References to football at Cambridge commence in 1574, with the game being forbidden, but despite this there are a number of mentions of the sport over the next two hundred years.[174] For most of the first half of the nineteenth century football was 'held to be undignified for University men' and although played on Parker's Piece, it does not appear to have been popular.[175] This meant that there was a willingness for students from a variety of public schools, notably, Eton, Rugby and Shrewsbury, to play together.[176] In 1846 two Salopians at Cambridge University, J. C. Thring and H. de Winter formed a football club in alliance with some old Etonians and Rugbeians, establishing a common code. Judging by the account from Thring, the old Rugbeians were bitterly opposed to the compromise code, which was possibly the reason why the club's existence was precarious.[177]

Given the lack of footballers, however, there was a strong incentive for the members of the various public schools to co-operate, and in 1848 fourteen men at Trinity College, Cambridge, representing Shrewsbury, Eton, Harrow, Winchester and Rugby debated for seven hours and produced a code that became the basis of the rules that were used by the University football club until 1858. The code, which largely excluded handling, had a permissive offside law, and insisted that goals could only be scored if the ball passed under the bar, was strongly opposed to the rules used in the Rugby School game.[178] This tendency to establish compromise codes that were based largely on association-type games continued in the 1850s, as with a club at King's College whose members stemmed from Eton, Harrow and Rugby, but whose rules resembled those of the Eton field game, albeit with some adaptations.[179]

It seems likely that as the period wore on there were growing numbers of footballers from the various public schools and this gradually enabled players from the same school to group together and play by the code of their old foundation, thus avoiding the need for compromise rules. Consequently, from the middle of the 1850s football at Cambridge was largely segregated according to code, with teams made up of individuals from the same public school either playing together or forming teams and periodically returning to their old foundation for a match. The most active of these were the old Etonians.[180] Players from Westminster often visited their old school.[181] Additionally old boys from Harrow and Sherborne returned to their respective institutions.[182] The tendency for those stemming from the same public school to mix together reached its logical conclusion with the creation of football clubs specifically devoted to particular public school codes. In 1856 some old Etonians formed a club for their own brand of football, having been stimulated to do so by the creation of a similar club at Oxford.[183] Within a short while the Cambridge Etononian football club was very active.[184] In 1857 old Rugbeians established their own football club at Cambridge, playing twice a week on Parker's Piece.[185] Finally, in 1863, the old Harrovians founded their own football club, which played at Parker's Piece and was very active.[186] Curiously, old boys from Shrewsbury, the school that had produced the best footballers at Cambridge between 1854 and 1860, did not endeavour to create their own club.[187]

In the face of such developments it was clear that it would be very difficult to hold together a football club that sought to embrace the different public schools that were represented at Cambridge University. Nonetheless, there were many at the University who believed that such a club should be established and in November 1863 a meeting was organised, made up of representatives from many public schools (see Table 2.6), to establish a general game and create a club. After some discussion a club was founded, it being agreed that the team could play on Parker's Piece, and that membership would cost one shilling a year. The rules did not represent a compromise between the various codes for they resolutely opposed many of the key practices of the game founded at Rugby School, notably running while carrying the ball. Given that old boys from Rugby had their own club, and that there were plenty of old Rugbeians and old Marlburians at Cambridge, it was predictable that confronted by a code that abolished many of the key elements of their game they simply rejected the compromise and returned to their own game. Nonetheless, the new code did at least provide rules that could be used for matches between Cambridge's various colleges, as with the fixture between Christ's College and Trinity.[188] More significantly, the code would be adopted by the newly founded FA in December 1863.

The strangest aspect about football at Cambridge was the almost complete lack of matches between players representing different public schools. Given that the Cambridge University Football Club embraced players from a range of public schools one might have expected that there would be far more interaction between the various foundations, but paradoxically this was far from the case. Throughout the entire period the author has only been able to uncover two such games that can be definitely dated. Both are fixtures between Eton and Harrow, one in December 1862 and the other in November 1863.[189]

Table 2.6 Members of the committee set up by Cambridge University FC to create a code of football rules in November 1863

Reverend Burn	Shrewsbury
W. R. Collyer	Rugby
W. P. Crawley	Marlborough
R. B. Blake-Humfrey	Eton
M. T. Martin	Rugby
J. T. Prior	Harrow
W. T. Trench	Eton
H. L. Williams	Harrow
W. S. Wright	Westminster

Source: *Bell's Life in London* 21 November 1863.

Oxford

The first reference to football at Oxford University was at St John's College in 1555, where the game was forbidden.[190] By the nineteenth century football was well established at Oxford, though largely segregated according to the code used by the particular old boys. During this period only Eton created their own football club, playing on Christchurch Cricket Ground.[191] However, there was a great deal of activity by many other schools. For instance, from 1857 forty or fifty Harrovians met and played every Wednesday and matches were often arranged between particular colleges, the teams being made up entirely of Harrovians.[192] Old boys from Winchester were also active, the Wykehamists of New College taking on the Wykehamists from the rest of Oxford.[193]

It was also very common for students from Oxford to return to their old school. The most prestigious of these events were the annual Varsity matches that occurred at Eton between old Etonians from Cambridge and Oxford.[194] Some of the teams of Oxonians returning to Eton were assembled by individuals, such as Bathurst and Lonsdale.[195] On occasions these included players from Cambridge and even army officers who were old Etonians.[196] During this period there were a great many visits by Etonians from Oxford back to their old school, and their results against the current College team were often regarded as a good indication of the relative strength or degeneration of the age. Generally the matches passed off without incident, and some were conducted with good humour, Coleridge being praised for the jokes he told, but on occasions tempers did flare and at least one player had his leg broken.[197]

While other foundations do not appear to have been as fond of visiting their old school as the Etonians, many did return. A team from Oxford visited Marlborough, the bulk of the Oxonians being old Marlburians.[198] In 1860 a side was assembled entirely from old boys from Radley who were based at Brasenose College, who revisited their old school and played a match.[199] Oxonians played a key role in the match at Sherborne between past and present pupils.[200] Old boys from Winchester also played at their former school.[201] While all the above trips came off without problems, the match conducted by the returning old

Harrovians was beset by wilful rule breaking which put some strain on the tempers of players.[202]

By comparison with Cambridge, there seems to have been relatively more interaction between players from different schools at Oxford, a number of inter-public school matches being played. The most common of these were Marlborough vs Rugby.[203] Additionally, in 1863 matches were played between Rugby vs Wellington, and Marlborough vs players from various schools.[204] Winchester played matches against Harrow (1859) and Radley (in 1859 and 1860).[205]

Interactions between elite institutions

The public schools and the universities of Cambridge and Oxford were socially elite institutions that commanded considerable attention. The various members of these bodies could interact at football in two ways. First, and most obviously, they could play against one another. Second, they could co-operate in establishing a code of laws that could regulate games. These two sides of their potential interaction represent the two sections of this part of the chapter. Let us begin with matches between these elite bodies.

Matches between the members of elite institutions

During the nineteenth century snobbery impeded the contact between various public schools. The most striking example of this occurred in 1818 when Westminster refused to accept a challenge from Charterhouse to play a cricket match, because for reasons of snobbery they did not recognise the foundation. This remained the case until 1850, when an old Carthusian became the headmaster of Westminster, thus prompting them to accept the status of Charterhouse. Westminster was by no means alone in such elitist attitudes. Until the 1840s Harrow only recognised Eton, Winchester, Westminster and Charterhouse as public schools; Rugby only obtaining admission to this pantheon when Vaughan, an ex-Rugbeian, became Harrow's headmaster.[206]

While there is no evidence of snobbery affecting the interactions between public schools on the football field, it is by no means impossible that it was a factor in determining the selection of suitable opponents. Contact between public schools on the football field appears to have been first suggested in 1827, when Wykehamists challenged Eton to a match on Egham racecourse. Eton rejected the challenge because Winchester had stipulated that both sides should 'dress in high gaiters and mud boots'.[207] Seven years later a match was arranged at Eton, for eleven players on each side, between Eton and Harrow, 'which excited a great deal of comment in both places'.[208] Although this appears to have been the very first football match between public schools, the result is unknown. The match does not appear to have coaxed other public schools into action and as the Table 2.7 shows in the years up to 1863 there were just twenty-five matches between public schools. Given that this includes six fixtures that were almost certainly never sanctioned by the authorities of either school, being conducted

Table 2.7 Football matches that were arranged between public schools up to 1863

Year	*Matches*	
1827	Eton vs Winchester[a,d]	
1834	Eton vs Harrow[e]	
1840s	Rugby vs Shrewsbury	Rugby vs Shrewsbury[f]
1852	Harrow vs Westminster	
1857	Haileybury vs Westminster	
1858	Westminster vs Winchester College	
1859	Harrow vs Winchester College[g]	Marlborough vs Rugby
	Harrow vs Westminster[h]	Radley vs Winchester College[i]
1860	Radley vs Winchester College[j]	
1861	Eton vs Westminster	Marlborough vs Rugby
1862	Eton vs Harrow[k]	Marlborough vs Rugby
1863	Charterhouse vs Westminster[l]	Eton vs Harrow[m]
	Eton vs Westminster[n]	Eton vs Winchester College[b]
	Harrow vs Westminster[c,o]	Marlborough vs Rugby (2 matches)
	Rugby vs Wellington[p]	

Notes

a Eton declined this match.

b Eton–Winchester two matches were arranged, eleven a side with Eton rules, and six a side with Winchester rules. In fact, both were postponed and evidently never played.[q]

c This is described as 'the great public school match between Westminster and Harrow, the sixth between them, there being one win each and four draws'. The author has only traced three during this period.

d *Eton College Magazine* vii (5 November 1832) 282.

e *Bell's Life in London* 7 December 1834.

f G. Fisher Annals of Shrewsbury School, pp 404–5. On p. 406 Fisher states that the first ever match between Shrewsbury and another school was in 1876–77 season.

g *Bell's Life in London* 4 December 1859.

h *Bell's Life in London* 11 December 1859.

i *Bell's Life in London* 27 November 1859.

j *Bell's Life in London* 2 December 1860.

k *Bell's Life in London* 21 December 1862.

l *Bell's Life in London* 5 December 1863.

m *Field* 7 November 1863.

n *Bell's Life in London* 26 December 1863.

o *Bell's Life in London* 12 December 1863.

p *Bell's Life in London* 14 November, 12 December 1863.

q *Bell's Life in London* 12 December 1863. *Field* 28 November 1863.

by teams of old boys who were at university, this means that there were under twenty football matches between public schools in a period of almost thirty years. The smallness of this figure is a graphic indication of exactly how little interaction took place between the various foundations. Nonetheless, attitudes were clearly becoming more flexible, for twelve of the twenty-five matches that did take place were staged between 1860 and 1863.

The dialogue between the elite over rules

As can be seen from Tables 2.8 and 2.9, during this period the most active school, Westminster, only played matches against half of the other foundations.

Table 2.8 Number of matches played between foundations up to 1863

	1	*2*	*3*	*4*	*5*	*6*	*7*	*8*	*9*	*10*	*11*
Charterhouse	x									1	
Eton		x		3						2	
Haileybury			x							1	
Harrow		3		x						6	1
Marlborough					x		5				
Radley						x					2
Rugby					5		x	2	1		
Shrewsbury							2	x			
Wellington							1		x		
Westminster	1	2	1	6						x	1
Winchester				1		2				1	x

Table 2.9 Overview of matches played between public schools up to 1863

School	*Total matches*	*Total opponents*
Westminster	11	5
Harrow	10	3
Rugby	08	3
Eton	05	2
Marlborough	05	1
Winchester	04	3
Radley	02	1
Shrewsbury	02	1
Charterhouse	01	1
Haileybury	01	1
Wellington	01	1

By contrast, over half of the foundations only played matches against a single opponent. While we cannot dismiss the possibility that snobbery influenced the decision to play football with particular schools, it appears likely that the most significant factor in determining the choice of opponent related to the code of laws that they used. As many public schools used codes that diverged widely from one another, matches were of two basic varieties. One type of game would be conducted purely with the code of one of the schools, the other side having to cope as best they could with strange rules. Alternatively, a compromise code could be agreed between the schools. Let us examine these two options.

During the period a number of footballers were sufficiently spirited to contest games using the rules of the other side. In the 1840s, Salopians at Cambridge drew 0–0 with Rugbeians despite using the latter's code and being outnumbered by twenty-five players to fifteen! The following year Shrewsbury managed to raise a full side but the game, using Rugby's rules, was again goalless.[209] At Oxford a team of Wykehamists played a side made up of former pupils from Radley, using both Radley's rules and Radley's ball.[210] On occasions visiting sides could do very well with rules that were comparatively alien to them. On

16 March 1856 *Bell's Life in London* recorded a match at Charterhouse School, using the foundation's rules, between the School eleven and an eleven made up of players from Rugby, Winchester, Eton, Oxford and Tonbridge. The visitors won 2–1, both goals being scored by Rugbeians.

The second approach to staging a match between rival schools was to establish a compromise code. On occasions it was difficult to find common ground, as with the match at Westminster between old Harrovians vs old Westminster, which was unsuccessful because the 'game of each is so different'.[211] The extent of the diversity of the games played by different foundations sometimes provided an opportunity for a comparatively easy compromise. For instance, a match was played at Christchurch cricket ground, Oxford, between Old Harrovians and Old Wykehamists using Harrow rules and a Winchester ball.[212] The most adventurous attempt at staging a match between public schools occurred at Cambridge in November 1862. The fixture was between Eton and Harrow, with eleven players on each side. A committee made up of the two clubs drew up rules that were surprisingly detailed, and this probably accounts for the lack of disputes during the match. The rules specified that the captains were to toss for choice of goals, kick-off and ball. The match, which consisted of two halves of three quarters of an hour each, was played on a pitch that was 150 yards long and 100 yards wide, with goals being twelve feet high and twenty feet long, with a string running along the top. A kick was to be taken from the centre at the commencement of each half and every time there was a goal. Charging was allowed but shinning, pushing with the hands, holding and such like were illegal. Players were not allowed to intentionally play the ball behind their own goal and if the ball went out of play it had to be kicked straight in again. Handling was forbidden and the offside law insisted that a player must have not less than four opponents between himself and the defender's goal.[213] It is rather strange that these rules did not become the basis for a more sustained code and certainly the influential journalist, Cartwright, was keen on obtaining them, but evidently without success.[214]

The most regular, and it would appear officially sanctioned, fixtures between different schools were Rugby–Marlborough matches. In many ways these games highlight the difficulties that confronted players from different schools who were attempting to play together. Ostensibly speaking, Rugby and Marlborough played the same football game, for the latter school's rules were based on Rugby's, but there were significant differences, stemming from the fact that 'Rugby are more under rules and assisted by traditional ideas'.[215] The evaluation of the difficulties resulting from this varied; some commentators claimed that 'slight differences in rules caused small problems', while others believed that there was 'too much mauling' and that 'the ball should be put down as soon as the carrier is held fast, to do otherwise is contrary to the spirit of the game'.[216] Matches between Rugby and Marlborough had a high-level of official countenance, typified by the large number of masters who played (in one fixture 'nine masters played').[217]

Given the presence of so many former public school boys at Oxford and Cambridge it is a surprise that there was not more contact between the different foundations on the football field. It is significant that during this period a number of varsity football matches do occur, but none involving teams that were drawn from more than one public school. While there were a number of Oxford–Cambridge clashes, both teams always came from a single institution. Varsity matches involving Etonians commenced from 1859.[218] Slightly later, in 1862, Harrovians began staging their own varsity matches.[219] As a consequence of all this, rules were not established to regulate football matches between the two most prestigious universities in the country.

As we have seen, from the 1840s the members of the Cambridge University Football Club had created a code of laws that were a compromise between the rules used by the various foundations from whence the members stemmed. Beginning in the 1850s there were periodic suggestions that the footballers from various public schools should form themselves into a committee and create a common code that they could all use.[220] In 1861 a writer from Westminster School urged that there should be a meeting of the captains of the various elevens with the aim of establishing a general code for football.[221] In common with many other commentators, the writer believed that newspapers such as *The Field* should assist this process by printing the various public school codes and allowing their columns to be used to ventilate ideas.[222] While theoretically such a debate seemed like an excellent idea, in practice many of the correspondents showed themselves to be extremely partisan and one editor was forced to bring the debate to a close because although he had received many letters from public schoolmen, 'they are so mixed up with abuse of each other that we consider the letters better unpublished'.[223] In only one area does there appear to have been a real unanimity of opinion between the various writers. It was agreed by correspondents from widely varying schools that the crucial criterion for the selection of a football game was the size of the school. It was argued that a game using the laws of Rugby School was ideal for larger institutions because of the almost unlimited number of players who could participate. By contrast, other forms of football were suitable for smaller numbers.[224] Naturally, such a *modus vivendi* was of no use in creating a unified code, but it did at least provide some consensus between former public school boys, no small achievement in itself!

The impact of public school rules on the wider society

In 1845 Rugby became the first public school to have their rules printed, followed in 1849 by Eton. While we are never told why either foundation decided to take such a step, the most likely reason for having their rules printed was the growth in the amount of football activity at the schools. While in Rugby's case, as we have seen, the evidence for this is less clear, there can be little doubt concerning Eton, where there is an abundance of documentation recording the growth in the practice of football.[225] After 1850 most public schools decided to have their rules printed, the process being almost completed by 1856.[226] Despite this, the various rule books remained obscure and Eton's rule book appears to have been the only one that was easily available.[227] The extent of the wider population's ignorance of the availability of particular public school codes can be gauged from a remark on 14 November 1858 by the editor of the foremost sporting paper of the day, *Bell's Life in London*, who wrote that he did not believe that Rugby's rules were printed. Within a few months, however, this situation was to change significantly when the laws of the football games at Eton, Harrow and Rugby were included in Fred Lillywhite's *Guide to Cricketers* thus making them easily available to the general population.[228]

Although the general public was now able to read the various codes, it was quite another matter whether they could understand them. It should be remembered that the various public school codes that were published made no effort to be either comprehensive or accessible to outsiders, being, like Rugby's, designed to resolve disputed points.[229] Clearly, such rules were intended for those who were familiar with the game and were not perceived as a vehicle for the wider dissemination of their version of football amongst the public. In 1861, in an effort to generate increased understanding of football's rules, the editor of *The Field* began printing various public school codes in the paper. Nonetheless, while doing so, he acknowledged that the rules of football were so obscure that outsiders were effectively put off the game. In his opinion, the rules of Rugby School were the most intelligible, whereas despite spending half an hour or so studying Eton's, their code remained a complete mystery to him.[230] In view of this, it is extremely unlikely that the printed codes of the various public schools had much impact on the wider population and at best they appear to have been very unsatisfactory mediums for the transmission of football.

Another possible avenue for the transmission of the public school games of football to the general public was former public school boys themselves. The vehicles for such dissemination would be matches between or involving public school boys and non-public school boys, or any form of active involvement between footballers emanating from the respective spheres. The author has never found a single example of either type of relationship previous to 1860. When such events appear, they do not stem from the great schools but rather the minor ones, Brighton College and Cheltenham College, whose boys take on teams of local players. This is the closest evidence of the potential transmission of public school football that the author has found. As it appears that the local players experienced considerable difficulty with the rules it is by no means clear whether they made much of the experience. Curiously enough, there is one excellent example of a case where the transmission of a public school football code to non-public school players does *not* occur despite the most promising of circumstances. In 1854 a noted old Rugbeian sportsman, Tate, was the master who supervised football at Richmond Grammar School. However, an examination of the game played by the boys shows that it was completely unrelated to that of Rugby School.[231]

An examination of the evidence reveals that while it is theoretically possible that public school football did exert an influence on the football played by the wider society, there is no reason for adhering to such a belief. Despite the fact that there is a copious amount of contemporary literature, ranging from reports in newspapers and periodicals, through to later articles by 'old boys' themselves, there is no evidence, previous to 1860, of public school football being transmitted to outsiders by means of either the printed or spoken word.[232] Ironically, while public school football was so obscure as to be without positive influence on the wider society, from the practical point of view, its status and reputation might well have had a profoundly negative effect on the game. First, the existence of so many different public school codes, which were often espoused with a ferocious partisanship, impeded co-operation between old boys from different foundations. Second, the existence of these codes, stemming as they did from such socially prestigious institutions, had the effect of intimidating outsiders and discouraging them from creating rules to regulate football. Cumulatively, it is possible that the existence of various public school codes impeded the growth of football and that the real development of the game would stem from players using rules that were unrelated to those of the great schools. We shall find such games in the wider society where they had probably been played since at least the eighteenth century and this quest forms the subject of our next chapter.

3 Football outside the public schools

From American Indians to *The Origin of the Species* – 1600–1859

In the seventeenth century, a British settler in New England recorded that the local American Indians were skilful football players whose game was far less violent than that of the English:

> so in sports of activitie at footeball though they play never so fiercly to outward appearance, yet angrier boyling blood never streames in their cooler veines, if any man be throwne he laughes at his foyle, there is no seeking of revenge, no quarreling, no bloody noses, scratched faces, blacke eyes, broken shinnes, no bruised members, or bruised ribs, the lamentable effects of rage; but the goale being wonne, the goods on the other side lost; friends they were at footeballe.[1]

Over the next hundred years British travellers recorded football at several other places. The most unlikely venue was Greenland; a visitor noting that amidst the snowy wastes two parties of Greenlanders would throw or kick the ball towards one another's goal.[2] Football was also quite popular in parts of Russia, notably Saint Petersburg. The ball they used was stuffed with feathers, and the aim was to catch it or pick it up. Judging by our account, Russian football was a violent game in which players were regularly subjected to kicks and cuffs from one another.[3]

The observations of these visitors make us aware that football had long been an international game, practised in a variety of ways by diverse peoples. The steady accumulation of such facts prompted the great Victorian anthropologist, Edward Tylor, to apply the evolutionary theory that Darwin had first set forth in his mould-breaking work from 1859, *The Origin of the Species*, to consider the history of games. Tylor believed that football was just one of a variety of pastimes that had developed from a very early game involving the use of a ball. By applying the concepts of evolutionary theory, Tylor rejected the idea of there being a straightforward relationship between ancient games and their modern descendants, believing that 'the line of change may be extremely circuitous' and that 'it will not do to assume that culture must always come on by regular and unvarying progress'.[4] For Tylor, the history of games was full of twists and turns, incorporating periods in which the sophistication of sports would experience comparative progress and regression. Tylor would have had little problem with the greater sophistication of the football game of the American Indians compared to their European contemporaries, for he saw history as being a complicated fusion of many different forces and certainly did not assume that a more developed material culture would manifest itself in increasingly sophisticated games.

Tylor's insights provide a helpful guide to the present chapter, which concerns itself with uncovering and assessing the football that was practised outside of the public schools between 1600 and 1859. Whereas in Chapter 1 we dealt with the history of one group of games that were played outside the domain of the public schools (those conducted on an annual basis generally known as Shrove-games) in this chapter we are concerned with the history of ordinary football games, unrelated to either Shrove-games or those played within the privileged confines of the public schools. The chapter consists of three sections. In the first, we consider the history of popularly conducted football games between 1600 and 1800. The second and third sections are devoted to nineteenth century football, primarily the years 1800–59. In the second section we consider the locations of the various teams existing throughout this period and the social and economic composition of their membership. The third section examines the rules that regulated the various games of football that were played by these teams. We commence with the first part of the chapter, a consideration of popularly conducted football between 1600 and 1800.

Football in Britain 1600–1800

Extensive research by Magoun has revealed that during the seventeenth century football was practised in a number of locations within Britain. In England it is recorded at: Hexham (1647), Penistone – two games (1648), Maidstone (1653), Manchester (1655), London (1656), Manchester (1656), Maidstone (1656), Manchester (1657), London (1664), Richmond in Yorkshire (1668), Burtersett (1669), Ousby (1672), Durham (1683), Aldeburgh (1692), London (1694) and Dartmouth (1696). In Scotland, references to football are found at: Elgin (which has extensive records of football between 1598 and 1653), Lochton (1601), Aberdeen (1605), Abernethy (1620), Banff (1629), Banff (1682), Glassford (1690s), Kipper (1700).[5] To an extent, the number of references to football in Britain comes as some surprise as one might have expected the appetite for the game to decline substantially because of the impact of the Puritan ascendancy in government, during which time many recreations, especially those conducted on Sundays, were subjected to attack. However, in practice, Sunday play had been criticised long before the Puritans and they appear to have had little impact on the game. Overall, far from football disappearing when the Puritans became ascendant in 1642, the game appears to have prospered from that time forth.[6] Nonetheless, football did suffer from some official proscription and this surely accounts for the fact that many of the references that

Magoun has uncovered are records of people being punished, or threatened with punishment, for playing football. Essentially speaking, in the seventeenth century football was not approved of by the government but despite this was sufficiently popular to continue. This situation was not unusual for the game, which had often been subjected to governmental strictures; monarchs such as Henry VIII believing that his population would be better employed practising archery in preparation for fighting the French than recreating themselves with a game of football.[7]

When one turns to consider football in Britain during the eighteenth century, the game appears to be concentrated in three regions: (1) East Anglia extending up into Lincolnshire, (2) Lancashire, (3) the London area. By contrast with the previous century, there appears to be no specific evidence of football play in Scotland during this period aside from annual Shrove-matches.[8]

The major stronghold for football in the eighteenth century was East Anglia, especially the distinctive local manifestation that was referred to as 'camp' or 'camping'.[9] Throughout the period, camping or football matches occurred at many fairs, with the consequence that certain people, such as Hugh Wright, who was a noted footballer in Suffolk between 1767 and 1773, became quite famous.[10] The likely promoters of these events were publicans, but gentlemen would also sponsor matches, as with the 10-a-side game on Cranley Green in Eye (Suffolk) in 1754.[11] Such was the popularity of football in East Anglia that in 1751 a crowd of over 6,000 watched a match at Newmarket.[12] However, as the eighteenth century drew to a close football appears to have lost some of its popular appeal. One reason for this was probably a match between Norfolk and Suffolk in which there was amazing savagery, it being alleged that a total of nine players were killed during the contest.[13] Football was also popular further up the coast, in Lincolnshire, though here it was often linked to social disturbance. In 1768 a total of three football matches were staged as a cover for a protest against land enclosures. The game was no more popular with the authorities in urban areas; at Louth in 1745, officials warned people that they would be fined if they played football.[14] However, the game was not always proscribed and a well-organised match occurred between Osbournby and Billingborough on Monday 13 July 1795, in which the latter team wore blue in order to be more easily distinguished from their opponents. The 'severe contest' lasted six hours and included 'several feats of agility'.[15]

Football was popular in areas of Lancashire, with both Rochdale and Bury holding annual tournaments between various parishes.[16] In addition to this, publicans at Bury sponsored occasional events, such as a 10-a-side match at Bury Racecourse. The game was stipulated to last for three quarters of an hour on Saturday 24 May 1755 and the prize was to be ten hats.[17] Football was also played at several locations by children though, as with the adult players in Lincolnshire, the boys found themselves falling foul of officialdom. In Manchester's Eccles district, a number of boys were summoned before magistrates for playing football in the streets.[18] At Colne (1713) and Preston (1801), boys were punished for playing football during the Sabbath.[19]

While occasional references have been uncovered to games elsewhere, such as Worcester (1743), Great Ness, Shropshire (1709), East Looe, Cornwall (1722), Worcester (1743) and Weatherby, Yorkshire (1773), the third focus of football action during the eighteenth century was around the London area.[20] To the north, one Wednesday morning in May 1789, there was an 'extraordinary match at Dunstable Downs – a young gentleman took the hill for a wager of two hundred guineas against eleven of the best footballers in the county. He won after four and a half hours play.'[21] Somewhat further south, two matches occurred in Hertfordshire. In the 1750s a game at Barnet was recorded in print, while in 1772 a match was mentioned between Hitchin and Gosmore. On at least two occasions, visitors to London commented on the football played there, primarily by apprentices (1716 and 1723).[22] The most important centre of footballing activity in the London region was at Kennington Common. During the latter half of the eighteenth century The Gymnastic Society, a club that was made up of natives of Westmoreland and Cumberland who were domiciled in London, met regularly to pursue two sports, wrestling and football. The centre for wrestling was the Belvedere Tavern in Pentonville, and football was centred on Kennington Common. Until 1789, football matches were regularly played for large and small stakes on Kennington Common. However, by 1789 most of the Gymnastic Society's members were about to retire from business and return north, and consequently it was decided to reduce the club's activity. By way of a grand finale, in 1789 the club played its final big match, a fixture for 1,000 guineas, 22-a-side, between the natives of Cumberland and Westmoreland. After this, although football did not cease entirely, the club's remaining members continuing to meet two or three times a year, activity was soon reduced to an annual match on Good Friday.[23] Occasionally, other matches would occur, such as one at Kennington Common between Westmoreland and Cumberland on Monday 4 April 1796, but by 1800 the fixtures appear to have ended.[24] Amusingly enough, information elsewhere indicates that 1800 was indeed a black year for football, for in that year *The Sporting Magazine* declared that as far as the amusements pursued by fashionable ladies went 'football is fast going out and leap-frog is now the full sport of the day'.[25]

As the first section of the chapter has shown, football was quite a popular game in various regions of the country between 1600 and 1800. However, in this, the second section of our chapter, we must examine the amount of football that took place between 1800 and 1859. We approach this in three ways. First we detail the established view of football activity during the period. Having accomplished this, we offer an alternative analysis of the period, paying particular attention to the geographical locations of teams that existed in the years between 1830 and 1859. Finally, we examine the social and economic composition of the membership of these teams. Let us begin by considering the established view of football activity in the wider society between 1800 and 1859.

The geographical, economic and social composition of football teams in Britain 1800–59

The prevailing view amongst social historians is that the growth of industrial and urban society in the years after 1800 led to the steady eradication of football, typified by the decline of the traditional Shrove-games, until by 1830 football had become quite rare beyond the confines of the public schools. The most prestigious exponent of this view was Magoun, who is generally agreed to have been the most assiduous researcher into the history of football. Magoun was unable to find any examples of football between 1827 and 1857 aside from the annual Shrove-games or the various types that were practised within the confines of the public schools. In consequence of this, Magoun declared that popular football was 'dead'. Modern scholars agree, Mason speaking of 'the final nail in the coffin' and Holt suggesting that 'the game survived primarily as a rural pastime which had been in slow decline over a long period'.[26]

Essentially, such views are fairly straightforward and may be summarised as follows. Changes in the social and economic environment of Britain, such as the increased application of the police against popular recreations, and the growth of urban and industrial life, which led to a decline of space and time in which to play, meant that by 1830 football had largely disappeared outside of the public schools. As a consequence of this, the future of football after 1830 was seen as resting with the public schools, where, as Walvin says, 'the game which we now know as football was to evolve'. Within each public school rules would be developed that were suitable for their particular circumstances, replacing the violence of the game with

Figure 3.1 Perhaps the earliest form of indoor association football was conducted as part of the gymnastics meeting at Exeter Hall in 1885. Taken from *The Illustrated Sporting and Dramatic News* 19 December 1885, p. 356. Of course, it was not uncommon for boys at public schools to play their particular brand of football indoors, notably at institutions such as Charterhouse.

skill and fair play.[27] This codified game would be disseminated into the wider society during the latter half of the nineteenth century.[28] As Young writes: 'The years between 1835 and 1857 were crucial for British football, for during these two decades the game, saving consequent refinements in detail, was reconditioned and made into an effective instrument for modern use.'[29] According to this view, the future of football lay with the public schools, for it was they who would codify the game and it was this game that would be disseminated to the wider public.

The question as to exactly how the new, refined, codified football was transmitted from the public school to the wider society has been answered in two ways. The first suggestion is that it occurred via printed books containing the rules of the various public school games. Alternatively, a second solution was that the public school versions of football were popularised by the activities of various former pupils. The first solution has few adherents, though Dunning and Sheard believe that one of the main incentives for Rugby and Eton to compile and then print their rules in the 1840s was that they wanted to ensure that their particular versions of football were adopted more widely, particularly in the newer public schools that were beginning to appear.[30] The second view, that the newly codified games were promoted by the initiatives of former public school boys, is held far more widely. Scholars often refer to the individuals who were responsible for introducing the wider population to public school football as 'missionaries'. Walvin is quite explicit about the process:

> But there were more deliberate and organised attempts by men who had passed through the public schools to transform the game of football they found in existence around the country. Where it did not exist, they introduced it. The most striking result of this drive to establish football throughout the country was to be seen in those urban, industrial communities which, in time, were to become the social bed-rock of the modern game.[31]

It was the middle- and upper-class individuals endeavouring to promote healthy leisure pursuits amongst the lower orders, who disseminated the new rationalised football, which the public schools had created, giving it a discernible impact on those beyond the previously small milieu of practitioners.[32]

Having completed our outline of the established picture of football up until the early decades of the second half of the nineteenth century, it is now time to examine the same period according to evidence that has been either overlooked or ignored by our predecessors. We commence with a detailed look at football in the years between 1800 and 1830.

In the early decades of the nineteenth century the local version of football, camping, continued to be popular in East Anglia; a match at Ranworth, Norfolk, on Monday 12 June 1815, attracting between two and three thousand spectators.[33] By 1831 the area's appetite for football 'seems to have fallen off', for although the match at Norwich cricket ground between Norfolk and Blofield drew a large crowd, it was the first match since one at Ranworth in August

1822.[34] In Lancashire, the football championships between the best players in Bury continued to be held every Easter until at least 1820, but by the 1830s these appear to have come to an end.[35]

Elsewhere, football made sporadic appearances. During the early part of the nineteenth century, football was played on Sundays in Howarth, despite the opposition of the local vicar.[36] In January 1816, there was a match at Newton Stewart in Scotland, held at Kiroughree racecourse, between the parishes of Penningham and Minnigaff. The event was well advertised, printed bills being posted all over the area, and attracted a huge concourse, including many aristocrats.[37] Similarly, in 1825 a festival in Huntingdonshire celebrating Lord Sheffield's marriage had a number of sports, including football.[38] While these events were clearly well organised, a match at Cobham in 1826 seems to have been considerably more informal, culminating in a huge fight between two players.[39] Judging by our sources, the fate of the game differed dramatically depending upon the region. For instance, a report from Herefordshire in 1822 claimed that 'foot-ball is now the most common sport, especially on Sunday afternoons'.[40] Alternatively, a year later, Litt declared that 'football has dwindled to nothing, it used to be common thirty years ago'.[41] In 1826, the chairman at the inaugural meeting of the London Gymnastic Society contrasted the lack of recreation available in the area with that of twenty years ago, declaring that in those days 'the fields to the north, south and west would be crowded every afternoon with cricket and football'. This, he claimed, had now disappeared, due to rapid growth in the amount of building that had taken place.[42]

Generally, the period between 1800 and 1830 contains fewer references to ordinary, as opposed to festival, football than the preceding century but this does not necessarily prove that it was in decline, let alone facing extinction, as some historians have maintained. Indeed, in July 1831 *The Sporting Magazine* declared that football was the most popular game in a range of northern counties, including Westmoreland, Cumberland, Yorkshire and Lancashire.[43] Were they right?

The alleged disappearance of football in the wider community between 1830 and 1860 has troubled a number of scholars, not least because of the rapid expansion of the game amongst the lower and middle classes in the 1870s. As we saw earlier, historians have attributed the upsurge in football activity in the 1870s to two causes. First, the dissemination of printed rule books. Second, the work of 'missionaries'. The first explanation can be easily dismissed, for as was shown in Chapter 2, the various written codes of public school football were effectively incomprehensible to outsiders and it is consequently extremely unlikely that the printed versions of them would have had any appreciable impact on the wider population. As to the second explanation, the work of 'missionaries', between 1864 and 1872 there were only five teams whose creation can be attributed to the efforts of former pupils from middle- and upper-class backgrounds. These were: Pennard (1864), Bradfield-on-Avon (1865), Edmonton (1866), Turton (1871), Darwen (1872).

More usually in this period, there was little social mixing at football, clubs remaining a strict preserve of the upper and middle classes. When, in the 1870s, teams with a significant working class input emerged, there was little indication that they were the product of 'missionaries'. On the contrary, the initiative seems often to have stemmed from members of an existing institution, such as a church or pub, which would utilise its facilities to develop a football team. Walvin stresses the role of the working class in promoting football: 'But football was not a simple transplant by middle class workers into working-class communities, for there was a powerful and spontaneous upsurge of working-class football'.[44] Mason agrees, and emphasises the role of the working class in promoting football.[45] Given the lack of 'missionaries', scholars are surely right in being sceptical concerning their influence. However, it is rather hard to understand how the working class assimilated football so rapidly, given that historians treat the game as being effectively extinct previous to the 1860s and 1870s.

Such facts have prompted Cunningham to doubt whether football's demise in the wider society in the years between 1830 and 1860 was anything like as complete as has been generally presented. On the contrary, he suggests that casual football probably did continue and noted that although such games were 'unlikely to leave behind any records…[this was] no indication that it was rare'.[46] Similarly, while generally inclined to accept the demise of football outside the public schools, Holt realised that its persistence would help to explain later occurrences and noted that:

> certainly if evidence of the continued popularity of football on any scale can be found before the arrival of the Association system, the rapidity with which the Northern working class teams took over the sport and their proprietary attitude towards it becomes more comprehensible.[47]

However, neither scholar could furnish much hard evidence in favour of football's persistence and consequently their observations remained essentially theoretical.

As it is, as we shall shortly show, there is an abundance of evidence of organised football activity between 1830 and 1859, stemming in the main from a previously overlooked source, *Bell's Life in London*.[48] For most of the period between 1822 and 1863 it was the third best selling stamped weekly. Despite its being quite costly, many pubs and clubs held copies. With the onset of the penny post in 1840, its columns filled with letters from readers incorporating all classes and stemming from a wide geographical area. Some of these related to football and were usually written by the competitors themselves, thus providing a wealth of information. While it is obviously impossible to assess the level of activity of the teams that we find mentioned, the information demonstrates that organised activity was present. Table 3.1 shows a list of teams, arranged geographically, with the dates when their activity commenced.

As we can see, in the thirty years between 1830 and 1859 there were at least ninety-three teams in existence. However, before we begin to consider these teams more fully, we must mention the presence of football in two other areas of British life. First, football amongst children, and second, the presence of football at adult festivals. Let us commence with football play amongst children.

While the picture we have of the childhood endured by the working class in Victorian cities is often one of long working hours in a place devoid of green fields and fresh air, it appears that even amidst these unpromising surrounds it was still possible to play football. In the 1830s, the Commission on Public Walks endeavoured to provide evidence that would demonstrate that children in Northern industrial towns lacked places in which to recreate themselves. As it was, Blackburn's Member of Parliament (MP) pointed out that children seemed fully capable of finding places in which to play and Bolton's MP rejected the notion that the local children lacked space for entertainment, declaring: 'they do play at football in these parks, children have plenty of space to play in Bolton, the town being not much more enclosed now than in the past'.[49] A few years later, a witness at another inquiry into the conditions of working class children wrote:

> Although Christmas Day and Good Friday were the only fixed holidays in the mining region of Yorkshire, children had at least one day off a week and a fair portion of time in the evening. This they could use to play sport on the considerable areas of wasteland in the neighbourhood. Their games included cricket, nur and spell and football.[50]

Football was certainly a game that the Victorian child was familiar with and was mentioned amongst the recreations that were laid on in 1850 at Burnage Hall, the residence of the industrialist Samuel Watts, when he was visited by 450 of his workers and their children.[51]

Football was present at a number of adult festivals during the period. For instance, in 1834 Earl Talbot held a Harvest Home festival at Ingestrie (Staffordshire?) and the chief entertainment was a football match between men employed in various farms, that was watched by a crowd of two hundred.[52] In that same year, the rural sports at Windsor featured a number of events, including single stick, donkey-racing and football.[53] Eight years later football was again part of the Windsor festival.[54] The game was also played in less formal settings. During a particularly cold spell in 1838, the Thames was completely frozen over and this prompted an entrepreneur at Richmond to provide a 'sheep to be roasted on the Thames for the benefit of labourers, bricklayers and other unemployed'. Admission cost a penny and a number of recreations were available, including sledges and footballs.[55] In Scotland the border games of 1841 included a football match between the south and north sides of the Tweed, that was conducted with 'much good feeling'.[56] The sports that were held at Dundee in 1849 concluded with a football match.[57]

Having noted the presence of football amongst children and at adult festivals, it is time now to examine the ninety-three teams whose existence we detailed in Table 3.1. Let us begin by looking at their geographical distribution, first according to their individual counties and then by broader divisions into regions (see Table 3.2).

As can be seen in Table 3.2, the most active counties for football during the period were Yorkshire and Lancashire, two of the most industrialised areas in

Table 3.1 Football teams active in the wider society between 1830 and 1859[a]

Scotland	
Edinburgh University (1828–35)	Blairdrummond Estate (1835)
Deanston Cotton Mill (1835)	Edinburgh Gentlemen's Servants (1841)
Edinburgh Chairmen (1841)	Edinburgh Waiters (1841)
Edinburgh University (1851)	Edinburgh 93rd Highlanders (1851)
Edinburgh Veterinary (1851)	Glasgow University (1851)
Academical Club (1858)	Glasgow Celtic Society (1859)
Merchiston School (1859)	
Cumbria	
Ulverston Leathermen (1839)	Ulverston Other Trades (1839)
Yorkshire	
Thurlstone (1843–45)	Totties (1843)
Thurstonland (1843)	Bilkerstone (1844)
Denby (1844)	Foolstone (1844)
Hoylandswaine (1844)	Penistone (1844)
Thurlstone Upper End (1844)	Southouse (1845)
Holmfirth (1845)	Hepworth (1845)
Leeds Grammar (1851*)	Holmfirth (1852)
Richmond Grammar (1854)	Bramham School (1855*)
St Peter's School, York (1856)	Hallam FC (1857?)
Sheffield FC (1857)	
Lancashire	
Sidney Smith's Tavern (1841)	Bolton Rifle Regiment (1841)
Cronkeysham Champions Society (1841)	Renamed Fieldhead Lads in 1842
Four Lanes End (1841)	Orrell (1841)
Body-guards Club (1841–42)	Fear-noughts Club (1841–42)
Whitford Lads (1842)	King's Guards (1844)
Bolton (1844)	Boston (1846)
Charlestown (1846)	Manchester Athenaeum (1849)
Liverpool FC (1858)	
Derbyshire	
Derby (1838)	Ashbourne Upwards (1846)
Ashbourne Downwards (1846)	Egginton (1849)
Willington (1849)	
West Midlands	
Barley Mow – Dudley (1839)	White Lion – Dudley (1839)
Birmingham Athenic (1842)	
Leicestershire	
Leicester (1838)	Great Leicestershire Cricket and Football Club (1840)
Enderby (1852)	Whetstone (1852)
Blaby Youth (1852)	Wigston (1852)
Northampton	
Staverton (1849)	
Warwickshire	
Bickenhill (1842)	Hampton-in-Arden (1842)
Flecknoe (1843)	Grandborough (1843)
Rugby Tailors (1845)	Flecknoe (1849)

Table 3.1 Continued

Suffolk	
Bury St Edmunds School (1550*)	
Bedford	
Bedford Grammar School (1856)	
Berkshire	
East Isley (1843)	West Isley (1843)
Hertfordshire	
Aldenham School (1825*)	
London Area	
Mill Hill School (1807*)	Royal Military Academy (1856)
St Bartholomew's Hospital (1856)	Blackheath (1858)
Forest School (1858)	Chigwell School (1858)
Forest FC (1859)	Grenadiers 3rd Battalion (1859)
Surrey	
Light Dragoons (1844)	Surrey FC (1849)
Sussex	
Brighton School (1852*)	
Hampshire	
Southampton FC (1852)	Winchester Football Club (1852)
Parkhurst Barracks (1856)	Sunbury Military College (1856–58)
Royal Naval Academy (1857)	HMS Illustrious (1857)
1st Battalion Rifles (1859)	Winchester Garrison Officers (1859)

Note

a *Athenaeum Gazette* 19 October 1849. *Bell's Life in London* 25 March 1838; 13 January, 31 March 1839; 8 March 1840; 11 April, 25 April, 5 December, 12 December, 26 December 1841; 2 January, 25 September, 2 October, 23 October, 28 November, 25 December 1842; 12 February, 26 February, 7 May, 31 December 1843; 15 December 1844; 26 January, 2 February, 21 December 1845; 8 February, 21 December 1846; 26 December 1847; 4 March, 22 April, 7 October 1849; 2 February, 9 March, 6 April 1851; 11 January, 29 February, 21 March, 28 March 1852; 19 March 1854. 19 October, 16 November, 23 November, 21 December 1856; 18 October, 8 November 1857; 31 January, 7 March 1858; 13 March, 30 October, 13 November, 18 December 1859. *Field* 26 February 1859. In his trawl through *Bell's* in search of references to football that the author originally made during the composition of his MA dissertation in 1990 he overlooked mention of the Great Leicestershire Cricket and Football Club. His first awareness of this was from a reference that he found in a work by John Goulstone; A. Collins, *Rugby's Great Split*, p. 8, R. Holt, *Sport and the British. A Modern History*, p. 43; *Stirling Journal* 6 November 1835; N. Tranter 'The first football club?' *IJHS* x (1993) 104–5. Those teams marked with * are schools mentioned as playing football in the period previous to 1860 in C. Alcock (ed.) *The Football Annual 1873* (London, 1873) pp. 65, 71, 76–7, 79. The author has been unable to find any additional evidence that substantiates these claims and is consequently unsure of how valid they might be.

Britain. In the 1840s, these two counties were completely dominant, between them containing 55 per cent of Britain's teams. By contrast, there was no activity at all in London and Hampshire. However, in the 1850s, Hampshire had more clubs than any other county, and London shared second place with Scotland, just ahead of Yorkshire. By this time Lancashire had just one team, Liverpool FC, a team assembled by old Rugbeians.

Table 3.2 Relative distribution of football teams by county 1830–59

County	*Pre-1830*	*1830s*	*1840s*	*1850s*	*Total*
Yorkshire			12	07	19
Lancashire			13	01	14
Scotland		03	03	07	13
Hampshire				08	08
London	01			07	08
Leicestershire		01	01	04	06
Warwickshire			06		06
Derbyshire		01	04		05
West Midlands		02	01		03
Berkshire			02		02
Cumbria		02			02
Surrey			02		02
Bedfordshire				01	01
Hertfordshire	01				01
Northamptonshire			01		01
Suffolk	01				01
Sussex				01	01
Total	03	09	45	35	93

Note
The teams listed in the first column, that is those that are described as pre 1830, are all schools whose footballing activity claims to be dated previous to 1830. As there appears to be no compelling evidence to support such claims the author has entered the information in a separate column. The three teams have been included in the final total of teams that existed between 1830 and 1859.

In order to get a broader perspective on the distribution of football activity throughout Britain let us divide the country into eleven geographical regions (see Table 3.3).

As Table 3.4 makes clear, in the 1840s the main regions for football were the Midlands, North West and Yorkshire. By the 1850s, the areas with the most teams were Home Counties, Scotland, London and Yorkshire. Two regions of England, the Western and West of England, were completely devoid of activity.

Broadly speaking, we can divide Britain into two distinct units based upon the predominant features of their economy. With its strong emphasis on manufacture, the North can be classified as industrial, and consists of the Midlands, Yorkshire and North West regions. By contrast, the economic basis of the South was more commercial and agricultural, and consists of the Home Counties, the Upper Home Counties and London. The result of such an analysis can be seen in Table 3.5.

Table 3.5 makes it clear that during the 1840s the North was the heartland of football, far surpassing the South. In the 1850s the situation was somewhat reversed, with the South taking the lead. Such facts are in sharp contradiction to the prevailing orthodoxy concerning the era. The dominant assumption amongst historians is that the 1840s, 'the hungry forties', were a time of great deprivation and turmoil, especially in industrial Britain. The population, it is claimed, were too tired and dispirited to play football. Indeed, even had

Table 3.3 Composition of football teams in various regions

Home Counties
Essex
Hampshire
Hertfordshire
Kent
Surrey
Sussex

London
London and Middlesex

Eastern
Cambridgeshire
Huntingdonshire
Lincolnshire
Norfolk
Rutland
Suffolk

Upper Home Counties
Bedfordshire
Berkshire
Buckinghamshire
Gloucestershire
Oxfordshire

Midlands
Derbyshire
Leicestershire
Northamptonshire
Nottinghamshire
West Midlands
Warwickshire
Worcestershire

Yorkshire

Scotland

West of England
Cornwall
Devon
Dorset
Somerset
Wiltshire

North East
Cumbria
Durham
Northumberland
Westmorland

North West
Cheshire
Lancashire

Western
Herefordshire
Monmouthshire
Shropshire
Staffordshire
Wales

Table 3.4 Number of football teams per region per decade

Region	*Pre-1830s*	*1830s*	*1840s*	*1850s*	*Total*
Midlands		04	13	04	21
Yorkshire			12	07	19
North West			13	01	14
Scotland		03	03	07	13
Home Counties	01		02	09	12
London	01			07	08
Upper Home Co			02	01	03
North East		02			02
Eastern	01				01

Table 3.5 Comparison of the number of teams in the North and the South 1830–59

Area	*Pre-1830s*	*1830s*	*1840s*	*1850s*	*Total*
North		04	38	12	54
South	02		04	17	23

Note
The pre-1830s figure is effectively irrelevant because it simply indicates those schools that claim to have been playing football previous to the 1830s. As there is no firm evidence of their playing football at any time during the period up to 1859, the author did not include them in any of the relevant decades.

they wanted to, they had neither the time nor the space in which to play. The following quote by Walvin is a good summary of these views:

> In the new towns of the midlands and north, football similarly began to fade away, but for different reasons. Dislocated and alienated people, whether natives of the town or immigrants from the countryside, were purged of their recreational traditions by the joint disciplines of urban and of industrial life.[58]

It was not until the 1850s that city life began to improve, the period 1852–67, '*The Age of Equipoise*', as Burn describes it, being one in which the social tensions of the previous decade become significantly diluted, producing a mood of optimism.[59]

As we can see, such statements are not supported by the facts concerning the existence of football activity. Far from the newly urbanised and industrialised areas of the Midlands and North being football deserts, by the 1840s they were the main centres for the game. It is in the following decade that they experience relative and absolute decline, a time when conventional wisdom would assume that they would start to enjoy growth. Cumulatively, such facts must prompt us to examine whether historians are correct in claiming that the growth in urban and industrial life meant that players had neither sufficient time nor space in which to play football. Let us first consider the question as to whether people had time to play football.

On only one occasion is there strong evidence of the amount of football being substantially damaged by the players' lack of sufficient leisure hours. In 1841, the team Whitford Lads were unable to arrange a match against Fieldhead Lads because the latter already had a game organised for that day and in consequence of this the teams had to wait a whole year in order to play.[60] While such qualitative data is interesting, as this constitutes the only example that we have, it is questionable how representative it was of the situation confronting working-class footballers. As it is, we are able to obtain an additional, more quantitative, idea of the availability of recreational time because we possess a substantial amount of information concerning the days on which matches occurred. Between 1830 and 1859 there were fifty-eight matches involving the clubs that are listed in Table 3.1. Of these, it proved possible to discern the day on which play took place in thirty-four cases, that is 58 per cent. Thus, we have a fairly good idea of the recreational timetable that was being used by footballers during this period and are consequently in a position to utilise this information in two ways.

Our first approach relates to the extent to which games were played during annual holiday periods. Such an analysis is based on the assumption that if players were short of recreational time in which to play, the bulk of football games would be staged during annual holiday periods. Correspondingly, a high incidence of matches during periods that could certainly not be classified as annual holidays would indicate a recreational timetable that was comparatively rich in opportunities for the sides to meet. The second insight that this information provides relates to the days on which games were played during an ordinary working week. For the bulk of the years between 1830 and 1859, Monday was the main recreational day of the week for those in the lower orders (many of whom would take the whole day off), and Saturday the busiest working day of the week. While from the middle of the 1840s this pattern was gradually changing, with the holiday on Monday being replaced by half-day Saturday, the new pattern did not become general until the 1860s. The situation was somewhat different for the middle classes, who appear to have had more leisure time on Saturday, especially by comparison with Monday. In view of this, we would expect that matches by teams from the lower orders would be concentrated on Mondays during an ordinary working week.

Unfortunately, when we endeavour to use our data to examine the incidence of play during established annual holidays, we confront one very significant problem: there were effectively no nationally established annual holidays. For instance, in Bolton Christmas Day was not a holiday, the factories working during all but the hours when the church service was on and the main holidays being taken during the first week of the New Year.[61] As a consequence of this, it is hard to determine whether particular days were holiday periods in an area, and inevitably this confuses the extent to which football activity can be seen as dependent upon established holidays. It was thus thought best to adopt as broad an approach as possible towards the definition of an annual holiday and consequently classify any festival day that was mentioned in the report that was provided of the game as being an annual holiday. Thus, during the period 1830–59 the following days are treated as annual established holidays: Christmas Day (3), Easter Monday (1), Good Friday (2), New Year's Day (1), Shrove Tuesday (3) (the figures in brackets represent the number of occasions on which they are mentioned). This amounts to ten, that is 29 per cent of those events where it was possible to discern the day on which play occurred. Clearly, annual holidays were important to the staging of football matches. The extent of influence exerted by annual holidays becomes still more apparent when we begin to analyse the social composition of the teams whose games were played during these possible holiday periods. Of the thirty-four matches for which we can discern the day of play, twenty were matches between working-class teams and fourteen between middle-class sides. Of the twenty matches conducted by working-class teams, ten occurred during annual holiday periods (50 per cent). By contrast, not one of the matches involving middle-class teams was held during a holiday period (see Table 3.6). Such facts indicate that annual holiday periods were particularly important for the holding of football matches involving working-class teams.

Our second approach to the information involves a consideration of the non-holiday recreational timetable. Table 3.7 lists the distribution of the twenty-four non-holiday events for which it was possible to uncover the day on which games were played. In terms of social class, these twenty-four matches break down into fourteen by upper-class players (58.3 per cent) and ten by working-class teams (41.7 per cent). While one might expect an analysis of the distribution of

Table 3.6 Use of ordinary days and holidays for match play by middle- and working-class teams

Social class	*Ordinary days*	*Holidays*	*Total*
Middle class	14 (100%)		14
Working class	10 (50%)	10 (50%)	20

Table 3.7 Days when matches were played

Day	*Mon*	*Tues*	*Wed*	*Thurs*	*Fri*	*Sat*	*Total*
Number of matches	4	2	4	1	2	11	24

Table 3.8 Distribution of games played by working- and middle-class teams during the working week

Day	*Mon*	*Tues*	*Wed*	*Thurs*	*Fri*	*Sat*	*Total*
Working-class team	4	1	0	1	2	02	10
Middle-class team	0	1	4	0	0	10	14

the teams according to their social rank throughout the various days of the week to break down roughly in proportion to the above ratio, this is not the case, as Table 3.8 makes clear. This is particularly noticeable on two days, Monday and Saturday. Of those teams whose playing day was discerned to be Monday, every one of them belonged to the working class. These were Cronkeysham Champions, Whitford Lads, Flecknoe and Dudley. By contrast, although games that were held on Saturday make up almost 50 per cent of the total, Deanston Cotton Mill vs Blairdrummond Estate Workers and Enderby vs Whetstone were the only matches held between working class teams on that day. Predominantly, Saturday was the time when middle class teams played, such as Edinburgh University, Edinburgh Veterinary College, Academical Club, Liverpool, Surrey, Manchester Athenaeum and various army officers. From this we can see that predominantly speaking the recreational timetable of the teams differed profoundly, depending upon their social rank, and that these reflected the timetable found elsewhere in the wider society.

Overall, our sources suggest that teams from the lower orders did experience some difficulties in obtaining sufficient leisure time in which to contest football matches. Judging by such information as we have been able to glean concerning the recreational timetable used by footballers during the period, teams from the lower orders were largely restricted to either annual holiday times or established free-days during the working week, notably Mondays. Of course, it must be remembered that the information upon which this is based is very incomplete and consequently we must not place too much emphasis upon it. Additionally, the fact that almost every match that was conducted by working-class teams involved stakes makes it clear that players had sufficient time to practise for matches, for otherwise they would surely not have risked playing for their own money!

Having examined the question as to whether people had time in which to play, we must now consider the other explanation that is usually provided for football's demise, lack of playing space. This view has been considerably strengthened by the vision that a number of very influential writers have presented of urban life around the middle of the nineteenth century, especially in the newly industrialised cities. Naturally, the embodiment of this is Manchester, a place that visitors such as Engels, Dickens, Disraeli and Carlyle condemned for its lack of greenery. As it is, however, an examination of our sources shows that footballers had few difficulties in finding space in Manchester in which to play. Essentially speaking there were two types of playing area. One type of provision was essentially private, on grounds that were attached to pubs, whose owners were happy to stage events in order to attract and retain customers.[62] Other places, such as Kersal Moor, Newton Common and the Stretford Road, were deserted, public land, containing ample available space in which to play.[63] The situation was similar elsewhere in the industrialised areas of Lancashire. For instance, in heavily urbanised Rochdale, footballers clearly regarded the availability of a playing area as an insignificant problem, suggesting to prospective opponents that they 'toss for choice of grounds'.[64] In Blackburn, a witness before a government inquiry observed that although there were no public areas in which football could be played, it was very common for players to trespass on to fields. These actions do not appear to have prompted hostility from the owners because during the wintertime 'they do not do much injury'.[65]

In Yorkshire's urban areas there were a number of private facilities available, such as Doncaster's Race Course and Sheffield's Hyde Park, both of which were suitable for football. In Edinburgh, the local hotels and pubs had land attached to them, and were the venues for matches between teams made up of servants. Rural areas contained even more space, games being played in fields. Of course, venues, whether in town or country, were sometimes less than perfect, as the following letter reveals,

> Shrove Tuesday. 10 single men of Willington v 10 single men of Egginton for £2 which was won by Willington, after one of the best games ever witnessed on the lawn of Egginton. It lasted two hours and 20 minutes and it was a fair kick and trip game. If the Egginton men are not satisfied the same ten men will play the other ten a return match £5 a side, but they hope the 'keeper' will be more cautious and see that the guard dog is properly secured or a muzzle put upon him, for should he break loose again he may get his head cracked.[66]

Figure 3.2 One of the earliest attempts at playing floodlight football was not a success. Still, as they said, 'Who wants to play football under artificial light?' Taken from *The Illustrated Sporting and Dramatic News* 16 November 1878, p. 204.

Predominantly, however, access to suitable playing space does not appear to have been a problem and in some instances goal frames were pitched and playing areas marked.

Having assessed the evidence concerning the time and space available for football play in the period between 1830 and 1859, we can draw the following conclusions. Overall, there is some evidence to suggest that while teams clearly were able to practise at football play, lack of free time meant that they experienced problems when trying to arrange match days. This was especially the case for those sides stemming from the lower orders. In contrast to these problems, there is no evidence to suggest that footballers experienced any problems in locating suitable playing areas. Ironically, according to our sources, the most pervasive difficulty experienced by teams did not stem from the expansion of industrial life, but rather from its limitations. Improvements in communications, notably letters and newspapers, meant that teams were in contact with sides from a much wider geographical area. However, difficulties stemming from travel impeded their contact with one another. A consequence of this was that teams restricted the geographical radius of prospective opponents; Rugby's tailors were probably typical in limiting themselves to teams within five miles. The two most common means used to try and remove the difficulties that the distance between teams created was either to arrange to meet the opponents half way, or to offer to 'give or take reasonable expenses'.[67] These practices probably persisted until the expansion of the availability of railway travel, whereupon teams such as Winchester, in 1852, were willing to journey up to fifty miles for a match.[68]

Having examined the geographical distribution of teams between 1830 and 1859, it is now time to consider the social composition of these sides. Broadly speaking, when analysed the ninety-three teams can be divided into five categories. These are as follows: (1) Local, (2) School, (3) Clubs, (4) Military, (5) Occupations. Let us examine these categories more fully.

The term 'Local' represents any team that appears to be primarily selected because of the area in which the players live. The term 'School' covers any educational institution, including universities and training hospitals. 'Club' refers to the term that the team use for themselves. However, there is one important exception to this. In Scotland, the teams representing Edinburgh University used to call themselves Edinburgh University FC. However, for the purposes of this study it was decided to classify them under Schools not Clubs because the club was regarded as being based upon the school. The term 'Military' incorporates all service personnel. 'Work' is a classification used for teams whose members appear to be selected primarily on the basis of their occupation.

Table 3.9 details the distribution of each particular type of team within a county.

While we might expect the types of team in each particular area to break down roughly in accordance with the overall ratios, this is rarely the case. On the contrary, many counties display a distinctive characteristic. Yorkshire and Lancashire have a heavy over representation of Local teams, while having no teams based upon Military or Work (Yorkshire) or Schools (Lancashire).

Table 3.9 Types of team in each particular county

County	*Local*	*School*	*Club*	*Military*	*Work*
Yorkshire	13	04	02		
Lancashire	08		04	01	01
Scotland		06	01	01	05
Hampshire			02	06	
London		04	02	02	
Leicestershire	05		01		
Warwickshire	05				01
Derbyshire	04				01
West Midlands	02		01		
Berkshire	02				
Cumbria					02
Surrey			01	01	
Bedfordshire		01			
Hertfordshire		01			
Northamptonshire	01				
Suffolk		01			
Sussex		01			
Total	40 (43%)	17 (18%)	14 (15%)	11 (12%)	10 (11%)

Table 3.10 Types of team in each particular region

Region	*Local*	*Schools*	*Club*	*Military*	*Work*	*Total*
Midlands	17		02		02	21
Yorkshire	13	04	02			19
North West	08		04	01	01	14
Scotland		06	01	01	05	13
Home Co.		02	03	07		12
London		04	02	02		08
Upper Home C	02	01				03
North East					02	02
Eastern		01				01
Western						00
West of Eng						00
Total	40	17	14	11	10	92

Scotland has no Local teams but six School- and five Work-teams. Military teams are heavily overrepresented in Hampshire, as are Schools in London. Neither area has any Local or Work sides.

In order to get a broader picture of the distribution of the types of clubs, Table 3.10 breaks the information down into regions, using the same geographical divisions that were adopted earlier as in Table 3.3.

The most striking point that becomes salient via this new perspective is the extent to which football teams in the Midlands were dominated by Local teams and their complete lack of teams from Schools or Military.

Table 3.11 A comparison of the distribution of teams between the North and the South 1830–59

Area	*Local*		*Schools*		*Clubs*		*Military*		*Jobs*		*Total*	
	No.	%	No.	%	No.	%	No.	%	No.	%	No.	%
North	38	70·3	04	7·4	08	14·8	01	1·8	03	5·5	54	100
South	02	8·7	07	30	05	21·7	09	39			23	100

Table 3.11 aims at comparing the North and the South by employing the same divisions that were previously used in Table 3.5. North consists of Midlands, Yorkshire and North West. South consists of London, Upper Home Counties and Home Counties.

As can be seen from Table 3.11 the football cultures of the North and the South differed significantly in terms of the composition of their teams. Almost three quarters of Northern teams were Local, that is, based primarily upon the locality of their members. By contrast, over 90 per cent of Southern were not Local. The most important nuclei for Southern clubs were official institutions, namely the Schools and Military. Between them, these two bodies accounted for almost 70 per cent of Southern teams. By contrast, under 10 per cent of Northern teams were based upon such institutions. In essence, the football culture of the North was based upon private groups, unrelated to any official organisations. In the South the situation was entirely different, sport appearing to be based upon official organisations in which people such as officers and teachers probably had important roles. The application of these organisational skills in the South might account for the surprising number of teams that are classified as Clubs that we find there. Whereas only 8 per cent of Southern teams are Local, almost three times this number, 21 per cent, are Clubs. In the North the figure is drastically reversed, with only 15 per cent of teams being classified as Clubs, while 70 per cent are Local.

Having examined the geographical distribution of the various sorts of teams, it is now time to concentrate our attention on a detailed analysis of each particular sort of team. We shall deal with these teams in order of magnitude, and therefore commence with those teams whose numbers account for the largest proportion of our sides, those we classify as Local.

Local

The principal basis for forty of the ninety-three teams extant during the period appears to have been the region in which they lived, whether it be an industrial town or a rural community. In rural areas, a number of teams were based on parish boundaries, especially in Warwickshire, where these divisions appear to have been used for selecting teams well into the 1860s.[69] Occasionally, as at both Ashbourne and Isley, two ends of a parish would compete. Somewhat surprisingly, throughout the period there is only one example of two villages playing one another, from 1852 in Leicestershire. Another surprising absentee was teams divided according to marital status, a pervasive distinction in Shrove-games. The only specification which approached that occurred in Derbyshire where the match was restricted to 'single men'.[70]

According to the letters that were submitted to newspapers the headquarters of local teams were invariably pubs in the vicinity. The involvement of pubs in football was multifaceted. In 1839, a match at Dudley occurred between two pubs. At Bolton, the noted athlete, Ben Hart, was also proprietor of the Sidney Smith's Tavern, recruiting a side there. More usually, publicans acted as stake-holders, a practice that was especially common in Yorkshire and Lancashire. The relationship between pubs and football teams was a two-way process. The team Cronkeysham Champions changed their name to Fieldhead Lads, the pub where they were based: correspondingly, Ashbourne had its 'Football Inn'.[71] Given that pubs were such important centres for recreation during this period, including a range of activities, it was natural that the publican would assist local footballers, for such activity would doubtless help to attract custom.[72] Indeed, it was not uncommon for publicans to sponsor events, especially in Lancashire, where amongst the prizes on offer was a pig. A typical example of such ventures was the following:

> On Monday 3rd of January, John Greenhough of Hare and Hounds Inn, Nr Bolton, in order to revive the old sport of football, will put up an excellent cheese of 40 lb weight, to be played for by an unlimited number of persons, the arrangements to be agreed upon by parties entering before going to the field, according to the old Lancashire fashion of drawing sides. A free ball will be given, and all entries must be pre 11 AM.[73]

Schools

While a number of schools in England claim to have played football during this period, it is often hard to find contemporary evidence that can confirm this, and naturally still more difficult to discern the rules they used. It appears likely that two of the schools, Bramham College and Forest School, played association-type games, for in the 1860s both were to belong to the FA.[74] Judging by reports, Richmond School in Yorkshire also played an association-type game, despite having Tate, a noted old Rugbeian sportsman, as the master supervising football.[75] Having examined the surviving evidence Tony Collins identifies the game played at St Peter's School in York as being based upon rugby.[76] Our evidence indicates that many students were flexible in their outlook towards rules, as with the team from St Bartholomew's Hospital, who journeyed down to Charterhouse in order to play the boys from that school at football in the cloisters, a game the visitors had never previously experienced.[77]

In Scotland, there was a great deal of football in places of education, especially universities. In the 1820s, a football club was established at Edinburgh University and during the eight years of its existence 291 members subscribed, mostly from the middle and upper classes. Despite this, the club collapsed in 1835 due to financial problems.[78] It is clear from the account books that the club played a football game that was akin to that practised generally in Scotland, which we shall describe later in this chapter. This sort of game persisted at the University and in 1851 provided the rules for an encounter between English and Scottish students. However, during the latter part of the 1850s the rugby game became ascendant and it is noticeable that those teams, such as the Academical Club, whose players had spent time in England perfecting certain skills, notably 'the drop kick', were superior to their rivals.[79]

Clubs

Football clubs stemmed from a wide diversity of backgrounds and incorporated a range of interests. The most straightforward were those clubs that were set up purely to play football. The simplest of these bodies, and probably the most ephemeral, were clubs based at a local pub whose members appear to have been drawn from the local working class. Two excellent examples of this were the Rochdale-based Body-guards and Fear-noughts clubs, which were probably composed of local operatives. Somewhat later, and further south, we find pub-based sides at Southampton and Winchester. While we have no way of assessing the activity of such bodies, it seems likely that they were rather short-lived groups, periodically assembled to conduct matches. By contrast with this, and in a very different social league, were the various clubs set up by old public school boys to enable them to play their particular type of football. A number of these appeared in the London area during the late 1850s and early 1860s, that were devoted to Rugby, the first of which was Blackheath in 1858, followed by Richmond, Civil Service and Harlequins in the years after 1860.[80] In 1858, another group of old Rugbeians formed Liverpool FC. However, the most influential team amongst contemporaries was created in 1859, Forest FC. Forest was formed by ex-Harrovians, including C. W. Alcock, J. F. Alcock, W. J. Thompson, A. Thompson, and C. A. Absolom. Despite commencing life using the code of Harrow School, Forest soon adjusted its rules, adopting those that had been established by the Cambridge University club in 1856.[81]

Unlike these bodies, that specialised in football, other clubs were more diverse. The Great Leicestershire Cricket and Football Club was keen to compete in a range of activities, challenging a local cricket team to a steeplechase of two miles.[82] The Athenic Institution at Birmingham had been founded by local Chartists, and offered a mixture of physical and intellectual recreations, including, by 1842, football. At the other end of the social spectrum, Manchester's elite Athenaeum created a Gymnastic Society in an effort to boost membership and by 1849 the available sports had been expanded to include football, regular games commencing on Saturday afternoons.[83] Football also formed part of recreations practised by The Glasgow Celtic Society, though they usually concentrated on shinty.[84]

While football remained one of a range of sports conducted at the above clubs, in three cases football clubs emerged out of institutions that had been originally set up to foster other sports. In 1849, the Surrey FC was created, with its membership being drawn largely from the various cricket clubs that were based at the Oval.[85] Around 1855 a number of young middle-class men began to meet in Sheffield to participate in various athletic sports, including football. By 1857, the decision was made to specialise in football and the Sheffield FC was created. Somewhat later, a similar transition occurred at nearby Hallam, producing another football club.[86]

Military

In 1846, troops were used to suppress the Shrovetide-game at Derby. More usually, the military were keen footballers. Broadly speaking, there were three varieties of contest involving military footballers: (a) contests with local civilians, (b) visits back to their old school for a game against current pupils and (c) games conducted between military sides.

While there are examples of the military playing local opponents, these appear to be comparatively rare. Such events were noteworthy because on at least one occasion, that of the 93rd Highlanders match against Edinburgh University, the former's shortage of players meant that their team, which was supposed to consist entirely of officers, contained members of the lower ranks. The rules used that day appear to have been those of the standard game found in Scotland throughout the period, and were unrelated to any public school model. It was altogether more common for the military, invariably officers, to return to their old school and play. Throughout the period there are many references to officers returning to Eton, and occasionally Winchester, to play football.

The majority of army football was internal and often had a strong element of conviviality. Additionally, during the Crimean war it is possible that the game might have been part of a programme of convalescence given to troops recuperating on the Isle of Wight.[87] By the 1850s, there are quite detailed reports of internal army matches, particularly in Hampshire, and the games appear to be based upon the rules from either Eton or Rugby public schools. While it is tempting to explain this as being due to the influence exerted by particular officers, who instructed the lower ranks in the various mysteries of their particular public school code, we really do not have sufficient information to evaluate such a theory. Ultimately, although we are sometimes informed, for example, that the matches were between England vs Ireland and Scotland, we have no hard information as to the rules used or the ranks of the competitors. In view of this, the role of the army in disseminating public school football to the lower orders remains theoretical.[88]

Occupations

During the period there is evidence that ten teams existed that were based upon the occupations of their members. These stem from four sectors. The rarest belonged to agriculture, just one team, Blairdrummond Estate Workers. Two teams were based amongst factory workers, Kings Guard Mill and Deanston Cotton Mill. Three sides came from Edinburgh's service sector, waiters, chairmen and gentlemen's servants. The largest group of workers were those we classify as skilled; Ulverston's printers, Ulverston's other trades, Rugby's tailors and Derby's printers.[89]

Having completed our survey of the types of teams that were functioning between 1830 and 1859, it is now time to turn our attention to the rules that the various clubs used.

The rules of football used by teams outside the public schools between 1830 and 1839

By utilising the reports of matches that appeared in the press and the accounts of contemporary writers, we are able to provide an insight into the rules that were used by those teams that were functioning outside of the public schools during the years between 1830 and 1859. Of course, we are only interested in teams whose rules were probably not derived from the public schools and consequently the Blackheath and Forest clubs are ignored, their codes being drawn from Rugby and Cambridge University respectively. Additionally, as it is possible that the rules used by the various military teams from London and Hampshire might have been derived from officers who were educated at public school and taught their variety of football to the troops, the following teams have been excluded: Royal Military Academy, Grenadiers 3rd Battalion, Parkhurst Barracks, Sunbury Military College, Royal Naval Academy, Royal Naval Cadets, HMS Illustrious, 1st Battalion Rifles and Winchester Garrison Officers. For similar reasons St Bartholomew's Hospital and St Peter's School (York) have been ignored.

Let us first consider the question as to exactly how matches were organised. On a number of occasions these games were arranged via the press, potential competitors submitting letters challenging one or more teams to a match, and specifying particular conditions. More commonly, one suspects, such letters were sent to the proposed opponent's headquarters, often a pub, detailing terms and conditions. The most elementary sort of challenge was the following, which appeared in *Bell's Life in London*, and was probably typical of the sort of letters that passed between clubs.

> The Holmfirth players will play Enderby youths at football, 10 or 12 men a side, two games out of three, for £20 a side, and meet them at Hyde Park, Sheffield, on Good Friday, April 9th between twelve and one o'clock. If £5 are sent to us, and articles to Mr J. Batty Red Lion Inn, Jackson Bridge near Holmfirth, the match can be made.[90]

The next phase, the teams having agreed to contest a match, was for the sides to meet and agree upon the terms. The main elements that they would discuss were usually; the date and time of the contest, the venue, the stakes, the numbers of players on each side, and the time limit to be played or the number of goals required for victory. Having reached an agreement those representing the sides would either acknowledge this verbally or in writing. Throughout the period it was common for contracts to be drawn up between the sides, specifying the conditions. The articles for the match between Hampton-in-Arden and Bickenhill were quite detailed, as can be seen:

> A meeting was held at the Clock public house, Bickenhill, Warwickshire on 15th instant, to draw up articles and decide upon the day and place for the match at football, between six gentlemen of the above parish and six gentlemen of Hampton, when it was decided to come off at Hampton in Arden, on the 2nd of November for a bottle of wine and dinner each. The length between goals to be ten score yards, width of goals ten feet, height six feet, and to be the best of three goals.[91]

On occasions the articles were very specific, as when it was stipulated that no one in the opponent's team was to weigh in excess of 10 stone 7 lb.[92] Team selection was in the hands of local experts. For instance at Bolton, the noted athlete Ben Hart had the final say as the following report reveals:

> Twenty Boltonians are prepared to play at football with twenty of the best men in the Rifle Regiment now stationed in Bolton, for £10 a side, to come off on New Year's Day, in the neighbourhood of Bolton, providing they are stationed in or near Bolton. The veteran Ben Hart is a player, and is appointed to pick out the men of Bolton, and unless approved by him such person or persons will not be allowed to play in the match. The money is ready at his house, where alone arrangements can be made.[93]

Evidently, as the following quote shows, players also had specific positions, such as Back groundsman:

> A match to take place at Charlestown near Ashton-under-Lyne on Friday 25th 8 of Charlestown heroes with John Greenwood from U.S.A. as back groundsman and 8 of Boston players with Samuel O'the Georges and Long Tom Kershaw of Waterhouse Lancashire, as back groundsman.[94]

In preparation for matches teams would often practice. An observer attributed the triumph of Deanston's cotton workers over Blairdrummond Estate Workers (nicknamed 'the Mossmen') to this:

> It must be told, however, that the Mossmen have had no practice of late, whilst the Deanston boys omit few opportunities of trying their agility in this manly game; and thus it is likely there may be a harder competition at another time.[95]

Table 3.12 Sums staked on matches 1830–59[a]

Sum	£1	£2	£3	£5	£10	£20	£25	£50
Matches	1	1	1	8	5	3	3	1

Note

a In 1848 there was a game at Holmfirth (Yorkshire) for a stake of £5. As the author is unaware of the circumstances relating to this match it has not been included in the table. The reference was from S. Chadwick, *The Claret and Gold* (Huddersfield, 1945) and was found in A. Collins, *Rugby's Great Split*, p. 53.

The key element in organising a match was the provision of stakes.[96] It appears likely that local publicans provided the stakes for some teams, but there were other sponsors, and prizes ranged from gold medals through to barrels of wine. On six occasions the stakes were clearly sociable – the teams dining together afterwards with the losers paying. More usually, the stakes were for money, as Table 3.12 shows.

On occasions betting also occurred, as with this match from 1843.

> Match for £3 a side, twelve of Flecknoe v Grandborough, came off on Monday April 17, in a meadow in the parish of Willoughby, Warwickshire. Grandborough has gained some notoriety from football playing, having played several matches with different parishes around, and always come off victorious, which caused their backers to put great confidence in them and to offer great odds to them; in fact, in the morning of playing they offered 100 to 1 and settled down to 12 to 1 against Flecknoe, which was freely taken. After playing eight hours, much to the surprise and mortification of the knowing ones, Flecknoe succeeded in gaining two games and therefore came off victorious.[97]

One suspects that local publicans took considerable interest in the commercial opportunities presented by some matches, for very large crowds were sometimes drawn, as with this game from Leicestershire in 1852:

> A match £5 a side, Shrove Tuesday. 15 a side Blaby Youth v Wygston Youth, in a field near to Countersthorpe, in the presence of several thousand people from two adjacent villages. The goals being pitched, the men stripped.[98]

While a match in Warwickshire was watched by a 'numerous and respectable assembly', who appear to have behaved impeccably, the crowd at Edinburgh in 1851 certainly did not: 'Nearly five hundred people had collected on the links, who in the most unpardonable and selfish manner, crowded over the ground so that the goals and players were perfectly unrecognisable'.[99] Interestingly enough, this appears to have been the only match during the period when the teams wore distinguishing marks that enabled their easier identification. The Scottish players had green badges, the English red badges.

As we have seen, most matches were based upon a series of rules that the teams had drawn up between them, which were agreed to either verbally or by a signed contract. Predominantly, these incorporated the provision of stakes and it was doubtless this element that was influential in ensuring that the rules were adhered to. However, signed contracts were not the only rules in existence at this time. From 1845 the public schools, led by Rugby, began to have their football laws printed, but as we saw in Chapter 2 it is unlikely that any of these would have meant much to the wider public, and consequently their influence on those outside the public schools, save for former pupils at the Blackheath and Forest clubs, was probably very slight indeed. During this period, however, two clubs outside the public schools that appear to have numbered one former public school boy between them, produced printed football codes. These teams were Surrey FC (in 1849) and Sheffield FC (in 1857). As we shall deal extensively with the Sheffield team in the Chapter 4, for current purposes it is sufficient to simply mention them and turn our attention to the other club, Surrey.

In 1849, a meeting was held to form Surrey FC. The prime mover was William Denison, who was famous as both a writer and a player of cricket, penning a number of books on the game. Denison was not an old public school boy, neither were Noad nor White, the other two officials who are mentioned, and it is quite clear that the rules Denison drew up were unrelated to any public school code.[100] Indeed, it is quite possible that he was referring back to a much earlier code of laws that had been used for football, those of the Gymnastic Society, the body that had existed in the area some fifty or sixty years before, for during his speech he specifically referred to the Gymnastic club, and one notes that the Gymnastic Society stipulated that teams should consist of twenty-two players a side, an idea that Denison included in his code. To the author's knowledge, the Surrey FC's rules were the first printed code that was ever produced outside the confines of the public schools. The report of the founding meeting of Surrey FC emphasised that Surrey was the only part of the metropolis in which football was still played and urged that the Surrey FC be established, its rules to be as follows:

1 The Club to consist only of such gentlemen as are members of the Surrey Cricket Club, Surrey Paragon Cricket Club, South London Cricket Club and the Union Cricket Club.
2 That subscriptions of 5 shillings to any of the above named gentlemen shall entitle him to all the privileges of Surrey Football Club. That the money so subscribed shall be appropriated to the defrayal of the expenses of the club, namely, the cost of balls and ropes, and the payment of a person who shall keep them in proper condition. The members shall dine together at the end of the season, and any surplus in subscriptions which may then be on hand, after the payment of expenses shall be applied to such dinner.
3 That the days for practice (weather permitting) shall be every Wednesday and Saturday in the afternoon, commencing on the first week of October and continuing until the last week of April in each year; the play to begin at 3 o'clock…

4 That the side shall consist of not more than 22 each, but if that number shall not be in attendance then of any smaller number to be arranged by those present.
5 That wilful kicking shall not be allowed.
6 That the ball shall be tossed up in the centre of the ground, and the game determined in favour of that side which shall first kick the ball over the 'goal ropes' of their opponents. Should the ball be kicked over the fence on either side of the ground, then the ball, when regained, shall be tossed up in the centre of the ground, in line with the place where it went out'.[101]

Having surveyed the first printed rules that were produced by a team outside of the public schools, it is now time for us to try and collate the various reports that we have relating to non-public school derived football, in order to uncover the type of rules that were used in popular football games in Britain.

During the period 1830–59, we have details on the numbers of players involved in thirty-three matches. In every case these were contests between fixed, equal sides, and there is no evidence of games being contested between uneven sides.[102] The numbers in each match vary substantially, as Table 3.13 shows.

The next facet of the rules to be considered concerns the objectives of the match. Essentially speaking, there were two distinct elements to this. The first, and more general, specified that a certain number of goals must be scored in order to obtain victory. A typical example was the following communication from the Totties team challenging Thurstone to a return, the winners being the first to score two goals:

> The latter is prepared to make a fresh match on the following terms, viz, six or eight players on each side, two goals out of three; to come off at Shrovetide, half-way between their respective homes; for £5 a side.[103]

However, the stipulations concerning the number of goals that were required for victory could vary substantially, ranging from the scoring of a single goal, up to eleven. The most common, occurring on eight occasions, was for matches for the best of three, the team scoring two goals first winning. Having no fixed time limit, their length varied widely. The quickest was about three hours but some were six or eight hours.[104]

An alternative mode of determining victory involved the introduction of a fixed time limit to the match, as with this one from Ashton-under-Lyne: 'the ball to be turned down at 11 o'clock a.m. and taken up precisely at three o'clock p.m. The party getting the most goals to be declared the winners.'[105] On occasions these

Table 3.13 Numbers on each side

Team size	01	02	03	04	06	08	10	11	12	15	20	22	24	30
Matches	1	1	1	1	2	3	4	5	6	2	4	1	1	1

two concepts were fused, as in the match between Edinburgh University and the 53rd Highlanders in 1851, which was for the best of five or whoever had the most goals by 5 p.m.[106]

We must now consider what constituted a goal, or 'game', as it was often referred to in some parts of Britain, especially Scotland. There were four principal types of goal. The first sort was objects, such as buildings or, as in a match for two hundred guineas recorded in *The World* 16 May 1789, a hill on Dunstable Downs. Second, and the most common by far throughout Britain, were areas of land referred to as 'bounds' in England or 'the hailing point' in Scotland. They were defined as follows:

> bounds are fixed 50 or 60 yards apart, or sometimes 100 when the numbers are large and the field will allow of it. These bounds are imaginary lines drawn between two sticks fixed in the ground, at the whole breadth of the field, if an ordinary one, and consequently the game is played in a square space, with a stick at each corner, two sides of which are the bounds and prolonged ad infinitum. The object of each party is to kick the ball over the other's bounds.[107]

These were the only goals in Scotland until the 1850s, and were widely used in England.[108] Given that these goals were so wide it would appear to have been very easy to score in them, but this was evidently not the case, for the matches, which often lasted for some time, were usually for the best of three goals. In view of this, it seems likely that 'bounds' were probably extremities of the field that were difficult to reach. The best evidence for this is a detailed report of a match from Rochdale in 1842:

> the Fear-noughts getting the first kick, and in two minutes put the ball on their opponents' headland (the term headland means, in Lancashire, each extremity of the field). This they did five times in about the same amount of time each, the browd being so dense that it was not possible to put the ball over the fence.[109]

The term 'browd' is possibly local slang for twisted brambles and might well represent the disused edge of a field in front of a fence.[110] Support for this interpretation can be derived from the descriptions of the word headland provided by a nineteenth-century dictionary: 'The strip of land left unploughed at the ends of a field. The grassy or waste borders of a field close to the hedge. Headlands are often the boundaries of property in open fields'.[111]

Given this, we can speculate that in this instance the bounds were the area on the far side of the fence. A third type of goal was represented by two markers, sometimes indicated by posts or the discarded clothes of the players. These were of varying widths, ranging between two and ten feet.[112] Walker describes them as follows: 'The goals are placed at the distance of 80 or a 100 yards from each other; and each is usually made of two sticks driven into the ground about 2 or 3 feet apart'.[113] However, Walker's account is so similar to that presented by Strutt in his classic work from 1801 that there is a suspicion that he was simply copying it. A fourth sort of goal included a cross bar, and scoring was dependent upon kicking the ball over this, as in the rules set out by Surrey FC in 1849.[114]

While the above were the principal means of scoring, clearly in some games there were subsidiary methods, most commonly referred to as byes or by-goals.[115] In Warwickshire, Bickenhill defeated Hampton-in-Arden by scoring two through goals and nine by-goals against two by-goals.[116] In Norfolk, somewhat earlier in the century, 'there were no goals and the result was decided by a single bye'.[117] What, one wonders, were byes? It is possible that 'bye' was derived from the term used in cock-fighting for battles that did not count as part of the overall struggle and were consequently subsidiary to the event. Alternatively, the definition of 'byes' presented by a nineteenth-century dictionary is suggestive: 'Byes: corner and ends of a field which cannot be reclaimed by the plough'.[118] This reminds us of the earlier term headland, which was described as 'the grassy or waste borders of a field close to the hedge'. Given that the match in Warwickshire employed goalposts and crossbars, the term 'through goal' is self-explanatory and it is tempting to suggest that 'by-goals' were touchdowns in an area behind the opponent's goal line but not in the goal area itself. Ultimately, of course, it appears impossible to define what exactly they constituted and 'by-goals', like the challenge in a communication from Yorkshire to 'kick three rises', will probably remain a mystery.[119]

Information on the length of pitches varies enormously, probably due to the numbers of players involved and the type of game played. In the game camping, which was predominantly played with the hands, pitches were between one hundred and fifty and two hundred yards long. Our two most detailed reports of football matches, from Deanston and Hampton-in-Arden, display a similar ratio of playing area to number of competitors; 20-a-side on a 620 yard pitch, 6-a-side on a 200 yard pitch. The most common figure, related in three general accounts that were independent of one another, was 100 yards.[120] We have very little information concerning the width of pitches and it is probably safe to assume that such boundaries as there were stemmed from natural obstacles. This was certainly the case in the football that was played in Scotland as the following quotation shows:

> There were no goal posts as in modern football and except when played in the sands at low tide there was no line drawn to indicate the bounds of the playing area, in other cases a footpath or some permanent mark was used.[121]

At Surrey FC touchlines were defined by fences running along either side of the pitch.[122]

Having defined the playing area it is now time to turn our attention to the game itself. Naturally, we begin with the commencement, the kick-off. There were four different ways of starting the game.

1 A place kick from the middle of the pitch by one of the teams. The writer on English sports, Stonehenge, provides our most detailed account of this:

> the ball is then placed on the ground, and the captain gives the first kick towards the opposite bounds, where the opposite party are mustered in line ready for the struggle, the ball is then placed on the ground, and the captain gives the first kick towards the opposite bounds, the other party meeting it, and returning it either by kick, or carrying it, if preferred, while ten are being counted by party.[123]

2 The ball was placed in the centre and at a given signal both teams, separated by an equal distance, raced for it: this was recorded three times, the last occasion being in 1862. A characteristic example is from Ulverston in 1839:

> The ball was placed about the centre of the ground and one from each side stood twenty yards from it. At a given signal the two opponents rushed forward and the representative of leather, Roger Gaskell, took the ball in grand style, thereby winning the gloves. The action then became general, but leather was forced to be content with the laurels already won, as the other party won every bye that was played.[124]

3 The ball was thrown up in the middle by a neutral person, usually the referee, between the teams, which were an equal distance apart: this was common in variants such as camping or hard ball, and was also found as late as 1849 in football games.[125] As we shall see in Chapter 5, it was one of the methods that the FA considered using to commence the game. The following is an account from 1842:

> The ball is thrown aloft in the air between two parties of players, equidistant from each other, on one side and on the other there is a fixed point or line called, as in the preceding case, the hailing spot. The object then, of each party is, by vigorous kicks, to propel the ball to the hailing place behind the adversaries, on the attainment of which object the game is won.[126]

4 The players pair off before the match and as soon as the ball is thrown up begin wrestling one another. This was part of the game in Ireland and the North East of England. Litt describes it thus: 'The ball is then thrown up and every man grasps the hand of his opponent and they begin to wrestle. That party which gains the most falls will out-number the other at the first onset.'[127]

The game having started, we must now examine the elements that constituted the general play. In the main, we are interested in two particular aspects: the extent to which the ball is handled and the role of physical contact between the players. As we shall see, these varied substantially depending upon the region in which the game was played.

Stonehenge described the response of one side whose opponents had just kicked the ball into their half:

> the other party meeting it, and returning it either by kick, or carrying it, if preferred, while ten are being counted by party, but in any case whether the ball is carried or being kicked out, the opposite party are privileged to throw down the ball carrier or kicker by any means in their power; and the usual practice is to run rapidly behind, and endeavour to put the foot inside his leg with a circular sweep which almost always succeeds, unless it is met by a jump in the air of a peculiar kind.[128]

Obviously, the ball could be handled at will and the player brought down by a type of wrestling throw. However, this was not the only type of football game practised in Britain, as the following account of the game from a similar period of time makes clear. The writer declared that the football game at Glasgow College which was played from 1820 to 1870 was a:

> dribbling one, the ball must be kicked and could not be carried or handled, no collaring or hacking was permitted and there was little rough play. If the ball was caught in the air a free, that is an undisturbed, kick was allowed. The player who held the ball dropped it from his hand and kicked it as he fell. The game was practically the same as Hand Ball as regards numbers and manner of playing; in the one case the ball was struck with the hand and in the other with the foot.[129]

In this game, handling was forbidden unless a player was able to make a 'fair catch', that is catch the ball while it was in the air. Wrestling and other direct physical contact was not permitted. As we shall see later, another account, also from Scotland shows that there were strict rules regulating the handling of the ball.

The extent and importance of physical contact, especially of a violent kind, vary dramatically. In 1839 a writer recorded that the violence of one team did them no good against their more skilful opponents: 'Many of the gentle craft were good millers, and carried on the contest toughly; but their opponents played more scientifically, and out manoeuvred them, and carried the day in triumph.[130] In 1842 Chambers evaluated football as being 'far less violent than hockey' and emphasised the near irrelevance of physical strength: 'skill in the application of a slight degree of force avails much more at this sport than greater strength unskilfully directed'.[131] A similar message emerges from the report of a match from 1851 between Edinburgh University Students and the 93rd Highlanders. After twelve minutes it was clear that the students' courage and desperation was not to be sufficient to combat the discipline and order of their craftier opponents.[132]

However, football could also be a game in which there was a substantial element of physical contact. As was mentioned earlier, certain football games, such as those in Ireland and the North East, were intimately related to wrestling.

A match played by Irishmen in the Islington area of London was recorded by an observer in 1820:

> As is usual in their sister kingdom, county play county; Some fine specimens of wrestling are occasionally exhibited, in order to delay two men who are rivals in pursuit of the ball. Meantime the others get on with the combat. The arrival of the ball in the goal is greeted with a lusty shout.[133]

Such displays of violence were obviously legitimate. However, much of the violence in football stemmed from players losing their tempers. In 1801, Joseph Strutt wrote: 'when the exercise becomes exceedingly violent, the players kick each others shins without the least ceremony, and some of them are overthrown at the hazard of their limbs'.[134]

A match from 1852 was probably typical of this, the losing side resorting to violence:

> Wigston won the toss and consequently had the wind in their favour. The play was excellent on both sides for half an hour. Wigston, finding they were losing, got out of temper, and began kicking the Blaby youths, but they smartly returned it. Blaby seemed to have the play entirely to themselves, winning the first goal. A rest then took place for half an hour, after which the ball being put down, Blaby having the wind the contest was very short, they winning easily.[135]

Judging by our reports there does not appear to have been a great deal of violence in football matches. Indeed, on at least six occasions, the teams dined together afterwards, with the losers paying the bill, an occurrence typified by an event from 1846: 'The parties will then adjourn to the Old Ship public house Charlestown to partake of a substantial dinner. The losing parties pay the piper.'[136]

As already noted, the provision of stakes was one crucial element in ensuring that the teams adhered to the rules that they had agreed to, the other was the use of referees. The use of neutral figures in football-type games probably preceded the nineteenth century. For instance, the football-variant game, camping, that was so popular in East Anglia, was commenced by a neutral man throwing the ball up. Beyond this, however, he had no further role. By contrast, some annual Shrove-matches, notably those at Derby and Scone had 'men of both sides attend to see fair play' was done. These cases long precede the first employment of officials to supervise football rules in public schools, which occurred at Eton in 1845. Although Young claimed that this was an important innovation, it had been anticipated at least three years earlier, in 1842, in a match between two Rochdale teams, the Body-guards and Fear-noughts.[137] Throughout the period there are a number of references to umpires.[138] Predominantly, two umpires, usually one from each side, supervised a match, though on at least one occasion, from Ashton-under-Lyne, the responsibility rested on one man's shoulders alone.[139] The umpire's role could often be very hard, and at Edinburgh in 1851 the officials were praised for remaining impartial, 'despite the party spirit remaining high.'[140]

The extent of the power of these umpires is hard to discern because the evidence is contradictory. In 1851, there was a match between the English and Scottish students at the University of Edinburgh. There, in order to prevent a goal, a Scottish player committed what we would now refer to as a professional foul, by claiming that he had caught the ball in a fair catch and was therefore entitled to a free kick, when actually he had simply dived on top of a ball that was moving along the ground. The incident is described as follows:

> After being in the hands of the Scots several times, the game turned in England's favour, and at a few minutes to five, had brought the ball to within a few yards of the goal, when another kick would have won it but for a Scotchman, who took the ball off the ground, and claimed a free kick, resisting every effort made to take the ball from him. The umpire, who saw the circumstances, immediately disallowed the claim, which, however, was poor satisfaction for losing the chance of the game.[141]

The Scottish player had got away with his act of sharp practice, for the referee was unable to punish him in a manner that would remotely compensate the English team for being deprived of the opportunity to score a goal. However, in Lancashire in 1841 a player was far less lucky. The arrangements between the competitors were as follows:

> The Body-guard Club, held at Baillie-street, Rochdale, accepts the challenge of the Fear-noughts Club to play them at foot-ball – for their proposed sum – two games out of three, twelve on each side. After that they will play them for half a barrel of Old Tom, one single game, the Fearnoughts to fix the time as early as possible.[142]

A couple of weeks later the match came off and with the score at 0–0 the following incident occurred:

> the sixth round, one of the Body-Guards (being tired) putting another person not connected with the game to kick for him, and their own umpire declaring it foul play according to the rules agreed to by both parties, decided the game.[143]

As we have seen, the articles of the match stipulated that a side had to score two goals to win. Yet as the above shows, the Body-Guards' own umpire declared that they were contravening the rules and consequently awarded victory to the Fear-noughts!

Table 3.14 The structure and properties of folk games and modern sports

Folk games	Modern sports
1 Diffuse, informal organisation implicit in the local social structure.	Highly specific, formal organisation, institutionally differentiated at the local, regional, national and international levels.
2 Simple and unwritten customary rules, legitimised by tradition.	Formal and elaborate written rules, worked out pragmatically and legitimated by rational, bureaucratic means.
3 Fluctuating game pattern, tendency to change through long-term and, from the viewpoint of the participants, imperceptible 'drift'.	Change institutionalised through rational, bureaucratic channels.
4 Regional variation of rules, size and shape of balls, etc.	National and international standardisation of rules, size and shape of balls, etc.
5 No fixed limits on territory, duration or numbers of participants.	Played on a spatially limited pitch with clearly defined boundaries, within fixed time limits, and with a fixed number of participants, equalised between the contending sides.
6 Strong influence of natural and social differences on game pattern.	Minimisation, principally by means of formal rules, of the influence of natural and social differences on the game-pattern norms of equality and 'fairness'.
7 Low role differentiation (division of labour) among the players.	High role differentiation (division of labour) among the players.
8 Loose distinction between playing and 'spectating' roles.	Strict distinction between playing and 'spectating' roles.
9 Low structural differentiation; several 'game-elements' rolled into one.	High structural differentiation; specialisation around kicking, carrying and throwing, the use of sticks, etc.
10 Informal social control by the players themselves within the context of the ongoing game.	Formal social control by officials who stand, as it were, 'outside' the game and who are appointed and certificated by central legislative bodies and empowered, when a breach of the rulesoccurs, to stop play and impose penalties graded according to the seriousness of the offence.
11 High level of socially tolerated physical violence; emotional spontaneity; low restraint.	Low level of socially tolerated physical violence; high emotional control; high restraint.
12 Generation in a relatively open and spontaneous form of pleasurable 'battle-excitement'.	Generation in a more controlled and 'sublimated' form of pleasurable 'battle-excitement'.
13 Emphasis on physical force as opposed to skill.	Emphasis on skill as opposed to physical force.

Table 3.14 Continued

Folk games	*Modern sports*
14 Strong communal pressure to participate; individual identity subordinate to group identity; test of identity in general.	Individually chosen as a recreation; individual identity of greater importance relative to group identity; test of identity in relation to a specific skill or set of skills.
15 Locally meaningful contests only; relative equality of playing skills among sides; no chances of national reputations or money payment.	National and international superimposed on local contests; emergence of élite players and teams; chance to establish national and international reputations; tendency to 'monetisation' of sports.

Source: E. Dunning and K. Sheard, *Barbarians, Gentlemen and Players* (Oxford, Martin Robertson, 1979) pp. 33–4.

Having completed our survey of the rules used by those teams who were functioning in the wider society and whose members appear to be completely untouched by any discernible influence from the public schools, we can see that their games were anything but the wild unregulated contests imagined by many scholars. Naturally, this leads us to reject the established view of football's emergence, which claims that the wild Shrove-type game was replaced by the imposition of the carefully codified version of football invented in the public schools. Tischler describes the change thus: 'English football was alternately the possession of the plebeian and patrician classes; it was an anarchic contest and a finely codified encounter; it served as an aspect of popular celebration and as a vehicle for discipline'.[144] Walvin emphasises the extent of the transformation: 'The new urban society required disciplined games, regimented by rules and timing. Football in the period after 1860 was as disciplined as its pre-industrial forbear had been lawless'.[145]

The most thoroughgoing and influential representation of these views stems from two sociologists, Dunning and Sheard, who maintain that in the period previous to the 1860s there were only two types of football. The first sort, and much the earlier, was typified by the games that were staged annually on Shrove Tuesday. These games involved very few rules and are described as 'rough and wild, closer to "real" fighting than modern sports'.[146] For Dunning and Sheard the Shrove-game was the only type of football practised outside the public schools, and they classify it as 'folk'. Such games are regarded as being completely different from the second sort of football that existed; these were the refined, codified varieties that had been created in the public schools. Whereas Shrove-games were football at its most basic, the football games found in public schools were carefully regulated by strict rules.

Using this assumption as their starting point, Dunning and Sheard have devised a typology that uses Shrove-football, which is classified as a 'folk' game, as the starting point in the evolution of sport, and contrasts it with its polarised opposite, 'modern sports', which are regarded as the final destination of their developmental model. Dunning and Sheard's developmental continuum is based upon the control and sublimation of violence via the imposition of formal and informal rules. This is illustrated in Table 3.14.[147]

As we have shown, the conception that Dunning and Sheard have of the football games that existed outside the influence of public schools during the period previous to 1860 are quite different from the picture that has been set forth in this chapter. Let us now examine the various criteria that Dunning and Sheard have proposed in order to assess the extent to which the various football games whose rules we have laid out correspond to their two ideal types, that is 'Folk Games' and 'Modern Sports'. We shall begin by examining the extent to which the popularly played football games can be described as 'folk' according to the criteria established by Dunning and Sheard in their typology.

The numbers in bold refer to the relevant categories in Table 3.14 set up by Dunning and Sheard.

1 While we do not know very much about most of the football teams, some were clubs and certainly cannot be described as 'informal social organisation[s] implicit in the local structure'.

2 As we have seen, the rules were often written, in codes or contracts, and were not necessarily related to tradition, often being agreed to via a debate with the other side over particular conditions.

3 While the game pattern certainly differed substantially depending upon area and period, changes in the rules need not necessarily have occurred over a long period, for they were subject to negotiation with the opposition.

4 These certainly were 'folk games' for they show sharp regional differences.

5 As the example of the articles drawn up for the match between Hampton-in-Arden and Bickenhill shows, very strict guide lines were established concerning the boundaries of the pitch.

6 Predominantly, the employment of rules and the selection of players according to their ability ensured that the influence exerted by 'natural and social differences on the game pattern' were minimal.

7 While we should not overemphasise the element of role differentiation, there were certain specific positions within some football games, such as 'back groundsman' in the game at Ashton-under-Lyne in 1846.

8 It would be absurd to maintain that a very strong distinction was not made between playing and 'spectating' roles. Indeed, when one side allowed a spectator to play in a match at Rochdale the umpire awarded the game against them.

9 While some games certainly included a variety of other sports within them, such as wrestling, and allowed substantial use of the hands, others restricted all such activity, even specifying that hands could only be used for a 'fair catch'.

10 Many of the matches used referees and did not depend on 'informal social control by the players themselves'.

11 While some games certainly did tolerate violence, though not necessarily 'high levels', predominantly they appear to have employed restraint.

12 It appears that many of our games outlawed unrestrained behaviour. For instance, Surrey FC stipulated 'wilful kicking shall not be allowed'.
13 As our sources make quite clear, in many games skill was far more important than physical force.
14 Far from there being any communal pressure to participate, teams were selected for their ability, as at Bolton's Sidney Smith's Tavern in 1841.
15 It would be mistaken to imagine that there was a 'relative equality of playing skills among sides', for they were selected according to their ability, and some players did obtain local reputations. However, they had no chances for obtaining a national reputation and certainly did not receive payment.

The above survey reveals that in only one instance, (4) 'Regional variation of rules, size and shape of ball, etc.' can the football games from this period be classified as 'folk games'. In two other cases, (7) and (15), the football games can be described as partly conforming to the definition of 'folk games'. By contrast, in twelve out of the fifteen categories, (1), (2), (3), (5), (6), (8), (9), (10), (11), (12), (13) and (14), the football games cannot be classified as 'folk games', and Dunning and Sheard's contention must consequently be rejected.

Let us now see how the popularly played games measure up against the typology that Dunning and Sheard have established for 'Modern sports'.

1 Clearly, the teams and clubs appear to have been far too rudimentary in terms of organisation to be classified as modern.
2 Substantially speaking, the creation of codes and contracts, often via a process of negotiation, meant that they can be classified as modern.
3 The lack of any overall supervisory administration means that they cannot be considered modern.
4 Obviously there was no national standard of rules and they cannot be considered modern.
5 Given that matches were played on strictly defined areas, with fixed time limits and equal, fixed numbers of players on each side, the game can be classified as modern.
6 Formal rules seem to have ensured equality and fairness and minimised the influence of 'natural and social differences on the game-pattern'. Consequently, the game can be classified as modern.
7 To a slight extent, the players did have specific roles, so the game might be described as partially modern.
8 Given that the matches were contested by fixed, equal sides, with outsiders (spectators) being specifically excluded, the game was clearly modern.
9 While certain rules did admit elements that belonged to other sports, such as wrestling, some games excluded these entirely. Consequently, they can be classified as modern.
10 As we have seen, referees were employed extensively, and certainly possessed some power. Of course, they were not certificated by a central body. In this sense, the game was partially modern.

11 Predominantly, the level of violence was limited and the emphasis was on restraint. While the types of football game obviously varied, generally the football game can be classified as modern.

12 As with the above, predominantly behaviour was sublimated and the game can be classified as modern.

13 The game was clearly modern, the emphasis being on skill as opposed to physical force.

14 Given that teams were selected according to a player's ability rather than due to any communal pressures, the game can be classified as modern.

15 The game was clearly not modern, having neither national nor international contests and with fairly minimal payment to players.

Our survey reveals that in nine of the fifteen cases, that is (2), (5), (6), (8), (9), (11), (12), (13) and (14), the football games that were conducted outside of public school influence fulfil Dunning and Sheard's definition of 'modern sports'. In two instances, (7) and (10), they partially fulfil the criteria for modern sports. In four instances, that is (1), (3), (4) and (15), they clearly do not. Cumulatively, this demonstrates that the popularly played games of football that we have detailed in this chapter fulfil many of the requirements of Dunning and Sheard's definition of 'modern-sports'. We can tabulate our findings as in Table 3.15.

From the above it is quite clear that the football games that we have identified as occurring outside the domain of any discernible public school influence in the years between 1830 and 1859 can scarcely be regarded as 'folk games' within the criteria established by Dunning and Sheard. Somewhat paradoxically, the football games can be seen as fulfilling two thirds of the criteria that are regarded as constituting 'modern sports'. As need hardly be said, this has very profound implications for the developmental model that Dunning and Sheard offer concerning the evolution of modern sport for it indicates that the changes were far less drastic than they maintain and that in many senses the football practised outside the domain of public school influence was already 'civilised'.

Table 3.15 The extent to which the football played in the wider community between 1830 and 1859 can be classified as a 'folk game' or a 'modern sport'

Extent of agreement with criteria	*Folk games*		*Modern sports*	
	No.	*%*	*No.*	*%*
Yes	01	(6·66%)	09	(60%)
Partially	02	(13·33%)	02	(13·33%)
No	12	(80%)	04	(26·66%)
Extent of agreement	02	(13·33%)	10	(66·66%)

Note
The maximum score is 15, a point being available in each category. In the case of a game conforming partially to a category a half point is awarded.

Between 1600 and 1859, a number of varieties of football were practised outside the domain of the public schools. While scholars have assumed that these were all based upon the wild, mob-like games that were conducted annually on Shrove Tuesday, we have seen that this is not the case. On the contrary, by the nineteenth century many football games contested outside the influence of the public schools were governed by rules and referees and contested by fixed, even, sides. We have also seen that the established view, which contends that from the onset of the industrial revolution football games outside the public schools were wiped out, is incorrect. Indeed, judging by the evidence, there was an increase in the activity of football play in the wider society between 1830 and 1859 by comparison with any previous era. However, having said all this, it is important not to exaggerate the extent of our findings. In large measure, the information that we have uncovered on football during this period is very fragmentary and while the existence of over ninety teams is obviously significant, it amounts to little more than three per year. Consequently, while during this period football was certainly far from being extinct outside the public schools, it was by no means a major sport, and its appeal was far from national, as a writer observed in 1842: 'now little known in some parts of the country, but keenly played in others'.[148] The best insight into the standing of the game is probably provided by a piece of legislation that was being considered in 1844, '*The bill concerning the encouragement of Manly sports*', which did not include football as one of the main areas of activity, listing it amongst the subsidiary recreations.[149] Such comments remind us of the 'knot of lads' whom we left playing football on the outskirts of Derby on Shrove Tuesday 1856. As the 1850s drew to a close football was a very minor recreation outside the public schools. Nonetheless, within a few years, this was to change dramatically and the seeds for this transformation were probably being sown while the Derby lads were taking advantage of their holiday to knock the ball about. At about this time, another group of youths from an altogether more prestigious social background, situated about two hours journey up the road, were beginning to meet regularly and practise various athletic sports, including football. These youths soon developed a taste for the game and in September 1857 Sheffield FC was founded. During the next ten years, Sheffield would transform football and it is to a detailed consideration of the World's first great football culture that we now turn.

4 'An epoch in the annals of sport'

Britain's first football culture – Sheffield 1857–67

It is a strange fact that the most important football culture that existed in the entire world during the 1850s and the 1860s, a time when the two varieties of the game, soccer and rugby, began to take on a distinctly modern appearance, has been largely ignored by historians. The culture was centred in Sheffield and its study provides a unique and detailed insight into the early history of the modern game. In this chapter we shall consider the emergence and fruition of the various elements that were to combine to create this. The chapter consists of four parts. In the first, we consider the foundations of Sheffield's football culture, primarily the years between 1857 and 1860. The next part examines the various clubs that existed between 1861 and 1867, particularly the amount of activity, their relative strength, the extent and composition of their membership, and their finances. In the part titled 'The evolution of Sheffield's code' we consider the crucial element that united these clubs, 'The Sheffield Rules', a playing code that embraced almost every club in the area, preventing many of the disputes over rules that caused such disruption in the London area. The final part concerns itself with Sheffield's impact on the rest of the country, both directly, via its contact with outside bodies, and indirectly, the impression made by the creation of the Sheffield FA and the staging of events such as the Youdan Cup. We commence with the first part of our study, an examination of the foundation of Sheffield's football culture.

The emergence of a football culture in Sheffield 1857–60

It is a sad fact that although Sheffield FC were to have an enormous impact on the history of the game, much of our information on their early days, especially their origins, is vague and contradictory. The most surprising aspect of this is that in 1907, when the club celebrated its silver jubilee, the three surviving members of the original side who were still involved with the team assisted in the composition of the *two* histories of the club that were commenced, one in manuscript and one in typescript. Given that the introduction of one of the histories describes the creation of the Sheffield club as 'an epoch in the annals of sport', one might expect that we would be well informed. Alas, neither history was completed and both are a mass of hand-written revisions. While this would not be overly problematic in itself, the histories offer contradictory accounts of significant events, such as the creation of the Club itself and the origins of the Club's code of laws. In the following account an effort is made to try and resolve many of these contradictions, sometimes by reference to other contemporary sources.

In Chapter 3, we saw that during the 1840s Yorkshire had been one of the most active regions for football in Britain. The first hard evidence of football in Sheffield stems from 1831, when the game was played at the city's main sporting venue, Hyde Park.[1] By a strange coincidence, it was also the year when one of the founders of Sheffield FC, Nathanial Creswick, was born. In 1852 the Yorkshire team Holmfirth arranged to meet their opponents from Leicestershire, Enderby, at Sheffield's Hyde Park to contest a football match for a stake of £20.[2] After this, judging by the publicly available record, football in Sheffield appears to go into some decline, and it is noticeable that it was one of the few sports *not* present at Sheffield's Hyde Park in 1856.[3] The origins of the Sheffield FC are unclear. As already noted, the Club's archive contains two histories that were composed in 1907. The typescript history maintains that the club was formed on 24 October 1857 and based at a greenhouse at Parkhouse, the residence of Mr Asline Ward. However, the typescript also contains a second account, in which a former secretary of the club, Chesterman, claims that the club was started in 1855–56 by a few old public school boys.[4] Intriguingly enough, a photo exists from 1855 that some have claimed to be of the Sheffield FC.[5] Alternatively, the manuscript history of the club states that:

> In the Autumn of 1857 a meeting of all the gentlemen enthusiastic for athletics, and especially as regards football, was called to form on a regular basis, The Sheffield Football Club. Games had been played before this time, but there had been no organised club for football.[6]

The mention of athletics was surely significant, because between 1858 and 1867 the most important events that the Sheffield FC would stage were her annual sports meetings. Given that many of the Club's founding members, especially Creswick and Prest, were fine all-round athletes, it is by no means unlikely that while still embryonic the future Sheffield FC did include a number of other sports.[7] The early history of the Sheffield FC may be summarised as follows. From possibly as early as 1855 athletes were meeting together in Sheffield and practising a range of sports, particularly football. By 1857 football was being extensively played and this resulted in the formation of the Sheffield FC on 24 October 1857. An insight into the Club's early activity is provided by a record of its finances from 1857 (Table 4.1).

While Table 4.1 shows that football was being enthusiastically conducted, it is far more difficult to discern the rules that the club were using, and the origin of these rules. In the next section we shall consider both these topics.

There are four accounts from contemporaries that describe the early days of the club and the processes involved in the creation of the code by which they played. These are (A) the history of the club that is written in manuscript, (B) the history

Table 4.1 Sheffield FC table of expenditure in 1857[a]

	£	s	d
Six footballs	2	6	0
Repairs to footballs		6	
Beer for servants	1	5	6
Beer for hostlers		13	6
Postage stamps		2	
Liniment		2	6
Balance	1	5	6
Total	4	15	6

Note
a FCRI (Sheffield City Archives).

of the club that is written in typescript with numbered pages, (C) the history of the club that is written in typescript on unnumbered pages and (D) a speech given by the club's co-founder at the dinner celebrating their silver jubilee. Let us first look at (A) the history of the club written in manuscript, paying particular attention to the means used to create a code of laws with which to play:

> As no other clubs existed no matches outside the club could be arranged, so the members met at the ground in Strawberry Hall Lane every Saturday afternoon to play such matches as 1st half of alphabet v 2nd half, or Law v Medicine. There was no limit as to the time to be played, or numbers of players on each side. There were no crossbars to the goals. and these goals were as wide as the sides agreed upon, anything from 12 feet up to 18 or 20 feet. Corner flag posts were the only limit on the field of play. After season 1857–8, the Hon Sec Nathaniel Creswick and committee drew up printed rules, regulations and laws for the club and from these is to be seen that game was half Rugby and half association.[8]

The typewritten history of the club offers two different accounts of the origin of the club's laws. The first, found on numbered sheets (B), was as follows:

> A knotty subject was the drafting of a set of rules. Copies of the rules in force at all the public schools were procured, and a new code, comprised of what was regarded as the best points of the whole, adopted. These rules were the forerunners of the present day 'soccer' rules, as the latter embody the main features of the former. It was then customary to play 20 a side and the duration of the game was two hours.[9]

Alternatively, on an unnumbered typewritten sheet (C), with a line through some of the text, we read the following:

> Mr W. Chesterman says the Club was largely made up of Public School boys, but there were no rules, and no other Clubs to meet, so sides were chosen at

> first. Then came Hallam, through the enterprise of Tom Vickers, and matches were arranged in which 'bull strength' was the principal feature. He had memories of seeing at these matches the ball lying quietly and groups of half a dozen butting each other like rams yards away. The idea was to charge 'if you could get a shot at him, whether near the ball or not'. Still, there were no rules. Rules had to be got piecemeal – bits from the rules of each public school as the boys came in; and one law which did not last very long was that players should carry half-a-crown in each hand to avoid pushing with the open hand.

Finally, we have a fourth account (D), derived from a seemingly verbatim copy of the speech that Creswick, the Club's co-founder, gave at a dinner celebrating Sheffield's silver jubilee:

> William Prest and himself, when it was decided to form this club, went for a walk into the country to discuss what rules of football they should use. They wrote to the leading public schools, Eton, Harrow, Winchester, Westminster, Rugby and some others, and a lot of different rules they obtained (laughter). One rule he remembered, he believed it came from Winchester, was that you should not old and hack a man at the same time (loud laughter). The number of players and the hours of play in those days were unlimited: they played generally until it was dark. One match he remembered was against Norton when they played four against six for three hours. He was one of the four and remembered that it became very personal (laughter).[10]

As Creswick was the co-founder of Sheffield his account (D) is probably the most reliable. By contrast, (C), which derives from Chesterman, who did not become a member until 1860, needs to be treated with caution and can be largely dismissed.[11] By piecing together (A) the manuscript history, (B) the numbered typewritten history and (D) Creswick's speech from 1907, we can obtain an insight into the processes used to create the first code of football laws that were used by the Club.

As earlier noted, football play commenced before the autumn of 1857, when it was decided to form a football club. History (A) provides us with some idea of the rules that the club used in its first season, 1857–58: 'there being no limit on the time played, the numbers on each side, or specifications relating to the size of the goals'. Judging by history (A), it was only at the end of the first season (1857–58), that is March 1858 at the earliest, that Creswick and the committee drew up printed rules for the club. The account offered by Creswick in (D) is somewhat different. Creswick states that 'when it was decided to form this club' they determined to compile some rules. Naturally, this would mean that the latest date on which the club's rules were created was October 1857, at least six months earlier than the account presented in history (A). The Club's minute books probably support Creswick, for although the first copy of the Club's code does not appear in manuscript until the committee meeting of 21 October 1858, there are two reasons for assuming that these laws must have been functioning previous to this. First, the players were surely using these rules between October 1857 and October 1858. Second, during the meeting many of the laws were changed, facts that suggest that the players had some experience of using them.

With regard to the source of Sheffield's code, four alternative suggestions have been advanced, three of which stem from the various historical accounts that have been presented of the club. The first is based upon the assumption that Sheffield FC was made up largely of former pupils of the area's most elite school, the Sheffield Collegiate. Scholars argue that while at the Collegiate the pupils played a brand of football, variously identified as either the Harrow or Eton code, which they had learned from their school masters, who were former public school boys.[12] The first point that these scholars make is substantially correct, for seventeen of the Sheffield FC's initial membership of fifty-seven stemmed from the Collegiate School.[13] Additionally, the Collegiate was certainly an elite school, and was able to provide pupils with space in which to play football, for it possessed 'pleasure ground of $3\frac{1}{2}$ acres'.[14] However, an examination of the various members of staff who worked at the Collegiate School from 1841 to 1852 yields the following: Reverend J. Bell, J. Deacon, W. Prior, G. A. Jacob, Reverend G. Sandford, W. Savigny, J. Singleton, H. Thompson.[15] Having scrutinised the registers for Charterhouse, Eton, Harrow, Rugby, Shrewsbury, Westminster and Winchester, it was discovered that Sandford was the only teacher who attended a public school. Until 1836 Sandford was at Shrewsbury, whence the twenty year old left for Cambridge, before becoming the deputy head of Sheffield Collegiate from 1843 to 1846.[16] It appears unlikely that Sandford was the source of Sheffield's rules because there is no indication of any interest in sport on his part. Additionally, Sandford left Shrewsbury before the school's football had become particularly organised. As for the Collegiate School, there is no indication of their paying any formal attention to the athletic recreation of their pupils. Indeed, it was not until January 1847, with the appointment of Mr Trown as drill master, that even the most basic provision was made for the physical exercise of the pupils.[17] In view of this, there is no reason for linking the code of the Sheffield FC with any game they might have experienced while pupils at the Collegiate.

A second, and related thesis, which also attributed Sheffield's rules to those that the players had learned while at school, was advanced by the former secretary of the club, Chesterman. Chesterman maintained that the various former public school boys who joined the club each contributed a particular element of their old school rules and that the Sheffield code was a collection of old public school derived rules. Once again, a comparison between a list of the founding members of Sheffield FC and the various public school registers reveals that only one player, Thomas Sale, an old Rugbeian, was from a public school. Although Sale was certainly a good sportsman while at Rugby, an examination of the Sheffield code reveals that it is largely uninfluenced by Rugby's version of football. Consequently, Chesterman's contention appears to be untenable.[18]

The predominant view amongst historians was that Sheffield's code was derived from studying those of the various public schools and adopting the rules that they found the most relevant.[19] As we have seen, the typewritten history of the club (B) that was produced in 1907 stated that 'copies of the rules in force at all the public schools were procured, and a new code, comprised of what was the best points of the whole, adopted'. Additionally, our most reliable source, the co-founder of the club, Creswick, stated in his speech at the Club's silver jubilee dinner (D) that he and Prest wrote to all the public schools for copies of their football laws, hoping to discover what rules to use. The result, it would appear, bewildered them, for as he says: 'and a lot of different rules they obtained (laughter)'. Of course, Creswick, a former politician, and one suspects general extrovert, might have simply been playing to the gallery. However, he continues by emphasising a brutal aspect of Winchester's code and how rudimentary Sheffield's game remained: 'The number of players and the hours of play in those days were unlimited'. Creswick then leaps several years and describes an acrimonious match against Norton that was from 1862.[20] Nowhere does he suggest that the various public school codes were studied. On the contrary, he is simply sarcastic towards them, giving the impression that neither he nor Prest (the club's co-founder) could derive much from the public school rules that they received. As we have seen in Chapter 2, this was a very common response to public school laws, the rules rarely being accessible to outsiders.

The fourth, and in the author's opinion, correct view of the origin of the Sheffield FC's code comes from the manuscript history that was written in 1907 and states: 'After season 1857–8, the Hon Sec Nathaniel Creswick and committee drew up printed rules, regulations and laws, for the club, and from these is to be seen that game was half Rugby and half association.' As we have seen, the various public school rules appear to have been almost unintelligible to Creswick and Prest, for they, like others both before and after them, were unable to grasp the meaning of laws that were not meant for outsiders but for those who were already familiar with the game.[21] In view of this, it appears likely that the Sheffield committee were unable to derive much assistance from the various public school laws and that the first set of rules was principally of local origin. The best evidence in support of this theory is an examination of the rules themselves. Let us now turn to consider the Sheffield code of 1858.

The Sheffield rules appeared in writing on 21 October 1858 and were as follows:

1 Kick off from the middle must be a place kick.
2 Kick out must not be from more than twenty five yards out of goal.
3 Fair catch is a catch direct from the foot of the opposite side and entitles a free kick.
4 Charging is fair in case of a place kick with the exception of kick off as soon as player offer to kick, but may always draw back unless he has actually touched the ball with his foot.

5 No pushing with the hands or hacking, or tripping up is fair under any circumstances whatsoever.
6 Knocking or pushing on the ball is altogether disallowed. The side breaking the rule forfeits a free kick to the opposite side.
7 No player may be held or pulled over.
8 It is not lawful to take the ball off the ground, except in touch, for any purpose whatsoever.
9 If the ball be bouncing it may be stopped by the hand, not pushed or hit, but if rolling it may not be stopped except by the foot.
10 No goal may be kicked from touch, nor by free kick from a fair catch.
11 A ball in touch is dead. Consequently the side that touches it down, must bring it to the edge of touch, and throw it straight out at least five yards from touch.

During the meeting laws 3, 5, 6, 9 and 10 were revised. In fact, laws 6 and 9 were struck out altogether and replaced by a new law: 'That the ball may be passed or hit with the hand – but holding the ball, except in the case of a fair catch is altogether disallowed'.

The amended versions of the other laws were as follows:

> 3: Fair catch is a catch from any player provided the ball has not touched the ground and entitles a free kick.
> 5: Pushing with the hands is allowed but no hacking or tripping up is fair under any circumstances whatsoever.
> 10: A goal must be kicked but not from touch nor by a free kick from a fair catch.

The resulting product became the first printed code of the Sheffield FC.[22]

Scholars have only been able to link three of the laws, 3, 4 and 7, to any public school model.[23] Far more striking than such tenuous suggestions, was the absence of any offside rule. This was a fundamental in all public school games, and a crucial element distinguishing them from those played outside. Not only that, Sheffield's sixth law, punishing illegal play with a free kick, was almost unknown in any public school code.[24] However, although our evidence, as set forth in Chapter 3, only provides us with a very fragmentary insight into the rules used by the various popularly played football games, the code produced at Sheffield in 1858 resembles them far more closely than any supposed public school model, as we shall now see.

Rule 1 of Sheffield's code can be found in the account given by Stonehenge in 1856 that reads: 'the ball is then placed on the ground, and the captain gives the first kick towards the opposite bounds'.[25]

The game played at Glasgow College, from 1820 until 1870, had rules resembling those of 3, 4, 5 and 7 in the Sheffield code as can be seen from the following quote: 'the ball must be kicked and could not be carried or handled, no collaring or hacking was permitted and there was little rough play. If the ball was caught in the air a free, that is an undisturbed, kick was allowed. The player who held the ball dropped it from his hand and kicked it as he fell'.[26]

Rules 3 and 8 might have been anticipated by those used at Edinburgh University FC as can be seen from the following quote: 'at a few minutes to five, they had brought the ball to within a few yards of goal, when another kick would have won it but for a Scotchman who took the ball on the ground and claimed a free kick, resisting every effort made to take the ball from him. The umpire, who saw the circumstances, immediately disallowed the claim, which, however, was poor satisfaction for losing the chance of the game'.[27]

Rule 6, which punishes illegal play, was anticipated by the umpire at Rochdale who awarded the match to the Fear-noughts when the Body-Guards started cheating as the following shows: 'the sixth round, one of the Body-Guards (being tired) putting another person not connected with the game to kick for him, and their own umpire declaring it foul play according to the rules agreed to by both parties, decided the game'.[28]

The code created by Surrey FC in 1849 anticipates rules 5 and 11 in the Sheffield code. Rule 5 in the Sheffield code forbids hacking and tripping and rule 5 of Surrey's code states '5. "Wilful kicking shall not be allowed."' Sheffield's rule 11 states that when the ball goes into touch it must be thrown out from the edge of touch. Surrey's rule 6 is similar, though declaring that the ball must be thrown up in the centre: '6. Should the ball be kicked over the fence on either side of the ground, then the ball, when regained, shall be tossed up in the centre of the ground, in line with the place where it went out.'[29]

In essence, only laws 2 and 10 lack any popularly played prototype, and no one has claimed a public school derivation for either.

As we have seen, there is no indication of any public school influence in the Sheffield laws that were discussed at the committee meeting of October 1858 and consequently no reason for assuming that the rules were derived from anywhere other than the ideas generally current in the wider society. In view of this, it would appear that the first set of rules that were used by Sheffield FC (i.e. in season 1857–58) and the revised versions that were approved for season 1858–59, were produced independently of any public school influence. As we have seen in Chapter 3, many football games beyond the influence of the public schools had rules that were at least as sophisticated as the first Sheffield code, and it is therefore likely that the rules used by Sheffield in 1857 were derived from the wider society and effectively uninfluenced by rules emanating from the public schools.

While the formation of Sheffield FC obviously meant that the game was making progress in the area, it remained a very minor sport. For instance, in March 1858 a crowd of 5,000 watched a nurr and spell match that was being staged for a stake of £50. Similarly, the first attention that the Sheffield FC received in either the local or national press was for its Gymnastic Competition, that was held at East Bank in April 1858. The general public were not admitted, entry being restricted to those members of the social elite who had been provided with tickets. Nonetheless, those outside this charmed circle were able to witness proceedings by standing on walls and hedges. The police controlled the crowd and commended their good behaviour. Given that the event was held to celebrate the completion of the club's first season, we might have expected the inclusion of a number of football-related activities. In fact, aside from a competition for the longest kick of a football, the activities were made up of athletics events.[30]

The Sheffield Club's officials were as follows: President F. Ward (1825–1908), vice presidents T. Sorby and J. Ellison. The committee were W. Prest, T. Pierson, W. Baker, J. Turner and T. Vickers. Secretary and treasurer N. Creswick.[31] In October 1858 the club appear to have had their first AGM.[32] The committee meeting that followed set out the mechanics of regulating membership. It appears that quite strict rules were employed to vet new members, who were required to furnish their address to the secretary, before having their membership balloted. The committee regulated every process carefully, and it was stipulated that at least three committee members had to be present when the balloting took place. At this point, candidates could be excluded if two black balls were registered. Having negotiated these hurdles, candidates paid a half crown for their year's membership, but had to have been members for at least two months before they were allowed to attend the annual athletics meeting.[33]

From its very inception, Sheffield FC were regarded as a socially elite institution, formed 'to provide recreation for the young gentlemen of Sheffield' and 'for several decades they were referred to by their opponents as the "Gentlemen"'.[34] An examination of the Club's officials from the early days reveals them to be elite members of the middle class. Ward, for instance, became chairman of Sheffield Forge and Rolling Mill, while Sorby was a merchant and manufacturer, Ellison a merchant and Pierson a solicitor. Pierson also became a captain in the artillery volunteers.[35] The co-founders of the Club, Nathaniel Creswick and William Prest, both came from wealthy backgrounds. The Creswicks were an old family in the area and Nathaniel was a solicitor and chairman of the Silver Plate Company. William Prest's father had moved to Sheffield from York and bought a wine business, which the son ran at one stage. Both Prest and Creswick were influential in founding the Hallamshire Volunteers in 1859, Prest rising to the rank of lieutenant colonel. In later years Creswick and Prest became Conservative politicians.[36] Socially, the membership of Sheffield FC were largely from the elite of the middle class, as Table 4.2 demonstrates.

The first hint of football's increasing popularity in Sheffield appeared during Christmas 1858, when Cooper's Hotel included the game amongst a range of sports that it was providing during a week of attractions.[37] Shortly after this, Sheffield FC contested their first match against external opposition (previously there had been games between various groups of the Club's members), their opponents being a team drawn from the local military, the 58th Regiment. Sheffield won quite easily, and during the match two of the soldiers suffered

Table 4.2 Occupations of the members of the Sheffield FC for seasons 1857–58 and 1858–59

Occupation	*Harvey*		*Mason*	
	1858	*1859*	*1858*	*1859*
Academic				02
Architect	01	01	01	03
Brewer	01	01	02	03
Dentist	01	01	02	
Doctor	02	01	02	
Gentleman	01	01		
Grocer				01
Joiner	01	01		
Land Agent	02	02	01	
Manager	01	01		
Manufacturer	07	08	11	18
Merchant	06	08		
Reverend	01	02	01	01
Silver Plater		01		
Solicitor	08	08	03	05
Spirit Seller	01	01		02
Stationer		01		01
Superintendent	01	01		
Surgeon	03	04	02	03
Tailor				01
Veterinary Surgeon	01	01	01	
Wine Merchant	01	01	01	01
Unknown	18	35	30	39
Total	57	80	57	80

Source: A. Mason, *Association Football and English Society 1863–1915* (Brighton: Harvester, 1980) pp. 22–3. *FCRI FCR2* (Sheffield city Archives). W. White *General Directory of Sheffield* (Sheffield, 1856). W. White *General Directory of Sheffield* (Sheffield, 1862).

Note
In this table the second and third columns give the author's findings regarding the occupations of the members of Sheffield FC for 1857/58 and 1858/59. The fourth and fifth columns give Mason's findings for the same periods. The discrepancies between the two sets of figures probably stem from the different sources that the scholars have used. Fundamentally, the differences are of no real significance, for both scholars demonstrate that a significant proportion of the members of Sheffield Football Club stemmed from the elite sections of the middle class. The above sources were used by the author.

fractured ribs.[38] Athletics remained the Club's chief event, and in April 1859 the Athletic Sports meeting was held at East Bank. As previously, admission was restricted to those privileged enough to receive tickets and despite the poor weather the event 'attracted a large and .fashionable attendance'. The events included a race going backwards and a competition for the most striking shirt, which Creswick, 'wearing an outrageous garment with all the colours in the rainbow', almost won. While this sounds quite good-humoured, most considered that the programme of events was too lengthy and their general quality poor due to the low standard of the competitors.[39]

While the membership of Sheffield FC expanded steadily throughout 1859, the game remained a very minor sport, completely dwarfed by activities such as cricket. Additionally, the increasing popularity of the Volunteer Movement, with its creation of local militias, probably dissuaded some potential footballers from joining the Club's ranks. Indeed, it distracted the attention of some of Sheffield's members, who played a vital role in creating the Hallamshire Volunteers. On 26 May 1859 the Hallamshire Volunteer Regiment was created, the first six members all stemming from Sheffield FC (the three Vickers brothers, Prest, Creswick and Flockton). While the various Volunteer groups certainly had an interest in sports, typified by the Newhall Volunteer athletic and military exercises of 1857 (an event that drew a crowd of 10,000), their penchant was for foot racing and single-stick rather than football.[40] Cattin maintained that the Volunteer Movement had a harmful effect on football in Sheffield, for it prompted many of Hallam FC's members to leave and join the Hallamshire Volunteers.[41] However, it appears likely that in the long run the opposite was true. First, it is by no means clear that Hallam FC existed in 1859 or even 1860. Second, while initially the Hallamshire Volunteer Regiment did distract attention from football, within a very short while this proto-military force was riven by serious disputes resulting in large numbers leaving (the Hallamshire Regiment was inaugurated in October 1859 and by December disputes had led many to leave).[42] It is quite possible that some of these disillusioned recruits might have joined a football club, especially as the game was becoming sufficiently popular to be staged at Newhall gardens in December 1859.[43]

In 1855 Bramall Lane opened and was available for all sports except pigeon shooting and whippet racing. Taking advantage of this, Sheffield held their annual Athletics meeting there on 7 May 1860, and attracted almost every major family in the neighbourhood. Although it was intended to be an exclusive entertainment, available only to those with tickets, some Club members evidently sold their tickets on to local firms, who snapped them up for re-sale. This appears to have been extremely lucrative, for it was common for ten shillings to be paid for admission vouchers that cost but a shilling.[44] For once, however, the most significant advance in the Club's fortunes occurred on the football field. At their AGM in October 1859 the Sheffield FC had appointed a committee to revise their playing laws.[45] It was probably at this point that the Club began to introduce many of the practices that they borrowed from Eton's code, most notably the rouge.[46] The extent of their success in grafting on these additions to their rules became apparent in December 1860 when they played a match on the rough playing surface of Hillsboro barrack ground against the 58th Regiment. Despite the fact that several members of the army team had been noted footballers while at public school, Sheffield, the rank outsiders, beat them, scoring one goal and ten rouges to their opponent's one goal and five rouges.[47] A few days later, on Boxing Day 1860, Sheffield defeated Hallam and Stumperlow 2–0.[48] At last, there was another team in the area for Sheffield FC to play besides the local military. Football was beginning to gain momentum in the area. Having reached this point it is time to commence the next part of the chapter, a consideration of the clubs that existed in the Sheffield area between 1861 and 1867.

Football clubs in the Sheffield area 1861–67

While the appearance of Hallam and Stumperlow in 1860 does not appear to have instigated a flood of football activity in the Sheffield area, we do at least find eight teams in 1861 and eleven the following year (Tables 4.3 and 4.4). In 1863 football became one of the area's more practised sports, and was referred to in the press as the 'now popular game'.[49] By then, crowds numbering the hundreds were sometimes drawn to spectate. These supporters displayed a range of emotions, from the violently partisan in the infamous Sheffield-Hallam match of December 1862, when fans joined players in the general free-for-all that erupted in the second half, through to the civilised sportsmanship of the match from 1863 between Mackenzie and Norfolk, 'one of the best matches of the season', which caused the crowd to 'applaud loudly at the end', such was their appreciation of the skill displayed by both sides.[50] Despite this, the coverage by the local, let alone national, press is comparatively slight for the bulk of this period and as a consequence many matches remained unreported and their results unattainable. Nonetheless, by comparison with any previous records relating to football we are remarkably well informed about the activities in the Sheffield region for we are able to draw on a range of sources, including local and national newspapers and the private archives of the Sheffield FC. Cumulatively, these provide us with a good insight into the world's first football culture.

In this part of our chapter, we are concerned with considering the football clubs that were present in the Sheffield region between 1861 and 1867. Our study will concern itself with three principal areas. First, we will consider the amount of activity of the various clubs and their relative strength. The second area that we shall explore relates to the composition of the various teams and the facilities that they offered. Finally, we devote ourselves to considering those revenue generating entertainments that were provided by the clubs, especially the annual athletics events. These became significant commercial ventures and will help us understand the extent to which football in Sheffield was motivated by commerce. Let us begin with the first area to be considered, the amount of activity of the various clubs and their relative strength. The following tables give an indication of the amount of activity and the relative standings between teams as recorded in the local press and in national sporting organs.

In 1861 Sheffield were regarded as being so strong that they were able to permit any of their opponents in the area to outnumber them on the field. The extent and significance of these odds varied substantially. On occasions, as with the match in which fifteen of Sheffield played eighteen of Stamperlow and Hallam, the large numbers involved probably prevented Sheffield being too severely affected, though they did lose 3–0.[51] By contrast, the match between 'three of the most celebrated Sheffield players' against six of Norton, must have seemed especially onerous for those who were outnumbered, especially as the match lasted two hours and they lost 4–0.[52] However, two months later when they played again, with the odds reduced to four against six, Sheffield routed Norton 5–0, though as the match lasted three hours 'it became very personal by the end'.[53]

Table 4.3 Results of matches in the Sheffield region in 1861

	1	*2*	*3*	*4*	*5*	*6*	*7*	*8*
1 Engineer	x	1						
2 4th West Yorkshire	0	x						
3 Hallam			x	?*			$1\frac{1}{2}$	
4 Norton			?	x			1?	
5 Pitsmoor					x		?	
6 Stamperlow						x	1	
7 Sheffield			$0\frac{1}{2}$	0*?*	?	0*	x	?
8 York							?	x

Note
A win = 1, loss = 0, draw $=\frac{1}{2}$, ? = result unknown, 2 = two wins and no losses, * are giving odds (deliberately playing with less men than the other side).

Table 4.4 Results of matches in the Sheffield region in 1862

	1	*2*	*3*	*4*	*5*	*6*	*7*	*8*	*9*	*10*	*11*
1 Artillery	x		$\frac{1}{2}$								
2 Collegiate Schl		x									$\frac{1}{2}\frac{1}{2}$
3 Engineer	$\frac{1}{2}$		x								
4 Hallam				x	1*				10		
5 Norton				0	x		?0		000	?	
6 Norwood						x		0			
7 Pitsmoor					?1		x		1?	1	
8 Pitsmoor Junior						1		x			
9 Sheffield				10	3*		0?		x	1*	
10 York					?		0		0	x	
11 York School		$\frac{1}{2}\frac{1}{2}$									x

Note
A win = 1, loss = 0, draw = $\frac{1}{2}$, ? = result unknown, 2 = two wins, 3 = three wins, * are giving odds (deliberately playing with less men than the other side).

At their pre-season meeting in October 1861, Hallam had modestly noted their own improvement and stated that they 'hope to be able to hold their own without the odds that we received last year'.[54] However, Hallam's improvement was such that whereas they had previously taken odds from Sheffield, they now were able to beat them in matches between numerically equal sizes.[55] Indeed, Hallam, themselves, were able to give other teams odds. On at least one occasion this proved to be a very bad idea. In March 1862 five of Hallam's twelve who were supposed to play the eighteen of Norton failed to show up and although Hallam borrowed three other players from Norton, the match was totally one-sided with the handful of Hallamites and their unlikely allies being completely outclassed.[56] By contrast with Hallam, who had improved substantially, Sheffield FC were no longer supreme in the area.

By 1863 newer sides were beginning to obtain the ascendancy in the region. The foremost of these was Pitsmoor, who in the season 1862–63 defeated every

Table 4.5 Results of matches in the Sheffield region in 1863

	1	2	3	4	5	6	7	8	9	10	11	12	13	14	15	16	17
1 Broomhall	x	1															
2 Christchurch	0	x					1										
3 Exchange			x								2		0				
4 Fir Vale				x			1					1					
5 Garrison					x										?		
6 Hallam						x							0				
7 Heeley		0		0			x		0								
8 Howard Hill								x			$1\frac{1}{2}$						1
9 Mackenzie							1		x	2	0		10				
10 Milton									0	x	0						
11 Norfolk			0					$0\frac{1}{2}$	2	1	x		0				
12 Norton				0								x	0		0		0
13 Pitsmoor			1			1			01		1	2	x		3		1
14 St Stephen's														x		0	
15 Sheffield					?							2	0		x		1
16 Tudor														1		x	
17 York								0				1	0		0		x

Note

A win = 1, loss = 0, draw = $\frac{1}{2}$, ? = result unknown, 2 = two wins and no losses. It should be noted that while these results provide some indication of the relative strength between teams, two other factors must be considered. First, the numbers on each side were not always equal. Second, matches between reserve teams have been included.

side in the area and managed to win all three of their matches against Sheffield.[57] Two other teams whose performances were worthy of note in 1863 were Norfolk, who won seven and lost just two of their ten matches, and Mackenzie, who won twelve of their fourteen matches (see Table 4.5).

In 1864 Pitsmoor was the leading club in the area, beating everyone that they played. On 26 September 1864 Sheffield's secretary reported on a dire season that had seen them accrue just two draws from six matches, the other games all being lost (Table 4.7). While he conceded that other teams in the area had improved, substantially speaking he thought that the poor results stemmed from the absence of key players and recommended that fewer fixtures be arranged so as to ensure that strong teams were fielded.[58]

At the AGM of the Sheffield club on 25 September 1865 the secretary observed with considerable pride that the addition of two or three good players to their ranks had meant that Sheffield had enjoyed a very good season, including *beating* Pitsmoor.[59] While Sheffield had certainly done quite well, many of their games had ended up 0–0, and their supremacy over the other teams in the area has surely been exaggerated by Young.[60] Retrospectively, the most notable achievement of Sheffield FC in 1865 was their entry on to the national stage, organising matches against clubs outside the Sheffield area, namely Lincoln and Nottingham. Interestingly, Norfolk also began to seek opponents from outside the Sheffield area, playing two matches against Leeds, one with the Sheffield rules and the other with Leeds code.

Table 4.6 Results of matches in the Sheffield region in 1864

	1	*2*	*3*	*4*	*5*	*6*	*7*	*8*	*9*	*10*	*11*	*12*	*13*
1 Attercliffe	x			0									
2 Broomhall		x	1	0				1	0	0			
3 Exchange		0	x										
4 Fir Vale	1	1		x		1	?	0	1		$\frac{1}{2}$		
5 Hallam					x			?		?		0	
6 Heeley				0		x		10		01			
7 Howard Hill				?			x						
8 Mackenzie		0		1	?	01		x	1	$\frac{1}{2}$	??	00	11
9 Milton		1		0				0	x	0			
10 Norfolk		1			?	10		$\frac{1}{2}$	1	x		$\frac{1}{2}0$	$\frac{1}{2}\frac{1}{2}$
11 Norton				$\frac{1}{2}$				??			x	0	
12 Pitsmoor					0	1		11		$\frac{1}{2}1$	1	x	$1\frac{1}{2}$
13 Sheffield								00		$\frac{1}{2}\frac{1}{2}$		$0\frac{1}{2}$	x

Notes
The Heeley team were known as Heeley Christchurch.
A win = 1, loss = 0, draw = $\frac{1}{2}$, ? = result unknown, It should be noted that while these results provide some indication of the relative strength between teams, two other factors must be considered. First, the numbers on each side were not always equal. Second, matches between reserve teams have been included.

Table 4.7 Results of matches in the Sheffield region in 1865

	1	*2*	*3*	*4*	*5*	*6*	*7*	*8*	*9*	*10*	*11*	*12*	*13*
1 Broomhall	x		$1\frac{1}{2}$		110	0011	1111	1	$0\frac{1}{2}$				?
2 Christchurch		x	?							00			
3 Fir Vale	$0\frac{1}{2}$	?	x					1	?		$\frac{1}{2}$		
4 Gleadless				x		0							
5 Hallam	001				x		101		0	$0\frac{1}{2}$		$0\frac{1}{2}$	
6 Heeley	1100			1		x							
7 Mackenzie	0000				010		x			$0\frac{1}{2}$	??	1	$\frac{1}{2}$
8 Mechanics	0		0					x	0			?	
9 Milton	$1\frac{1}{2}$		?		1			1	x	1			
10 Norfolk		2			$1\frac{1}{2}$		$1\frac{1}{2}$		0	x			?
11 Norton			$\frac{1}{2}$				??				x		$?\frac{1}{2}\frac{1}{2}$
12 Pitsmoor					$1\frac{1}{2}$		0	?				x	
13 Sheffield	?						$\frac{1}{2}$			?	$?\frac{1}{2}\frac{1}{2}$		x

Notes
A win = 1, loss = 0, draw = $\frac{1}{2}$, ? = result unknown, 2 = two wins and no losses. It should be noted that while these results provide some indication of the relative strength between teams, two other factors must be considered. First, the numbers on each side were not always equal. Second, matches between reserve teams have been included.
Mechanics were generally known as United Mechanics.

By 1866 Pitsmoor had again established themselves as the best team in the area.[61] Sheffield had almost turned their back on the other local sides and become involved in matches on a national stage, notably against the FA.

As can be seen from the above Table 4.9, there was a great deal of football in the Sheffield area that was recorded by the press. Aside from these general

Table 4.8 Results of matches in the Sheffield region in 1866

	1	*2*	*3*	*4*	*5*	*6*	*7*	*8*	*9*	*10*	*11*	*12*	*13*	*14*
1 Broomhall	x	1	1	2	2	2½	1	1	100			3		
2 Fir Vale	0	x				1?	2	2	0					?
3 Garrick	0		x					?						
4 Gleadless	00			x		?								
5 Hallam	00				x	1	0??			00	3	00		
6 Heeley	00½	0?		?	0	x	?2	?		1?				
7 Mackenzie	0	00			1??	0?0	x		0?	?$\frac{1}{2}\frac{1}{2}$	0			
8 Mechanics	0	00	?			?		x	?			00		
9 Milton	20	1					1?	?	x	??1	0			
10 Norfolk					2	0?	?$\frac{1}{2}\frac{1}{2}$		??0	x		??2½		?
11 Norton					000		1		1		x	½01		
12 Pitsmoor	000				2			2		?00½	½10	x	10	1
13 Sheffield												01	x	
14 Wellington		?								?		0		x

Note
A win = 1, loss = 0, draw = ½, ? = result unknown, 2 = two wins and no losses. It should be noted that while these results provide some indication of the relative strength between teams, two other factors must be considered. First, the numbers on each side were not always equal. Second, matches between reserve teams have been included.

Table 4.9 Results of matches in the Sheffield region in 1867

	1	*2*	*3*	*4*	*5*	*6*	*7*	*8*	*9*	*10*	*11*	*12*	*13*	*14*	*15*	*16*	*17*	*18*	*19*
1 Brightside	x									1									
2 Broomhall		x			2		3	1	2	1	1	1	2		4		1		
3 Collegiate			x					2											
4 Exchange				x		2		1											2
5 Fir Vale		2			x	1	2		1	2	1								
6 Garrick				2	1	x			3	1					2		3		1
7 Hallam		3			2		x		1			2	3		2				
8 Heeley		1	2	1				x	1	1		2			2		1		2
9 Mackenzie		2			1	3	1	1	x			3	1		2				2
10 Mechanics	1	1			2	1		1		x		1	2		2		1	1	
11 Milton		1			1						x	1	2				2		
12 Norfolk		1					2	2	3	1	1	x			3				1
13 Norton		2					3		1	2	2		x			1			
14 Owlerton														x				1	
15 Pitsmoor		4				2	2	2	2	2		3			x				2
16 Sheffield													1			x			
17 Sheff Wed		1				3		1		1	2						x		1
18 Tapton										1				1				x	
19 Wellington				2		1		2	2			1			2		1		x

Note
This table lists the amount of fixtures between clubs, not their results. By now, the extent of matches involving reserve teams, including matches between first teams and second teams, means that match results are often not representative of the relative strength of teams.

matches, early in 1867 a knock-out competition was staged, the Youdan Cup, which was won by Hallam. By this time, three clubs could claim to be the strongest in the region. The club who probably had the most justification for doing so were Hallam, who had won the Youdan Cup. However, their most obvious rivals, Sheffield, had declined to take part in the tournament and appeared to be grooming themselves for the national stage. At their AGM on 30 September the club voted to stop playing matches against local teams, declaring that 'they are most unsatisfactory', and that it would be better to spend the time practising because too many players fail to show up and play.[62] As noted earlier, this complaint was articulated at the meeting three years earlier (26 September 1864) and it is therefore clear that the primary reason for Sheffield ceasing to play local sides was the failure of players from the Club to represent the team. Oddly enough, in later years, a completely different, and surely fallacious, explanation was provided of the Club's decision to withdraw from local matches, for it was claimed that Sheffield ceased playing other local teams because such opponents always strengthened their elevens by including the best players of other clubs.[63] As we have seen, such a problem was never hinted at during Sheffield's AGMs and consequently such claims must be rejected. Either way, Sheffield's match against Norton in early 1867 appears to have been their last for some time against local sides.[64] The third side who might reasonably claim to be the strongest in the region was Norfolk. Unlike Sheffield, who had effectively withdrawn from local football, Norfolk had an impressive match record in 1867, having won thirteen, drawn seven and lost just two. Additionally, like Sheffield they sought opponents from further afield. Having earlier played Leeds, Norfolk had begun practising with Nottingham's code and had arranged fixtures with them. Norfolk had over two hundred members and was in a good financial position. While it is unclear who were the strongest team in the area, there is little doubt that Wellington was one of the weakest and possess the unwanted distinction of having lost the quickest match in the area's history. Amidst terrible weather, Wellington went 4–0 behind against Norfolk in just 20 minutes and decided to pack up, seeing little point in getting both drubbing and soaking.[65] Wellington were unusual in as much as they were one of the few teams in the area who did not practise regularly. By contrast, teams such as Broomhall were typical of the dedicated nature of most clubs, practising on Monday and Saturday. As we have seen, in their early years Sheffield had to stage intra-club matches because they lacked opponents, and until 1863 this was probably the motivation for many such matches. However, by 1867 practice sessions usually stemmed from one of two impulses. Generally, the aim was to improve skills. Towards the end of the period, however, such sessions focused increasingly upon ensuring that new and different codes were understood. Cumulatively, such devotion to practice and training reflects the serious attitude that many clubs and players entertained towards the sport.

The second area that we shall deal with is concerned with the composition of clubs, the size of their membership, and the facilities that they offered. Let us begin by examining the social profile of the various clubs.

The blueprint for football in Sheffield was established by the first major club in the region, Sheffield FC. As we have seen, the founding members of this body were regarded as representing the elite amongst the middle class and candidates for membership had to undergo a fairly strict vetting before being admitted. During the 1860s many other football clubs were created in Sheffield and judging by the evidence, such as the hours of play and the cost of membership, these clubs were, predominantly, middle-class organisations.[66] While, theoretically, one might imagine that they perceived themselves as the equals of Sheffield FC, in at least two senses they behaved in a clearly subordinate manner. In the first place, they spoke deferentially about the members of Sheffield FC. An example of this can be found in an advert from York Athletic and Football Club, stating that the 'Gentlemen players of Sheffield FC will take part' in their opening game of the season[67] Second, and more profoundly, clubs would install key personnel from Sheffield FC to act as officials. This occurred at York FC, who made Creswick their president, even though he simultaneously held important positions in Sheffield FC.[68] In part such deference was probably due to Sheffield FC being the oldest and richest club in the region, but it probably stemmed from the high social status of the membership. Such evidence does much to substantiate a broader observation that was recently made by Mike Huggins concerning Victorian recreation. He observed that 'the middle classes were riven by divisions', notably the 'vertical fracture between business and professional classes'.[69] In Sheffield this process was obviously present, for there was a distinction between the socially elite members of the Sheffield FC and the other teams in the region, despite the fact that they could all be classified as middle class.

Given that Sheffield FC are the only club for whom we have detailed membership records, it is very hard to assess the extent to which individuals from working class or lower middle class backgrounds participated in the area's football culture. From the very outset, one of the cruder indications of social class, dress, must be dismissed from the equation, for footballers appear to have had a taste for the raffish. In 1863 a directive from York FC reminded members that they were required to play in the club uniform.[70] Four years later, the secretary of Sheffield bemoaned the fact that in the match against Nottingham no two players were dressed alike and declared that 'the result is unpleasing to the eye'.[71] Another possible insight into the presence of different social classes within a club was the practice matches that were so common in the early 1860s. In 1862, for instance, matches occurred at the Sheffield, Pitsmoor and Hallam clubs between two groups of players who were classified as gentlemen vs players.[72] It is very difficult to know how seriously to take such a division and it is unlikely to have been as meaningful as some of the other criteria that were employed in such matches, such as 'Old Collegers v the rest', 'old v young', 'under 30s v over 30s'.[73] By 1866 there is hard evidence that the lower orders were beginning to participate in the running of sporting clubs within the area. For instance, Milton FC presented a gift to their honorary secretary, Joseph Rowbothom, who was due to commence his professional cricket career for Yorkshire.[74] In that same year, Rotherham Athletics Club introduced a new committee in which 'all classes [are] represented'.[75] In 1867 there is substantial evidence of less economically wealthy individuals being involved in football. The rules of the Youdan Cup specified that there would be no waiting for players to arrive, a strong indication that we are dealing with people whose time is regulated by work and who are in no sense leisured amateurs. Significantly, during a Youdan Cup game a player broke his nose and a collection was made for him, the report continuing 'doubtless something will be awarded him out of the funds weekly while unable to work'.[76] By then, efforts were being made to establish a player's accident fund into which players paid small weekly subscriptions in order to be able to draw eight shillings a week during periods when injury rendered them unable to earn a living.[77] Obviously, the people that such a fund was intended to cater for did not belong to the comfortable middle class, being altogether more precariously situated financially. By 1867 the social boundaries of football in the Sheffield region appear to have expanded and embraced groups who would never have been admitted to the Sheffield FC at its inception.

The popularity of football was such that by 1865 even villages, such as Heeley and Gleadless, had teams. However, the most common organisations from which clubs emerged were cricket clubs. Between 1861 and 1867 eight football clubs in the Sheffield area were based upon existing cricket teams. In 1861 a meeting was organised at York Cricket Club to create a football club and within a very short period of time fifty of the cricket club's 386 members had joined this new body. Pitsmoor Cricket Club did likewise. The principal aim of both ventures was to use the football club as a way of maintaining fitness during the Winter, but it seems likely that in Pitsmoor's case these rather limited aims were soon superseded, for the football team became very successful.[78] York appears to have remained more wedded to its parent body, admitting all members of the related cricket and archery clubs to its matches.[79] In 1862 Howard Hill Cricket Club created a football team, as did Mackenzie Cricket Club the following year. By 1864 such was the popularity of football that the well-established Attercliffe Cricket Club became Attercliffe Cricket and Football Club and in 1866 United Mechanics Cricket and Football Club was founded.[80] In 1867 both the Exchange and Sheffield Wednesday football clubs were created, based upon established cricket clubs. On occasions the same personnel were used in football and cricket clubs, for instance in 1865 the secretary of Hallam FC and Hallam Cricket Club was H. Bramall.[81]

The Hallam FC, of course, had probably been influenced by the local Hallamshire Volunteer Regiment, and military sources were certainly influential in the area's football culture. As earlier noted, the first matches of the Sheffield FC against external opposition in 1859 and 1860, were with the local military. Indeed, it is even possible that the introduction of the use of the rouge into the Sheffield code was derived from this source. Unquestionably the military produced one of the most bizarre episodes in Sheffield football when during a match at Sheffield barracks Creeswick, the Sheffield FC captain, became perturbed at the numerical size of the military team. Although the match was supposed to be for twenty players-a-side, when the officer, responding to Creswick's complaints, had his team parade, it was found that they numbered thirty eight! Despite this, Sheffield continued to arrange matches against military sides and as late as 1864 were accepting the challenge of the Riflemen Club.[82] More usually, one suspects, military teams played one another, and certainly local volunteer regiments, such as the West Yorkshire Artillery and the West Yorkshire Engineers, arranged public matches in order to generate revenue via gate money.[83] Socially, many of these military sides were probably made up of officers.

The extent of the membership numbers of the various sides during the period is largely a mystery and Table 4.10 sets out such information as we have. However, as Table 4.11 shows, there is strong evidence that the membership of clubs grew steadily, for as we can see by the end of the period eleven sides were fielding second teams and three third teams. However, it must be remembered that it was not uncommon for teams to be unable to raise a full side.

The facilities offered by clubs can be broadly divided into three groups; a ground on which to play or watch football, privileges available to members, a range of additional entertainments. Let us first consider the matter of a playing ground.

During the 1860s Sheffield FC was constantly trying to obtain decent playing and practice grounds. Given that Bramall Lane had been opened in 1855 one might have thought that this would have been the natural home of such a wealthy and influential club. However, the committee of management that ran Bramall Lane opposed Sheffield FC vehemently and it was not until 29 December 1862 that football was permitted, a charity game between Sheffield and Hallam.[84] Far from ushering in peace and understanding, this fixture did little to ease relations between the Bramall Lane authorities and Sheffield FC and the club continued to be deprived of a decent ground.[85] The club was no luckier with its training ground, the dreadful nature of which was referred to during the AGM of 1865. In the 1870s the lack of a decent playing area was to prove a serious handicap to Sheffield FC and Cattin believes that it was the principal reason for this influential body failing to retain their position in the area.[86] By contrast with all Sheffield's troubles over obtaining a decent playing area, the ground that Heeley FC used was loaned free to them by a patron.[87]

Members of Sheffield's various football clubs were eligible for a range of privileges that expanded steadily as the period progressed. Initially speaking, football matches appear to have been very private affairs, characterised by the attitude of Sheffield FC, whose advert for their fixture against Norton at the East Bank ground reminded the public that 'none but members and their friends may enter the ground'.[88] A year later, Sheffield began providing an omnibus to carry Club members and their friends to their opponents' ground.[89] Other sides soon began to emulate this and by 1867 the provision of an omnibus to away matches was pervasive. Sheffield FC also provided beer and tobacco for playing members at home games.[90] As to away games, Sheffield paid 5 shillings each player who had a free dinner at another club.

From their very inception FCs in the Sheffield area were not perceived as commercial ventures and in the beginning at least, their main source of revenue

Table 4.10 The membership of clubs in the Sheffield area

	1862	*1863*	*1864*	*1865*	*1866*	*1867*
Howard Hill		070				
Mackenzie		100				
Norfolk					120	200
Sheffield	200		252[a]		260	
York	050					

Note
a 28 of these were women.

Table 4.11 Clubs in the Sheffield region who had second and third teams

Team	*1863*	*1864*	*1865*	*1866*	*1867*
Broomhall		2nd	2nd	2nd	2nd, 3rd
Exchange					2nd
Garrick					2nd, 3rd
Hallam					2nd
Heeley				2nd	2nd
Mackenzie			2nd	2nd	2nd, 3rd
Mechanics					2nd
Milton		2nd		2nd	
Norfolk		2nd		2nd, 3rd	2nd
Pitsmoor	2nd		2nd	2nd, 3rd	2nd
Sheffield	2nd				
Sheff Wed					2nd
Wellington					2nd, 3rd

Note
If a club had a second or third team during a particular year it is mentioned in the relevant column.

was the members' subscriptions. As the period went on, additional events were provided for members to either participate in or watch, but with the exception of their annual athletics meetings, with which we shall shortly deal, none of these had any discernible commercial purpose. From 1864 some clubs began to hold a paper chase. In no sense were these competitive events, the emphasis being on fun, typified by the wearing of ridiculous multi-coloured shirts.[91] Another source of entertainment was the musical concert presented by Fir Vale in 1865.[92] Of a somewhat more serious nature, it appears, was the athletics match between Pitsmoor and Fir Vale that was held, ironically, on Shrove Tuesday in 1864.[93]

By contrast with these entertainments, some recreations did generate significant sums of money and it is to these that we now turn.

It was no accident that the very first reference that we have to Sheffield FC in either the national or local press relates to the athletics event that they held to round off the first season of their existence. For almost this entire period athletics events proved to be the most popular aspects of a football club's programme, generating crowds, revenue and publicity. The contents of such events usually fell into two categories. The first sort, which were dominant in the earlier period, placed an emphasis on amusement, often of a somewhat slapstick variety.[94] A characteristic example of this was an event from the Sheffield FC's meeting of 1864 in which it was stipulated that the 'water jump has to be crossed twice for the amusement of the visitors'.[95] The organisers would introduce various novelties into their programmes in the hope of causing amusement, such as a 'smoking race' that was held at Milton's sports event in 1866.[96] Increasingly, however, programmes began to cater for a wide range of tastes, including events where the onus was on fun, such as races for wheelbarrows and donkeys, and demanding, high quality athletic competitions, to which expert entrants were drawn by the offer of large prizes.[97] By 1867 Hallam's athletics meeting was one of the few where events were predominantly for fun, with competitors running with buckets of water on their heads and such like.[98] Elsewhere, things were becoming more serious.

A wide variety of prizes was offered at the annual sports meetings during the early part of the 1860s, incorporating both cups and useful items.[99] Such prizes were obviously regarded as being attractive, and were displayed in shop windows.[100] In many senses there was neither need nor desire to attract expert competitors from afar, for although disappointment bordering on concern was sometimes expressed over the rather poor quality of competitors, as at the AGM of Sheffield FC in 1864, rules ensured that an external competitor's access to almost every event was restricted. Until 1867 most events at the sports meetings throughout the area were limited to either military personnel or the members of local football, athletics or cricket clubs.[101] Alternatively, social criteria were sometimes employed, notably at Sheffield's meeting for 1865, where certain events were set aside for 'gentlemen amateurs'.[102] By 1866, however, there was a new level of seriousness about competitors, which even manifested itself in the clothes they wore or rather failed to wear. Increasingly, spectators complained that 'many players wear drawers and singlets', and umpires keen on trying to limit the amount of flesh that was being displayed emphasised that 'competitors are required to wear loose shirt and trousers'.[103] By contrast with the light hearted knock-about of earlier years there was a new seriousness to these events, with disputes occurring over the accuracy of the timing of races.[104] The probable cause of this sharper competitiveness was the decision, in 1866, to open Sheffield FC's Athletic meeting to anyone and increase the available prize money. These innovations had the effect of enticing distinguished competitors from Surrey, Nottingham and Northumberland and inevitably improved the standard.[105] By the following year most of the area's athletic events were drawing competitors in larger numbers and of better quality. For instance, over one hundred people entered the programme that Mackenzie staged, and sixty enlisted at Broomhall's. The battle against unusual apparel persisted and at Norfolk's event competitors were forbidden to wear tights. Disputes had now become quite common, heated discussions occurring over such issues as 'what is walking?'[106]

The athletics meeting that Sheffield FC conducted at the end of every season was a 'fashionable' affair, attracting most of the area's elite. Until 1862 the general public were not admitted, access to this social event being restricted to Club members, their friends and a number of the well connected. The decision to admit the wider public, at sixpence each, was a great commercial success, some 3,000 spectators attending.[107] From that time forth, the social parameters continued to be rolled back and by 1867 many children were attending, their parents paying three pence to secure their admission. Elsewhere, similar commercial expertise was being deployed, programmes at York, for instance, being sold for three pence, and evidently unless clubs were unlucky with either the weather or some rival attraction a reasonable profit could be made. Unfortunately, we lack detailed information concerning the admission prices that were charged, the numbers attending and the amount of receipts generated from the gate money. The following Tables 4.12 and 4.13 set out such information as we have.

The gate money generated by annual athletics events rapidly became a major, if not chief, source of income for many clubs.[108] By contrast, on the rare occasions when gate money was taken at football matches it was donated to charitable purposes. During the early 1860s a number of matches were staged on behalf of particular charities. The group who appears to have received the most regular donations were the Volunteer movement. In 1861 two Volunteer regiments played football on a dreadful pitch with spectators being charged sixpence to watch, the receipts being shared equally between the funds of the two regiments.[109] A year later, and somewhat more expertly, Sheffield played Hallam, with the proceeds being donated to the Volunteers. Admission cost either sixpence or a shilling, though Volunteers who were wearing their uniform were admitted free.[110] The Volunteers, along with local cricket clubs, also received money that was donated by Rotherham Athletics club.[111]

As fears of a French invasion relented and were replaced by concern over the effect that the Union blockade of Confederacy ports was having on the Northern cotton towns, Sheffield and Hallam organised another charity match, this time on behalf of the Lancashire Relief Fund. The match was held at Bramall Lane and admission charges were the same as for an ordinary cricket match, ranging between three pence and sixpence.[112] Four years later Bramall Lane was again the venue for a charitable match, this time between teams representing the town and the country. Admission charges were sixpence and the receipts were shared between Sheffield Infirmary, the public hospital and the dispensary.[113] Towards the end of the period Milton had begun to charge spectator's admission money to watch an ordinary match, non-members having to pay a penny to watch them play Norfolk. The proceeds, seven shillings, were donated to the local orphanage.[114]

As we can see, football was not a commercial game during this period. The one possible exception might be the gate money generated by the Youdan Cup. As we shall see later, this attracted substantial attention, crowds of up to 3,000 being drawn, and must have produced something in the region of £50 gate money. While the precise fate of the money is unclear, it seems likely that Thomas Youdan, who was a music hall proprietor, devoted the bulk of it to providing prizes for local FCs. It is certainly the case that he bought the silver cup that was awarded to the runners up in the competition out of the gate money,

Table 4.12 The cost and attendance at athletics events in the Sheffield area 1862–67

	1862	*1863*	*1864*	*1865*	*1866*	*1867*
Attercliffe			3d	x		
Broomhall						
Christchurch		good			x	
Collegiate		6d, big		x		large
Fir Vale						
Garrick						
Hallam		x		x	x	x
Heeley				x		1,000
Mackenzie		x	6d	thousands	large	x
Mechanics					800	x
Milton					1,500	x
Norfolk		3d	6d	6d	3,000	x
Pitsmoor	moderate	numerous	large, 6d	x	x	1,524
Sheffield	3,000	x	5,000	4,000	x	7,000
York	6d	x				

Note
x = event was staged. The cost of admission for spectators is indicated by price. Crowd size is indicated by figure or expression used in the report.

Table 4.13 The receipts from annual athletic sports meeting

	1862	*1863*	*1864*	*1865*	*1866*	*1867*
Norfolk					75	
Pitsmoor						38
Sheffield	150		250	200		259[a]

Notes
The figures are in pounds.
a was based on treating each spectator as paying 9d admission.

and he also provided a silver cup and a silver cigar case as prizes for the athletic sports that were held at Mackenzie and Norfolk respectively.[115]

While a variety of sports in the area were conducted for stakes, the chief commercial sport was cricket. For instance, in 1866 the cricket match between Hallam and Wednesday was contested for a £50 stake in front of a huge crowd.[116] In the Sheffield area the wealthiest sporting body seems to have been Sheffield United Cricket Club whose receipts for season 1862–63 were £317, producing a balance of £650.[117] Three years later their condition was still healthier.[118] By contrast, football was a very uncommercial activity, whose members often donated money to other sports and charities.[119] Predominantly, the impression is that for the bulk of the period football regarded itself as an essentially private activity, focused upon club members and their friends, and it is instructive to observe that fixture lists advertising the coming matches for the season in the local newspapers did not appear until 1865–66.[120]

We might sum up the situation of the various clubs in Sheffield between 1861 and 1867 as follows. The amount of organised football played in the Sheffield area expanded throughout the period with clubs appearing that were based upon a variety of bodies, particularly cricket clubs. Socially, the composition of these clubs appears to expand, incorporating members from rather lower in the social scale, perhaps including some from the working class. While Sheffield FC remained the dominant commercial and social entity in the region, in competitive terms they rapidly lost their position and were generally overshadowed by their rivals. Football was not organised commercially, and such profits as were produced were donated to charity. However, a high level of expertise was deployed when organising the annual athletics events that the various FCs staged and these were exploited commercially in order to generate profits. By the latter part of the 1860s the revenue from such events represented the chief source of most clubs' incomes. Previous to this, clubs had relied on the fees paid by their members. Between 1861 and 1867 football in Sheffield was in no sense commercial and in this differed sharply from most other sports, notably cricket.

The evolution of Sheffield's code 1861–67

In this part of the chapter, we examine the changes that occurred in the code of football laws that regulated most of the games between clubs in the region between 1861 and 1867. Our approach is essentially chronological but before commencing it should be emphasised that throughout this period the rules of football used in the region were based on the code of one team, Sheffield FC. This fact produced a great uniformity within the area, ensuring that it was not beset by the fragmentation that afflicted other regions, such as London, where a spectrum of widely different codes impeded interaction between clubs.

As we saw in the part 'The emergence of a football culture in Sheffield', having established a very rudimentary code in 1858, Sheffield FC initiated a number of meetings over the next few years during which they introduced a variety of changes. It seems likely that many of these changes stemmed from an improved understanding of the various public school games, which enabled them to introduce refinements where relevant. This last point must be emphasised, for because the composition of Sheffield FC was almost devoid of former public school boys their attitude towards the various public school codes was entirely pragmatic, adopting such components as they perceived as being useful.[121] This objectivity was characteristic of the Club's flexible attitude towards rules which manifested itself in several areas, such as the giving of 'odds' in matches, that is allowing the weaker side to use more men, as in a match between Sheffield FC and Norton, in which the latter had eighteen men to Sheffield's twelve.[122]

While we have no real idea about the rules used by clubs other than Sheffield FC in the years previous to 1862, it is possible that some teams in the area might have used rules that were quite distinct. However, in 1862, after another series of meetings, Sheffield published a far more sophisticated and comprehensive code than that of 1858 and made the bold pronouncement that from now on these would be the only rules that they would use in matches.[123] As it was, the supremacy enjoyed by Sheffield FC, in terms of the social standing of its members, the wealth of the club and the ability of its players, meant that every club in the area adopted 'The Sheffield Rules', thus producing an important uniformity. As can be seen from the following laws, the code that was printed in 1862 was far more sophisticated than that of 1858. Of particular interest are the following laws:

11 A rouge is obtained by the player who first touches the ball after it has been kicked between the rouge flags, and when a rouge has been obtained one of the defending side must stand post two yards from the front of the centre of the goal sticks.

12 No rouge is obtained when the player who first touches the ball is on the defending side. In that case it is a kick out as specified in law 2.

14 A goal outweighs any number of rouges. Should no goals be scored or an equal number be obtained, the match is decided by rouges.

16 In setting out the ground, the goal sticks must be placed 12 feet apart, and the cross bar 9 feet from the ground. The rouge flags must be placed one on each side and in line with the goal, and 12 feet distance from the goal.[124]

The rouge was introduced as an additional mode of scoring because the small size of Sheffield's goals led to a proliferation of goalless draws.[125]

While the adherence of every FC in the region to the same code of laws guaranteed that games were less likely to be afflicted by disputes over rules, the rules themselves admitted a considerable amount of physical contact and on occasions this precipitated violent confrontations. During the period the most notable of these occurred, ironically, during a charity match that was staged at Bramall Lane in December 1862 between Sheffield and Hallam. The robust play admitted by the Sheffield rules, coupled with the tension existing between two well-established rivals, ensured a series of niggling incidents that finally boiled over into a fight that engulfed both spectators and players. Early in the game Hallam's Waterfall clattered into Creswick of Sheffield while charging him. The force of the contact was such that Creswick, who appears to have been a fairly rumbustious competitor, threatened Waterfall with his fist. While Creswick apologised soon afterwards, tension lingered and somewhat later, while the players were awaiting the umpire's decision, Creswick knocked the ball unfairly from the Hallam players' hands and kicked it towards their goal. The game continued in this fractious vein, stirred on by the crowd who indulged in 'much partisan cheering, especially when "downing" a man', and almost inevitably culminated in a clash between Creswick and Waterfall. The initial foul was by Waterfall, who held Creswick illegally. In response, Creswick hit Waterfall so hard that it made his mouth bleed, whereupon Waterfall 'threw off his waistcoat', charged at Creswick and struck him. A general melée followed, including both spectators and players, and it was some time before calmer heads prevailed and installed a truce, with Waterfall being sent to play in goal. While some of the Hallam players and supporters were sorry that Creswick had been hurt, many appear to have relished the incident, gleefully regarding it as a suitable punishment, especially as 'Creswick happens to have many of these unfortunate incidents with his fist'.[126]

Episodes like the above conflagrations were not typical of the interactions between clubs in the Sheffield area. On the contrary, committees appear to have met on a regular basis to discuss the rules and where necessary adaptations and revisions were made in order to 'iron out defects as they appear', a fact much praised by the influential journalist Cartwright.[127] By 1863 the football culture in Sheffield was very strong and confident and consequently when they learned of the creation of the FA in London they contacted them, submitting a copy of their own printed code and some suggestions concerning the proposed laws of the FA The letter of 30 November 1863 from Chesterman, the Sheffield secretary, to the FA noted that the Club had just begun to use an offside rule, which was as follows:

> any player between the opponent's goal and the goalkeeper unless he has followed the ball there, is offside and out of play. The goalkeeper is that player in the defending side who is for the time being nearest his own goal.[128]

Predominantly speaking, the rules advocated by Sheffield were far more akin to what was eventually to become association football than those that were being espoused by the FA in 1863. In regard to this, it is of particular interest that Sheffield was violently opposed to the practice of players 'running in', that is running holding the ball in their hands, behaviour that was to become a defining characteristic of the rugby code but was then enjoying substantial support from the FA. A further example of Sheffield's support of a law that would later be adopted by the FA was their advocacy of crossbars in order to render it more easy for umpires to determine whether a goal had been scored. It would be many years before the FA adopted this idea fully.[129]

While, as we have seen, since 1862 the code created by Sheffield FC had been adopted by the other clubs in the region, two elements of the game remained unstandardised throughout the period, the length of games and the numbers on each side. The Sheffield rules provided no guidance as to the length of time of matches, and these could range from anything between one and three hours, depending upon the agreement concluded by the competing teams. From October 1863 Sheffield insisted that they would not play matches in which there were more than eleven players on each side.[130] In practice, of course, they were flexible, and on 26 September 1864 endeavoured to arrange a fixture against Mackenzie FC at either eleven or fourteen players a side.[131] Generally, as Table 4.14 shows, Sheffield's attempt at standardising the numbers on each side did not enjoy success.

Sheffield FC endeavoured to promote the adoption of important components of the FA's code throughout the Sheffield region. Consequently, in season 1865–66 they used the FA's astonishingly restrictive offside law, which insisted that anyone who was in front of the ball was out of play. The product of this was

Table 4.14 The numbers on each side in matches within the Sheffield area 1865–67

Numbers per side	*10*	*11*	*12*	*14*	*15*	*18*	*24*
1865		02	08	03	01	01	01
1866	01	04	05	18	01		
1867		04	09	10			
Total	01	10	22	31	02	01	01

an abundance of goalless draws and much disquiet, with clubs such as Hallam experimenting with their own offside law. Predictably, at the end of the season the FA's offside law was abandoned in the Sheffield area and replaced by the more liberal rule that the Yorkshire clubs had previously adhered to.[132] Paradoxically, Sheffield's decision to abandon the London body's offside rule persuaded the FA to significantly dilute the offending rule: the provinces were influencing the metropolis. Indeed, during 1866 Sheffield's rules increasingly diverged from those of the FA, with practices such as offside and the awarding of a free kick for a 'fair catch' being abandoned.[133]

The vigour of Sheffield's football culture grew in inverse proportion to the declining influence of the London-based FA. While the latter's code was scarcely adhered to anywhere, the number of games using Sheffield's rules multiplied. Naturally, this did not prevent disputes, such as the controversy that erupted in the match between Heeley and Norfolk in 1866. Generally, throughout Britain, matches were administered by two umpires, one from each side, but the absence of an official from Heeley meant that on this occasion both officials belonged to the Norfolk club. However, when a Heeley goal was disallowed the offended parties refused to accept the umpire's decision, prompting a Norfolk official to declare that Heeley now have: 'the unenviable reputation of being the only club in Sheffield who refuse to abide by the umpire's decision'.[134] While, retrospectively, it seems strange that there were not more of such incidents throughout Britain, the first sustained attempt to introduce a neutral official occurred at Sheffield in 1867, as one of a raft of novel laws that were introduced by the committee administering the Youdan Cup.

The Youdan Cup was the inspiration of a local entrepreneur and while the event is notable for a number of developments, including the large numbers of paying spectators that were drawn to matches, perhaps the most startling innovations related to the rules that were used. The committee who created these were extremely pragmatic, one rule, for instance, declaring 'No waiting for players to arrive'. Whereas it would be some years before the FA would punish fouling, in true Sheffield fashion the Youdan committee stated that the 'referee has the authority to award a free kick if any club makes three fouls or kicks out when the ball is thrown in, if he believe it intentional'.[135] Anticipating the 'Golden Goal' rule that was used in Euro 96, the Youdan Committee declared that 'the first side to score in extra time win the match'.[136] However, the most significant novelty was the use of neutral referees rather than umpires from each side. While the latter functionaries were retained in some matches, notably the final, they were subordinate to the other official, who came from a third club.[137]

As we can see, officials in the Sheffield area selected rules in a very pragmatic fashion and although in March 1867 the embryonic Sheffield FA discussed the laws of the FA and showed some interest in adopting them entirely as their own, ultimately they decided to retain their own laws, emphasising the fundamental similarities between the two codes.[138] The meeting considered a number of disputes that were present in the Sheffield rules, such as whether one goal was worth five rouges.[139] Predominantly, their decisions were very pragmatic. Thus, it was decided that if the shirt colours of the teams clashed the side who had been in existence the longer were entitled to retain their strip.[140] Similarly, if a match in which odds were given went to extra time the sides were to be numerically evened.[141] These were very uncontentious, common-sense decisions, that corresponded fully with the general sentiment of the footballing community. As was usual throughout this period, the rules regulating football in Sheffield accorded with the consensus and were thus able to unify the region.

Essentially, there were two key elements in Sheffield's outlook towards rules that were vital. The first of these was that the entire area used a single code, that devised by Sheffield FC. The second major element was the immense pragmatism displayed by the committee of Sheffield FC when devising and adjusting rules. It appears that decisions were made according to the problems that were encountered in everyday play and the aim was always to find a practical solution from any source that should prove applicable. The product of such pragmatism was the creation of a practical code that was far in advance of that of the FA, anticipating many laws that the London based association would later come to adopt.

Sheffield and beyond: contact with outsiders and the emergence of an association

In this section, we look at the impact that Sheffield had on the wider footballing community and the increasingly organised nature of the game in the region. This section consists of four components. The first two are concerned with Sheffield's relations with the wider world, namely the provinces and the FA. The sections 'Developments in Sheffield's football culture' and 'Sheffield FA' deal with developments within Sheffield, namely the Youdan Cup and the creation of an embryonic Sheffield FA, respectively. We begin with the provinces.

Sheffield and the provinces

The first contact that Sheffield had with outsiders on the football field occurred in January 1865 when they visited Nottingham and played the local team in an eighteen-a-side match. Sheffield's lack of familiarity with the Nottingham rules meant that they played 'warily' at first but eventually took the lead via a 'very scientific goal' and according to the Sheffield papers won the match.[142] In the return Sheffield achieved victory via the solitary goal of the game, when Nottingham's lack of familiarity with Sheffield's code meant that they failed to cover their goal properly.[143] The following year an effort was made to establish a compromise code, with Sheffield agreeing to use Nottingham's offside law in return for like concessions.[144] Despite this, the match that followed at Nottingham was beset by difficulties over the rules. These culminated when Chesterman retrieved the ball from amongst the crowd and touched it down, thus equalising Nottingham's earlier score. The goal was disputed and the 'decision remained in abeyance', the game coming to a premature end.[145] Sheffield won the return at home in March 1866 but the match was more notable for the appalling weather that it was played in. The local paper was struck by the absurdity of the spectacle of: 'Thirty players dressed in very light costume under a blinding shower of sleet'.[146] It appears that by 1867 matches with Nottingham had lost their appeal and Sheffield could only persuade seven players to visit Trent Bridge. Although Nottingham loaned them two of their reserves, Sheffield's team never numbered more than nine against Nottingham's eleven and the home side won the match inside the hour.[147]

While until 1867 matches with Nottingham had generally accomplished the basics, both sides turning up with the requisite numbers, games against Lincoln rarely attained even this. The first match between them, in 1865, set the tone, Lincoln failing to raise a team because many players preferred to attend a rival attraction, the Lincoln races, which were being held on the same day. Lincoln compounded the problem by omitting to notice that they were a man short and in consequence of this efforts were not made to adjust the numbers on each side. Given that Lincoln was also unfamiliar with Sheffield's rules it was unsurpising that the home side won.[148] Lincoln's code was very different to that of Sheffield, resembling a rugby-type game, and to compensate for this Sheffield staged practice matches using these rules. However, it did them little good, Lincoln winning the return 2–0.[149] Once again, when Lincoln visited Sheffield they were a man short but this time they had the sense to enlist one of the spectators. Amidst appalling weather, Sheffield won two rouges to nil.[150] The next match, played at Lincoln using the home side's rules, was the most satisfactory of the fixtures, both sides raising full teams and the game, which finished 1–1, being contested in good spirit, uncontroversially supervised by an umpire from each side.[151] By contrast, the match in December 1866 was especially dismal, the weather being so terrible that only fifty spectators attended, and the match ending prematurely after a dispute over a goal.[152] Such appetite as Sheffield had for visiting Lincoln had clearly dwindled by February 1867, for no fewer than twenty-one Sheffield players refused to play. Eventually the visitors did manage to raise a team of eight, and despite using the home side's code, pulled off a surprising victory over the ten men of Lincoln.[153] In November 1867 Sheffield achieved another victory over Lincoln, though proving themselves to be considerate hosts – at half time both sides enjoyed some sherry![154] During this period Sheffield also defeated another provincial side, a fifteen from Manchester, a victory that was assisted by the visitors' lack of familiarity with Sheffield's rules.[155]

Sheffield FC was not the only team from the region who played outsiders. The Norfolk club played two matches against Leeds in 1865, on the home and away principle, with the visitors adopting the home side's code.[156] As we have seen, the problems over rules could spoil such matches, but despite this the game at Leeds was excellent, the crowd applauding warmly despite it finishing goalless. The umpires were Skinner, president of Norfolk Club and Curzon of the *Leeds Mercury*.[157] By 1867 Norfolk ventured further afield, and prepared to take on Nottingham by practising with the Midlander's code.[158]

Given that Lincoln used a rugby-based code, and Nottingham a rather robust association one, the matches that Sheffield and Norfolk arranged with them did at least provide these areas with examples of an association-type game along the lines advocated by the FA. However, as we have seen, the matches themselves were often beset by problems and efforts to create compromise codes do not appear to have succeeded. Predominantly, the impact of Sheffield's 'missionary' ventures was slight.

Sheffield and the FA

By contrast with their lack of impact in the provinces, Sheffield had a substantial influence on the London-based FA. Throughout this period, it was Sheffield which took the initiative in their dealings with the FA. These commenced with Chesterman's letter to the London body on 30 November 1863 and continued through to the arrangements for a match between Sheffield and the FA for 6 April 1867.[159] Sheffield were probably the staunchest supporters that the FA had during this period and did as much as they could to try and promote the Association's interests. In 1866 Sheffield sought to arouse the dormant FA by proposing that there should be a match between London and Sheffield. In London this was misrepresented as a match between the FA and the Sheffield FA, the latter body representing twenty-three clubs.[160] The Sheffield Association had not been formed, and the match was essentially between Sheffield FC and the London FA.[161] Not only that – Sheffield did not wish to play the whole FA, but simply one London club. The two sides established the following basic framework for the game:

1 The ground was to be 120 yards long and 80 yards wide.
2 London are to wear white jerseys or flannel shirts and white trousers.
3 A Lilywhite no 5 ball to be used.
4 The game shall kick off at 3 p.m. and finish at 4:30 p.m.
5 Notices of the match shall be placed in *Bell's Life in London, The Sporting Life, The Sportsman*.[162]

The rules that were used would be those of the FA, and it appears that some in Sheffield regarded the club's secretary Chesterman as having been wrong to do this.[163] In preparation for the match Sheffield practised using the FA code.[164]

While the match was important for fostering greater co-operation between the two bodies, aside from the fact that London won it is rather hard to assess the impact that the game made on the players. According to one source, London objected to the rough play of Sheffield.[165] Alternatively, Sheffield believed that there was far too much hacking from the London side.[166] A third source gives the impression that the game was quite pleasant.[167]

By 1867 the FA was in deep trouble and at their meeting in February there were only three pieces of good news, all stemming from Sheffield. The Sheffield delegate, Chesterman had brought proposals that they should arrange another match with London in order to help generate publicity. Chesterman also alerted the few delegates (for only six people in total attended the meeting) that the region was keen on creating a local association, containing large numbers of players and clubs, that would be affiliated to the FA. Finally, as the FA officials observed, the sporting papers had recorded that 3,000 spectators had paid to watch the final of the knock-out cup competition that was being staged in Sheffield. It is to these matters, the blossoming of Sheffield's football culture, that we now turn.

Developments in Sheffield's football culture

In March 1867 the representatives of thirteen clubs from the Sheffield area met at the Adelphi Hotel, with H. W. Chambers in the chair, to discuss the creation of a Sheffield Association. The rules that were used in Sheffield differed from those of the FA in three principal ways: (1) Sheffield's code had no offside rule (2) Sheffield's code awarded a penalty against offenders for handling (3) Sheffield counted rouges if the scores finished level. After much discussion at a later meeting on 9 October 1867 it was decided to effectively leave Sheffield's code unchanged, while acknowledging the validity of the FA's rules.[168] The following year, the Sheffield FA was formally constituted and the long process of harmonising Sheffield's rules with those of the FA commenced with the removal of the clauses admitting the rouge from the Yorkshire-based code.[169] The constitution of the Sheffield FA as issued in 1868 was as follows:

1 The body shall be called the Sheffield FA.
2 All clubs of one year standing are eligible to join.
3 Annual subscriptions are 10s 6d per club.
4 Its officials shall consist of a president, vice president, treasurer and secretary, and a committee consisting of one member from each club. Seven officials constitute a quorum.
5 Officials will be elected at the AGM.
6 AGM to be held on the second Wednesday in October.
7 In the event of an attempt to alter a law, it must be sent to the secretary by the first Wednesday in October, and he will advertise it in the local papers.
8 Each member must forward a statement on colours and costume.
9 Clubs joining must nominate a delegate.
10 All clubs must play by the Association rules.[170]

Table 4.15 The Youdan Cup knock-out competition in 1867

First round	*Second round*
Hallam beat Heeley Norton beat Mechanics	Hallam beat Norton
Norfolk beat Fir Vale Broomhall beat Pitsmoor	Norfolk beat Broomhall
Mackenzie beat Garrick Milton beat Wellington	Mackenzie beat Milton

Note
In the finals Hallam beat Norfolk and Mackenzie and finished second.

The second aspect of Sheffield's progress was the Youdan Cup (Table 4.15), the final of which was between Hallam and Norfolk in February 1867, was the most high profile football match that had occurred anywhere in Britain up until that point. The match attracted 3,000 spectators, each paying 3d admission, and was regarded as astonishing proof of football's substantial potential popularity.[171] The idea of staging a cup competition had been initiated by the Alexander Music Hall's proprietor, Thomas Youdan, who offered both a silver cup and prize money. As it was, although Youdan awarded a £2 prize to the person who submitted the best design for the silver cup, it proved impossible to have the trophy made in time for it to be presented to the winners, Hallam.[172] However, at least the trophy for the runners-up, a two-handed silver goblet encircled with athletic figures that had been purchased with the proceeds of the gate money, had been completed. Sadly, Youdan was unable to present it personally because he was ill.[173] In the finals Hallam beat Norfolk and Mackenzie to finish first, while Norfolk beat Mackenzie and finished second.

As has been earlier noted, the Youdan Cup was regulated by rules that were drawn up by a committee. The first two rounds were on a knock-out basis. However, the final was contested between three teams playing one another in their turn. The results in the various matches ranged between victory by a solitary rouge through to four goals to nil. In some matches extra time was needed to obtain a result.

From the earlier discussion we can see that by 1867 football in the Sheffield region was full of vitality. Indeed, efforts were being made to place the game on a more financially secure footing for its players by creating a 'Players Accident Fund' which would pay eight shillings a week to those of its subscribers who were prevented by injury from working.[174] At this stage the idea appears to have been still-born because attempts to establish a basis for such a fund by staging charity events, such as a match between the Town and the Country, failed. The match occurred at Bramall Lane but insufficient spectators paid the three penny's admission charge to prevent the fixture suffering a financial loss.[175] The failure of such a scheme meant that injured players who were prevented from working had to rely on collections being made on their behalf.[176]

Sheffield FA

While Sheffield appears to have had little impact on the provinces, between 1863 and 1867 they exerted a substantial influence on the FA, generating a number of initiatives that were designed to publicise the game. In 1867, as we shall see in Chapter 5, it is likely that the successful nature of football activity in Sheffield encouraged the FA to continue at a time when its officials were considering disbanding the organisation. The creation of the Sheffield FA, an affiliate body whose members outnumbered the FA, provided the London association with important support. Similarly, the Youdan Cup gave an insight into the size of football's potential audience. Cumulatively, this provided hope for the FA at a time when it was struggling to continue.

As we have seen, between 1857 and 1867 a large football culture blossomed in the Sheffield region. The area's clubs all played by the same code and selected their rules in a very pragmatic fashion. While, as yet, commercial expertise was only being applied to the annual athletics meetings that the clubs held, with football being governed on non-profit-making lines, events such as the Youdan Cup had revealed that football had a large potential paying audience. Consequently, there is much evidence to support the contention that by 1867 the football culture of Sheffield was in many senses modern, especially as in the following year, 1868, the Sheffield FA, a body that had to all practical purposes long been in existence, was formally constituted. Having established this, it is time now to examine the fate of football elsewhere in Britain in the years between 1860 and 1867, the subject of Chapter 5.

5 Footballing backwaters?

London, the FA and the rest 1860–67

As we saw in Chapter 3, in the years between 1830 and 1859 there was no more football activity in the Sheffield area than in many other regions, especially elsewhere in the north, but between 1860 and 1863 this changed substantially, with football in the Sheffield region tending to account for about a third of the total of the game's activity in Britain as a whole. Additionally, there was great homogeneity in the rules used by teams in the Sheffield area which meant that they avoided the problems that fragmented the football cultures elsewhere in Britain. Cumulatively, as was shown in Chapter 4, the years 1860–67 were ones in which the football culture of Sheffield led the way, leaving the rest of the nation toiling in the rear. In this chapter we shall examine the fate of football outside the Sheffield region between 1860 and 1867, particularly the attempts to create a national association to unify and regulate the game. The chapter consists of six parts. In the first we shall consider the football that occurred outside the Sheffield region between 1860 and 1863 and the ideas that were being advanced concerning the establishment of a unified code of rules. The next part examines the creation of the FA in 1863 and the reasons behind its failure to establish a common set of laws. The part titled 'Football at Public Schools' picks up the story where we left it in Chapter 2, and examines football in the public schools and Cambridge and Oxford universities from 1864 to 1867. In the next part we assess the football in the wider community outside the Sheffield region between 1864 and 1867, particularly the problems relating to the myriad of codes that were practised. The part 'The Football Association 1865–67' is devoted to the events surrounding the meeting that the FA held in 1867, when the Association very nearly disbanded. In the concluding part we assess the impact that the football culture of Sheffield had on the game in Britain and suggest that had it not been for the strength and vitality of the Sheffield region the FA might have taken on an entirely different structure. We commence with the first part of our study, an examination of the football practised outside of Sheffield between 1860 and 1863 and the ideas that were being discussed relating to the creation of a unified code.

Football in London and elsewhere, 1860–63

This, the first part of the chapter, consists of three sections. The opening section considers the basis and composition of the various teams existing in London and the provinces (excluding the Sheffield area) between 1860 and 1863. In the next, we assess the various codes of rules that were utilised by these sides. The section titled 'unified code of football laws' considers the views that were advanced over the creation of a unified code of football laws that would embrace the entire country. We commence with our first section, the basis and composition of the various teams existing outside of the Sheffield area between 1860 and 1863.

Basis and composition of the teams

During this period teams were generally based upon three organisations, (1) schools, (2) private clubs, (3) military. Let us begin by considering the largest category, schools.

1 *Schools.* The most pervasive structure upon which teams were based was the school. While considerable attention is justifiably paid to sides made up of old public school boys, it appears that the ordinary school was more important as a basis for clubs. During this period a large number of teams appear who directly represented their schools. For instance, in the London area there were Wimbledon School, Kensington Grammar and Forest School; while Hampshire had Queenswood College and Romsey; and Lincolnshire – Mr Roger's School and Louth Grammar. Scotland had a number of such institutions, the most famous being Merchiston School and Edinburgh Academy. Alternatively, the membership of a number of clubs was based almost exclusively on former pupils of a particular school. Prominent examples of this were the Civil Service and Harlequin clubs and the Worlabye House team, the last being drawn almost exclusively from former pupils of Baty's School.[1]

The public schools were extremely important nuclei for teams, and the strongest side in the London area during the early 1860s was Forest FC, or Forest-Leytonstone as they were often called. The club was created by old Harrovians and played at Epping Forest (Snaresbrook). Alcock classified them as the first attempt 'to extend football on any definite fixed system'.[2] From 1862 Forest scored heavy wins against Crystal Palace, Barnes, Richmond, Kilburn and others, obtaining six victories in as many weeks at the very end of 1863.[3] This occurred despite the fact that they were not always able to raise a full team and were sometimes outnumbered by their opponents.[4] Many of Forest's matches drew large crowds, numbering the hundreds and while the majority of these spectators were doubtless attracted by the football, some, particularly women, appear to have regarded it as a social occasion as the following description of the ground on which the match between Barnes and Forest was staged suggests: 'a large field with a noble avenue of trees running through it which made a pleasant promenade for spectators and attracted many of the fairer sex'.[5]

The composition of the Forest FC illustrates how intimate and homogeneous, even incestuous, the football culture of the London area could become. A number of players from the Forest club also represented a further team that was made up of old Harrovians, No Names of Kilburn. In their turn, the No Names club played against Harrow old boys and Harrow school, who probably contained members of the Forest Club! However, although the tendency was for teams to commence life as comparatively homogeneous, consisting largely, if not entirely, of old boys from a particular foundation, as time progressed the diversity of membership increased as former public school boys from other institutions were admitted. This transition is characterised by the transformation that occurred in the various informal 'pick-up' teams of old Etonians, such as Cleasby's XI and Thompson's XI, that were present in the London region in the early years of the 1860s. In 1863 the people who had previously assembled such teams, notably Cleasby, Malken and Berens, created a formally structured team, Crusaders, with a more varied membership, including non-Etonians.[6] Additionally, the Crusaders had a broader range of opponents.[7] This transition from a team based upon players from a single school to one unrelated to the educational origin of its members represents the replacement of schools by clubs.

2 *Private clubs*. The Crusaders had been anticipated by the most influential team in the London area during this era, Dingly Dell, a side who were made up of old public school boys from various foundations.[8] The comparative diversity of the club's make-up, typified by their pragmatic attitude towards rules, which incorporated elements from many school football games, coupled with their social status and the fact that they played both public schools and suburban clubs, meant that potentially Dingly Dell could have exerted a substantial influence on football in the London region. However, although Dingly Dell was regarded by some as the best of the non-public school sides, their results were indifferent and in season 1861–62 their match record was three wins, five draws and four defeats (losing three matches to Westminster and one to Harrow).[9] In many ways Dingly Dell's matches serve to underline the embryonic condition of football in the London region. For instance, it is instructive that when they played Surbiton it was at the local cricket rather than football ground, and the match, which was contested using the Dingly Dell rules, was terminated when a serious accident occurred that left two players badly injured. The rules themselves, though generally praised, were criticised for allowing 'too much sneaking'.[10]

The Crusaders and Dingly Dell were not the only sides that were based on private clubs in the metropolis. The Barnes team was made up largely of oarsmen, especially those from the London Rowing Club and maintained strong links with that sport. The club were fortunate in being loaned a playing field by a local man, a facility which ensured that within weeks of being formed Barnes had a large membership.[11] Barnes enjoyed a substantial following, their two matches with Richmond, for instance, drawing hundreds of spectators, including some ladies.[12] While Barnes, like other London clubs, were made up predominantly of old public school boys, in the provinces most clubs seem to have lacked this prestigious intake. One of the few exceptions to this was Liverpool Rugby Club (created 1862), who were made up largely of old Rugbeians.[13] By contrast, there is no indication of the New Swindon, Louth and Lincoln clubs having any former public school boys, though this lack of elite connections did not prevent

Lincoln from kitting themselves out in an elaborate uniform consisting of white jersey with a heraldic crest, and a cap.[14]

3 *Military*. Football was played at a number of military colleges and army bases. For instance, a match was staged on Saint Patrick's Day at the Royal Military College at Sandhurst between the English and a combined Irish and Scottish team.[15] Football was particularly popular at Richmond's military college, where local cadets, (who were generally old Rugbeians) were especially active.[16] However, the regular changes in personnel at the institution impeded the establishment of a permanent club and even in November 1863 Richmond's secretary, Ash, stated that they were not an organised club.[17] It appears that for similar reasons it was difficult establishing a football club at Aldershot Camp in Kent, for although the officers and men regularly played in the same teams, transfers within the army deprived the club of a settled membership.[18] Military football also appears to have been very popular with the wider public, the match at Chatham in December 1863 between the Royal Engineers and RMA attracting a large crowd that included 'many ladies'.[19]

The codes

While it seems likely that other organisations besides schools, private clubs and the military were influential in the creation of teams, the sparsity of our information prevents us from expanding upon this.[20] When it comes to considering the matter of the rules used by the various clubs during the period, these appear to fall into three broad categories: (a) purely belonging to one code, such as one of the public schools, (b) based upon a mixture of codes that is, selecting rules from various public schools, (c) based upon a mixture of distinct codes (i.e. fusing elements of a rugby game – one in which the primacy is on handling the ball, with those of an association game – one on which the emphasis is on kicking the ball). We shall now examine these three broad categories.

(a) During this period 'pure' codes were effectively derived from the elite institutions, primarily the various public schools and Cambridge University.[21] The various public school codes were largely adopted by teams of 'old boys', though probably with some level of modification. For instance, Forest Football Club, which was composed of old Harrovians, commenced life by using a modified version of the Harrow rules but soon replaced these by a fairly pristine version of the Cambridge University code.[22] It appears that various pick-up teams used the Eton rules, as did the War Office side. Teams that were made up of old Rugbeians generally used the football rules of their foundation.[23] However, judging by Scotland, where rules based upon those of Rugby School were rather loosely interpreted, notably in the annual match between Merchiston Castle and Edinburgh Academy, Rugby's laws were subject to local interpretation.[24]

(b) There were two types of mixed codes. The first sort were conscious creations by clubs. The most notable exponents of this were Dingly Dell and the Crusaders, though it appears likely that the components of their games were drawn only from those public schools whose football was association based (giving primacy to the feet rather than the hands). The second type of mixed codes were not intended to last for a season or so, but were drawn up for the exigencies of a single match between sides whose rules were substantially different. Let us look at this latter group more closely.

The existence of the various 'pure' codes, notably the two distinct types that we would classify as association, those from Charterhouse, Eton, Harrow, Westminster and Winchester, and rugby, based upon the rules of Rugby School, meant that on occasions the rules used by competing teams were almost completely distinct. Inevitably, unless the clubs were comfortable with both types of code this could cause particular problems for one or other of them would be playing a type of football that was very strange to them. Judging by our sources, it appears that it was very rare for clubs to have a sufficiently catholic outlook towards rules to play pure versions of both rugby and association football. One of the few that did so was the newly formed Civil Service club who within the space of a week in November 1863 played matches using polarised codes. In their first match they lost 2–0 at Charterhouse, with the home side's association game, and a few days later 2–0 at Blackheath with that team's rugby-based laws.[25] Predictably, the Civil Service club had difficulty understanding these rules and journalists attributed their defeats largely to this lack of familiarity. While the extent of the problem in this instance was unusually extreme, due to the diversity of the codes, it was common for teams to have difficulty in understanding one another's laws, and consequently the construction of compromise rules based on mutual agreement and sacrifice was pervasive.

Generally, a substantial amount of dialogue was required to establish compromise rules between two clubs who played by different codes. However, despite this matches were often afflicted by disputes, such as that between Elizabethans and Old Charlton, in which the various compromises continually broke down.[26] Such difficulties appear to have beset matches between sides that entertained the kindliest mutual feelings, for instance the fixture between Forest and Barnes. Although the game was conducted with compromise rules that the clubs had carefully agreed between them, this did not prevent disputes, a report noting that on occasions 'some little temper was displayed'. This experience prompted Forest FC to declare that from that time forth they would adopt the newly created FA rules, save in matches in which they had already agreed to play using a compromise code.[27]

(c) Mixture of distinct codes. A number of clubs were very catholic in their adoption of rules, integrating elements that were derived from both rugby and association games. It is noticeable that predominantly such clubs were from the provinces and this might be explained by two reasons. In the first place, the lack of appreciable public school influence in such clubs enabled them to approach the selection of rules in an altogether more catholic fashion, integrating elements from diverse sources. A second possible reason might be the isolated nature of these clubs. As such teams lacked external opponents, with almost all their matches being internal affairs, they had greater freedom to select elements from various codes that suited them, unconcerned with the impact such rules might have on outsiders. Whatever the reasons, during this period the provinces produced three clubs whose games appear to have been a hybrid of rugby and association – New Swindon, Louth and Lincoln.

The New Swindon FC appear to have used a rugby-based code in which a touch down was referred to as a 'rouge' and was worth a point, as with Eton's game, and the scoring side then permitted an attempt to kick a goal.[28] The Louth club were established in February 1862 and like New Swindon appear to have lacked opponents.[29] In 1863 Louth wrote to the *Field* stating that although they had been in existence for two seasons they were struggling to resolve 'the knotty question of rules'. As it was, a committee made up of club members did revise the rules, which numbered twenty, and the club secretary, Tupholme, sent a copy of these to the *Field*. Rule fourteen read as follows: 'He who catches a rebound, may kick or throw the ball anywhere he please (except as provided in rule 17, that is, into goal), but so long as he holds the ball he is liable to be shinned'.[30]

The Louth game appeared to be largely rugby-based and the *Field* urged them to replace these with the new Cambridge University rules that were being embraced by the FA. By a strange irony, but a few months earlier a club had been formed by Louth's neighbour Lincoln. The rules used by Lincoln were essentially based upon those of Rugby School, though the influences included elements that stemmed from Marlborough and Eton.[31] An insight into the diverse range of Lincoln's rules can be obtained from listing some of their features. As with virtually all public school games, Lincoln's rules included a very strict offside law, forbidding passing to anyone who was in front of the ball. Like Rugby School, Lincoln used a crossbar, but as with some association-based codes they permitted goalkeepers and outlawed hacking.[32] The club were clearly in turmoil over the selection of rules and a meeting designed to resolve this problem was only able to agree upon their first law that read: 'That the game should be commenced by throwing the ball up in the center of the ground by the side winning the toss, neither side approaching within ten yards of the ball until thrown up'.[33]

In September 1863 Lincoln and Louth played two matches, both of which appear to have been good tempered affairs.[34] However, as we shall later see, in the following year they were both persuaded to adopt the new code established by the FA, a move that does not appear to have helped football to flourish in the area.

Unified code of football laws

This section considers the views that were expressed in the years between 1860 and 1863 concerning the establishment of a universal code that could regulate football. In the early 1860s the question of establishing unified rules, which as we saw in Chapter 2 had periodically exercised the attention of commentators both inside and outside public schools, bubbled to the surface. While the arguments often concerned themselves with the precise minutiae of exactly which elements should be included in such a code, a considerable amount of attention was devoted to considering the thorny question over whom such a code was intended for. Predominantly, and somewhat paradoxically given their relative social standing, the universal code was regarded as being of particular value to two groups, the lower orders and public school boys. Let us now consider the arguments that were debated concerning these two very diverse groups, beginning with those relating to the lower orders.

The impulse for teaching football to the lower orders was derived from the Volunteer Movement of 1859. The Volunteer Movement involved the creation of a number of militias who would help repel an invading French army that it was feared would cross the Channel under the belligerent leadership of Napoleon III. While the invasion scare soon vanished, the Volunteer Movement had an obvious appeal for the establishment because it meant that whereas in the past the working class would entertain themselves in a variety of rowdy pursuits, these would be replaced by free time that was dominated by drill and discipline under the direction of their social betters. For the more idealistic, the Volunteer Movement provided a model in which social harmony could be created by a combination of benevolent discipline and mutual respect. Inevitably, sport was regarded as having a role to play in this transformation, with games such as cricket fusing self-discipline and manly exertion. However, whereas in most areas of the country cricket could only be played during the summer months, football was presented as the ideal winter game, which could foster the same virtues as cricket and provide a suitable meeting ground in which the different social classes could mix on a friendly basis.[35] The major problem that prevented football accomplishing this, according to its advocates, was the lack of an easily understood, uniform code. In order to create this football's advocates urged that a committee should create football rules that were simple enough to ensure that even 'uneducated villagers could play'.[36]

While, as we have seen, advocates of the creation of a universal football code that could render the game accessible to the lower orders used a rhetoric that stressed the social virtues of such a development, the sole concern of those pressing for a code that could embrace every public school was to facilitate the growth of football as a sport. While this might have seemed an altogether more achievable goal than the somewhat far-fetched claims that were being advanced concerning the social virtues that would be promoted by disseminating football to the lower orders, in practice it was an unsolvable problem. Whereas the lower orders were assumed to be sufficiently docile to render the imposition of a common football code a simple matter of education, commentators were aware that the social standing of the various public schools meant that they were a far less malleable proposition. In order to create a football code that could embrace the public schools a body had to be uncovered who enjoyed sufficient social standing to be taken seriously by such influential and status-conscious institutions, and whose knowledge of the various football codes was such that the laws they constructed could be successfully adhered to. In the early 1860s some commentators felt that the Dingly Dell club, which was made up of old boys from a variety of foundations, and whose code was based upon an amalgam of the laws of the various public school codes, presented the best opportunity of establishing a universal code and urged them to publish their rules.[37] However, this did not achieve fruition and prompted another commentator to suggest that the universities (i.e. Cambridge and Oxford) were the only bodies that possessed sufficient expertise and prestige to create a universal code for football that could establish itself throughout the kingdom.[38] This, to an extent, was what happened with the laws that were adopted by the FA in 1863, which stemmed from Cambridge University, having been assembled by a committee of old boys from various foundations. However, as we shall see, this venture was largely a failure, as could be easily predicted from the two main objections that were ventilated by commentators from public schools in the period leading up to the creation of the FA. It is to these objections that we now turn.

The first, and most fundamental objection, was the innate conservatism of the public schools, which made them extremely reluctant to compromise their rules in any way.[39] An old Rugbeian, with an assurance that appears to have characterised the pronouncements from that particular foundation, observed that his school would certainly not countenance any compromise code but believed that it might be suitable for some of the other schools.[40] A second, and in many senses more practical objection, that was voiced by present and former public school boys, was that the whole idea of encouraging the public schools to mix with one another at football was unsound and only likely to increase tension between them. An old Etonian wrote to the *Times* as follows: 'The feud between Eton and Harrow is sufficiently well known to make an increase of hostile feeling very undesirable'.[41] In essence, the less contact public schools had with one another on the football field the better they were likely to get on!

The only grain of encouragement that the public schools offered to the creation of a universal code stemmed from the occasionally voiced desire that a new set of laws should be created to regulate matches between schools. The impulse for this was derived from the failure of the compromise rules that had been established to govern the matches between public schools, notably those that had been used in the matches between Westminster and Eton in 1861 and 1862.[42] Naturally, the universal code would be rarely used, for predominantly the various foundations would continue using their own individual laws of football. Limited though such a conception was, to an extent these views found an ally in Thring, who rejected the whole idea of a code being created by fusing components from the rules of the various public schools, which he condemned as producing 'a mongrel game'. He urged that a completely new, distinct, version of football should be established.[43] For Thring, however, such a code was not to be a rarely used stand-by, but the bedrock of football, superseding all other laws. Socially, Thring did not intend that the universal code would be restricted to the elite from the public schools, but hoped that it would embrace the lower orders as well. In an effort to attain this, Thring's universal code was a simplified version of football, quite unrelated to the abstruse esoterica that pervaded public school codes, and between 1862 and 1864 Thring often expounded his views in print, even publishing a book *The Winter Game*.[44] As need hardly be said, public school boys were largely indifferent to Thring's rules, their general attitude being effectively summed up by an old Rugbeian who classified football rules into two categories, those that were simple in which there was little risk of injury and those games that were more complicated in which the laws allowed plenty of opportunity for wounding.[45] Public school boys much preferred the latter, complicated varieties, and were consequently uninterested in simplified versions of football that were designed to attract mass appeal. It appears that for quite different reasons the indifference of the public school boys was shared by the lower orders, who do not appear to have become involved in football clubs. As a consequence of this, the only group who could realistically be expected to adopt a uniform code in large numbers were those members of the middle class who had not been to public school and whose attitudes were therefore sufficiently flexible to accommodate change. So far as can be seen, between 1860 and 1863 there do not appear to have been many of such people in the various teams that operated in the London area, facts which did not bode well for the FA, a body that was being created to establish a universal code, and whose fortunes are our next subject. It is to this, a study of the early years of the FA, the next part of our chapter, that we now turn.

The early years of the FA 1863–64

While, as we have seen, from at least the 1850s there had been suggestions that a universal code should be established for football, the impetus to create the FA in October 1863 appears to have stemmed largely from a debate that was generated in *The Times* newspaper. On 5 October a letter from an Etonian supported the creation of a universal code that could be used to regulate inter-school matches, while in no sense interfering with the existent public school varieties of football. Over the next few days *The Times* published further letters from correspondents representing Eton, Harrow, Charterhouse, Westminster, Winchester and Rugby, which showed an interest in the increased dissemination of football laws, but no sustained enthusiasm for the creation of a universal code.[46] At this stage there does not appear to have been much idea of involving those outside the public schools but the impulse having been given, on 26 October 1863 (Table 5.1) a meeting was assembled of those interested in creating the FA.[47]

The acting chairman of the FA's inaugural meeting was A. Pember who stated that the Metropolitan clubs needed to create a definitive code of rules for football in order to facilitate increased activity. The acting secretary, Ebenezer Morley continued by maintaining that an increased attendance would have certainly been obtained had there been greater publicity. Nonetheless, he believed that the quality of those attending was sufficient to justify the assembled body establishing itself as an association and it was agreed that subscribing clubs would pay £1 10s annual membership fees. A committee was created to discuss rules but Hartshorne of Charterhouse declined to join because he was the only representative from the public schools and was consequently unwilling to commit himself. The acting chairman, Pember, attributed the absence of the other public schools to their reluctance to initiate action and determined that the Association would write to

Table 5.1 The list of delegates at the first FA meeting (held at Freemasons Tavern 26 October 1863)

Alcock	Forest Leytonstone
Bell	Surbiton
Day	Crystal Palace
Gordon	Blackheath Proprietary School
Mackintosh	Kensington School
Moore	Blackheath
Morley	Barnes
Pember	NN Kilburn
Shillingford	Blackheath Perceval House
Stewart	Crusaders
Wawn	War Office

Table 5.2 The list of delegates at the second FA meeting (10 November)

J. Alcock	Forest Leytonstone
F. Brand	Royal Naval School (New Cross)
F. Campbell	Blackheath
A. Fawkes	Blackheath Perceval House
T. Gregory	Barnes
C. Hawker	War Office
W. Johnston	Royal Naval School (New Cross)
A. Mackenzie	Forest Leytonstone
L. McIver	Kensington School
F. Moore	Blackheath
H. Morley	Barnes
A. Pember	NN Kilburn
T. Redgrave	Kensington School
W. Shillingford	Blackheath Perceval House
J. Turner	Crystal Palace

them seeking their co-operation in the creation of a code of rules. Additionally, efforts were organised to publicise the Association, notices of the next meeting being sent to *Bell's Life in London*, *The Field* and *The Sporting Life*.[48] Overall, the Association had probably made a reasonable start, and while the absence of the public schools was somewhat ominous *The Times* believed that they would probably intervene later.[49]

A notice from the FA that appeared in *Bell's Life in London* on 7 November stated that almost twenty clubs had enrolled in the Association and invited communications from anyone who was interested in football. Three days later, on 10 November, the second meeting of the FA was held at the Freemason's Tavern (Table 5.2), though commencing rather later than was scheduled. Predominantly, the news was bad, with the various public schools that Morley had written to either ignoring his letters, as in the case of Eton, Rugby and Winchester, or rejecting contact with the Association. While collectively this was disappointing, Harrow, who sent two letters, did at least

Mr MORLEY, hon secretary, said that he had endeavoured as faithfully as he could to draw up the laws according to the suggestions made, but he wished to call the attention of the meeting to other matters that had taken place. The Cambridge University Football Club, probably stimulated by the Football Association, had formed some laws in which gentlemen of note from six of the public schools had taken part. Those rules, so approved, were entitled to the greatest consideration and respect at the hands of the association, and they ought not to pass them over without giving them all the weight that the feeling of six of the public schools entitled them to. The laws to which he (Mr Morley) referred seemed to embrace every requisite of the game with great simplicity, and before passing the laws that had been proposed it would be well that they should consider every phase of the matter [hear, hear].

Mr ALCOCK thought that the association could not do better than fall into the views of the gentlemen at Cambridge who had put forward the laws which the hon secretary had referred to; and as there were several members of the public schools who had taken part in the matter, he deemed it well worthy the earnest consideration of the association. Having those views, and feeling that it would be well to have the support of the Universities, he should move "That the rules of the Cambridge University Football Club, which have been lately published, appear to be the most desirable code of rules for the association to adopt, and therefore it is proposed that a committee be appointed to enter into communication with the committee of the University, and to endeavour to induce them to modify some of the rules which appear to the association to be too lax, and liable to give rise to disputes."

Mr TURNER would willingly second that resolution.

Mr CAMPBELL proposed as an amendment that the words "The most desirable code of rules for the association to adopt," be omitted, and to insert instead thereof "worthy of consideration."

Mr LAWSON seconded.

Mr MORLEY would suggest the words that they "embrace the true principles of the game with the greatest simplicity." He moved the insertion of those words in the resolution as a further amendment, in lieu of the words proposed by Mr Campbell.

Mr GREGORY seconded.

On a division there were eight voted for each amendment, and the President gave a casting vote in favour of Mr Morley's amendment.

Mr LAWSON moved, and Mr GREGORY seconded, the following resolution:—"That the committee be empowered not to insist on the clause in the association's proposed rules which allows running with the ball." This was carried.

Some further discussion then took place upon the appointment of the committee suggested in the foregoing resolution, and several representative members of school clubs said they had misunderstood the purport of the amendments, and therefore had not voted. They wished to know whether it was not competent for them to ignore the Cambridge rules altogether, which had been referred to as the basis of any proposed rules?

The PRESIDENT said that the question had been decided by the amendment being carried.

A member said that he presumed the non-voters wished to go on with the rules as they had been proposed by the association, and discuss them.

Several members: Yes, yes.

The PRESIDENT said that in the proper course of business the appointment of the committee ought to proceed.

Another member thought that the hon sec should put himself in communication with the Cambridge players, to ascertain whether they would enter into any negociations on the subject.

The proposition received 7 votes, none being held up against it.

Mr. ALCOCK then moved, and another gentleman seconded, the appointment of the committee as follows:—Messrs Moore, Campbell, Lawson, and Alcock.

On the question being put a member observed that, with many others near him, the resolution had been passed without their fully understanding the matter, but as the President had decided that it had been properly carried, and he (the speaker), with several friends, should certainly have voted against that resolution, he should move as an amendment to the appointment of a committee the addition of the following words, "And that the committee *do* insist upon 'hacking,' when running with the ball, in their communications with Cambridge."

On a division the numbers were—for the amendment, 10; against it, 9.

The PRESIDENT pointed out that the vote just passed to all intents and purposes annulled the business of the evening, whereupon Mr. ALCOCK said it was too late to proceed further, and moved that the meeting do adjourn till Tuesday next, Dec 1, and it was so resolved.

Subjoined we give the laws as proposed to be settled by the association, subject, however, to discussion, and probably some alteration:—

1. The maximum length of the ground shall be 200 yards, the maximum breadth shall be 100 yards, the length and breadth shall be marked off with flags, and the goal shall be defined by two upright posts, eight yards apart, without any tape or bar across them.

2. The game shall be commenced by a place kick from the centre of the ground by the side winning the toss, the other side shall not approach within 10 yards of the ball until it is kicked off. After a goal is won the losing side shall be entitled to kick off.

3. The two sides shall change goals after each goal is won.

4. A goal shall be won when the ball passes over the space between the goal posts (at whatever height), not being thrown, knocked on, or carried.

5. When the ball is in touch the first player who touches it shall kick or throw it from the point on the boundary line where it left the ground, in a direction at right angles with the boundary line.

6. A player shall be out of play immediately he is in front of the ball, and must return behind the ball as soon as possible. If the ball is kicked past a player by his own side, he shall not touch or kick it or advance until one of the other side has first kicked it or one of his own side on a level with or in front of him has been able to kick it.

7. In case the ball goes behind the goal line, if a player on the side to whom the goal belongs first touches the ball, one of his side shall be entitled to a free kick from the goal line at the point opposite the place where the ball shall be touched. If a player of the opposite side first touches the ball, one of his side shall be entitled to a free kick from a point 15 yards outside the goal line, opposite the place where the ball is touched.

8. If a player makes a fair catch he shall be entitled to a free kick, provided he claims it by making a mark with his heel at once; and in order to take such kick he may go as far back as he pleases, and no player on the opposite side shall advance beyond his mark until he has kicked.

9. A player shall be entitled to run with the ball towards his adversaries' goal if he makes a fair catch, or catches the ball on the first bound; but in the case of a fair catch, if he makes his mark, he shall not then run.

10. If any player shall run with the ball towards his adversaries'

Figure 5.1 A report of the FA meeting of 24 November 1863 that appeared in *Bell's Life in London* 28 November 1863, p. 6. The report shows that attempts were made by a force who appear to have been led by the secretary, Morley, to introduce laws that were similar to those of the newly created Cambridge university FC, whose game was one that forbade elements that were central to the rugby version of football. As the following photographs from the FA minute book show (Figures 5.2, 5.3, 5.4) these attempts failed, being rejected by the meeting. Indeed, a resolution insisting upon retaining 'hacking' when running with the ball was passed by ten votes to nine (Figure 5.3). Morley, the secretary of the FA, was very unhappy with this and declared that such a decision 'to all intents and purposes annulled the business of the evening'. At this point it was decided to adjourn the meeting and arrange to reconvene the following Tuesday (see Figure 5.4).

show some interest, and although electing to 'cling to our present rules' sent a copy of their laws and stated that their headmaster would not allow them to attend meetings during term times. Hartshorne of Charterhouse and Lane of Westminster drew attention to a meeting that was being arranged between the captains of the various public school elevens, stating that it would be inappropriate for any public school to pre-empt such a body. The FA's officials, Pember and Morley, put a brave face on this and insisted that they had never envisaged that the public schools would abandon their laws but believed that the code that the FA established would be suitable for such inter-school matches that these foundations might choose to hold in the future. Despite the rejection of the public schools Morley stated that he believed that the Association would have sufficient authority if twenty or thirty clubs joined.[50]

Once the various letters had been read and discussed 'it was then unanimously resolved that the Association should proceed to make general rules as to length of pitch, width of goals, height of goals, cross bar or tape, when a goal should be won'. There were then a series of points relating to starting the game: 'place kick from half distance, place kick from quarter distance, throwing the ball in the air, rolling the ball down the centre, throwing the ball in between two lines of

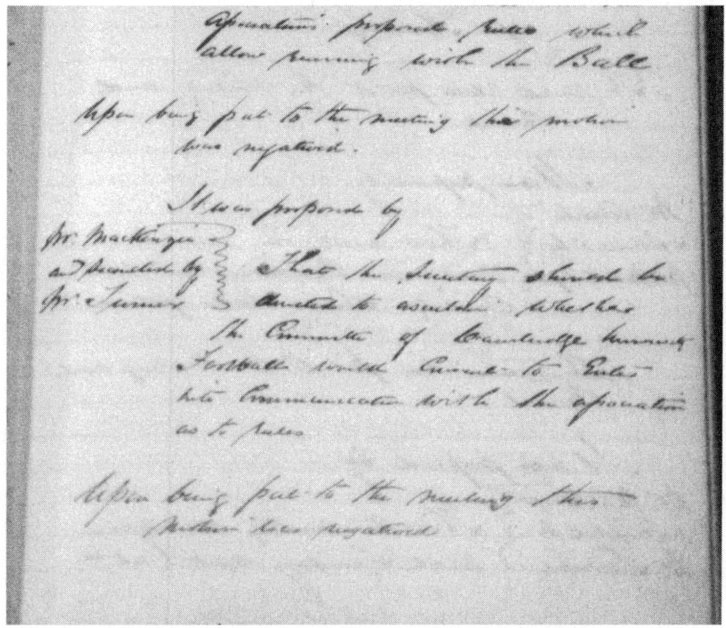

Figure 5.2 Section from the FA minute book of 24 November 1863.

It was proposed by Mr Mackenzie *and seconded by* Mr Turner
'That the secretary should be entitled to ascertain whether the committee of Cambridge University FC would consent to enter into communications with the aforementioned as to rules'.
'Upon being put to the meeting this motion was negatived'.

The attempt by the FA to enter into dialogue with Cambridge University FC was rejected by those attending the FA meeting.

Table 5.3 The list of delegates at the third FA meeting (17 November)[a]

Brackenberry	Blackheath
Brand	Royal Naval School (New Cross)
Campbell	Blackheath
Gregory	Barnes
Johnson	Royal Naval School (New Cross)
Lawson	NN Kilburn
Lloyd	Crystal Palace
McIvar	Kensington School
Moore	Blackheath
Morley	Barnes
Pember	NN Kilburn
Redgrave	Kensington School
Stenning	Blackheath Perceval House
Turner	Crystal Palace

Note

a The list was taken from the F.A. *Minute Books 1863–1874* 17 November 1863. However, *Bell's Life in London* 21 November 1863 gives an additional delegate G. Mariette (War Office).

players, some other method'. The next points the meeting considered were: 'offside, touch, behind the goal-lines, hard play, hacking, mauling, holding, packs, running with the ball, fair catch, charging, settlement of disputes, boots, throwing the ball, knocking on.'[51]

As can be seen, this was a comprehensive approach to football and shows that the delegates had a very catholic outlook concerning the constituent elements of the game. After some discussion, and under their direction, the secretary of the FA, Ebenezer Morley, drew up nine rules, whereupon they adjourned until the following week (17 November).

On the 17 November the meeting (see Table 5.3) opened with letters being read from Thring, who wanted to enrol his school in the FA and had a number of suggestions concerning laws; Graham, who sent a copy of the rules that his club (Lincoln) had drawn up, and Lieutenant Colonel Clifford of Aldershott (*sic*), who stated that he would try and establish a regular club based upon the Association's rules. The following delegates were present.

The president, Pember, declared that he expected that many other clubs would join once the FA established a code of laws and publicised them. Morley, the secretary, read out the nine laws that the Association had agreed upon at the previous meeting and then added a further fourteen that he had composed in accordance with the debate that had occurred at that meeting. This being done, there was much 'animated discussion' about the proposed rules, especially relating to hacking, tripping and holding.[52] By the end of the meeting the following twenty-three laws had been provisionally agreed:

1 The length of the ground should not exceed 200 yards.
2 The width of the ground should not exceed 100 yards.

3 The goals should be defined as two upright posts without any tape or bar across the top of this.
4 That a goal should be scored when the ball was kicked between the goal posts or over the space between.
5 That the goal posts be 8 yards apart.
6 That the game be commenced by a place kick from the centre of the ground.
7 The losing side should be entitled to kick off.
8 The goals should be changed after each goal is won.
9 That the ball is out of bounds it should be kicked or thrown in straight by the person who should first touch it down.
10 A player is 'out of play' immediately he is in front of the ball and must return behind the ball as soon as possible. If the ball is kicked by his own side past a player he may not touch or kick it, or advance until one of the other side has just kicked it, or one of his own side on a level with it, or in front of him, has been able to kick it.
11 In case the ball goes behind the goal line. If the side to whom the goal belongs touches the ball down one of that side to be entitled to a free kick from the goal line opposite the place where the ball is touched down. If touched down by one of the opposite side, one of such side shall be entitled to a free kick (place or drop) from a point 15 yards outside the goal line opposite the place where the ball was touched down.
12 A player is to be entitled to run with the ball in his hands if he makes a fair catch or catches the ball on the first bound.
13 A player may be hacked on the front of the leg below the knee while running with the ball.
14 Tripping shall not be allowed except when running with the ball.
15 A player may be held when running with the ball.
16 Hands shall not be used against an adversary except when he is running with the ball.
17 A fair catch is to be when ball is coming directly off an adversary's foot or body. A catch from behind goal or out of touch is not a fair catch.
18 Any player is to be allowed to charge another player provided they are both in active play, a player may charge when out of active play.
19 No one wearing projecting nails, tin plates, or gutta perches on soles or heels of his boots, be allowed to play.
20 A player may pass the ball to another player if he makes a fair catch or takes the ball on the first bound.
21 A knock on is from the hand only.
22 A fair catch to entitle the player to a free kick provided he makes a mark with his heel at once, and he may go back as far as he please.
23 A goal is to be scored when the ball passes over the space between the goal posts at whatever height – not being thrown, knocked on or carried.[53]

It was decided that a final settlement of the laws that would constitute the association's code would be decided at the next meeting, which was to commence at 6:30 p.m. on 24 November (Table 5.4).

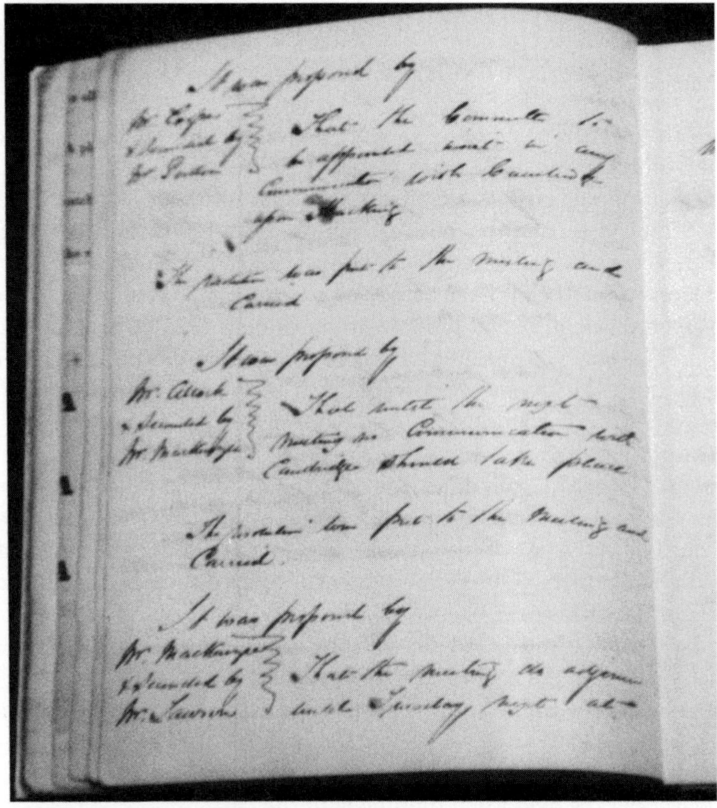

Figure 5.3 The smoking gun (copy of photo from FA minute book).

It was proposed by Mr Cooper and seconded by Mr Gordon
'That the committee to be appointed must insist on any communication with Cambridge upon hacking'.
'The resolution was put to the meeting and carried'.

The meeting commenced with a number of letters being read, generally relating to the laws that the Association was considering adopting. Amongst the correspondents were Steward (Shrewsbury School), Thring (Uppingham), H. C. Moore (Royal Engineers) and Chambers (Lincoln FC). It was then decided to collate the twenty-three rules that they had provisionally agreed into fourteen laws that would constitute the Association's code.[54] These included the following:

9: 'A player shall be entitled to run with the ball towards his adversaries' goal if he makes a fair catch, or catches the ball on the first bound; but in the case of a fair catch, he makes his mark, he shall not run.'

10: 'If any player shall run with the ball towards his adversaries' goal, any player in the opposite side shall be at liberty to charge, hold, trip or

Table 5.4 The list of delegates at the fourth FA meeting (24 November)

Alcock	Forest
Campbell	Blackheath
Cooper	Blackheath
Cruikshank	Wimbledon
Daltry	Wimbledon
Fox	Blackheath Proprietary
Gordon	Blackheath Proprietary
Gregory	Barnes
Lawson	Kilburn
Lloyd	Crystal Palace
Mackenzie	Forest
Morley	Barnes
Pember	Kilburn
Powell	Kensington School
Redgrave	Kensington School
Shillingford	Blackheath Perceval House
Tawke	Blackheath Perceval House
Turner	Crystal Palace
Wawn	War Office

hack him, or to wrest the ball from him; but no player shall be held and hacked at the same time.'

11: 'Neither tripping or hacking shall be allowed and no player shall use his hand or elbow to hold or push his adversary, except in the case provided for by law 10.'

As can be seen, these rules were heavily influenced by the practices of the football played at Rugby School. However, during the meeting the secretary, Morley, drew attention to a code of laws that had just been produced at Cambridge University by a committee of nine public school boys stemming from Eton (2 delegates), Harrow (2), Marlborough, Rugby (2), Shrewsbury and Westminster. Two of these laws specifically outlawed key elements of Rugby's version of football, hacking and running with the ball. The relevant Cambridge laws were:

8: 'The ball when in play may be stopped by any part of the body, but may not be held or hit by the hands, arms or shoulder'.

9: 'All charging is fair; but holding, pushing with the hands, tripping up and shinning are forbidden'.

Morley urged that the FA enter into communication with Cambridge and Charles Alcock and James Turner proposed that a committee be created for this purpose. After some debate Morley and T. Gregory put forward an amendment that the Association should declare that the Cambridge rules 'embrace the true principles of the game with the greatest simplicity'. Curiously, a formal vote was never

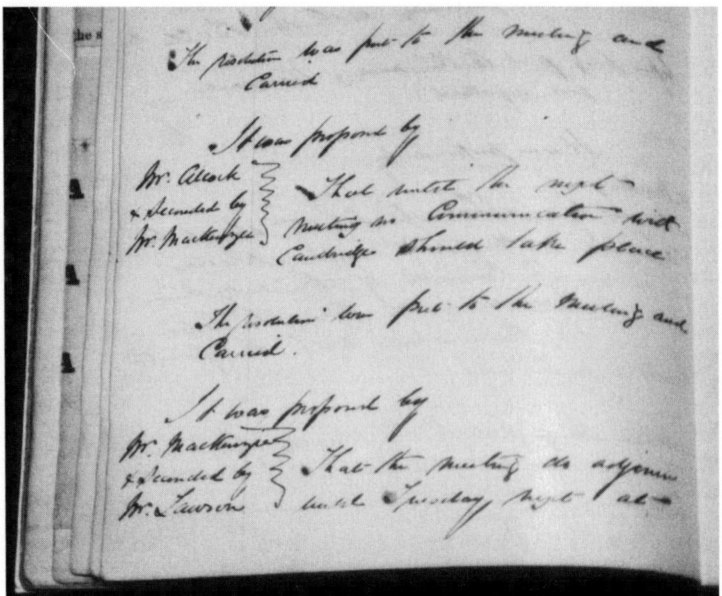

The resolution was put to the meeting and
Carried

It was proposed by
Mr. Alcock & seconded by Mr. Mackenzie } That until the next meeting no communication with Cambridge should take place

The resolution was put to the meeting and
Carried.

It was proposed by
Mr. Mackenzie & seconded by Mr. Lawson } That the meeting be adjourned until Tuesday night at

Figure 5.4 *It was proposed by* Mr Alcock *and seconded by* Mr Mackenzie
'That until the next meeting no communication with Cambridge should take place'. 'The motion was put to the meeting and carried'.

As we saw in Figure 5.3 the meeting of the FA on 24 November 1863 passed a motion that hacking was a non-negotiable item in the communications that the FA would have with Cambridge University FC. As it was, a proposal by Mr Alcock that was seconded by Mr Mackenzie deferred this until the next meeting.

taken on this motion, the chairmen only asking those in favour to show their hands (a total of eight). A further amendment was advanced by Lawson and Gregory: 'That the committee to be appointed be empowered not to insist on the clause in the association's proposed rules which allow running with the ball'. While this was carried, it is quite clear from a contemporary report that many delegates were confused over the meaning of the amendment and upon realising the implications of what they had done, especially when taken in conjunction with the previous motion, protested. At first, the chairman, A. Pember, and secretary, Morley, attempted to steamroller ahead, but the clamour in the room was such that they had to allow further debate. At this point F. Campbell put forward a motion: 'And that the committee do insist upon "hacking", when running with the ball, in their communication with Cambridge'. This motion was passed by ten votes to nine, thus ensuring that hacking was a non-negotiable component of the FA code. Morley and Pember were clearly upset at this, the latter declaring 'that the vote to all intents and purposes annulled the business of the evening'. At this point the meeting adjourned, agreeing to meet the following week.[55]

Table 5.5 The list of delegates at the fifth FA meeting (1 December)

Alcock	Forest Leytonstone
Bouch	Forest School (Walthamstow)
Campbell	Blackheath
Campbell	Blackheath
Daltry	Wimbledon School
Fox	Blackheath Proprietary
Gordon	Blackheath Proprietary
Gregory	Barnes
Lawson	Kilburn
Mackenzie	Forest Leytonstone
Morgan	Forest School (Walthamstow)
Morley	Barnes
Pember	Kilburn
Siordet	Crystal Palace
Urwick	Crystal Palace

The fifth meeting of the FA (Table 5.5) commenced on 1 December with a series of letters being read, the correspondents including Chambers (Lincoln), Tupholme (Louth), Ash (Richmond) and Chesterman (Sheffield). The last correspondent sent a copy of the rules that were used by his club and alerted the FA to the football played in the Sheffield area.[56] Upon this being concluded, Morley, the secretary, read out the minutes of the last meeting, that of 24 November. As we have seen, the very last amendment adopted by the FA during that meeting insisted that hacking and running holding the ball were fixed components of the Association's code and consequently not negotiable. However, although this amendment had been passed by a vote involving all the delegates, and had been written in the Association's minute book, Morley did not read it out. It was therefore predictable that when the time came for the meeting to vote on the accuracy of the minutes, Campbell 'asked on behalf of the Blackheath club that a protest against the minutes being so should be seconded by the meeting'. However, Campbell's protest was in vain, and his motion that the minutes be rejected was lost.

The opponents of a game based upon the code of rules from Rugby School then pressed home their attack, Alcock proposing that laws 9 and 10 of the FA code be removed. Despite Campbell declaring 'that the Blackheath club would probably withdraw from the association if the proposal was carried', laws 9 and 10 of the FA code were expunged and replaced by:

> 9: No player shall carry the ball.
> 10: Neither tripping or hacking shall be allowed and no player to use his hand to push adversary.

In response to this Campbell proposed that 'the meeting be adjourned until the vacation so that the representatives of the schools who are members of the Association be enabled to attend'. This motion was lost by thirteen votes to four.[57]

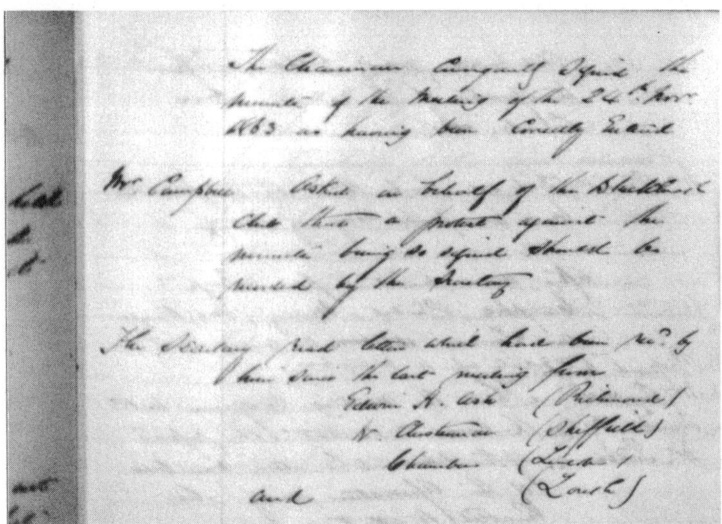

Figure 5.5 Campbell, the delegate representing the Blackheath club, protests against the moves to excise rugby elements from the code of the FA and declares that the club will withdraw. This caused the split between the rugby and association version of football.

The chairman having read minutes of the meeting for 24th November as having been correctly stated
'Mr Campbell asked on behalf of the Blackheath Club that a protest against the minutes being so defined should be entered by the secretary'
The secretary read letters which came from
Ash (Richmond), Chesterman (Sheffield), Chambers (Louth)

It is curious that historians have never drawn attention to the reality of the events that occurred during the fifth FA meeting of 1 December 1863. In large measure Pember and Morley staged what was effectively a coup against the existing consensus regarding the rules by taking advantage of the non-appearance of a number of delegates who were sympathetic to the football played at Rugby. As we have seen, at the fourth meeting of the FA on the 24 November, the nineteen delegates who were present voted narrowly in favour of preserving hacking and running carrying the ball, both crucial elements of the game for those who favoured football based upon that played at Rugby School.

Although we lack details concerning the way delegates voted, by examining the names and affiliations of delegates and the record of the final tally of votes we can arrive at a fairly clear picture of exactly how each delegate cast his vote at both meetings. To begin with, it is easy to infer that delegates from Blackheath and Blackheath Proprietary supported the rugby-style game at both meetings, because both teams were strong supporters of games based upon that of Rugby School. By contrast, as all the remaining delegates who were present at the fifth meeting voted against a game involving hacking and running with the ball their voting intentions at both meetings can also be easily inferred.[58] Similarly, the fact that the following sides, Kensington School, Perceval House and War Office were present at the fourth meeting but absent at the fifth meeting is a strong indicator that they were amongst the group who voted on behalf of the rugby-type game at the former meeting. The most interesting votes appear to have been those cast by the delegates representing Wimbledon School. At the fourth meeting Wimbledon School was represented by two delegates, Daltry and J. Cruikshank, and the analysis of the voting tally indicates that the votes were split, one supporting a rugby-type game and the other condemning it. At the fifth meeting, however, Daltry was the sole representative of Wimbledon School, casting his vote against the rugby-style game.

Our analysis of the voting patterns of the delegates at the fourth and fifth meetings of the FA (as set forth in Table 5.6) demonstrates that many of those clubs and delegates who had supported the Rugby School game at the fourth meeting were absent from the fifth meeting. Additionally, the Forest School club, a team who opposed hacking and running with the ball, and who had been absent the previous week, sent two delegates. In essence, six of those delegates who were sympathetic to the Rugby School game were absent, and two new delegates who favoured the association game were present. From this it is quite clear that Morley and Pember took advantage of the absence of Rugby School's supporters to bulldoze those supporting hacking and running with the ball out of the Association.[59]

Table 5.6 The relative representation of clubs at the fourth (24 November) and the fifth (1 December) meetings of the FA

Club	*Fourth meeting*		*Fifth meeting*	
	Votes	*Distribution*	*Votes*	*Distribution*
Barnes	2	2a	2	2a
Blackheath	2	R2	2	R2
Blackheath Perceval House	2	R2		
Blackheath Proprietary	2	R2	2	R2
Crystal Palace	2	2a	2	2a
Forest Leytonstone	2	2a	2	2a
Forest School			2	2a
Kensington School	2	R2		
Kilburn	2	2a	2	2a
War Office	1	R1		
Wimbledon School	2	1a R1	1	1a
Total	19	a9 R10	15	a11 R4

Notes
The figure in the vote's column indicates the number of votes that a club had. The figure in the distribution column indicates the number of votes that the club cast. If the votes were cast on behalf of an amendment supporting the inclusion of hacking and running with the ball they are classified as R. If the votes were cast against hacking and running with the ball they are classified as 'a'.

The following week, 8 December, the sixth meeting of the FA was convened and letters from Thring (Uppingham) and Moore (Royal Engineers) read. A formal vote was taken by the assembled delegates on the rules that they had agreed at the last meeting and as those supporting a rugby-style game were again largely absent the new code was adopted and permission given to Lillywhite to publish the new laws. A committee was then appointed, consisting of Pember (president), Campbell (treasurer), Morley (secretary) and Alcock, Steward, Turner and Wawn. It was then agreed that the new rules would be tried at a test game on Saturday, 2 January 1864. In response to this Campbell insisted that he would be unable to attend the test game because it was vacation time and regretted the establishment of the new laws which he regarded as spoiling the game.[60] Upon being reminded by Pember that the new laws had been adopted by a majority decision Campbell stated that he had been 'instructed by Blackheath' to withdraw if such laws were adopted and consequently tendered the resignation of his club. Curiously, however, Campbell agreed to continue as treasurer of the FA and in a seeming effort to compromise Pember and Morley stated that the issue of rules would be reconsidered at the next meeting in September 1864, by which time they would have had sufficient trial. A list was then drawn up by the secretary of the clubs who were members of the Association. They numbered eighteen and were as follows: Aldershott, Blackheath, Blackheath Perceval House, Blackheath Proprietary School, Crusaders, Forest Leytonstone, Forest School, Kensington School, Lincoln, NN (Kilburn), Royal Engineers (Chatham), Royal Naval School (New Cross), Sheffield FC, Surbiton, Uppingham School, Walthamstow, War Office, Wimbledon School.[61]

The earlier list was quite ironic because the decision to outlaw hacking and other aspects of the game found at Rugby School ensured that many of those clubs left the FA, throwing the whole status of the Association into question. Indeed, it was not until 1868 that the membership of the Association would surpass eighteen and for much of the period between 1864 and 1867 subscribing clubs would scarcely reach double figures. This could scarcely have come as a surprise to Pember and Morley who had obviously engineered the split between what eventually came to be the association and rugby games by taking advantage of the non-attendance of opposing delegates to frame laws that suited their purpose. In many ways, of course, it might be argued that the two varieties of football were largely incompatible, for the practice of hacking would have almost certainly prevented any other type of football but the game based upon that of Rugby school being played.[62] In view of this, those favouring a more dribbling based game had little alternative than to seek the removal of hacking if they were to practise their game. However, had the officials, particularly Pember and Morley, shown more flexibility it is certainly possible that a tenable compromise might have been reached.

The correspondent from *Bell's Life in London* stated that the delegates from Blackheath had told him before the first meeting of the FA that they had no intention of stopping hacking.[63] However, the attitude of Blackheath was in no sense representative of those playing a game based upon Rugby School's code.[64] For

FOOTBALL.

THE FOOTBALL ASSOCIATION.

The fourth meeting of the members of this recently-formed association was held on Tuesday evening, Dec 1, at seven o'clock, at the Freemasons' Tavern, Great Queen-street, Lincoln's Inn-fields, for the further consideration of the laws, and perfecting generally the working arrangements of the association. In our impression of Saturday last we gave a full report of the meeting which was held on the previous Tuesday, and at which meeting considerable discussion arose on a question calculated to lead to a sudden disruption of the association, and the tone taken on Tuesday last evidenced that the Blackheath members were fully bent on preserving their time-honoured institution of "hacking," although, as will be seen, the "non-hackers" carried their point. The meeting was numerons, and comprised the following members, the names of the clubs they represented being also specified:—Blackheath Club, Messrs F. M. Campbell and L. A. Campbell; Blackheath Proprietary School, Messrs W. H. Gordon and T. P. Fox; Forest, Leytonstone, Messrs J. F. Alcock and A. W. Mackenzie; Forest School, Walthamstow, Messrs J. Morgan and J. Bouch, jun; Crystal Palace, Messrs F. Urwick and J. L. Siordet; Barnes, Messrs W. C. Morley and T. D. Gregory; N. N. Kilburn, Messrs A. Pember and G. Lawson; Wimbledon School, Mr A. E. Daltry. The President (Mr A. Pember) took the chair, and called on the hon sec (Mr W. C. Morley) to read the minutes of the last meeting. The hon sec accordingly read the minutes as entered by him, and the president put the question, "That the minutes as read are correctly entered, and that they be signed accordingly."

Mr F. M. Campbell (the treasurer) said: I wish to call the attention of the meeting to what took place on the last occasion. It would be remembered that Mr Alcock proposed, "That the rules of the Cambridge University Football Club, which have been lately published, appear to be the most desirable code of rules for the association to adopt, and therefore it is proposed that a committee be appointed to enter into communication with the committee of the University, and to endeavour to induce them to modify some of the rules which appear to the association to be too lax, and liable to give rise to disputes." I then moved an amendment that the words, "The most desirable code of rules for the association to adopt" be omitted, and to insert instead thereof "worthy of consideration." Upon that Mr Morley made another amendment for the insertion of the words in the place of those proposed by me, "and that they embrace the true principles of the game with the greatest simplicity." The president, when he put the first amendment, took the number in favour of it, seven, and then put the second amendment, for which eight hands were held up. On neither of those amendments did he take the votes against either of them, and as the number present was 19, if the resolution had been put in the proper form the amendment would have been negatived.

Mr Mackenzie: But everybody might not have voted.

The President: I really think Mr Campbell that you are in error. There certainly was something said, and I replied, "Why, you did not vote," on which the gentleman—I think it was Mr Gordon—replied to the effect that the purport of the resolution had not been properly understood, and most certainly I put it again, and they did not vote again. I certainly put the question both ways, and I appeal to the recollection of those gentlemen who were present at the last meeting. Besides, I gave a casting vote for Mr Morley's amendment. What is your plan now, then? Do you move that these minutes are not correct?

Mr Campbell: No, I will not say that, but I want the resolutions of Mr Alcock and Mr Morley to be expunged.

Mr Lawson: Then you can move that so much of the minutes as relate to that matter be not confirmed.

Mr Campbell accordingly moved, and Mr Gordon seconded—"That so much of the minutes as relate to the resolutions moved by Mr Alcock and Mr Morley be not confirmed."

The President put the question, which was negatived, and the minutes were then confirmed and signed, Mr Campbell entering a formal protest on behalf of the Blackheath players.

The Hon Secretary then read the following letters, which had been received since the last meeting:—

"Lincoln, Nov 30, 1863.

"Dear Sir: Herewith I beg to send you copy of a letter I have received from the hon secretary of the Louth Football Club in reply to mine, inquiring whether they had joined the association, and recommending the propriety of their doing so without delay. I shall write to him by to-night's post referring him to you, and in the mean time, perhaps, you will be good enough to give him some information in the matter, as he desires. Our acquaintance with the Louth Club arises from our having played matches with each other. Hoping that we may succeed in obtaining the club as one of the members, and begging you will send me a list at your earliest convenience of the members of the association, believe me to be, yours very truly,

"E. A. Chambers, Hon Sec Lincoln Football Club."

The enclosure was as follows (said Mr Morley), with the exception of the last paragraph, which referred to a private matter:—

"Louth, Nov 26, 1863.

"Dear Sir: I saw the first meeting of the Football Association reported in the papers, and ever since have been on the point of writing to you to ascertain the opinion of your club as to the association, as we have now a sub-committee formed for revising our rules of play, and I judged it advisable, whether or no the two clubs joined the London association, to have rules of play in common for the greater facility of arranging matches, &c. With reference to the association, my own predilections are entirely in favour of it, and I shall do my best to induce our club to join it after our next meeting. With respect to what clubs have already joined I am in partial ignorance, and shall be glad to learn that the foundation schools of Harrow, Eton, and Rugby have done so, as their joining or holding back must have, any way, a great amount of influence, looked up to as are those schools for their practice of the game.—Believe me, yours truly,

The President: I must be allowed to interpose a word. At the outset I must remind Mr Campbell that several of the London clubs were invited to attend to talk the matter over, and when we first started it was agreed that the rules should be arranged upon a certain basis, and put into proper form by Mr Morley, who kindly undertook to do it, but that nothing was to be considered finally settled till they had been confirmed at a subsequent meeting, as appears by the heading of the printed laws, which is in these words, "to settle the laws, which are proposed to be as follows." Several gentlemen came, and you, Mr Campbell, amongst the number, and if those who attended and put down the names of their clubs as proposing to join the association, with the intention of adhering to it if all their principles were carried out, or immediately seceding if their notions were not adopted, it certainly is not, in my opinion, a fair and honest way of dealing. You virtually say, "I will come and join your association, and see if I can get my notions adopted, and if so go on with you, but if not we will secede, and form an association for ourselves."

Mr Campbell: In reply I will just say that when the Blackheath clubs joined the association they were prepared to carry the laws such as the majority of the meeting agreed to. When the last meeting was held for the express purpose, as the president had said, of settling the proposed laws, they ought to have gone on with the rules as proposed by the association, and not taken the course they did as to the Cambridge rules, but the resolution and amendments had been proposed and passed in the way they had been without being properly put to the meeting, because it was found that the "hacking" party were too strong.

The President: That is, I think, an accusation of ungentlemanly conduct to which I am not willing to submit, added to which it is not the fact.

Mr Morley: I certainly thought that any member had a perfect right to propose any resolution he though fit.

Mr Alcock: Let me explain that I moved the resolution upon the subject of the Cambridge rules without any previous communication with any one until just prior to the meeting, when they were brought to my notice quite unexpectedly on my part.

Mr Lawson: I saw the rules in one of the sporting papers, and thinking they were just the rules that were wanted, I certainly submitted them to one or two; but I emphatically deny that I had any intention of delaying any fair discussion of the laws. I may observe that the division on the question, "That the committee *do* insist upon 'hacking' in their communications with Cambridge" was very close, the numbers being 10 to 9, and certainly I had no idea that we should be in a minority.

The President: Well, gentlemen, there is a motion before the meeting, "That Nos. 9 and 10, of the proposed laws be expunged."

Mr Campbell: I beg to move as an amendment, "That this meeting do adjourn until the vacation, so that the representatives of the schools who are members of the assocation may be enabled to attend."

Mr Gordon seconded, and on the amendment being put to the vote it was lost by 13 to 4, and the original motion carried.

The President observed that though the rules 9 and 10 were expunged, it was quite competent for Mr Campbell to bring the matter up at the next annual meeting, by which time it would be seen how the laws worked.

Mr Morley said that before the meeting proceeded any further he would suggest that having the Cambridge rules before them the association should, in forming their own laws, see what consideration the others deserved. No communication had taken place with Cambridge since the last meeting, but he (Mr Morley) thought that their hands would be strengthened if the laws of the association were made nearly identical with the Cambridge rules. He thought it a matter worthy of consideration, especially with reference to the influence it might have on some of the public schools.

The President thought it would be better to go on with their own rules.

Mr Alcock would be glad if they could so assimilate the rules as to bring all players within the scope of the association.

The meeting then proceeded to settle the proposed laws, which will have to be confirmed at the next meeting, and we give them now *in extenso* as they will be submitted *verb et lit* for adoption, so that any non-contents may not be able to say they did not know, and there are several very important differences from the code published last week.

Figure 5.6 Despite the resolution to retain the rugby elements of football (running holding the ball and hacking) having been passed at the meeting of the FA on 24 November and inserted in the minute book (see Figure 5.3) the secretary does not include it in his list of resolutions passed at the previous meeting This prompted Campbell, the delegate of the Blackheath club, to protest. Due to the fact that most of the supporters of hacking were absent, Campbell's protest was lost and this soon resulted in the withdrawal from the FA of those who supported a rugby-style version of football. Although previous historians have always condemned Campbell, it is clear that he was in the right morally and that it was the FA officials, largely Alcock and Morley, who were acting unfairly. This report appeared in *Bell's Life in London* 5 December 1863, p. 3.

instance, an old Rugbeian wrote to the *Field* criticising Blackheath for retaining hacking and urged that unnecessary hacking be discouraged, for he regarded tripping as being the only necessary violence.[65] Similarly, The Royal Engineers continued to subscribe to the FA but retained running holding the ball, which they considered to be a necessary part of the game.[66] Essentially speaking, it would be erroneous to regard all those who adhered to a game that was based upon Rugby School's rules as being incapable of compromise. At this point it is instructive to consider the activities of Richmond FC between November 1863 and January 1864. Although Richmond was made up largely of old Rugbeians, and would eventually adopt the rugby code, during the period when the FA were debating their initial laws Richmond contested matches under no less than three different, and in large measure adversarial, codes.[67] On 7 November, 21 November and 5 December Richmond played matches against Forest FC, using the rules of Cambridge University, that is, the code most opposed to the Rugby School game. On 19 December they played against Barnes under the code that the FA had just produced. Two weeks later, 2 January 1864, Richmond played Blackheath under rugby rules.[68] As the example of Richmond shows, there was clearly room for manoeuvre and every reason for believing that a tenable compromise could have been reached. Given the make-up of the FA it would have been perfectly plausible to create two distinct codes, one excluding hacking and running carrying the ball, and the other permitting them, that would be administered under the rubric of the FA.[69] In essence, there would have been two rationalised football codes, one rugby, one association, under the auspices of the FA, thus standardising the two principal types of football. This would have had the effect of considerably simplifying football by removing the plethora of different variants. However, Pember and Morley determined that a game which excluded hacking and running carrying the ball should establish itself as the sole model of the FA game and consequently evicted those supporting a code that was based upon that of Rugby School.

The final attempt at establishing a compromise between the FA and those favouring a code influenced by that of Rugby School occurred at Battersea on 2 January 1864. As earlier mentioned, a decision had been made at the sixth meeting of the FA to experiment with the new code with the express intention of finally resolving the question of rules at the AGM in September 1864. To this end, a trial match was organised at Battersea, the teams being led by Pember and Morley, in which there was plenty of catching and running holding the ball.[70] However, by then those favouring the inclusion of elements of Rugby School's game appear to have largely abandoned the Association, whereas the attitudes of many of the supporters of the FA had hardened. The most notable of these was the influential writer Cartwright, who was a columnist for *The Field*. A month or so earlier he had regarded the Cambridge rules as being too extreme in their exclusion of handling, and supported the use of touchdowns, but after watching the match at Battersea he urged that running holding the ball be excluded.[71] By January 1864 compromise between those favouring holding the ball and the use of hacking and those excluding both such elements had become impossible, the former being effectively excluded from the FA.

Although the new laws that had been created by the FA in 1863 were made easily available to the public by Lilywhite, whose firm printed them in a pocket book that cost just sixpence, there is very little evidence of the Association winning support.[72] Indeed, their decision to evict those favouring a game based on that of Rugby School ensured that support haemorrhaged at an alarming rate, as a gleeful former public school boy observed in January 1864.[73] In the face of this the FA did nothing.[74] It was little wonder that concerned supporters, such as Cartwright, urged that students from the universities of Cambridge and Oxford should promote the FA by staging matches against various county teams, 'otherwise football will remain a game that is only practised by schoolboys'.[75] As for the public schools, they regarded the code created by the FA as being irrelevant because 'prejudices are the very basis of our public schools'. The individual games of football that each had established were an intimate part of the school's identity and would not be replaced by the code of the FA However, the writer believed that the FA rules would be suitable for those who had not been to public school.[76] By the end of 1864 far from unifying football the FA had left the game more divided than ever and appeared to have neither the ideas nor the appetite to change such a situation, a reality that was summed up in October 1864 when the Association's minute book recorded that during its main meeting of the year 'no business was conducted'.[77]

Football at the public schools, Cambridge and Oxford universities 1864–67

As the reader will recall, in Chapter 3 we examined football in Britain's elite institutions up until 1863. It is now time for us to rejoin these foundations in order to assess their activity in the years between 1864 and 1867. This subject is represented in this part and consists of two sections. The first section focuses on the public schools, while the second deals with Cambridge and Oxford universities.

Football in the various public schools

The fundamental structure of football at the various public schools was the house match. The majority of these, as we saw in Chapter 3, were well established by 1863 and between 1864 and 1867 this activity continued. Three internal events deserve some notice. While from the 1850s a number of masters had begun playing sports with their boys, the first occurrence of this in a house match at Shrewsbury was in 1864, when the Reverend Luckott participated.[78] In that same year at Uppingham a champion's cup for the best house at football commenced and the following year one of the pupils at Cheltenham College donated a cup that could be contested for annually by the boys.[79] By comparison with the earlier period another set of internal matches expanded; these were visits from teams assembled by old boys, sometimes from either Cambridge or Oxford universities. Over the period there was an increasing tendency for the teams assembled by old boys to include outsiders and schools such as Charterhouse were often visited by these pick-up elevens, notably a team in 1866 that included Alcock.

This last development blended with a tendency that became increasingly manifest during this period, matches between the public school team and outside clubs. With the exception of Winchester, who appear to have had very little to do with outsiders, every public school interacted with those from other foundations.[80] For instance, Charterhouse often played clubs in the London area, such as Dingly Dell (1864) and Wanderers (1865). Similarly, Eton played a number of London teams, most notably the Amateur Athletics Club in 1867.[81] In 1865 a team of old Etonians visited London and played the Civil Service club, using the latter's rules, with which Eton was unfamiliar.[82] Harrow's opponents included Forest FC and Kensington in 1864 and Civil Service in 1865.[83] Marlborough played Blackheath in 1865 and Old Marlburians took on Wimbledon School in 1867.[84] Rugby played Blackheath Proprietary School and Old Rugbeian's took on Richmond.[85] The most active team appears to have been Westminster, who played a lot of matches against Charterhouse, Brighton College, Civil Service, Crusaders, Hertfordshire Rangers and West Kent. [86]

As can be seen from the list of Westminster's opponents, by this period it was common for them to play against another public school, Charterhouse. Indeed, although *The Field* rather curiously described the Charterhouse–Westminster fixture in 1866 as the 'only match between public schools', between 1864 and 1867 there were a number of matches between different foundations.[87] The most common fixtures between different schools were Rugby–Marlborough matches. The majority of these matches took place at Oxford but a number were staged at Marlborough and the substantial attention that was focused on these fixtures, including the active participation of schoolmasters (in 1864 'six masters played'), demonstrate the extent of official acknowledgement.[88] Oxford also hosted a match between Rugby and Wellington and Clifton College vs Rugby.[89] Cambridge hosted at least two inter-public school matches, namely Eton–Westminster and Rugby–Haileybury.[90] Other matches between elite institutions were Harrow vs Cambridge (1864) and Brighton College vs Westminster (1866).[91] However, the match that has attracted the most attention was the infamous 'match between Marlborough and Clifton College which in 1864 ended in a ferocious hacking match'. It has been claimed that 'English school authorities were long frightened by the traditions of this historic fixture'.[92]

The activities at Cambridge and Oxford universities, 1864–67

Having reviewed the activities involving public schools, it is now time to consider of the activities at Cambridge and Oxford universities between 1864 and 1867. The majority of football that occurred in the universities was based upon the distinctive varieties of each particular public school. As mentioned in Chapter 3, former public school boys from Harrow and Rugby who were at Cambridge set up clubs that were devoted to their old school game, and old Etonians had football clubs at both Cambridge and Oxford. Additionally, particularly at Oxford, old boys from the same foundation regularly played football using their school rules, though outside the structure of a formally constituted club. The three main examples of this were Harrow, Marlborough and Rugby.[93] Old boys from Oxford often visited their schools and took on the current team, notably at Charterhouse and Eton.[94] This was particularly common at Cambridge, former pupils from Charterhouse, Eton, Haileybury, Harrow and Westminster returning to play matches at their respective schools.[95]

In terms of the codes used, the above matches were entirely insular. Potentially, Cambridge and Oxford provided an excellent opportunity for footballers from different public schools to interact, though in practice, as we have seen, only a few such matches occurred. Another potential opportunity for contact with different codes occurred when teams of outsiders visited. During the period at least three outside teams visited Cambridge; Crusaders, Wanderers and Eton.[96] Oxford was visited by Harrow Chequers and Wanderers (twice).[97] Of course, the most fertile opportunity for old boys from various public schools to interact while at university was the university football club. As we saw in Chapter 3, from at least the 1840s Cambridge had a football club that used a compromise code, and in 1863 a committee created a set of rules that were to be adopted by the FA. Despite this, however, there is little indication of these rules being employed in matches between various colleges.[98] At no stage during this period is there any indication of either a common code or a football club being established at Oxford. Indeed, aside from the occasional visits by pick-up teams, there is little evidence of football matches between the various Oxford colleges.[99]

While as the above shows, there was far more contact between footballers from public schools than most historians have ever hinted at, cumulatively it does not amount to much. During this period some public schools, notably Charterhouse and Westminster, began to interact with other clubs on a more regular basis. Predominantly, however, public school teams used their own rules and there is little indication of dialogue. It appears likely that most of the teams they played, even if they did not stem from their foundation, were made up of public school boys. With regard to contact with non-public school boys, during the period the author has only uncovered two fixtures in which the opponents were almost certainly unrelated to a foundation, a match that Harrow played in 1865 against a team made up of outsiders from the area, using Harrow rules, and a game between eleven public school boys assembled by Marshall, a student from Emmanuel College Cambridge, and Lincoln FC.[100] In view of all this, it appears likely that elite institutions such as Oxford and Cambridge and the public schools contributed comparatively little to the dissemination of football amongst the wider public.

Football in London and elsewhere 1864–67

This part concerns itself with football activity in the years between 1864 and 1867. It consists of two sections. In the first we analyse the basis of the various clubs and their social composition, the sorts of problems that they confronted

Table 5.7 The activity of major teams in the London area 1862–67

	1862	*1863*	*1864*	*1865*	*1866*	*1867*
Barnes	01	05	03	03	04	04
Blackheath	01	04	04	10	04	10
Blackheath Perceval		01	04	03		
Blackheath Proprietary		01	02	04	07	11
Blackheath School			08		02	
Charterhouse School				06	12	15
Civil Service		02	06	11	17	11
Crusades		04	07	06	08	02
Crystal Palace	03	02	05	06	02	01
Dingly Dell	07	07				
Elizabethans	03	03				
Forest FC	03	14	06	02		01
Forest School		03	01	02	02	11
Harrow Chequers				07	10	11
NN (Kilburn)		05	05	04	03	05
Richmond	03	04	07	13	19	17
St Bartholomew's Hospital	01	01	02		03	03
Wanderers			02	09	16	21
Westminster School				07	07	12
Wimbledon School	01			03	09	10

Source: A number of teams in the London area seem to have existed by 1860, notably Blackheath, Blackheath Propreitary and Harlequins, who are not mentioned in the press until 1862 at the earliest. It seems likely that this was because they did not submit reports of their activity to the sporting press, and this indicates that there was probably a substantial amount of under-reporting of football in 1860 and 1861.

Note
Table 5.7 gives an indication of the amount of activity in the London area between 1862 and 1867. The reason for omitting data relating to the years 1860 and 1861 is that until 1862 the football played beyond the confines of the public schools did not receive much coverage in the sporting press. The figures indicate the number of matches that the sporting press records as being played by the particular team in that year.

and the extent of the popular support that they generated. The next section concentrates on the types of rules that were used. Before commencing this, in order to highlight the growth in recorded activity in the London area between 1862 and 1867, Table 5.7 records the number of matches played by the major teams in that region.

Basis of clubs and their social composition

The first section commences with an examination of the basis of the various clubs and their social composition. From 1864 two changes appear within the membership of football clubs: (a) the creation of clubs with a membership based on the lower orders, (b) increased attention to other sports.

Although commercially the bare elements of the game had become financially accessible, the price of a football ranging between five shillings and twelve shillings and sixpence, a sum that teams from the working class would have generally been able to afford, there do not appear to have been any teams created by the lower orders.[101] However, the initiatives of members of the elite in three areas resulted in the creation of football clubs that specifically catered for the lower orders, at Edmonton, Pennard and Bradford-on-Avon. Edmonton was a country village on the periphery of London, in which Jackson, a keen middle-class footballer, created The Mutual Improvement Recreation Society, which included a range of activities, amongst which was a library and a football club. Jackson was aided by the 'county folk', especially a 'sporting parson', through whose support regular football play was permitted on Sundays, providing that the competitors went to church.[102] At Bradford-on-Avon, Forster, an old Wykehamist, drew up a code and created a local club.[103] In 1864 Thring was influential in creating a football club at Pennard which enabled the villagers to join the squire and parson in a game.[104]

As earlier mentioned, the Barnes club had close links with the local rowing club, and this relationship expanded after 1863 to the point of their having to postpone their opening fixture of the season 1865–66 because a number of the members were involved in an eight-oar rowing match.[105] Barnes extended their involvement in other sports by purchasing a gymnasium and by 1866 had commenced staging an annual athletics meeting.[106] An examination of the various criteria used to designate those who were eligible to attend the athletics event gives an insight into the elite social profile of Barnes membership. The only people who were granted access were the members of any amateur football or rowing club, students from Cambridge, Oxford, and the public schools, and employees in the civil service.[107]

In the provinces both the Nottingham and Lincoln clubs were linked to local sporting bodies. The Nottingham team had close ties with the local cricket clubs and in their early days played at the Meadow Cricket Ground. Within a very short time the football club were drawing large crowds, and by 1867 their popularity had grown sufficiently to enable them to hire Trent Bridge Cricket Ground. By then, several well-known cricketers played in the football side.[108] Lincoln FC incorporated a number of other sports bodies and matches were arranged such as rowing club vs the rest.[109] The Club appear to have seen themselves as the centre for sports in that area and held an athletics meeting in 1866.[110]

Aside from these two changes, the appearance of teams containing the lower orders and the increased connection with other sports, the general basis and social composition of teams in the years between 1864 and 1867 was much the same as in the preceding period. It appears that the composition of teams was still strongly based upon membership of a particular institution, especially a school. The Harrow Chequers team were probably typical of many clubs, being made up of 'old boys', in this case Harrovians, several of whom were still at Harrow School.[111] The Forest FC was a similarly elite institution, with strong ties to Harrow School, a foundation they visited early in 1864, contesting a match using the Harrow rules.[112] A year later they again visited, defeating a team assembled by the Harrow master Bowen.[113] In the case of Forest FC, however, change was underway. The gradual decline of club membership prompted Forest to disband and reform themselves as the Wanderers. Although the Wanderers maintained their close connections with Harrow School, the club broadened its membership to include those from other public schools. Indeed, the Wanderers' constitution gave them the monopoly of the best public school players from any foundation, and thus their membership included Etonians such as Kinnaird, Bonsor, Lubbock, Thompson, Hogg, Harrovians such as Alcock, Betts and Bowen, Vidal of Westminster, Birley and Londsay of Winchester, Wollaston from Lancing and Nepeau of Charterhouse. Naturally, the inclusion of such widespread talent, many of who went on to join other clubs, meant that the Wanderers were the parent of many metropolitan teams.[114]

By this period football was far more organised, typified by the fixture lists which appeared on a weekly basis in newspapers from February 1864.[115] Naturally, the matches advertised were invariably in the London area, and provincial teams, aside from those around Sheffield, were afflicted with the profoundest problem of all, lack of opponents. As a consequence of this much of the football activity was devoted to internal matches and practice sessions, hence the keenness of clubs such as Lincoln in obtaining an improved training ground.[116] The general lack of opponents and the extent of their reliance on internal matches meant that teams were concerned to adopt a code that was both entertaining and understood by outsiders. It was for this reason that the clubs at Lincoln and at Louth, who played games that were more akin to that of Rugby School's, adopted the FA's code, with some minor adjustments, in early 1864.[117] Despite these changes, Lincoln does not appear to have been able to arrange many matches with outsiders and were thus restricted to internal games. In October 1864 Lincoln discussed abandoning the FA's code because they regarded the rules as being unexciting and preferred 'a more animated and plucky game' and consequently set up a committee who could construct a code that they could use.[118] The code as formulated included matches between unequal sides and many ingredients that belonged to a version of football based upon the game found at Rugby School.[119] Judging by reports, Lincoln appears to have found it easier to arrange external fixtures after this, and it is notable that they appear to have been the first provincial side to contest a match against a team of old public school boys, an eleven assembled by Marshall, a player from Emmanuel College Cambridge.[120] Lincoln also took advantage of improving transport facilities, catching the 12:15 p.m. steam-packet to Hull for a match. It appears that the club's itinerary was quite crammed that day, for their match with Hull was preceded by a lunch, though Lincoln does not appear to have suffered any ill-effects from this, the contest finishing 1–1.[121] Towards the end of 1867 football in the Lincoln area was prospering. Ironically, however, given Lincoln's unhappy experience with the rules of the FA, the Club's rules were regarded as being too violent by most of the newly emerging sides in the locality, even though they, too, played a game that was based upon that of Rugby School. Such facts forced the Lincoln team to tone their rules down in order to conform with those of other local sides.[122]

While lack of opponents and tight travelling schedules were not problems that beset clubs in the London area, metropolitan matches were often afflicted with two sets of difficulties. The more trivial stemmed from clubs being unable to raise a full team. The Civil Service club were particular sufferers, having to borrow three players from Barnes in order to contest their eleven-a-side match with them.[123] The following month it was even worse, the Civil Service only managing to assemble six players against the Wanderers.[124] Nonetheless, such odds were not always problematic. Blackheath Proprietary could only raise two-thirds of their fifteen man team against Richmond but despite being so heavily outnumbered won the match.[125] A second and rather more serious problem was that of rules. As we shall see later, differences in rules afflicted matches employing both association and rugby based codes. Of course, these problems were not always decisive, in 1864 the Wanderers defeated Civil Service at Battersea Park, despite being unfamiliar with the rules. In this match, however, the players confronted a problem that was largely beyond their resolution, the game having to terminate early because the park gates were about to be shut![126]

The last point reminds us that most matches were staged in public areas and easily accessible to spectators. A number of matches did attract large crowds, consisting of several hundred spectators, particularly Civil Service–Eton in December 1865 and Richmond–Blackheath in January 1867.[127] The crowd at the match between Blackheath School and High House in February 1864 were particularly noisy, with plenty of 'deafening cheering'.[128] While such observations sound quite promising, suggesting that football appears to have been quite a popular sport, it must be remembered that admission to matches was free and as match reports rarely mention the size of the crowd it might well be that the majority of matches attracted comparatively few spectators.

Having examined the composition of clubs during this period, it is now time to focus attention on the rules that they used. As we saw in the part titled 'The early years of the FA', the attempt in 1863 to create a body that would incorporate the two main types of football, that is the association variety as represented by the codes used by public schools such as Charterhouse, Eton, Harrow, Westminster and Winchester, and the rugby variety, a game that was derived from Rugby School, had failed, prompting the two varieties to split into rival camps. As it was, this had done little to improve the clarity of either code and by 1867 both games were in a real mess. Let us first consider the association game.

Initially speaking, there was a good deal of optimism concerning the introduction of the new FA's code and a report of the match between Barnes and Richmond in December 1863, a contest that was conducted 'in good temper' by both sides, stressed that the competitors had found the Association's rules easy to play.[129] Unfortunately, however, the code of the FA was soon revealed as being difficult to understand. Indeed, far from accelerating the interaction between teams using different codes, the FA's rules created further difficulties, even sides who played association-based games remaining baffled by them. For instance, a match under the rules of the FA between CCC, a team playing an association-type game, and Crystal Palace, who used the FA's code, was spoilt because the

CCC team could not understand the FA rules.[130] A still more serious problem was the weakness of particular aspects of the FA's code, especially the offside law, which tended to interfere with the enjoyment of both players and spectators, as was evident in the match between Barnes and Crystal Palace in March 1866.[131] As a consequence of this, very few sides used the 'London Association' (i.e. FA) rules outside London, and the match between Darlington and Richmond (Yorkshire) was unusual as being one of the few such fixtures to take place previous to 1868.[132]

A week after playing their fixture with Richmond using the FA code, Darlington contested their annual match against Durham University using rules that included 'bullies', indicating that the game was probably an association-type.[133] Throughout the country far more clubs appear to have played an association-type, rather than a FA game. The ingredients of such rules varied substantially, incorporating elements from various public school brands of association football and other local innovations. These teams were found in both the provinces and the London area and included some of the oldest and most influential clubs. For instance, Forest School joined the FA in 1863 but by 1867 a commentator described their rules as being full of 'peculiar combinations'.[134]

The main 'pure' association games were from the various public schools and the FA. A number of clubs did adopt one of these codes and adhere to the rules without any significant modification. However, some clubs cross-fertilised the various rules, selecting and applying elements from a range of association-based codes. A number, however, went still further, for in addition to utilising practices from association codes they borrowed rules that were based on the laws emanating from Rugby School. The rules that such clubs produced can be classified as a hybrid between the association and rugby games. During this period there were at least four such clubs: Bradford-on-Avon, Edmonton, Essex Calves, Leeds Athletic and Rossall.

The rules of the club at Bradford-on-Avon forbade charging unless the ball was nearby and were very strict concerning offside, preventing the ball from being passed forward. Handling was kept to a minimum, though touchdowns were recognised.[135] While the code used by Edmonton was a mixture of Harrow, Eton and Rugby rules, it is significant that the game was played with a round ball rather than the oval shaped one beloved by Rugby. A player catching the ball before it had bounced could run with the ball in his hands but if he was touched by an opponent he had to bounce the ball. Charging was forbidden unless it was directed at a player who was dribbling with the ball at his feet. Goals had to be kicked, they could not be carried.[136] While the games played by Bradford-on-Avon and Edmonton were essentially based on association-type laws, with the primacy being given to kicking rather than carrying the ball in the hands, the rules used by Essex Calves and Rossall School indicate that they might be more accurately described as playing a rugby-based game that included elements that were derived from association-type football. The bulk of the rules played by the Essex Calves team were derived from rugby, but the club commenced the game with Eton's version of bullying.[137] Rossall School used rugby rules but their game involved bullies and rouges, practices linked with Eton's game.[138] The rules played by Leeds Athletic were most intriguing, for although they called their game Rugby football, they contained elements that were distinctively those of the association game, as the following outline makes clear:

> players were not allowed to run with the ball [that is carrying it], though they could handle it, make a fair catch, and were compelled to observe the law of on-side. A goal was scored, however, whenever the ball passed between the posts, irrespective of height, there being no crossbar.[139]

The above examples of teams who adopted a catholic attitude towards rules, embracing elements from across the ostensible divide between the rugby and association games, suggest that these two types of football were far less polarised than might be assumed. As it was, it was very rare for matches to occur between teams that were based upon the rugby and association models respectively, and during this period the author has only uncovered two such fixtures: Blackheath School vs Forest School and Blackheath vs CCC. Naturally, the plausibility of such matches depended upon the rules that both sides generally used. As earlier noted, the code used by Forest School, though association-based, contained many diverse elements, but despite this their lack of familiarity with Blackheath School's rugby-based rules handicapped them substantially, enabling Blackheath to secure a comfortable victory.[140] An altogether more promising test occurred in December 1864 in the match between Blackheath (rugby-based) and CCC (association-based) using the code of the former. Given that the CCC team included 'several old Rugbeians' it might be assumed that disputes over laws would be minimised. However, the CCC team were quite unable to understand Blackheath's offside law, which they declared to be different to anything that they had ever experienced, and completely baffling to the old Rugbeians in their side! Unfortunately these disputes spilt over into the crowd and Blackheath's supporters, who were numerous, constantly hissed the CCC team and obstructed their efforts at every available opportunity.[141] It would appear that in this match the difficulties that were experienced over rules were due to a very profound problem: the lack of uniformity in the code of laws that were ostensibly based on those of Rugby School.

In the period between 1864 and 1867 disputes over the rules that constituted the code of Rugby School became increasingly salient. For instance, in March 1864 conflict erupted over a goal that Blackheath Proprietary School scored against High House, which the latter claimed was contrary to the rules that the sides had agreed between them. A good deal of mutual recrimination followed on both the field and in the press columns, where it emerged that High House and every other team in the area did not permit players to 'catch the ball on the bound' (i.e. after it had bounced once) and then run holding it, whereas Blackheath Proprietary did.[142] The rules used by clubs varied substantially, with some, notably Brighton FC, being condemned for their violence, a writer suggesting that they buy a copy of Rugby School's laws in order to remove brutal hacking and other excesses.[143] The charge that teams were systematically ignoring many aspects of the Rugby School rules was a common one, as with the match in Scotland between Merchiston and Edinburgh Academy, a contest afflicted by 'too much mauling', which the sides promised to remove in future by adhering more rigorously to the Rugby School code.[144]

In many ways this was a naive outlook because as a commentator observed in December 1864, Rugby needed to resolve its disputed laws.[145] Given that the Rugby School code was sufficiently ambiguous to embrace a wide variety of practical interpretations, it was little wonder that there was often limited uniformity between clubs. The focal point of these difficulties was the London area and the issue around which opinion divided was the same one that had prompted the secession of a number of Rugby-supporting delegates from the FA in 1863, hacking. The attitudes of clubs in the London area towards hacking varied substantially and, as we shall now see, were typified by the polarised extremes of the Blackheath and Richmond clubs.

Opinions on hacking varied amongst old Rugbeians, one writer claiming that most believed that hacking ensured that Rugby's game remained distinct from 'less exciting variants'.[146] Predominantly, however, most commentators agreed that the version of rugby played in the London area was far more violent than the game at Rugby School and consequently believed that it needed to be toned down.[147] It was generally agreed that the most robust form of the Rugby School game that was found in the London area stemmed from Blackheath, whose game differed substantially from the rules of the foundation that had invented the game! The Rugby School game was far less violent than that played by Blackheath, with players putting the ball down when tackled, while at Blackheath they clung on.[148] The violence of Blackheath's game was contrasted with that played by the Richmond Club, the latter being described as using 'pure Rugby rules'. One writer maintained that the dangerous elements in rugby stemmed from the failure to obey the pristine rules of the School's code which he believed would eliminate the necessity for 'pads' and other forms of protection.[149] The tide of public favour was supporting Richmond's version of rugby and in November 1866 Richmond sent copies of their proposed laws, which outlawed hacking, to all London clubs. The relevant laws were as follows:

1 That in the opinion of this meeting all unnecessary hacking should be put stop to.
2 That all hacking in scrummages, except by those immediately on the ball, is contrary to the spirit of the Rugby game and is forbidden.
3 That no player be hacked over except he has the ball in his hands.[150]

It appears that such a movement had considerable momentum and whereas in March 1864 Blackheath clung tenaciously to hacking, declaring that it had not caused a single injury that season, by December 1866 the club's rules forbade hacking.[151] Despite this, consensus was still a long way from being established and by 1867 even officials from Rugby School conceded that the rules needed to be completely overhauled.[152]

By 1867 there were five types of football games. (1) Teams strictly adhering to a single code of an association game, such as Eton College, Harrow, the FA and such like. (2) Teams using rules based on those of an association-type game, that was derived from cross-fertilising various association codes. (3) Teams whose attitude to rules was catholic, integrating elements from both association and rugby codes. (4) Teams who used the Rugby School laws in their purest and least contentious forms. (5) Clubs playing a type of game *based* upon the rules of Rugby School but including a number of practices that could not be described as conforming to the essence of the code.

By 1867 neither the association-based nor rugby-based games were in any sense unified, monolithic blocks. On the contrary, both embraced groups that diverged widely, particularly with regard to the levels of permissible violence and the amount of handling that was allowed. Indeed, there were groups in the middle who were promiscuous in their selection of rules, freely mixing elements that were regarded as typifying rugby and association. Given this, the association and rugby games might be better viewed as extreme points of a continuum rather than distinct and separate entities. This matter is best understood by a practical example, that of hacking. In 1863 a large number of delegates who supported a game based upon that of Rugby School's seceded from the FA when that body outlawed hacking. However, by 1867 hacking had ceased to be a matter of contention for many clubs using rules that were based upon those of Rugby School, for they had agreed to curb hacking, which they regarded as an abuse. Potentially, such a development offered the possibility of some rapprochement between the FA and those clubs playing a form of the Rugby School game in which hacking was banned. The manner and extent of this rapprochement could manifest itself in a variety of ways. At one extreme the two versions of football might be fused, including elements of each. Alternatively, the rugby and association games might remain completely separate though being administered under the rubric of a single authority, the FA. Of course, much of this depended on how matters had developed within the FA between 1865 and 1867, the fifth part of this chapter, and the matter to which we now turn.

The FA 1865–67

At the end of the part on 'The early years of the FA' we left the FA having quoted from their minute book for 28 October 1864 that 'no business was conducted'. The following year the Association appears to have been entirely dormant and the next entry is dated 22 February 1866! As the reader might guess from this, between 1864 and 1867 the Association was generally very passive, taking almost no initiatives. As a consequence of this the FA shrank to almost nothing and was seriously considering disbanding. In this part of the chapter, we shall move chronologically though the history of the FA during 1866 and 1867.

From today's perspective the prevailing attitude of the FA between 1863 and 1867, in which they made no attempt to organise the football community, beyond establishing a code of laws, seems hard to understand. However, the FA was created to produce a code of laws for football and regarded this as its primary, indeed very probably its only, objective.[153] It is somewhat harder to understand why the FA was so limited in the bodies that it chose to interact with. Given that the ostensible aim of the FA was to provide a national code for the game, its officials displayed a surprising lack of interest in the opinions of those outside the social elite. From the very first, the only people the FA bothered contacting were the elite institutions, such as the public schools and Cambridge and Oxford universities. While these prestigious institutions obviously had a wealth of experience and expertise in football, and clearly needed to be consulted, it is baffling why the FA ignored Sheffield. As we have seen, in 1862 Sheffield FC had produced a printed code that was based upon five years of practical experience, integrating ideas from a variety of influences. Additionally, Sheffield's rules were used by a large number of teams within its area and were clearly a significant component of the national football culture. However, the FA appear to have been totally ignorant of this and it was the Sheffield secretary, Chesterman, who in November 1863 initiated contact between the two bodies.[154] While one might have assumed that having become aware of the football culture of Sheffield the FA would interact with them in a vigorous manner, this was not the case. On the contrary, the FA remained dormant, scarcely interacting with anyone, let alone initiating contact with the provinces.

By 1866 criticism of the code of laws that the FA had established in 1863 had reached such a point that on the 22 February a meeting was convened to overhaul them.[155] By then, far from attracting members, the rules were actually driving clubs away. The Kilburn team complained that so few clubs adhered to the code of the FA that they were only able to play matches against Crystal Palace and Barnes with the Association's rules. Despite this, Morley, the chairman of the FA, insisted that all the Association's members should try and use its code at all times.[156] In reality, such sentiments were meaningless, for the Association's rules were virtually ignored by all London-based teams and consequently the few clubs who had adopted the code were forced to compromise on rules in order to obtain opponents. Outside of Sheffield, the FA had few supporters in the provinces, especially as Lincoln, a club who had joined in 1863, withdrew because their members preferred a 'more animated and plucky game'.[157] Upon hearing of Lincoln's objections, the president of the FA, Pember, had responded in a very undignified manner, sneering at the barbarity of Lincoln's game, and the club's addiction to uncivilised practices such as hacking. A letter from Lincoln's secretary, H. Garnham, revealed that Pember's assumption was erroneous, for the Lincoln club did not leave the FA because of their love of hacking but because their players found the Association's code unexciting.[158] They were not alone in this. A number of clubs urged that the very strict offside law that was used by the FA be relaxed. Retrospectively, one can scarcely blame them. Law 6 of the FA code that was established on 1 December 1863 reads as follows:

> When the player has kicked the ball anyone of the same side who is nearer to the opponents goal line is out of play and may not touch the ball himself nor in any way whatever prevent any other player from doing so until the ball has been played: but no player is out of play when the ball is kicked from behind the goal line.[159]

Many clubs thought this far too strict and at the meeting of 1866 it was decided that a player was not offside providing that at least three opponents were between him and the opposing goal when the ball was first played. Interestingly, some delegates from London clubs wanted the offside law scrapped entirely, particularly as Sheffield did not use it. In essence, they wanted the FA to alter its code to conform with that of Sheffield's![160] Such an attitude was not uncommon, and in a letter to the FA the Lincoln secretary, Garnham declared: 'Now, would it not be well for the association to shift headquarters to Sheffield and then, under Mr Chesterman's superintendence, endeavour to frame a code of laws'.[161] While he was obviously being sarcastic, given the strength and coherence of Sheffield's football culture, especially by comparison to the weak, divided London-based FA, Garnham had a point. As it was, during the meeting various proposals were made concerning the rules and were recorded in the minute book as follows:

rule 1: introduce tape across the goal.
rule 4: goal scored by ball passing under the tape.
rule 5: the first player to touch the ball when it goes out of play is to throw it in.
rule 6: A player is not offside provided that he has three opponents between himself and the opponent's goal.
rule 7: in the case of drawn games the number of touch downs decides the result.[162]

After much discussion the meeting abolished the try at goal for a touch down, the awarding of a free kick for a fair catch, changed the offside law and introduced a piece of tape as a crossbar.[163]

Six days later (28 February 1866) the FA received a letter from Sheffield proposing that a match be played at Battersea Park between the two associations. On 13 March the rules for the Sheffield match were arranged and on 24 March London's team was selected. It is noticeable that not only did Sheffield take the initiative by proposing the match, but made all the concessions concerning rules in order to ensure that the event took place.[164] This resulted in a fixture that helped to expand the public profile of the FA and also provided a model that was later to assist the London-based body to expand.[165] In no sense was this the first time that Sheffield had taken the initiative in promoting the FA. As was earlier observed, in 1863 it was Sheffield who contacted the FA and in the years that followed (especially 1865 and 1866) Sheffield sought to promote an association-type game in the provinces, by playing a number of matches against teams from outside their area, such as Lincoln, Nottingham and Manchester.

Despite the efforts of Sheffield to promote the FA in the provinces, the popularity of the Association declined. The extent of this became brutally apparent at the Football Association's AGM on 12 February 1867. By then, the membership of the FA consisted of just ten teams: Barnes, Crystal Palace, Civil Service, Kensington School, London Scottish Rifles, NN (Kilburn), Royal Engineers, Sheffield FC, Wanderers, Worlabye House.[166] Geographically, this amounted to nine teams from the London region, and from the provinces just Sheffield (whose laws, though different, shared substantial structural similarities).[167] Given that by 1867 there were about seventy football clubs in the London region, such evidence demonstrates that even in its supposed heartland the FA was almost an irrelevance. As for the meeting, only six people attended; Alcock, A. Cathill, Graham, Morley, W. Willis and Chesterman, who was Sheffield's representative. The chairman, Morley, was particularly disappointed with the poor attendance, especially by comparison with the very early meetings in 1863. As he said, in those days 'there was much more enthusiasm than has ever been displayed since'. Morley believed that the prevailing apathy stemmed from an 'assumption that the FA had accomplished the object for which it was established', by creating a code governing football. He continued by stating that he was very pleased that these laws had been adopted in Sheffield 'the greatest stronghold of football in England'. As far as Morley was concerned, the Association's purpose was accomplished and he concluded by saying:

> He thought they should seriously consider that night whether it were worth while to continue the association or dissolve it: if after discussion hey considered they had made the rules perfect, what was the utility of meeting again to do nothing?[168]

As need hardly be said, the statement bordered on the absurd, for it was fairly clear that if the Association's rules were so good why was almost no one using them? Alcock endeavoured to perform a similar act of sophistry when he emphasised the progress that football had made in the London area. In 1860, he claimed, only two clubs, Dingly Dell and Crusaders, had played 'foreign' (i.e. against other teams) matches, and in 1866 there were 122 'exclusive of public schools'. He omitted to mention that the vast majority of these were not conducted under the Association's rules and that the FA was almost irrelevant to the spread of football. However, he did observe that the FA was regarded 'with a certain amount of distrust by the public schools', a fact that he regretted. Indeed, he stated that he would 'gladly assist in the establishment of one game', even suggesting that efforts should be made to amend aspects of the FA's code in order to render it more appealing to the public schools.[169] Alcock was not alone in criticising the existing rules, for although there were only five other people in the room, Morley was soon disabused of the idea that anyone regarded the rules as being 'perfect'. On the contrary, there were a number of important amendments suggested, including the abolition of the offside law.[170]

It is ironic that the FA's existence was saved by its own failure, for clearly, had the assembled few agreed with their president, Morley, that the code was essentially sound, the Association would have disbanded there and then! In certain respects, of course, the lack of delegates attending the meeting of 1867 was in itself sufficient argument for dissolving the Association, a factor that clearly influenced the attitude of Morley. However, the mood of the meeting was lifted by two initiatives undertaken by Sheffield. The first was a letter from Chambers, who was representing the 'Sheffield Association', in which he stated that 'whatever was done that evening would receive every attention at the hands of the Sheffield players'. Given that, as Willis, the secretary of the FA, observed, the Sheffield Association consisted of fourteen clubs and between 1,000 and 1,200 members, the support of such a body was vital, for they clearly dwarfed the London based FA. The other piece of good news was that a return match was to be arranged between London and Sheffield, thus offering the FA an opportunity of promoting itself.[171]

It appears that had it not been for Sheffield's enthusiastic endorsement of the FA at the meeting of 1867 the London based Association might well have decided to disband even though they were still dissatisfied with the code that they had established. After all, if one removes Sheffield, the FA consisted of just nine clubs, of whom only three could be bothered to send a delegate. Who, exactly, would such a body be legislating for? Under such circumstances, what possible reason could there be to continue? The addition of Sheffield, representing as it did the most vibrant football culture in the world, was a significant morale booster to the FA, an organisation that was at its lowest ebb, and probably decisive in ensuring its continuance. The support, and indeed example, of Sheffield almost certainly had a significant practical impact on the FA. An examination of the FA's meeting in 1867 reveals the limited role envisaged for the Association by its officials. As far as people such as Morley and Alcock were concerned the FA's sole purpose was to create a set of rules that clubs could utilise and obviously no one envisaged any role for the Association in promoting, organising and regulating activity. At best, the FA was a very loose federation of clubs who adopted a similar code. However, as we shall shortly see, within a matter of months the Association adopted an altogether more positive attitude towards the wider football world.

Whereas previously the FA had considered that its sole objective was to frame a code of playing laws, in the aftermath of the meeting of February 1867 it began to act decisively in three directions. In the first place, the Association's code was changed, resulting in greater harmony between the rules of the FA and those used by Westminster and Charterhouse.[172] Second, the Association's new secretary, Graham, sent a circular to every club in the country advertising the new laws. Finally, on 2 November 1867 a match was arranged between two home counties teams, Middlesex vs Surrey and Kent, at Battersea, in an effort to educate players in the use of the new rules.[173] It appears likely that the inspiration for this was Sheffield's suggestion at the FA meeting in February 1867 that a match be staged between the two Associations. As a consequence of these initiatives, by 1868 Westminster and Charterhouse had joined the FA, along with a number of other mainly London-based clubs, bringing the FA's membership up to thirty.[174]

Although such promotional measures might seem fairly mundane, by comparison with the passivity displayed by the Association in the past it was extremely unusual. As we have already seen, since its inception the FA had been extremely passive in promoting itself, with every important initiative having stemmed from outsiders. It is surely no coincidence that this attitude changed shortly after the news of the extent of the vibrant football culture in Sheffield percolated to

London. Both football writers and officials in London were pleasantly astonished at two developments within the Sheffield region. In the first place, the extent of the coherence of Sheffield's football culture invited admiration, especially as it had established a 'branch association' made up of fourteen very active clubs, all of who played by the same code. Second, and in many ways more spectacularly, they were very pleased at the number of paying spectators attracted to the Youdan Cup fixtures, particularly the fact that 3,000 people attended the final.[175] This was a clear demonstration of the potential popularity of football and an encouragement to those who were endeavouring to expand and organise the FA. At this juncture it is interesting to speculate on the possible shape of football in 1867 had the vibrant culture that was rooted in Sheffield not existed. This represents the sixth and final part of our study.

The structure of British football in 1867

As we saw in the earlier part titled 'The FA 1865–67', it is likely that the strong support and inspiration provided by Sheffield prompted the London-based FA to adopt a far more dominant organisational role. Indeed, it is even possible that but for Sheffield the FA might have disbanded altogether, leaving a meagre legacy that consisted of a body of rules and a handful of clubs who adhered to them. If the FA had disbanded in 1867, it seems likely that sheer pragmatism would have prompted the handful of clubs adhering to the Association's laws to adopt a more conciliatory attitude towards other football codes. As has already been noted, the majority of clubs playing an association-type game did not use the rules of the FA, preferring instead to draw on a spectrum of influences, some of which would later be regarded as belonging, distinctively, to the rugby game. It is therefore fully conceivable that supporters of an association-type game, keen on reviving or re-energising a supervisory organisation, might have created a new FA, or expanded the parameters of the old one, in order to integrate elements from a whole range of football games, including rugby.

The plausibility of this contention is substantially increased by evidence from the rugby game. As was shown earlier, by 1867 many influential rugby playing clubs were beginning to reject hacking, having taken their lead from Richmond FC, who were numerically the largest of those clubs using rules based on those of Rugby School's. In view of this it can be sensibly inferred that by 1867 the issue of hacking, which in 1863 had proved sufficiently contentious to split the early FA, was showing signs of being defused. This development increased the possibility of the establishment of a common code between those playing the association and rugby varieties of football. Additionally, the remit of the FA might have been broadened to include the supervision of rugby, rendering the organisation the chief arbiter of the laws of both association and rugby football. While such a possibility sounds absurd, in 1867 it gained support from a surprising quarter: Rugby School! As part of his effort to promote the new rules of the FA and encourage teams to join, the Association's secretary, Graham, wrote to every football club in the country, inviting them to join the FA and adopt the new code. Predictably, the representative of Rugby School, F. Ellis rejected these overtures. Nonetheless, he commended the FA's efforts and 'wished, however, [that] a code of rules could be drawn up which might be used by all playing the rugby game' and urged that 'if the FA wish to complete thoroughly their good work, they might turn their attention to this subject'.[176] Clearly, Rugby School was happy to allow the FA to draw up the rules governing rugby football.[177] In view of this, it is fully conceivable that had the FA adopted a more conciliatory approach towards other varieties of football in 1867 a body could have been created embracing both the rugby and association games. There were two principal ways in which this could have been done. First, a compromise code might have been created in which hacking was either totally excluded or significantly diluted, but running with the ball permitted. Alternatively, the FA might have supervised two separate codes, one rugby and one association, treating them as equals.

As it was, of course, bolstered by the existence of and strong support from, the football culture of Sheffield, in 1867 the FA consciously elected to exclude elements within their rules that had affinities with the rugby game, namely touchdowns (rouges), the use of the hand to knock the ball on. They also reaffirmed the stipulation that they had introduced in 1866 that a goal can only be scored by the ball passing under a tape instead of 'at whatever height'. The consequence of this for the FA's rules was to 'bring{ing} them still more into conformity with the several non-handling games'. As the FA's secretary of the time, R. Graham, stated,

> it was hoped that these alterations might conciliate many clubs and schools other than those who followed the Rugby game. It had become evident that to amalgamate the two classes was impossible and the Association decided to throw its lot entirely with the opponents of Rugby.[178]

This, effectively, killed off all possibility of the two varieties of football co-operating. and from that time forth both codes became increasingly distinct and well established. Indeed, the momentum of both games was such that compromise became an irrelevance. It thus appears that the football culture of Sheffield ensured that the two varieties of football that became known as rugby and association remained segregated.

In conclusion let us review the changes that occurred during this period. In 1860 there was very little organised football activity outside of the public schools but by 1867 organised football games, whether of the association or rugby varieties, had become considerably more common in the wider community. To a considerable extent, these football teams were focused in two geographical sites, the Sheffield region and the London area. The most important change that had occurred during this period was the appearance and transformation of the FA. Between 1863 and 1867 the FA had been an extremely weak and limited organisation but by 1868 it had adopted an altogether more aggressive stance, initiating activity and actively promoting itself. The product of this was that a very solid foundation was laid for the expansion and organisation of association-type football, as opposed to the variant that was based upon that found in Rugby School. The next few years would witness the creation of many important institutions, notably the FA Cup and the Rugby Football Union, and these form the topic of our next chapter.

6 Football splits up but goes national

The creation of a national football culture (1868–73)

The period between 1868 and 1873 witnessed four significant developments that served to establish the football culture that in many ways we still have today. In 1868 the FA at last began to resemble a credible body, possessing both members and purpose. To an extent, however, the very desire of the FA to define itself so rigorously in terms of rules ensured that it effectively denied a place within the Association to those clubs whose game was based on a model derived from the football of Rugby School. Thus, by 1871, in a desperate attempt to bring order to a game that had become increasingly anarchical due to the widely divergent interpretations of rules, the RFU was established. The sole purpose of the RFU was to regulate rugby and its creation effectively severed football into two separate, and to a certain extent adversarial, games – association and rugby football. While it could certainly be argued that such a state had existed de facto, since the split in December 1863, as late as 1867 it was possible that a reintegration of sorts might have occurred. In 1871, at almost the same time as the rugby game was establishing itself as a separate entity, the FA initiated its most adventurous project, the establishment of a cup competition, which would help to spread interest in the game beyond the London area. The project does seem to have enjoyed some success and in 1873 the Scottish FA was founded, effectively bringing the whole of the British mainland under the rubric of football associations of one type or another.

This chapter examines football in Britain between 1868 and 1873 and consists of five parts. The first relates to the bolstering of the FA and one of the unlooked for consequences of this process, the creation of the RFU. In the next part we consider the creation of the FA Cup. The part titled 'Provincial football' relates to football in the provinces, while the following part deals with the emergence of the Scottish FA. The concluding part examines football at the elite institutions of Cambridge and Oxford universities and the public schools.

Creating a strong FA and forming the RFU

On 17 January 1868 there was a meeting of the committee of the FA in the chambers of the secretary; Morley, attended by Alcock, Graham, Morley and Willis.

Figure 6.1 By the 1890s footballers were endorsing products. In this advert Forfar football club were amongst the list of those giving a testimonial on the benefits of Elliman's Embrocation from *The Illustrated Sporting and Dramatic News* 26 September 1891, p. 91. It would be interesting to know how much they were paid for such endorsements.

Table 6.1 List of the clubs that were enrolled as members of the FA in 1868

Club	County
Amateur Athletic FC	
Barnes	
Bramham College	Yorkshire
Brixton	
Charterhouse School	
CCC Clapham	
Civil Service	
Clifden House (Brentford)	
Cowley School	Oxford
Crystal Palace	
Donington Grammar School	Lincolnshire
Forest School	
Hitchin	
Holt	Wiltshire
Hull College	Yorkshire
Kensington School	
Leamington College	Warwickshire
London Athletic	
London Scottish Rifles	
Milford College	South Wales
N. N. (Kilburn)	
Reigate	
Royal Engineers (Chatham)	
Sheffield	Yorkshire
Totteridge Park	
Upton Park	
Wanderers	
West Brompton College	
Westminster School	
Worlabye House (Roehampton)	

Note
Where a county is not given for a side the team stem from the region covered by London and the Home Counties.

By this time, due to a range of initiatives that were discussed in the Chapter 5, a total of thirty clubs had enrolled as members of the FA (see Table 6.1).[1] Administratively, this was one of the last acts undertaken by the old structure of the FA for a decision was made to increase the committee, which had been previously limited to four members, by adding another five, the new additions being: W. J. Dixon (former captain of Westminster), Lord Edmund Fitzmaurice (Eton), G. Kennedy (old Harrovian), A. Kinnaird (Eton) and Muir Mackenzie (Charterhouse), all of whom were formerly at either the universities of Cambridge or Oxford. By the following year the FA indicated that it was attempting to embrace a geographically wider group, four members of the committee stemming from the provinces. The FA officials in 1869 were: President E. Morley (Barnes), Secretary C. Alcock (Harrow), the committee consisted of W. Chesterman (Sheffield), W. Cuthill (Crystal Palace), W. J. Dixon

(Westminster), R. G. Graham (Charterhouse), A. Kinnaird (Eton), J. Kirkpatrick (Civil Service), A. Padley (Lincoln), C. Rotherd (Nottingham), R. W. Willis (Barnes), V. Wright (old Harrovian member of the Newark club).[2]

While such changes in both administration and personnel doubtless helped the FA to become more appealing, ultimately such success as the Association enjoyed stemmed largely from their increasing pragmatism concerning rules. As we saw in the Chapter 5, the rules that had been selected by the FA in 1863 had shown themselves to be highly unsatisfactory and by the end of 1867 they had undergone substantial revisions. The most significant of these changes had occurred in the season 1865–66, when it was decided that a player was onside providing that he had at least three opponents in front of him when he received the ball. Cumulatively, the changes meant that by the end of 1867 the rules of the FA were 'synonymous with those which for years have been practised by the Westminster boys at Vincent Square, and represent the least complicated form of the "dribbling game"'.[3] By disposing of the strict offside rule, and replacing it with the less stringent provision in use at Westminster and Charterhouse, the FA had ensured itself of the co-operation of these two prestigious schools.[4] Additionally, as Alcock wrote, the change had helped to clarify significantly the various football rules that were in use in the London area: 'Of late years, however, the practice of the sport in the metropolis, and outside the immediate pale of the public schools, has drawn the points of difference into much narrower limits'.[5] Alcock went on to distinguish the two groups as the 'Guelphs' who were 'dribblers' and the 'Ghibelines', who favoured the 'running and hacking style'. Essentially, outside of the public schools there were two football codes, games that would later come to be known as rugby and association. However, the FA still regarded itself as an Association for all footballers 'whether they be of the hacking or non-hacking persuasion' and their aim was:

> To effect a code of rules that shall unite all the various differences under one recognised head, may emphatically be described as the ruling principle of those who, under its management, seek a healthy reform of what may be regarded as football abuses.[6]

This principle was reiterated the following year, the FA retaining the belief that it was the national association for all footballers.[7]

In truth, however, the plausibility of such an ambition had been undermined in 1867 when the Association had rejected the request from Ellis, of Rugby School, that it should resolve and clarify the rules of the game used at Rugby. The immense diversity of interpretations of the laws regulating the football game of Rugby School had reached such a point that

> before commencing a match, the captains of the sides always needed a conference in order to settle the points upon which there was a probability of their being some difference on the mode of play of their respective clubs.[8]

Consequently when, in 1870, a spate of serious injuries during games regulated by the football laws of Rugby School led to demands for the creation of a set of rules that would curb such violence, players did not turn to the FA for guidance, or suggest that the two codes co-operate.[9] On the contrary, a decision was made on 26 January 1871 to establish the RFU, with a committee of thirteen men. The 'sole object of the RFU is the promotion of one uniform game after the Rugby model'.[10] To this end, three officials, all old Rugbeians, E. C. Holmes, L. Maton and A. Rutter, then created the new laws of the Union, which were established on 26 July 1871 and included an unambiguous declaration that hacking was forbidden:

> Law 57: 'No hacking or hacking over or tripping up shall be allowed under any circumstances'.[11]

Predominantly, with the exception of the exclusion of hacking, the RFU's initial rules were quite conservative.[12] Despite this, and the fact that the RFU's laws were drawn up by Old Rugbeians, Rugby School refused to join the RFU, and continued using laws that permitted hacking! Indeed, the school did not join the RFU until the 1890s.

The FA Cup

With the creation of the RFU in 1871 the game of football became fundamentally split into the association and rugby varieties. Curiously enough, just six days before the final creation of the RFU, the FA began initiating its most ambitious attempt yet to publicise itself, a knock-out cup competition that was to become known as the FA Cup. The event occurred on the 20 July 1871 in the offices of *The Sportsman*, a paper that Alcock wrote for. During a meeting involving seven men (C. Alcock, D. Allport, M. Betts, J. Giffard, Captain Marindin, A. Stair, C. Stephenson) Alcock suggested that a cup competition be held, the others appearing to have readily adopted the idea. Three months later, 16 October 1871, the rules for the competition were drafted.[13] According to Alcock he got the idea for the FA Cup from the cock house competition of Harrow School, the foundation that he had attended.[14] Although by then the FA was in a healthy condition, with a membership of fifty clubs, Alcock intended that the cup should act as a further stimulus, accelerating the Association's prestige.[15] Given that subscriptions to the FA were only five shillings a year, the £25 necessary to purchase the FA Cup was raised by donations. The most notable contributors were the Queen's Park club from Glasgow, who subscribed a guinea despite only having an annual revenue of £6.

In many ways the deeds of Queen's Park and their supporters were the most positive aspect of a competition in which four matches were decided by the non-appearance of teams and drawn games usually resulted in both teams progressing to the next round (see Table 6.2). Queen's Park were granted byes until the semi-finals, when a subscription from the citizens of Glasgow supplied the funds necessary for their journey to London. Unfortunately, the funds ran out after the first match, which was drawn, and Queen's Park had to withdraw.[16] The final on 16 March 1872 was watched by a crowd of 2,000 (predominantly classified in social terms as gentlemen) who paid one shilling entrance money each. Although the Royal Engineers were 7 : 4 on favourites, an injury to one of their

Table 6.2 The FA Cup 1871–72

1st round
Harrow Chequers scratched vs Wanderers
Clapham Rovers 3 Upton Park 0
Reigate Priory scratched vs Royal Engineers
Barnes 2 Civil Service 0
Maidenhead 2 Great Marlow 0
Crystal Palace drew vs Hitchin
Donington School drew vs Queen's Park
Hampstead Heathens Bye

2nd round
Hampstead Heathens 1 Barnes 0
Crystal Palace 3 Maidenhead 0
Royal Engineers 3 Hitchin 0
Donington School scratched vs Queen's Park
Wanderers 1 Clapham Rovers 0

3rd round
Wanderers drew vs Crystal Palace
Royal Engineers 3 Hampstead 0
Queen's Park bye

4th round
Wanderers drew vs Queen's Park. Queen's Park then scratched
Royal Engineers 3 Crystal Palace 0

Final
Wanderers 1 Royal Engineers 0

Table 6.3 Attendance records of FA Cup finals 1872–78

Year	1872	1873	1874	1875	1876	1877	1878
Attendance	2,000	3,000	2,000	3,000	3,000[a]	3,000	4,500

Note
a While the figures in the table were drawn from B. Butler, *The Official Illustrated History of the FA Cup* the author has some doubts concerning their veracity and notes that according to the official annual of the Football Association, C. Alcock, *Football Annual* 1875/6, p. 87, only, 1,500 people attended the FA Cup final of 1876.

players meant that a goal by Morton Peto Betts won the game for the Wanderers team. Farcically enough, Betts played the match under the alias of A. H. Chequer, because he had been a Harrow Chequer player (a team that had scratched in the first round when paired against Wanderers).[17] Throughout the competition Wanderers had only won two games in their progress through five rounds, a fact that scarcely resembles a knock-out competition. Nonetheless, for all its inadequacies, the staging of such a competition was an achievement.[18] It would, of course, be some years before the FA Cup became a major sporting attraction and it is noticeable that it was not until 1878 that the crowd watching the final exceeded the 3,000 paying spectators that had been drawn to the Youdan Cup final in Sheffield in 1867 (see Table 6.3).[19]

Provincial football

As we have seen in Chapters 3 and 4, between 1860 and 1867 the centre for football in Britain was Sheffield. Naturally, the growth enjoyed by the FA after 1868 meant that Sheffield lost this status, though still continuing to be immensely important. By 1868 the Sheffield FA had constituted itself as a legislative body and over the next few years steadily refined its rules.[20] Predominantly, the Sheffield code was far more sophisticated than that of the FA, who would often belatedly introduce similar legislation. Indeed, in 1869 Sheffield introduced the idea of corner kicks and these were adopted, at Sheffield's suggestion, by the FA in 1872:[21]

> rule 8: when the ball is kicked over the bar of the goal, it must be kicked off by the side behind whose goal it went, within six yards from the limit of their goal. The side who thus kick the ball are entitled to a fair kick-off in whatever way they please; the opposite side not being allowed to approach within six yards of the ball. When ball is kicked behind the goal line a player of the opposite side to that which kicked it out shall kick it off from the nearest corner flag. No player shall be allowed within six yards of the ball until kicked.[22]

The relationship between the FA and the Sheffield FA does not appear to have been entirely easy, possibly because of a certain sensitivity on the part of the FA In 1870 the FA were happy to admit the sixteen clubs that belonged to the Sheffield FA as members while allowing them to retain their own rules.[23] However, a year later, in December 1871, the FA refused to allow a representative team to play a match using Sheffield's rules because they regarded it as diluting the standing of their code. As a consequence of this Alcock had to assemble a side privately to contest a game in Sheffield using the home-side's rules.[24]

Sheffield, of course, was the highly organised face of provincial football. By contrast, many sides were effectively untouched by wider organisations. A good example of this was the Turton club. Around the same time as the RFU and the FA Cup were being organised, two old Harrovians, the Kays, returned to Turton and fostered a football club. The Kay brothers, J. C. and Robert, aided by the village school master, W. T. Dixon, created Turton FC, holding their first AGM on 1 December 1871. The club was an excellent example of the type of patronage that the socially significant could provide. The Kays' father, James, was president and also supplied the club with a reading room.[25] J. C. Kay was captain and W. T. Dixon secretary and treasurer. The club had forty-eight playing members, mostly from the lower orders, who paid annual subscriptions of one shilling. Between 1871 and 1873 Turton used both Harrow's rules and ball (a cheese-shaped object).[26] At no stage was this club ever mentioned in *The Football Annual* that Alcock produced and it was probably typical of many similar ventures. In many ways such clubs demonstrated the limitations of the FA, for they were effectively oblivious to the Association's code and largely unreached by external organisations.[27]

The Scottish FA

One of the areas in which football enjoyed substantial growth after 1867 was Scotland. In 1868 John Lillywhite had been given permission to issue *The Football Annual*, which contained the laws of all the various codes, especially that of the FA, and it was from Lillywhite that Glasgow's Queen's Park club obtained their copy of the Association's rules. In 1870 Queen's Park joined the FA.[28] By 1872 a number of Scottish clubs had begun to organise themselves, namely: Queen's Park, Airdrie, Kilmarnock, The Thistle, The Eastern, Third Lanark Regiment, Vale of Leven, Dumbarton, Renton and Clydesdale. The Queen's Park club, particularly their secretary, A. Rae, were vigorous promoters of the FA rules and encouraged their adoption by Scottish clubs. In 1873 the Scottish FA was created, as was a cup competition. After this a rapid expansion of the game took place in Scotland, typified by the growth experienced between 1875 and 1880, when the number of clubs increased from 27 to 140.[29]

The growth of the Scottish FA had been anticipated by international matches between England and Scotland. The first international match between England and Scotland occurred on 18 November 1871 at the Oval in Surrey. The Scottish team had only one player who was not drawn from an English club. The first instance of a Scottish team travelling to London for a football match occurred on 4 March 1872 when the Queen's Park team visited the Oval to play Wanderers in the FA Cup.[30] 'The first match of any importance that took place over the border according to the rules of the FA', was the goalless draw between Scotland and England in Glasgow on 30 November 1872. The Scottish side only had one player who was from an English club.[31] The match attracted a crowd of 4,000, including many women.[32] Nonetheless, it was still rare for players from Scottish clubs to travel to England for international matches, and only three of the team came from Scottish based clubs in the international match at the Oval on 8 March 1873.[33]

Football and the socially elite

By the late 1860s, the disciplinary problems that had afflicted most public schools in the first half of the nineteenth century had largely vanished.[34] Despite this, the wide-scale promotion of athletics, which had gained much of its intellectual and practical rationale from its perceived capacity to assist the preservation of order within schools, expanded, coming to dominate the curriculum. By then, education in many foundations consisted largely of classical learning and sport and the new gentleman was regarded as being the product of a process of education rather than the content of it.[35] Consequently, football was practised extensively at almost every public school. While one might have imagined that there would be an increased amount of contact with outsiders, this does not appear to have been the case. Judging by the evidence, Harrow appears to have been the only school that played extensive amounts of 'foreign' matches, against Wanderers, Harrow Chequers, Cambridge Harrovians, Oxford Harrovians,

Bowen's team and such like. Football at the other schools appears to have been a remorseless procession of internal, generally house, matches. However, participation was not always compulsory, and from 1868 reluctant school boys at Eton could opt out of football.

An idea of the regularity of organised football play can be gleaned from Table 6.4. As for the timetable, the following details of the games routine of various schools are instructive. At Cheltenham College football was played between 12 a.m and 1 p.m and 5 p.m and 6 p.m every day. By 1867 there were generally twelve 'Field' games being conducted at Eton every day, mostly by house teams. Marlborough College football consisted of house matches of twenty-a-side and two or three big games every week, that were played from 2:45 p.m to 4:15 p.m. Rossall's football occurred on Wednesday and Saturday, 2:15–3:45 p.m. At Winchester College a game was played every day during the football season, with teams being divided into three sections, College, Commoners and Tutors Houses.

By contrast with the prevailing outlook of football at public school, which was insular, players at university showed a much greater willingness to interact with those from other foundations. Predominantly, players appear to have almost been swept up by the popularity of the game and by 1868 even the smallest colleges at Oxford and Cambridge had teams. Teams consisted of two types, those made up of old boys from a particular public school, playing the game of their foundation, and those drawn from a range of public schools using the FA code. At both Cambridge and Oxford old boys from Eton, Harrow and Rugby established clubs

Table 6.4 Football games in public schools 1868–73

Foundation	*1868*	*1869*	*1870*	*1871*	*1872*	*1873*
Brighton College	08		08	06	07	
Charterhouse	19	12	12	15	13	16
Cheltenham College	17	23	25	25	21	23
Clifton School	07					
Eton College	40	19	28	37		
Haileybury College	08	14	16	14		04
Harrow School	16	19	19	20	12	20
Lancing College						12
Marlborough College	11	15		13	24	14
Merchant Taylors' School						
Radley College	08	16	09	10	09	06
Rossall School	24		12	07		25
Ryl Military College					11	
Rugby	24	23	20	22		
Shrewsbury College	13					
Tonbridge College					12	
Uppingham	18	19	17	17	17	15
Wellington College				24	11	
Westminster School	17	19	19	17	12	16
Winchester College	19	19	26	16	12	09

Table 6.5 Football games by major British clubs 1868–73

Club	*1868*	*1869*	*1870*	*1871*	*1872*	*1873*	*Code*
Belsize Park					24		R
Blackheath				16			R
Brighton Wasps					11		R
Cambridge Eton	06						a′
Cambridge University			07				a
Christ's College (Finchley)			16	16	15		R
Clapham Rovers			22*	29*	36*		a R
Clapton				18			R
Edinburgh Royal High School					12		R
Essex Rifles (twenty-first)			04				a
Flamingos			17	18			R
Forest School			12				a
Gipsies				18			R
Gitanos						17	a
Glasgow Academicals			07	07	16		R′
Hampstead		12	20				R
Harlequins				25	19	27	R
Harrow Chequers						11	a
Hornsey					16		R
Kettering						03	R
King's College					17		R
Lausanne			12				R
Manchester Athletic	09						R
Marlborough Nomads					17	19	R
Nottingham			14				a
Old Paulines					06		R
Oxford University Association						08	a
Queen's House				18			R
Ravenscourt Park		28	19	20	36	32	R
Richmond	30	35	24	20	25	38	R
Royal Engineers	14	17		15	20	20	a
Streatham					08		R
Upton Park			12	12	14	15	a
Walthamstow			13				a
Wanderers	29	29	34	35	32		a
Wasps			15	18	18		R
West Kent					18		a R
Woodford Wells						18	a

Notes
R game based on that of Rugby School.
R′ game based on code of RFU.
a game using the rules of the Football Association.
a′ game using an association based code.
* Clapham Rovers played about half their matches under association rules, the other half under the rugby code.

to conduct their variety of football. Generally, university students were very flexible in their outlook towards rules. Thus, the club established by Etonians at Cambridge played internal matches under the Eton rules three times a week, but also took on outsiders, such as Harrow, Charterhouse, Westminster and

The Wanderers, using other codes.[36] Some teams of old boys enjoyed immense success with codes that were unrelated to that of their old schools. However, this rarely impacted upon their foundation. For instance, in the 1870s Oxford's Wykehamists were very successful when using the laws of the FA but the association game was not introduced at the school.[37] Significantly, enough, three university teams were very active in the wider community during this period, Cambridge Eton, Cambridge University and Oxford University Association (see Table 6.4).

Between 1868 and 1873 football became considerably more organised and this manifested itself in four components of its culture. In the first place, greater expertise was deployed in the selection of rules and the creation of codes. Second, an increasingly effective structure had been developed to administer football, enabling problems to be more easily resolved. Third, there was an increasing tendency for clubs to have larger and more organised programmes of fixtures than in the past (see Table 6.5 and compare it to Table 5.7 in Chapter 5). Finally, and only as regards association football, a cup competition had been created. Cumulatively, these changes meant that by 1873 a football culture that incorporated the whole of Britain had been created. However, this geographical breadth was significantly less imposing than might appear because football had become split into two fundamental groups, the rugby and association varieties of the game. After 1871 these distinctions, which had been present since the original fracture that had occurred at the FA meeting in December 1863, became more pronounced, with the two varieties of football being administered by separate, and in certain senses, adversarial institutions.

In Chapter 7 we shall take a detailed look at the growth in the number of clubs between 1860 and 1873, paying particular attention to the rules that they used.

7 Kicking and carrying

The geographical distribution of sporting rules 1860–73

As we have seen in the earlier chapters, while there were many printed codes in existence previous to 1860, predominantly they were not understood by outsiders and this restricted their impact. In view of this, much of the transmission of rules was probably oral and dependent upon local interpretation. In this chapter we have divided Britain into four areas, (1) London and the home counties (consisting of Essex, Hertfordshire, Middlesex and Surrey), (2) the provinces (excluding Sheffield), (3) Scotland, (4) Sheffield, and set out the football rules that were adopted by teams in each of these areas between 1860 and 1873. The chapter itself is divided into three parts. In the first we consider the rules that were used by the teams in the various regions between 1860 and 1867. In the next we focus attention on the differences between the various codes of football rules, subjecting them to detailed comparison. In the part titled 'The geographical distribution of rules 1868–73' we consider the rules that were used by the teams in the various regions of Britain between 1868 and 1873. Finally, we conclude with an overview of the rules used during the entire period, 1860–73.

The geographical distribution of rules 1860–67

The first part of the chapter, Tables 7.1–7.4 (for detailed records of clubs during this period see Tables 7.24–7.27 at the end of the chapter), is based upon an examination of a variety of sources between 1860 and 1867 and displays three sets of information. In the first place, it details the years in which particular clubs were recorded as playing at least one match. Second, where possible, a club's membership of the FA is recorded (with the letter A). Finally, an effort has been made to distinguish, broadly, the type of game that was played.

All three sets of information are afflicted by certain weaknesses that must be taken into consideration. The most obvious relates to our first category, the activity of a club in a particular year, for this depends entirely on the attention paid to a club in our sources. With reference to the second category, an effort to record those clubs who were members of the FA, we confront two different sorts of problems. First, it is often impossible to determine how long a club's membership of the FA lasted, because such records were not preserved. Second, it is important not to overstate the significance of a club belonging to the FA. Many clubs appear to have belonged to the FA but rarely, if ever, used the FA's code. This last point leads us into two important issues that must be appreciated in relation to our third objective, the attempt to classify the rules used by a club. In the first place, we often lack detailed information on the rules that were used and consequently such decisions are based on inference from the reports of matches and such like. Second, it must be remembered that the football played by clubs who are classified as belonging to the same category often differed significantly. While this is most apparent in those games classified as association, which incorporated a substantial diversity of codes, it must not be overlooked that rugby's rules varied significantly between some clubs. The only code in which there appears to have been a significant uniformity was Sheffield. This was an association-type game in which the clubs, all of whom were based in the Sheffield area, adhered to substantially the same rules.

Tables 7.1–7.4 collate the information on the broad classification of rules into three geographical divisions, London and the home counties (Table 7.1), the provinces, Scotland and Sheffield (Table 7.2), and a national overview (Tables 7.3 and 7.4).

Table 7.1 Overview of London and the home counties 1860–67

Code	*1860*	*1861*	*1862*	*1863*	*1864*	*1865*	*1866*	*1867*
Association			08	14	10	14	22	33
Rugby	03	05	07	12	18	25	30	36
Unknown		01			04	02	02	06
Total	03	06	15	26	32	41	54	75

Table 7.2 Overview of the provinces, Scotland and Sheffield 1860–67

Code	*1860*	*1861*	*1862*	*1863*	*1864*	*1865*	*1866*	*1867*
Association	01	04	06	08	06	11	14	18
Rugby	05	07	06	11	09	03	09	09
Sheffield	04	08	12	17	13	13	17	16
Unknown					02	01		03
Total	10	19	24	36	30	28	40	46

Table 7.3 Grand total of the codes used in Britain 1860–67

Code	*1860*	*1861*	*1862*	*1863*	*1864*	*1865*	*1866*	*1867*
Association	01	04	14	22	16	25	36	51
Rugby	08	12	13	23	27	28	39	45
Sheffield	04	08	12	17	13	13	17	16
Unknown		01			06	03	02	09
Total	13	25	39	62	62	69	94	121

Table 7.4 The number of association- and Rugby-based clubs 1860–67

Code	*1860*	*1861*	*1862*	*1863*	*1864*	*1865*	*1866*	*1867*
Association based	05	12	26	39	29	38	53	67
Rugby based	08	12	13	23	27	28	39	45
Unknown		01			06	03	03	09
Difference	R+3	=	A+13	A+16	A+2	A+10	A+14	A+22

Note

For the purposes of Table 7.4 the figures for those clubs adhering to the Sheffield rules are included amongst those playing an association-based game.

Overview of codes used by teams 1860–67

The situation in London during 1860 and 1861 was probably not quite as grim for association football as Table 7.1 might suggest, for there is evidence that Forest FC were playing a brand of game that was based upon the code used at Cambridge University. However, it appears that their games must have been internal affairs for there was no one for them to play! The first evidence that the author has uncovered of an external match involving Forest FC is from 1862. As has been observed in Chapter 5, there was very little football in the London area in 1860–61. Predominantly, aside from a slight advantage enjoyed in 1863, teams practising association-type football (based upon giving primacy to the feet) were heavily outnumbered by those pursuing a rugby-based game (giving primacy to the hands) until 1867, when the reforms advocated by the FA served to generate interest. The immense popularity of the rugby version of football in the London area is very clear from Table 7.1 and the figures for 1864 and 1865 provide eloquent testimony to the failure of the FA to create a code of laws that could satisfy the requirements of potential members.

As Table 7.2 makes clear, between 1861 and 1866 the code used by Sheffield represented the most popular rules outside London and the home counties. By contrast with London, the rugby game was not particularly popular, especially from 1865 to 1867, when it was surpassed by both the association and Sheffield codes. It was only after the reforms in 1867 that the number of clubs playing association-type games, essentially based upon those of the FA, surpassed those using Sheffield's rules.

The number of clubs playing rugby grew steadily throughout the period, whereas both Sheffield and association-based games experienced fluctuations.

After the early years of the 1860s the number of clubs based upon an association-type football, whether using the model of Sheffield or some other source, surpassed those using the rugby game. Given that rugby confronted the well-organised culture of Sheffield, and from 1863 the FA, an association ostensibly devoted to promoting its version of football, this is scarcely surprising. In many ways it is remarkable how many teams did use a rugby-based game, given the lack of any central organisation that could promote and regulate such a distinctive brand of football.

The Grand Stand
Band of Pipers (Cameron Highlanders.)
A long throw out from touch
A scrimmage near touch line
1. Making his mark.
The Goal for England
2 The Kick. —

Figure 7.1 England–Scotland rugby match from 1890. *The Illustrated Sporting and Dramatic News* 25 March 1890, p. 5.

Having discussed the relative experiences of the different codes between 1860 and 1867 it is now time to look at aspects of the codes themselves. This is best done from the vantage point of 1868, by which time most of the rules, particularly those of the FA, had become considerably more popular. In this, part of the chapter, we detail the differences between the various sets of printed rules.

The chief points of difference between the various codes in 1868[1]

Certain aspects of the FA's code seem very strange from today's perspective, not least the fact that they did not use referees! The FA recognised the 'fair catch' but did not credit the 'rouge', an additional mode of scoring usually obtained by either touching the ball down behind the opponent's goal or kicking it through an area on either side of the enemy goal. It would appear that football was a rather more robust game in those days, for only the FA and Sheffield forbade tripping. It seems very strange that Sheffield's was the only code in which it was specified that a ball that had gone into touch should be played out by the opposite side to the team that had last played it.

Table 7.5 Ground length

200 yds × 100 yds	FA, Sheffield
150 yds × 100 yds	Cambridge, Harrow
80 yds × 27 yds	Winchester
No fixed length	Brighton, Charterhouse,[a] Cheltenham, Eton, Haileybury Marlborough, Rossall, Shrewsbury, Uppingham, Westminster[a]

Note

a Having adopted the FA code Charterhouse and Westminster generally use a pitch of 200 yds × 100 yds.

Table 7.6 Goal size

8 yds × 8 ft	FA
4 yds × 9 ft	Sheffield
11 ft × 7 ft	Eton
27 yds	Winchester
12 ft × 10 ft	Brighton
12 ft	Harrow
$18\frac{1}{2}$ ft × 18 ft	Cheltenham, Haileybury, Marlborough, Rugby[a]
11 ft × 8 ft	Rossall
43 yds	Shrewsbury
6 paces wide	Uppingham
15 yds	Cambridge
10 ft × 6 ft	Charterhouse, Westminster

Notes

Where only one figure is given it indicates that there were no height restrictions.

a Rugby has a cross bar 10 ft from the ground.

Table 7.7 Additional methods of scoring

Rouge if kicked through area on either side of goal 4 yds × 9 ft[a]	Sheffield
Rouge if touched down in area 20 yds from either side of goal	Cambridge
Rouge if touched down in area 15 yds from either side of goal	Brighton
Scoring a rouge allows 'bully' in front of goal sticks[b]	Brighton, Eton, Rossall, Uppingham

Notes

a This area was usually marked by flags.

b The 'bully', like the Winchester 'hot' is akin to a Rugby scrum in which the players lower their heads and try to push the ball through the opposing party.

Table 7.8 Referees

Use referee	Cambridge, Eton, Harrow, Rossall, Sheffield
Decisions made by captains	Brighton, Cheltenham, Haileybury, Rugby
Decisions made by contending parties	Charterhouse, Westminster

Note

Where a body is not mentioned, for example, the FA, no referees were used.

Table 7.9 Handling

Allowed	Brighton, Charterhouse, Cheltenham, FA, Haileybury, Harrow, Marlborough, Rugby, Shrewsbury, Uppingham, Westminster, Winchester
Forbidden	Cambridge, Eton, Rossall

Table 7.10 What constitutes a 'fair catch'?

Only if ball has not hit the ground	Cambridge, Shrewsbury, Uppingham
May be stopped with hands	Charterhouse, Eton, FA, Rossall, Sheffield, Westminster, Winchester
If ball is bouncing	Brighton, Cheltenham, Haileybury, Marlborough, Rugby

Table 7.11 Rewards for a fair catch

Free kick with 3-yard run	Harrow, Shrewsbury
Kick at once	Charterhouse, FA, Sheffield, Westminster
Allowed to run carrying the ball	Brighton, Cheltenham, Haileybury, Marlborough, Rugby, Uppingham,[a] Winchester

Note

a At Uppingham a player must drop the ball if he is held.

Table 7.12 Physical contact

Allow holding	Cheltenham, Haileybury, Marlborough, Rugby, Uppingham, Winchester
Allow tripping	Only FA and Sheffield forbid it
Allow hacking	Cheltenham, Haileybury, Marlborough, Rugby[a]
Allow charging	All codes permit it

Note
a Of course, in 1871 the new laws constituted by the RFU would ban hacking.

Table 7.13 Kick-off

Place kick from the centre	Brighton, Cambridge, Charterhouse, FA, Haileybury, Harrow, Rugby, Sheffield, Shrewsbury
Kick from 30 yds in front of the side's goal	Cheltenham, Marlborough
Kick from a quarter of the way up the pitch	Uppingham
A 'bully' in the centre[a]	Eton, Rossall
A hot[a]	Winchester
Ball being thrown up in the centre	Westminster

Note
a The 'bully', like the Winchester 'hot' is akin to a Rugby scrum in which the players lower their heads and try to push the ball through the opposing party.

Table 7.14 Changing ends

At half-time if no goals have been scored	Brighton, Eton, Rossall, Sheffield, Winchester
Changed every time that a side scores	Cheltenham, FA, Harrow, Marlborough, Rugby, Shrewsbury, Uppingham

Table 7.15 The ball in touch behind the goal

Kicked out by the defending side	Charterhouse, FA, Harrow, Shrewsbury, Westminster, Winchester
Attacking side, having touched the ball down behind their opponents goal, are permitted a free kick which can then be caught and kicked again by them	Cheltenham, Haileybury, Marlborough, Rugby

Table 7.16 The ball in touch

When the ball goes out of bounds a 'bully' occurs	Eton
When the ball goes out of bounds a 'hot' occurs	Winchester
The first side reaching the ball kick it out	Cambridge
The first side reaching the ball throw it out	Cheltenham and Rugby
The first side reaching the ball must throw it out at right angles	FA and Rossall
The opposite side to the one that played it into touch must throw the ball out at right angles	Sheffield

The geographical distribution of rules 1868–73

In this part, Tables 7.17–7.23 (for detailed information on the various clubs see tables 84–87 at the end of the chapter), lists the codes that each club used and is based upon the very detailed information provided by various editions of *The Football Annual*. These volumes, edited by Alcock, specifically list the codes used by clubs and are consequently far more reliable than the inferences found in part one of this chapter. Concomitant with this, the classifications are less broad and considerably more specific. For instance, whereas in part one the classification a – association, could represent a club playing any form of association-type game, albeit using the FA's rules or those of one of the public schools, such as Winchester, in part two the classification a – association only represents clubs using the FA code. Those clubs using an association-type code but not that of the FA will be classified as a′ – association type, unless they happen to fall under the rubric of one of the other association-type codes which are exclusively specified, such as Uppingham, whereupon they will be represented by the appropriate symbol. While the advantages of the information presented in *The Football Annual* are obvious, it must be remembered that it only covers those clubs who either forwarded information to Alcock, or were members of either the FA or RFU, and that a number of bodies, particularly those stemming from the universities of Oxford and Cambridge, are not adequately represented.[2] The author has not attempted to include this missing data in the resulting tables. An additional problem relates to the body known as the South Derbyshire Association. *The Football Annual* for 1870 records South Derbyshire as a club playing the united rules. The following year a body, The South Derbyshire Association, is mentioned, consisting of eleven clubs and using the Sheffield Association code. In 1872 and 1873 the South Derbyshire Association are again listed, containing eleven clubs and twelve clubs respectively. As none of the clubs are listed their identities remain a mystery but it is presumed that they were unrelated to any of the clubs from the area that are mentioned in the relevant volumes of the *Football Annual*.

In Table 7.1 we saw that by 1867 the gulf between the number of teams in London and the home counties playing association-based football as compared to rugby-based football had narrowed substantially. However, as Table 7.17 shows,

Table 7.17 An overview of the rules used by clubs in London and the home counties 1868–73

Rules used by clubs	*1868*	*1869*	*1870*	*1871*	*1872*	*1873*
Association	26	28	29	26	37	36
Association-variants	01	01	01	03	03	02
Rugby	29	21	19	29	40	84
Rugby-variants	04	18	19	28	27	05
Use both association and rugby	01	01	04	03	02	02
Mix of association and rugby	01	02	01			
Special (rugby-based)	01	01	01			
Marlborough college	01	01				
Total	64	73	74	89	109	129

Table 7.18 The clubs playing association-based and rugby-based football in the London area 1868–73

	1868	*1869*	*1870*	*1871*	*1872*	*1873*
Association	27	29	30	29	40	38
Rugby	35	41	39	57	67	89
Difference	−08	−12	−09	−28	−27	−51

Table 7.19 Comparing rugby with rugby-variants in the London area 1868–73

	1868	*1869*	*1870*	*1871*	*1872*	*1873*
Rugby	29	21	19	29	40	84
Rugby-variant	06	20	20	28	27	05
Difference	+23	+01	−01	+01	+13	+79

from 1868 the gap between them tended to widen, often quite dramatically. This can be seen more clearly in Table 7.18 which groups both association and association-type games and rugby and rugby-type games together in separate blocks.

Additionally, Table 7.17 demonstrates how divided the game of rugby had become, with rugby-variants becoming increasingly prominent. This is seen more clearly in Table 7.19 where the various rugby-variants are grouped together. From this it would appear that once the reforms that were introduced in 1871, when the laws of rugby were clarified, had been assimilated, the game of rugby attained a significant unity in terms of the rules that it used.

The effect that the laws introduced by the Rugby Football Union in 1871 had on rugby in London and the home counties, which we identified in the previous table (Table 7.19), is amplified in the provinces, where until 1872 the amount of clubs playing rugby and a rugby-variant was effectively equal. In 1872, however, the established rugby laws attained significant ascendancy and this precluded the immense expansion that the sport experienced in 1873.

For the bulk of this period those clubs in the provinces, Sheffield and Scotland who played an association-type game were fairly evenly split between the codes of the Football Association and Sheffield Association (see Table 7.20). It was only near the end of the period, in 1872 and 1873 that the London-based association enjoyed a significant ascendancy. Previous to then, the Sheffield code had been largely responsible for the numerical advantage that clubs using association-type rules enjoyed over clubs playing rugby and its variants.

Table 7.21 demonstrates how significant the Sheffield code was amongst those playing association-type football, amounting to over a quarter of the clubs. The impact of the rule changes introduced by the RFU in 1871 can be seen clearly by 1873, where scarcely any sides are now recorded as using variants. An examination of the other years, especially 1869–71 reveals the extent of the split within rugby.

In many ways the most remarkable aspect of Table 7.22 is the similarity in the number of clubs playing association and rugby football throughout the period.

Table 7.20 An overview of the rules used by clubs in the provinces, Scotland and Sheffield 1868–73

Rules used by clubs	*1868*	*1869*	*1870*	*1871*	*1872*	*1873*
Association	14	15	21	24	36	57
Association-variants	01			01	02	03
Cambridge		01		01	01	01
Derbyshire						01
Sheffield	13	18	18	33	32	34
Association and Sheffield					01	01
United			05	01		
Uppingham						01
Use both association and rugby	01	01	01	04	04	03
Rugby	05	11	12	13	24	41
Rugby-variants	06	11	08	11	08	04
Marlborough			01			
Special code (rugby-based)	01	01	01			
Total	41	58	67	88	108	146

Table 7.21 An overview of the rules used by clubs in Britain 1868–73

Rules used by clubs	*1868*	*1869*	*1870*	*1871*	*1872*	*1873*
Association	40	43	50	50	73	93
Association-variants	02	01	01	04	05	05
Cambridge		01		01	01	01
Derbyshire						01
Association and Sheffield					01	01
Sheffield	13	18	18	33	32	34
United			05	01		
Uppingham						01
Use both association and rugby	02	02	05	07	06	05
Mix of association and rugby	01	02	01			
Rugby	34	32	31	42	64	125
Rugby-variants	10	29	27	39	35	09
Marlborough	01	01	01			
Scottish-variants of rugby	02	02	02			
Total	105	131	141	177	217	275

As we have seen, these two different codes were concentrated in distinct areas, each enjoying a considerable local ascendancy. Given that the FA's headquarters were in London it was probably somewhat embarrassing for them that its rival game was so strong in that area.

Table 7.23 demonstrates the significant growth that occurred in the number of football clubs between 1860 and 1873. Predominantly, both types of football, association and rugby, enjoyed growth throughout the period, and it appears likely that the slight fluctuations that do occur are principally due to the failure

Table 7.22 The relative popularity of the association and rugby-based codes 1868–73

Code used	*1868*	*1869*	*1870*	*1871*	*1872*	*1873*
Association based codes	55	63	74	89	112	136
Play both association and rugby	02	02	05	07	06	05
Play mix of association and rugby	01	02	01			
Rugby based codes	47	64	61	81	99	134
Total clubs	105	131	141	177	217	275
Difference between association and rugby	+08	−01	+13	+08	+13	+02

Note

In this table the broad group of criteria that were used in Tables 7.5–7.7 and especially Table 7.4 in order to distinguish association and Rugby football are employed. The games classified as association are: Association (FA) and its variants, Cambridge, Derbyshire, Sheffield, United and Uppingham. The games classified as Rugby are: Rugby (RFU) and variants, Marlborough, Scottish rugby, Special Code.

Table 7.23 An overview of the number of teams using the association and rugby codes 1860–73

Year	*Association*	*Rugby*	*Both*	*Mix*	*Unknown*	*Total*	*Association (%)*
1860	005	008				013	38.5
1861	012	012			01	025	48
1862	026	013				039	66.6
1863	039	023				062	62.9
1864	029	027			06	062	46.8
1865	038	028			03	069	55
1866	053	039			02	094	56.3
1867	067	045			09	121	55.3
1868	055	047	02	01		105	54.3
1869	063	064	02	02		131	49.6
1870	074	061	05	01		141	56
1871	089	081	07			177	54.2
1872	112	099	06			217	54.3
1873	136	134	05			275	51.3

Notes

Table 7.23 employs the same set of criteria as used in Table 7.22. The significant decline in the number of clubs in 1868 as compared to 1867 suggests that many teams did not send their details to Alcock and were consequently not included in *The Football Annual* for that year.

The figures for the percentage of teams using an association-based code include those sides who adopt both rugby and association codes on different occasions. Such figures do not include those teams whose game is a mixture of the two codes.

of the sources to provide a sufficiently accurate picture of reality. By 1873 the rules of both types of football had been provided with a solid basis, and with the creation of the Scottish FA organisations regulating football games existed on a national level. Additionally, potentially attractive matches were being organised, such as international games between teams representing England and

Scotland. Most important of all, however, from 1871 the FA began holding an annual challenge cup competition. Potentially, such a competition had immense appeal, having a capacity to generate intense local pride and emotion. In 1873 there was no indication that anyone saw this as having a particular commercial value. Indeed, as we observed in Chapter 4, the event that could be seen as the forerunner of such ventures, Sheffield's Youdan Cup competition, does not appear to have been staged as a commercial speculation. Contemporary reports, while taking an obvious delight in the fact that thousands of fans were willing to pay money to watch football matches, simply regarded this as a proof of the game's popularity; there was no indication that football might become a commercial proposition (Tables 7.24–7.31). However, this attitude would soon change and in Chapter 8 we shall examine the impact of this.

Table 7.24 The activity of clubs in London and the home counties and the predominant code used 1860–67

	1860	*1861*	*1862*	*1863*	*1864*	*1865*	*1866*	*1867*	*Code*
Admiralty					x				R
Alexandra								x	a
Amateur Athletics Club								x	a
Avengers								x	a
Barnes			x	A	x	x	A	A	a
Bishop Stortford Grammar School (Herts)						x			?
Blackheath Club[a]	x	x	x	A	x	x	x	x	R
Blackheath Perceval House				A	x	x			R
Blackheath Proprietary School	x	x	x	A	x	x	x	x	R
Blackheath School					x	x	x		R
Brackenbury's							x		R
Bradford School							x		?
Brentwood School							x	x	a
Brixton								x	a
Byculla Club (Croydon)								x	a
Camberwell Collegiate						x			R
Carlton Club					x				R
Carshalton House								x	R
CCC					x	x	x	x	a
Charlton							x	x	R
Charterhouse							x	x	a
Chigwell							x		a
Chislehurst				x				x	R

(Table 7.24 continued)

Table 7.24 Continued

	1860	*1861*	*1862*	*1863*	*1864*	*1865*	*1866*	*1867*	*Code*
Cholmeley School (Highgate)[b]						x			R
City of London School						x	x		R
Civil Service[c]				x	x	x	A	A	a
Civil Service College						x	x	x	R
Clapham						x		x	a
Clapham Grammar					x	x	x	x	R
Colchester Grammar (Essex)					x				?
Colchester Volunteer Corps (Essex)					x				?
Croydon								x	?
Crusaders				A	x	x	x	x	a
Crystal Palace			x	A	x	x	x	A	a
(8th) Depot Battalion (Essex)							x		R
Depot Battalion								x	R
Dingley Dell			x	x	x				a
Dr Bridgman's School						x	x	x	R
Durham House (Clapham)								x	?
Eccentrics							x		a
Edmonton[d]							x		a
Elan Grove					x	x			?
Elizabethan Club			x	x					a
Epsom College								x	R
Essex Calves							x		R
(21st) Essex Rifle Volunteers								x	a
Flamingos								x	R
Forest Club (Leytonstone)			x	A	x	x	x	x	a
Forest School				A	x	x	x	x	a
Grasshoppers								x	R
Great Ealing School					x				?
Guy's Hospital							x		R
Harrow							x	x	a
Harrow Chequers						x	x	x	a
Hatfield (Herts)								x	a
Hertfordshire Rangers							x	x	a
Highgate School					x	x	x	x	R
High House (Charlton)					x	x			R
Hitchin (Herts)							x	x	a
Hitchin School						x			a
Keir House								x	R
Kensington Common						x	x		R
Kensington Grammar		x			x			x	R
Kensington School				A			A	A	a
King's College				x	x	x	x	x	R
Kingston School			x	x			x		R
London Athletic Club								x	a
London Hospitals							x	x	?

Table 7.24 Continued

	1860	*1861*	*1862*	*1863*	*1864*	*1865*	*1866*	*1867*	*Code*
London Scottish Rifles								a	a
Merchant Taylors' School					x	x	x	x	R
Montague					x	x			R
No Names (Kilburn)				A	x	x	A	A	a
Old Charlton			x						R
Old Etonians							x	x	a
Old Felstadians								x	?
Old Harrovians								x	a
Oxford House								x	R
Ravenscourt Park								x	R
Red Rovers							x	x	R
Red Tapes								x	a
Reigate and Redhill						x	x		a
Richmond			x	x	x	x	x	x	R
Richmond Inn							x		R
Royal Artillery								x	R
Royal Marines								x	?
Royal Military Academy					x	x	x	x	R
Royal Military College	x							x	R
Royal Naval School		x		A				x	R
St Andrew's College (Bradfield, Essex)						x	x	x	R
St Bartholomew's Hospital				x	x	x	x	x	R
St George's Hospital						x	x	x	R
St Mary's Hospital							x	x	R
St Pauls School						x		x	R
St Peter's College (Battersea)								x	R
St Thomas's Hospital							x		R
South Middlesex Volunteers		x							?
Spring Grove (Isleworth)							x	x	R
Spring Grove (Islington)							x		R
Surbiton			x	A					a
Tottenham and Edmonton								x	?
Tulse Hill Academy				x	x				R
Twickenham						x			R
University College								x	R
United Hospitals								x	R
Upton Park								x	a
Victoria Rifles							x		?
Walthamstow			x	A				x	a
Walthamstow Rifles							x	x	a

(Table 7.24 continued)

Table 7.24 Continued

	1860	1861	1862	1863	1864	1865	1866	1867	Code
Wanderers					x	x	A	A	a
War Office			x	A					a
Wellesley House						x	x	x	R
Westminster School						x	x	x	a
Wimbledon			x	A					R
Wimbledon School		x	x	x	x	x	x	x	R
Worlabye House							A	A	a

Keys
A Member of the FA.
x Indicates that the club played at least one match that year.
The final column headed code in the Tables 7.1–7.3 attempts to divide the clubs into two categories according to the codes they played.
a Association.
R Rugby.

These are very broad classifications based upon the author's impression that a game was played predominantly with the hands (rugby) or feet (association) and are not restricted to the pristine varieties of each particular game such as the code established at Rugby School or the rules drawn up by the FA. On the contrary, they incorporate a wide variety of codes. For instance, the games found at Eton, Winchester and Harrow are all classified as a – association. Likewise, the Scottish versions of rugby, despite differing substantially from the rules established at Rugby School are classified as R – Rugby.

? On occasions the author was unable to make even this very broad distinction between Rugby and Association playing clubs and classified the clubs ? – to indicate this.

It must be appreciated that the division of clubs into two mutually exclusive categories, though providing a useful overview of activity, is extremely simplistic because clubs were often promiscuous in their selection of rules, freely mixing elements that would later be regarded as belonging, distinctively, to opposite codes. Additionally, clubs sometimes played more than one code. For instance, on 26 March 1864 *The Field* reports a match, using rugby rules, between the Blackheath and Forest schools. This was very unusual for the Forest School, who almost invariably played by an association-based code.

Notes
a The author has decided to treat both Blackheath and Blackheath Proprietary School as being active in the years between 1860 and 1862, although he has uncovered no indication of this in contemporary publicly available records such as newspapers and periodicals. According to a number of sources, notably the foundation dates provided by Lillywhite's *Football Annual*, both teams existed from the late 1850s. In the case of Blackheath, the author is inclined to believe that there are sufficient references to the club to render such an assumption uncontentious. However, this does not appear to be the case with Blackheath Proprietary School and the author would alert the reader to this. The author has excluded Harlequins from Table 7.24 because he has been unable to find any mention of activity by them throughout the entire period 1860–67, despite the fact that there appears to be fairly strong evidence that the club was founded in 1860.
b While teams are often heavily identified with a particular code on occasions there is strong evidence to suggest that they were not using it in particular matches. For instance, Cholmeley School beat Saint Paul's 9–0 and Merchant Tailors' 5–0, scores that suggest the games were not played under rugby rules, though this was the code that was generally used by all three schools. *Field* 11 November 1865.
c The Civil Service club is a good example of the problems involved in trying to classify the type of football played by a club. Originally speaking, they were created by old boys from a rugby playing school. H. Vassall, 'Rugby Union football', *English Illustrated Magazine* vii (1889–90) p. 430. In 1863 they played Blackheath and in 1867 Richmond, both well-established rugby clubs. Predominantly, however, their opponents were clubs using an association-based code, such as Charterhouse.
d Strictly speaking, the Edmonton club were named 'The Mutual Improvement Recreation Society' but the author suspects that they were generally known as Edmonton. N. Jackson *Sporting Days and Sporting Ways*, p. 21.

Table 7.25 The activity of provincial clubs and the predominant code used 1860–67

	1860	*1861*	*1862*	*1863*	*1864*	*1865*	*1866*	*1867*	*Code*
Aldeburgh School (Norfolk)							x		a
Aldershot				A					a
Beccles Grammar (Suffolk)				x					R
Bedford Commercial School			x						a
Bedford Grammar School			x						a
Blue Mantles (Kent)					x				a
Bradford (Wilts)						x	x		a
Bradford (Yorkshire)[a]								x	a
Bramham College (Hull)[b]								x	a
Brighton						x			a
Brighton College			x	x	x	x	x	x	a
Brighton FC							x		R
Brighton Schools		x							a
Bungay (Norfolk)				x					R
Cheltenham College	x	x	x	x	x	x	x	x	R
Cheltenham (Glocs)	x								R
Clifton College (Avon)				x		x			R
Darlington (Durham)[c]							x	x	a
Durham University and College						x	x	x	a
Eastman Naval Establishment (Hampshire)								x	a
Eltham								x	R
Fleetwood School of Musketry (Lancashire)			x				x		R
Holt (Wilts)							x		a
Hove (Brighton)						x			?
Hull[d]								x	a
Hulme Athenaeum								x	a
King Edwards School (Birmingham)							x		R
King's School (Sherborne)								x	R
Leeds					x	x	x	x	a
Leeds Grammar								x	a
Lincoln[e]				x	x	x	x	x	R
Liverpool			x						R
Louth (Lincs)[f]			x	x	x				R
Louth Grammar School				x					R

(*Table 7.25 continued*)

Table 7.25 Continued

	1860	*1861*	*1862*	*1863*	*1864*	*1865*	*1866*	*1867*	*Code*
Manchester							x		R
New Swindon (Wilts)	x								R
Norfolk Grammar					x				R
North Grove House (Hampshire)								x	a
Nottingham[g]						x	x	x	a
Nottingham Forest								x	a
Pennard Village (Somerset)					x				?
Queenswood College (Hants)		x							R
53rd Regiment (Hants)		x							R
85th Regiment (Aldershot, Hants)		x							R
Richmond (Yorkshire)							x		a
Roger's School (Louth)				x					R
Romsey (Hants)		x							R
Rossall School							x	x	R
Rossall 65th Rifle Corps (Lancs)					x	x	x	x	R
Royal Engineers (Chatham)				A			A	A	a
St John's College (Hurstpierpoint)								x	R
Sale (Lancs)								x	a
Shrewsbury County (Salop)				x					a
Shrewsbury School	x	x	x	x	x	x	x	x	a
Shropshire			x						a
Somersetshire College (Bath) (Avon)								x	?
Stockton on Tees (Cleveland)								x	a
Sydenham College (Birmingham)							x		R
Tonbridge Castle (Kent)				x	x	x			a
Tonbridge Grammar (Kent)						x			a
Tonbridge School (Kent)				x					a
Tonbridge Town					x				a
Trowbridge (Wilts)							x		a
Uppingham School		x	x	A	x	x	x	x	a
Wellington College (Somerset)				x					R

Table 7.25 Continued

	1860	*1861*	*1862*	*1863*	*1864*	*1865*	*1866*	*1867*	*Code*
Wellington School							x	x	R
West Kent								x	a
Wrexham FC[h]					x				?

Keys
See keys in Table 7.24.

Notes

a According to F. Marshall (ed.) *Football: The Rugby Union Game*, p. 423 players began playing football at Bradford cricket ground. c.1863, the rules being 'a cross between the present rugby and association games'. The author has classified Bradford as being Association because of remarks in *The Field* 20 April 1867.

b F. Marshall (ed.) *Football: The Rugby Union Game*, p. 421 indicates that Bramham College played rugby. This was certainly not the case in their match against Hull in 1867. *Field* 7 December 1867.

c F. Marshall (ed.) *Football: The Rugby Union Game*, p. 457 has the claim that Darlington existed in embryonic form in 1863 and that a club had been created in 1865, when they merged with the local cricket side. It is also recorded that 'Darlington claim to be the oldest rugby club in Durham'. While this might be the case, so far as the publicly available record goes it is clear that in 1866 and 1867 Darlington were playing an association game, see *Field* 1 December 1866 and 23 November 1867.

d In F. Marshall (ed.) *Football: The Rugby Union Game*, p. 421 it is stated that the Hull club were founded in 1865 and that the 'game was something resembling rugby, though running with the ball was only permissible after a catch'. It is certainly the case that in their match against Bramham College Hull used the FA rules. *Field* 7 December 1867.

e As is shown in Chapter 4, during this period Lincoln did use the FA code, though generally they much preferred their own rugby-oriented game. Strictly speaking they should probably be classified as a = association for 1863/64 and thereafter R.

f In 1863/64 Louth adopted the Cambridge University/FA rules, though as with Lincoln there is no evidence of them using the same against external opposition.

g Catton claims that the Nottingham team were founded in 1862 mainly by bankers and lawyers. J. Catton, *The Real Football* (London, 1900) p. 159. While Catton might be correct, the author doubts this because the earliest reference that he has uncovered of the Nottingham club is from 1865. Both the Nottingham and Nottingham Forest clubs appear to have played a hybrid of rugby and association rules. In 1865 a journalist contrasted Nottingham with Lincoln, stating that the former's game was more akin to association football, the latter's rugby. *Field* 18 March 1865.

h J. Catton, *The Real Football* (London, 1900) p. 200. It is stated that Wrexham was founded in 1864. The author has found no reference to them and has no idea as to the code they might have played.

Table 7.26 The activity and codes of clubs in Scotland 1860–67

	1860	*1861*	*1862*	*1863*	*1864*	*1865*	*1866*	*1867*	*Code*
Edinburgh Academicals								x	R
Edinburgh Academy	x	x	x	x	x				R
Merchiston Castle	x	x	x	x	x				R
St Andrews University					x				R
West of Scotland								x	?

Keys
See keys in Table 7.24.

Table 7.27 The activity of clubs in Sheffield 1860–67

	1860	*1861*	*1862*	*1863*	*1864*	*1865*	*1866*	*1867*
Attercliffe Cricket and Football club					x			
Brightside								x
Broomhall				x	x	x	x	x
Christchurch				x				
Collegiate School			x					x
Engineer Volunteer Corps		x	x					
Exchange				x	x	x	x	x
Fir Vale				x	x	x	x	x
Garrison				x				
Gleadless						x	x	
Hallam	x	x	x	x	x	x	x	x
Hallam and Stamperlow	x							
Heeley				x	x	x	x	x
Howard Hill Steel Bank			x	x	x			
Loxley Cricket and Football Club							x	
Mackenzie				x	x	x	x	x
Milton				x	x	x	x	x
Norfolk				x	x	x	x	x
Norton		x	x	x	x	x	x	x
Norwood			x					
Owlerton							x	
Pitsmoor		x	x	x	x	x	x	x
Pitsmoor Junior Club			x					
(58th) Regiment	x							
St Stephen				x				
Sheffield FC	x	x	x	A	x	x	x	x
Sheffield Wednesday								x
Stamperlow		x						
Tapton							x	
Tudor				x				
United Mechanics'						x	x	x
Wellington							x	x
West Yorkshire Artillery Volunteers			x	x				
York Athletic and Football Club		x	x	x				
York School			x					

Keys
See keys in Table 7.24.

Note
All the clubs in this list played by the Sheffield rules, which was the earliest association-type code that was used outside of the public schools.

Table 7.28 The codes used by clubs in London and the home counties region 1868–73

	Founded	*1868*	*1869*	*1870*	*1871*	*1872*	*1873*
Addison	1869				R	R Æ	R Æ
Aldenham School	1825			a	a	a	a
Amateur Athletics Club	1866	a A	a A	a A	a A	a A	a A
Arab	1871					R	R
Balham	1871						R
Barnes	1862	a A	a A	a A	a A	a A	a A
Bayswater Hornets	1871				R*	R*	R
Bedminster							Æ
Bedouins	1868		a				
Belsize	1870				R*	R*	R
Belsize Park					R*	Æ	
Blackheath	1858	R	R	R	R	R	R
Blackheath Proprietary	1856	R	R	R	R	R	R
Black Heatherns						R	
Blackheath Rovers	1870				R		
Black Rovers	1870				R*	R*	
Brentwood School	1865	a	a	a	a	a A	a
Brixton	1867	A	a A	A	A	A	
Brondesbury	1871					a	a A
Burlington House	1867		R	R	R	R	R
Bute House (Petersham)	1870				R	R	R
Carlton	1870				R*	R*	R Æ
CCC (Clapton)		a A	a A	A	A	A	
Charlton	1868	R					
Charterhouse School		A	A	A	A	A	A
Cheshunt	1869			R*	R*	R*Æ	R*Æ
Chesterfield (Blackheath)	1870				R*	R*	R
Cholmeley School, Highgate	1862	R	R*	R*	R*	R*	R
Christ's College, Finchley	1862				R	R	R
City of London School	1862		R*	R*	R*	R*	R*
Civil Service	1862	O A	O A	O A	O A	OA Æ	OA Æ
Civil Service College	1862	R	R				
Clapham Rovers	1869		a	O A	O A	OA Æ	OA Æ
Clapton	1866	R*	R*			Æ	R Æ
Clapton Pilgrims	1871					a A	
Clevedon	1870					R Æ	R Æ
Clifden House (Brentford)		A					
Cranbrook Rovers	1872						R
Crescent	1868		R*	R*	R*	R* Æ	R Æ
Crescent Rangers	1873						R

(*Table 7.28 continued*)

Table 7.28 Continued

	Founded	*1868*	*1869*	*1870*	*1871*	*1872*	*1873*
Croydon Oakfield	1867		R*				
Crusades	1859		a				
Crystal Palace	1863	a A	a A	a A	a A	a A	a A
Dartmouth	1872						R Æ
Dulwich College	1858		R*	R*	R*	R*	R
Ealing Rovers	1870					a	
East Sheen	1873						R
Eaton Rovers	1870				R*	R*	R*Æ
Epsom College	1865	R	R	R	R	R Æ	R Æ
(3rd) Essex Rifle Volunteers	1868					a	
(21st) Essex Rifle Volunteers	1868			a A	a A	A	a A
Farningham	1872						a
Flamingos	1865	R	R*	R*	R*	R* Æ	R Æ
Football Company	1871				R		
Forest FC	1869 re	a′	a′	a′	a′ A	a′ A	a′
Forest School		A	a A	a A	a A	a A	a A
Gipsies	1868	R	R	R	R	R Æ	R Æ
Gitanos[a]	1864		a	a	a	a	a A
Godolphin School	1854	R	R*	R*	R*	R*	R
Grafnel	1872						R Æ
Grasshoppers	1867			R*	R*		R
Great Marlow	1870				a A	a A	a A
Grove Park	1871						R
Guy's Hospital	1843	R	R	R	R	R Æ	R Æ
Hampstead	1867	R	R	R	R	R	
Hampstead Heathens	1868			A	a A	a A	
Harlequins	1860						R Æ
Harrow Chequers	1865	a	a	a	a A	a A	a A
Harrow Pilgrims				A			
Hendon	1872						R
Hertfordshire Rangers	1865	a	a	a	a	a	a
Highgate School			R*				
High Wycombe	1871					a A	A
Hitchin	1865	a A	a A	a A	a A	a A	a
Holbroke House School (Richmond)	1869					R	R
Hornsey	1869				R	R	R Æ
Hurstpierpoint College	1850				R	R	R
Indian Civil Engineering Office							Æ
Keir House	1860	R					
Kensington Foundation School	1861				R		
Kensington Grammar School						R*	
Kensington School		A	A	A			

Table 7.28 Continued

	Founded	*1868*	*1869*	*1870*	*1871*	*1872*	*1873*
King's College	1862	R	R	R*	R*	R*	R
King's College School	1863	R	R*	R*	R*	R*	R
Lausanne	1867			O	OA	RAÆ	RÆ
Law	1869			R	R	RÆ	Æ
Leighton (Leyton)	1868				a	a A	a A
London Athletic Club		a A	a A	A	A	A	A
London Hospital	1866	R	R	R	R	R	R
London International College	1869					R	R
London Scottish Rifles		A	A	A	A	A	A
Maidenhead	1870				a	a A	a A
Maidstone				R	R	R	
Marlborough Nomads	1868		R*	R*	R*	R* Æ	R
The Mars	1867	R	R				
Melrose	1869			R			
Merchant Taylors' School	1859	R	R*	R*	R*	R*	R
Mill Hill School	1807					R	R
Mohicans	1869			R*			R
Mortlake	1872						R
No Names (NN) (Kilburn)	1863	a A	a A	A			
Oakfield (Clapton)	1871					R Æ	R Æ
Oakfield (Croydon)	1867	R		R*	R*	R*	R
Old Cheltonians							Æ
Old Etonians						A	A
Old Paulines	1871					R	R Æ
Olympics	1871						R
Owls	1867	M	M				
Pilgrims (Clapton)	1871						a A
Pirates	1869		R*				Æ
Putney	1871						R
Queen's House (Greenwich)	1867		R*	R*	R*	R*Æ	R Æ
Rams	1871						R
Rangers (Clapton)	1871					R	R
Ravenscourt Park	1865	R*	R	R	R	R Æ	R Æ
Red Rovers	1865	R*	R*	R*	R*	R*	R*
Red White and Blue	1870				R	R Æ	R Æ
Reigate		A	A	A			
Reigate Priory	1871					a A	A
Richmond (Surrey)	1862	R	R	R	R	R Æ	R Æ
Rob Roy	1873						R
Rockets	1871						R Æ
Royal Engineers[b]	1867 re	a A	a A	a A	a	a	a A
Royal Miltary Academy	1865	R	R	R	R	R	R
Royal Miltary College		R	R	R	R	R	R
Royal Naval School	1842	R			R	R	R

(Table 7.28 continued)

Table 7.28 Continued

	Founded	*1868*	*1869*	*1870*	*1871*	*1872*	*1873*
Saint Albans Pilgrims	1869					a	a A
Saint Andrews Rovers	1869				R*	R*Æ	R Æ
Saint Bartholomew's Hospital	1866	R	R	R	R	R	R Æ
Saint George's Hospital	1863	mix	mix	mix	R	R	R
Saint Mary's Hospital	1865	R	R				
Saint Paul's School	1862	spec	spec	spec	R*	R*Æ	R Æ
Saint Thomas's Hospital	1865	R	R	R	R	R	R
Skyrockets	1871					R	
Smugglers	1840	R	R				
Somerset	1870						R
Southall	1872						a A
South Norwood	1871					a A	a A
South Park (Ilford)	1867	a					
Spartans	1873						R
Spring Grove School Club	1867	R					
Stars							Æ
Streatham	1871					R Æ	R Æ
(1st) Surrey Rifles	1869				a A	a A	a A
Sutton	1872						R
Swifts	1868				R	R	a
Sydenham	1870			O			
Tollebridge Park (Herts)		A	A	A			
Tonbridge School				R			Æ
Trojans	1869					a A	a A
Union							R*
United Hospitals	1867	R*	R				
University College			R*				
University College Hospital							R
University College School					R*	R*	R
Upton Park	1866	a A	a A	a A	a A	a A	a A
Uxbridge	1870					a A	a A
Walthamstow	1867	R	mix	R*	R*	R*	R
Wamba	1872						R
Wanderers	1864	a A	a A	a A	a A	a A	a A
Wasps	1868		R*	R*	R*	R*Æ	R Æ
West Brompton College		A	A	A			
Westminster School				A	A	A	A
Wey-side	1870				a′	a′	a′
Whitton Club		a	a				
Wimbledon Hornets	1868		R*	R*	R*	R*Æ	R*Æ
Wimbledon School		R	R	R	R	Æ	R Æ

Table 7.28 Continued

	Founded	*1868*	*1869*	*1870*	*1871*	*1872*	*1873*
Windsor Home Park	1870				a′ A	a′ A	a A
Woodford Wells	1869			a	a	a A	a A
Woolwich Royal Military Academy							Æ
Worlabye House (Roehampton)		A	A	A			

Keys

A Registered members of the Football Association. On occasions a club are classified as members of the FA but are recorded as using a different code. In this case they are treated as using that code rather than the rules of the FA.

a FA code.

a′ Modified Association. An association-type game that does not fall into the categories represented by a, C, D, S, U or UN.

Æ Registered members of the RFU. In 1873 Chesterfield were classified as using the rules of the Derbyshire FA but of belonging to the RFU. For the purposes of this study they are treated as playing by the Derbyshire code.

a S Association and Sheffield – clubs who played matches with either the FA or Sheffield codes.

C Cambridge University (an association variety).

D Derbyshire FA (a code almost identical to Sheffield).

mix The club used a mixture of rules, drawn from the rugby and association codes.

M Marlborough College code. Rules based on rugby.

O The club played matches with either the association or Rugby codes. It should be observed that not only did the clubs Civil Service and Clapham Rovers play by both codes but they were also members of the FA and RFU simultaneously.

R Rugby. Previous to the establishment of the RFU rules in 1871 this classification relates to those club's playing a game that substantially conformed to the rules agreed upon at Rugby School. After 1871 this usually means those clubs conforming to the laws of the RFU.

R* modified Rugby. Predominantly this means that hacking and tripping are excluded. After the introduction of the reformed code of 1871 clubs rarely included such a specification in their rules. Generally, when they did it indicated that a number of additional local rules were included. It must be remembered that in Scotland the rules used for rugby remained different from the standard English game. The area in which this made itself most felt was hacking, a practice that 'is not much indulged in and by many of the clubs is entirely abolished'. The growth of international matches between Scotland and England increased the adoption of uniform laws.

re Re-established club. It should be noted that it is very common for the dates that Alcock provides for the foundation of clubs to vary substantially within the various handbooks. Generally, the author has simply inserted the first date that he has come across, though on occasions he has attempted to select the most plausible amongst those that Alcock offers. The author should emphasise that predominantly he is sceptical about many of the foundation dates that are provided.

spec special rules. These seem to have been based on a modification of rugby.

S Sheffield rules, an association-variant that are described as 'practically indistinguishable from those of the F.A.' in *The Football Annual* (1869, p. 63).

U Uppingham School code (an association variety).

UN United rules, an association-variant used in the Midlands.

Notes

a Gitanos were described as 'a strong club and public school combination'. R. M. Ruck, 'Football in the early "seventies"', *Royal Engineers Journal* xlii ns (December 1928), p. 640.

b The game played by The Royal Engineers throughout this period reveals a great deal about the similarities between the Association and Rugby varieties of football. The team contained many old Rugbeians and as late as 1873 hacking was very common. The Royal Engineers scored a large number of goals by literally barging the opposing goalkeeper through his own goal. R. M. Ruck, 'Football in the early "seventies"', *Royal Engineers Journal* xlii ns (December 1928) p. 638.

c John Alcock, *The Football Annual 1870–71*, p. 73.

Table 7.29 The codes used by clubs in the provinces 1868–73

	Founded	*1868*	*1869*	*1870*	*1871*	*1872*	*1873*
Barnard Castle (Durham)	1870					a A	A
Birmingham Athletic Club	1866	R*	R*				
Blue Mantle (Trowbridge Wells)	1865			R			
Blundell's School (Devon)			R	R	R	R	R
Bradford (Yorkshire)	1864	R	R				
Bramham College (Hull)	1855	a A	a A	a A	a A	a A	a A
Brighton School	1862					a	a′
Brighton Wasps						R	
Broughton High School (Manchester)	1867		R*	R*	R*	R*	
Burton on Trent	1870					a	a′
Bury St Edmunds Grammar	1550						a
Cambridge Eton Club		a					
Cambridge University							A
Cambridge University Association							a
Castleton							S, a
(8th) Cheshire Rifles	1872						a
Chesterfield	1866				a A	a A	D Æ
Christ's College Cambridge	1862		C				
Congleton Rovers	1860			a	O	O	O
Cowley School (Oxford)		A	A	A			
Darlington	1865	R*	R*	R*	R*	R*	R*
Dartford	1871					R	R
Derwent (Derby)	1871						S
Donnington Grammar (Lincoln)	1870	A	A	A	a A	a A	a A
Edgbaston	1867		R	R	R	R	
Farningham							A
Free Wanderers (Manchester)	1870				R	R	R
Gravesend and Milton	1872						R
Hampton Common	1869				a	a	a
Harrogate	1871						R
Hereford	1870					R	R
Heversham Grammar	1865			R			
The Holt (Wiltshire)	1864	a A	a A	a A	a	a	a
Horncastle	1866	R*	R*	R*	UN	a′ A	a A
Hull	1865	spec	spec	spec	R	R	R Æ
Hull College		A	A				A
Hulme Athenaeum	1863	a	a	a	a	a	a
Ipswich	1870				R*		
Kettering	1872						U
King's College (Rochester)	1866					a	a
King's Lynn							A
King's School (Sherbourn)		a	R*				
Lancing College						a	a
Leamington College (Warwickshire)	1867	A	A	A		a	a

Table 7.29 Continued

	Founded	*1868*	*1869*	*1870*	*1871*	*1872*	*1873*
Leeds Athletic	1864	a	a		R*	R*	a
Leeds Grammar School	1851	R	R	R	R	R	R
Leek	1868	R					
Lincoln	1861	R	R*	a A	a A	a A	a A
Liverpool	1866		R	R	R	R	R Æ
Manchester Athletic	1866	R	R				Æ
Mansfield	1870				a		
Marlborough	1871				O	O	a A
Milford, College (South Wales)		A	A	A			
Milksham	1865			a	a	a	a
Newark	1868			a A	a A	a A	a A
Norwich	1868				C	C	C
Nottingham	1863	a	a	a A	a A	aSA	
Nottingham Forest	1865	a	S	S	SA	SA	aA
Nottingham Foresters	1867		a				
Nottingham Law	1869				a	a	a
Nottingham Town	1863				a	a	
Ockbrook and Borrowin Church Union	1867			a	S		
Ockbrook School	1867			UN	S	S	S
Oxford University							Æ
Oxford University Association				A	A	A	A
Plymouth Grammar	1869			a			
Pontypool	1870				a ′	a′	a′
Preston Grasshoppers	1869				R*	R*	R
Rangers (Swindon)	1868			M	R*		
Reading	1871					a	a
Reading School	1872						R
Rochdale	1867	R*	R	R	R	R	R Æ
Rochdale Athletic	1871					R	R
Rochdale Hornets	1871				R*	R	R
Rochester	1868		a	a	a	a	a
Rugeley Association Athletic Club	1871					a A	a A
St Andrews (Derby)	1867			UN	S	S	S
St John's College (Hurstpierpoint)	1858	R*	R*	R*	R*	R*	
St Peter's School (York)		R*	R*	R*	R*	R*	R*
Sale	1861	a	R	R	R	R	R
Sawley	1867			a			
Sherborne School	1556					a	a
Shrewsbury School							A
Shropshire Wanderers							A
Sleaford	1871						a
South Derbyshire	1869			UN			
Southsea	1873						R
Spondon House School (Derbyshire)	1867			UN		A	

(Table 7.29 continued)

Table 7.29 Continued

	Founded	*1868*	*1869*	*1870*	*1871*	*1872*	*1873*
Stoke on Trent	1867					a	a
Stoke Ramblers	1869		a				
Teeside Wanderers	1870				a	a	a
Tredegarville (Cardiff)	1870				O	O	R
Trent College	1869			UN			
Trinity College (Dublin)							Æ
Trowbridge	1864		R*				
Trowbridge Wells	1865			R			
Truro	1871						R
Wellington College							Æ
West Kent	1867	O	O	O	OA	OAÆ	OAÆ
Whitchurch (Salop)	1866		a			a	a
The Wick (Brighton)	1850					R*	R*
Wigan	1872						R Æ
Worcester	1871					R	R

Keys
See keys in Table 7.28.

Table 7.30 The codes used by teams in Scotland 1868–73

	Founded	*1868*	*1869*	*1870*	*1871*	*1872*	*1873*
Alexandra Athletic	1873						a
Annan	1867	a	a	a	a	a	a
Callander	1873						a
Cambuslang	1873						R
Carlton							R
Clydesdale	1872					a	a A
Dalhousie	1871						R
Dumbarton	1873						a
Dumbreck	1872						a A
Dumfries	1869		R	a			a
Dundee	1871					a	R
Eastern	1872						a A
Edinburgh Academicals	1858		R*	R*			R Æ
Edinburgh University	1866				R*	R*Æ	R*
Edinburgh Wanderers	1870					R	R Æ
Gilbertfield Academy							R
Glasgow Academical	1865		R*	R	R	R Æ	R Æ
Glasgow University	1871				R	R	R
Granville	1872						a
Highlanders (93rd)	1872						Æ
Kilmarnock	1872						R
Kinmount	1866			a	a	a	a
(3rd) Lanarck Volunteers	1872						a
Lanarkshire (1st)							a
Loretto School				R*	R	R	R
Madras				R	a	a	a
Merchiston School	1850			R*	R*	R	R
Paisley	1870					R	R
Queens Park	1867				a A	a A	a A
Royal High School Edinburgh	1868					R	R Æ

Table 7.30 Continued

	Founded	*1868*	*1869*	*1870*	*1871*	*1872*	*1873*
Saint Salvatore	1848		R	R		R	R
Southern	1871						O
Springkell				a			a
Trinity College (Glenmorland)					R	R	
Vale of Leven	1872						a A
West of Scotland	1864		R		R	R Æ	R Æ

Keys
See keys in Table 7.28.

Table 7.31 List of teams in Sheffield area using the Sheffield code 1868–73

	Founded	*1868*	*1869*	*1870*	*1871*	*1872*	*1873*
Artillery	1870						S
Brincliffe	1868			S	S	S	S
Broomhall	1868	S	S	S	S A	S A	S A
Christchurch	1870			S	S	S	S
Crookes	1870						S
Dronfield	1869		S		A	A	A
Exchange	1863				S A	S A	S A
Fir Vale	1862	S	S	S	S A	S A	S A
Garrick	1866	S	S	S	A	A	A
Hallam	1857	S	S	S	S A	S A	S A
Heeley	1862	S	S	S	S A	S A	S A
Mackenzie	1862	S	S	S	S A	S A	A
Milton	1862	S	S				
Norfolk	1861	S	S	S	S A	S A	S A
North Woodhouse			S				
Norton	1861		S	S	S A	S A	A
Oxford	1869		S	S	S	S A	S A
Parkwood Springs	1870			S	S A	S A	S A
Perseverance	1870				S	S	S
Pitsmoor	1861	S	S		A	A	A
Rotherham	1870			S	S	S	S
Sheffield	1857	S	S	S A	S A	S A	S A
Surrey	1870			S	S	S	S
United Mechanics	1863	S	S	S	S A	S A	S A
Walkley	1870						S
Wednesday	1867	S	S	S	S A	S A	S A
Wellington	1866	S	S		A	A	A

Keys
See keys in Table 7.28.

Note
In the above table the United Mechanics team were known as Mechanics during the period up to 1870.

The Sheffield FA was listed as an affiliate of the FA from 1871 to 1873. As a consequence of this for the last three years of our table most of the region's clubs are listed as members of the FA. The Sheffield rules were adopted by a few clubs outside the region but the only large scale use was by the South Derbyshire FA, founded in 1871. In 1871 and 1872 all 11 of the clubs affiliated to the Association used Sheffield's rules and by 1873 all 12 of the clubs used the Sheffield code. As noted earlier, it appears likely that the clubs in the South Derbyshire FA were not listed in Alcock's *Football Annual*, and as such their identities are a mystery.

8 Cups, leagues and professionals

Rugby and association football 1874–1901

The final quarter of the nineteenth century saw both varieties of football create structures that would persist for well over a hundred years. In this chapter we survey the period in a broadly chronological fashion; it consists of five sections, each relating to a particular theme. The first section focuses on the growth of two types of framework that were devoted to organising football, clubs and associations. In the second section we consider the changes in the various law codes that governed football games and the impact that they had on the way the games were played. The third section is concerned with the substantial commercial growth that football enjoyed, while the fourth section focuses on the way professionals took over association football and the impact that this had. In the last section we view a parallel issue, the effect that professionals had on the rugby game and the split that this engendered within the supervisory organisation. We commence with the first section of the chapter, the growth of clubs and associations.

The growth of clubs and associations

In the first section of this chapter we examine two key elements in the expansion that occurred within rugby and association football. These were clubs and the larger, local bodies that collected them together, generally known as associations. We begin with a consideration of the most fundamental building block of all, clubs.

In Chapters 4 and 5 we noted that many of the football clubs that existed in the 1860s were made up predominantly of players from the middle and upper classes. Additionally, football teams were often based upon clubs that already existed for other sports. This was especially the case in Sheffield, where during the 1860s many of the local football teams were based on the area's long-standing cricket clubs, to whom they were completely subordinate. From the middle of the 1870s the structure of English football clubs underwent a profound change that had the effect of transforming the social composition of many teams and completely altering the relationship between football and other sports.

Judging by the evidence, a large number of the football teams that were created after the middle of the 1870s were based on existing local institutions,

Figure 8.1 Blackheath did not die with their exit from the FA. Picture from *The Illustrated Sporting and Dramatic News* 14 October 1893, p. 182; from Blackheath vs Middlesex Wanderers.

particularly churches, one of the most notable examples being Aston Villa, which was founded in 1874.[1] While the vast bulk of the membership of these new teams stemmed from the lower orders, the leading roles within the organisations were occupied by middle- and upper-class patrons. This was particularly the case for clubs that were based on churches, where clergymen who adhered to a doctrine of 'muscular Christianity' used this direct involvement with the local community as a means of spreading the Gospel to the lower orders. While theoretically it might be thought that the working class members of such organisations would adopt the beliefs and values espoused by their patrons, in practice there is little indication of their being permeated by such ideals. Indeed, the evidence indicates that the working-class members of the teams simply used the access that the club facilities provided and were fully prepared to abandon the institution when they felt that those supervising such activities were becoming too intrusive.[2] The origins of Bolton Wanderers provides an excellent case study of the limitations of middle-class patronage. In 1874 Ogden, a schoolmaster, formed the Christchurch FC at Bolton, with each player subscribing 6d in order to purchase a five shilling football. The Reverend Wright, who was sympathetic to the venture, became president, and Ogden himself, captain. The team played in various places, including a cemetery, using a mixture of rules, though mainly those of Harrow School and the Football Association (FA).[3] In the early stages, the middle-class patrons, namely the vicar and the schoolmaster, kept a strong grip on the club, with meetings being held at Christchurch School, the vicar stipulating that the club was forbidden to assemble without him. However, as the team became more organised the players came to resent this supervision and this culminated in a walk out, the team relocating itself at the Gladstone Hotel and selecting new officials. On 28 August 1877 Christchurch FC became Bolton Wanderers.[4]

It was significant that the Bolton players chose a pub as their new headquarters, for as we saw in Chapter 3 pubs were a key focus for the football teams of the 1840s and 1850s. While Bolton was an association football club, similar developments were occurring in rugby football where clubs were appearing based upon a variety of organisations, including church, workplace and pub.[5] From the late 1870s working-class players in the north began making significant inroads into rugby teams and within ten years most of the players in Yorkshire's rugby clubs were from the lower orders.[6] Cumulatively, in both rugby and association football, the period between 1875 and 1885 was one in which the lower orders attained a numerical ascendancy in most clubs. Additionally, the relationship between football, particularly the association variety, and other sports was changing significantly. Whereas in the 1860s cricket clubs had been the major sporting organisations within an area, onto which football teams were occasionally grafted as a means of enabling cricketers to retain their fitness during the winter, from the middle of the 1870s cricket clubs came to depend increasingly on the revenue generated by their football sides, and at Darwen, Bolton and Bradford, for example, the money created by the admission charges levied on football spectators enabled the cricket teams to survive.[7]

While the appearance of large numbers of clubs was a key element in disseminating football, the emergence of local associations was no less crucial. Between 1875 and 1885 almost every football club in Britain was embraced by a local association, some of which conducted fiercely contested cup competitions. As we have seen in Chapters 4 and 6 the oldest of these was the Sheffield Association, an organisation that was very highly developed, including, from 1873, the Sheffield Football Accident Fund, an insurance scheme for contracting players. From the middle of the 1870s the Sheffield Association consisted of between thirty and forty subscribing clubs and a membership numbering as many as 5,000 players. Naturally, the revenue generated by such numbers was sufficient to enable the Sheffield Association to purchase a fifty guinea trophy in 1876 and establish a challenge cup competition.[8] The major problem afflicting football in the Sheffield area was the inability of the Sheffield Association to cope with the influx of clubs that wanted to join and as a consequence of this in March 1878 the Sheffield New Association (known as The Hallamshire FA) was formed. This new association supervised the activities of these new clubs.[9]

As we have seen in Chapters 3 and 4, the rules used in Sheffield were different from those of the FA and this remained the case until 1877, when the Yorkshire body determined to adopt the same laws as their metropolitan counterparts. Elsewhere, other associations were appearing. Perhaps the most surprising of all of them was the Birmingham and District Association, a body that was created in 1875 to supervise the association variety of football. A letter from the secretary of the newly created body emphasised the significance of this development, for as he pointed out until 1873 the rugby game had been completely dominant in the area. However, although the Birmingham and District Association played association football they did not use the rules of the Football Association. On the contrary, despite the wishes of the secretary of the Birmingham and District Association, who wanted the Association to adopt the FA rules, the various clubs in the area insisted on a compromise code being established, containing elements of the different laws that the various clubs subscribed to.[10]

From its very foundation the Birmingham and District Association commenced a challenge cup competition and while the attendance figures for the final of 1876/77 competition (2,000 producing £15 gate money) did not quite surpass that of the FA Cup, the body rapidly prospered and by 1880 fifty clubs were affiliated. Other Associations followed – notably, in 1878, the Lancashire FA, which was particularly assisted by advice from the Scottish FA.[11] Within a short while the Lancashire FA were organising a cup competition and in 1879 paid over £140 to purchase what became the Lancashire Cup.[12] Cup competitions were a key reason for the progress of the various Associations within England and were just as popular elsewhere, the Welsh Challenge Cup being instituted in 1877.[13] The most popular competition of all, at least if we were to go by the number of entries, was the Scottish FA Cup, which attracted 126 entries in the season 1878–79.[14]

Table 8.1 gives an idea of the number of clubs that were in the various associations that appeared towards the end of the 1870s. The growth of such bodies accelerated during the first half of the 1880s and while it is sometimes difficult to glean the number of clubs belonging to each association, Table 8.2

Table 8.1 Number of clubs belonging to the various local associations 1877–80

Association	*1877*	*1878*	*1879*	*1880*
Sheffield	35	38	49	50
Birmingham	17	20	41	44
Staffordshire		14	23	no figure
Lancashire		22	33	40
Berks and Bucks				15
Northumberland				12
Wales				17

Source: Information taken from C. Alcock, *Football Annual* 1876/77 onwards.

Note
In 1877 the only information recorded concerning the Welsh is that four clubs belong to the English FA. In 1880 there is no information for the Staffordshire Association.

Table 8.2 Number of clubs belonging to the various local associations 1884–85

Association	*Number of clubs*	*Code*
Berks and Bucks	10	Assn
Birmingham and District	63	Assn
Cheshire	24	Assn
Cheshire Union		Rugby
Cleveland	12	Assn
Derbyshire	24	Assn
Durham County		Rugby
Hallamshire	22	Assn
Lancashire	84	Assn
Lincolnshire	25	Assn
Liverpool and District	28	Assn
London	79	Assn
Midland Counties	10	Rugby
Northumberland	50	Assn
Northumberland County	06	Rugby
Nottingham	25	Assn
Scarborough and East Riding	06	Assn
Staffordshire	19	Assn
Surrey		Assn
Sussex		Assn

Source: C. Alcock, *Football Annual* 1884–85 (London, 1885) pp. 59–62.

Note
The table provides such evidence as there is concerning the number of clubs in the various bodies. On occasions the author simply added up the number of clubs that had entered the cup competition of the particular body. The information in the final column indicates the code used by the body, either rugby or association.

provides a snapshot from season 1884–85. The primary aim of these local associations was to ensure that clubs had a plentiful supply of fixtures but in certain areas they had an ancillary role, assisting in the organised recreation of schoolchildren. The Sussex County FA was formed in 1882, at precisely the time when parents in the area were pressing local schools to introduce games on Saturday, with the intention of keeping children out of mischief. In 1892 the Brighton Schools FA was created, with teachers providing football instruction in their spare time. In this they were aided by facilities that were provided by the local corporation and cumulatively such initiatives enabled junior football to spread rapidly despite the fact that until 1906 state schools were forbidden to teach games as part of their curriculum.[15]

Codes and tactics

The appearance of local associations helped to standardise the rules used for football, both rugby and association, in various areas, though on many occasions the rules adhered to by the local association differed from the main supervisory body of that particular brand of football. This section of the chapter is divided into three segments. In the first we consider the variety of rules that existed in particular areas and their relationship to the official bodies that administered the sport. In the second, we detail some of the main changes that occurred in the codes of the FA and the Rugby Football Union (RFU) during the last quarter of the nineteenth century. In the third we consider the ways in which the tactics of association football changed, relating these where possible to transformations in the rules. We begin with the effect of local practices on the rules of football.

In Chapter 5 we saw that there was a substantial variation in the rules used by clubs, whether playing association-type or rugby-type games. To an extent, the reforms instituted by the FA and the RFU in 1868 and 1871 respectively, established greater uniformity but despite such efforts a large number of football variants continued to be played. A good deal of football was largely untouched by what were essentially seen as metropolitan developments, and was typified by the football played in the mining villages of Northumberland where the FA's codified game was not introduced until 1882.[16] The RFU were no more successful in Barrow, where rugby was not played by the usual rules, which were seen simply as providing a guide. Such facts meant that within Barrow the visiting clubs, that were expected to play under the home team's code, experienced considerable problems and this produced many disputes. By 1875, after a violently biased referee had cranked the friction level up to near breaking point, clubs within Barrow decided that in all future matches both sides should provide referees in order to iron out disputes.[17]

At an altogether more organised level many clubs rejected the codes of the FA and RFU because they played under the rubric of their local association, that had framed distinctive laws. The most prominent of these was the Sheffield Association, whose rules were generally reckoned to be better than those of the FA.[18] It was certainly the case that Sheffield was regarded as being a very significant force within association football, and on 19 December 1874 this manifested itself in a match between Sheffield and the Royal Engineers that was conducted under two different sets of laws. In the first half the Sheffield code was used and that of the FA in the second.[19] In 1877 Sheffield adopted the code of the FA and by so doing brought a substantial portion of those provincial teams who played an association-type game within the fold of the metropolitan body.[20] Inevitably, this helped to make the laws more uniform and assisted in the centralisation of the game. Such an attitude was characteristic of the pragmatism of many football teams within Britain and was typified by the behaviour of two southern teams in the 1870s. In 1876, the Lyminington Club was formed and decided to adopt both the FA and RFU codes. Previous to playing a game, the team members would decide by a show of hands which particular set of rules they were going to use.[21] Two years later, the Andover club showed itself to be no less pragmatic, for having commenced its life by using the rules of the RFU, it elected to replace them with those of the FA because it regarded rugby as being too dangerous.[22]

Figure 8.2 One hundred and ten years on the teams in Figures 8.2, 8.3 and 8.4 are major powers in the English game. Match between Arsenal and Middlesbrough.

During this period the rules of both the FA and the RFU underwent significant change and a few of the more notable developments are detailed as follows. In 1874 the rules of the FA contained their first mention of umpires. A year later, because so many players were failing to score with place kicks, rugby players were in deep discussion over whether to decide drawn matches by tries at goal. The problem had arisen because having left school, players no longer had time to practise place kicking regularly and were consequently often failing to score.[23] In 1875 the FA began to permit cross bars to be used instead of a tape (though they were not compulsory until 1882) and insisted that teams change ends at half time.[24] It is surprising that the first mention of the referee in the laws of the FA does not occur until 1881, when the official was empowered to award a goal against any team whose player was guilty of wilful handling in order to prevent a goal being scored. Despite the fact that the accession to the FA of the various local associations meant that the rules of association football within England became significantly unified, substantial differences existed between the English and Scottish FAs, and in December 1882 a meeting took place at Manchester, when a series of compromises were concluded.[25] In the early part of that year, March 1882, rugby players undertook the experiment of having the England–Scotland match refereed by an official from a neutral country.[26] Also in 1882 the referee's power to award a goal as punishment for a player wilfully handling the ball to prevent their opponent's scoring was rescinded. Previous to 1883 the rules of the FA had allowed players to take throw-ins with just one hand, but from that year a law stipulated that the player must use both hands. In 1890 the penalty kick was first introduced by the FA and from 1892 the Football League insisted that every match must have a referee. The powers of the referee were quite circumscribed and it was only in 1894 that the FA permitted the referee to make decisions without first having been appealed to by one or other of the sides. The following year, perhaps following the example of the FA, the RFU innovated by 'entrusting the control of play to the referee without appeal'.[27] In 1897 the FA decided that handling was only illegal if it was intentional.[28] As we shall later see, in 1895 disputes over the issue of paying players led to the emergence of two rival supervisory bodies for rugby football. Although initially both organisations adhered to the same rules, from 1897 the new body, that was to later become the Rugby League, introduced significant changes to the laws of the game and in the succeeding years both varieties of rugby developed along distinct lines, producing very different types of game.[29]

Changes in the rules of football had an inevitable effect on tactics and it is no accident that a game based on passing rather than dribbling developed in Sheffield, where the offside law was considerably more lenient than that of the FA (requiring just one defender rather than three to be in front of the attacker when he received the ball).[30] It took some time for defensive strategy to adapt to the passing game and as late as 1874 it was common for only three defenders to be used. However, the exploits of teams such as Shropshire Wanderers, who in the season of 1874–75 became masters of the 'passing on' game that had been developed by Sheffield, meant that by 1875 further defensive players were required and before long positions such as centre half became crucial.[31] Alcock certainly seems to have regretted this, for he believed that dribbling was 'the most effective kind of play'.[32] However, passing had become the key to association football, whether the short passes beloved by Queen's Park, or the long passes that proved so effective for Blackburn Olympic in 1883.[33] Curiously, the side that was generally credited with transforming the tactics of association football and almost single-handedly inventing the modern game was not a professional team but the Cambridge University XI of 1883. Contemporaries described Cambridge as being the first 'combination' team in which each player was allotted an area of the field and played as part of a team in a game that was based upon passing.[34] This hardly sounds like the behaviour of the dashing individual that was to be later extolled by romantic advocates of the amateur game!

Football becomes a business

During the 1870s football became an increasingly popular game and this was reflected in the large numbers of spectators who were prepared to pay to watch matches. The effect of this was that by the early 1880s football was beginning to become a business with an increasing use of semi-professional players, particularly in the association game. In this the third section of our chapter we outline some of the ingredients of this culture.

During the 1870s the appetite for football, of both the association and rugby varieties, blossomed in the north, with large crowds being drawn to important matches. The creation of regional associations, and especially the cup competitions that many of them staged, generated intense local rivalry, making football a very lucrative commercial industry. Curiously enough, the impact of the competition that might be expected to attract the most interest of all, the FA Cup, was somewhat diluted in the provinces during the 1870s because of the stipulation that matches had to be played in London. In order to circumvent the considerable expense involved in making the trip to London, it was arranged that until the final two rounds ties should be organised on a zonal basis. Inevitably, this limited the number of clashes between top Northern and Southern teams, but probably encouraged more provincial sides to enter. In terms of the representative nature of the FA Cup the season 1877–78 was crucial, for it was the first time that a number of top provincial sides, namely Darwen, Manchester and Nottingham, entered. Within a short while the Northern teams had taken the measure of the competition and by 1883 the Blackburn Olympic club lifted the trophy itself.[35]

In terms of the attendances drawn to matches during the 1870s, Glasgow was the chief city for association football. On 2 February 1875 a crowd of 10,000 watched Glasgow play Sheffield and on 9 October 1875 12,000 people paid one shilling admission for the match between Queen's Park and Wanderers, producing receipts of £600.[36] Most extraordinary of all, in March 1876 Scotland's international match with Wales attracted 20,000 people. Towards the end of the decade some matches in England proved almost as attractive. The visit of the Glasgow team to play Sheffield was watched by a crowd of nearly 10,000 on 9 February 1878.[37] Less spectacularly, local cup competitions had a capacity to draw reasonable sized crowds to a large number of games. In 1878, the twenty-seven ties of the Birmingham and District Cup competition were watched by a total of 48,000 people.[38] The first match in England that really attracted attention because of the profits that were generated was the clash in 1880 between Darwen and Blackburn Rovers, that was watched by a crowd of 10,000, producing receipts that exceeded £250, 'the largest gate ever seen for an association game'.[39] Between 1874 and 1880, association football became an important spectator sport in various northern areas, such as Lancashire.

During the 1870s, Rugby football proved to be no less popular in many areas of the North, with internationals, county matches and local cup competitions, attracting large crowds. Judging by our sources, however, there was an increasing awareness of the relative disparity between the crowds drawn to matches in the North as compared to the South. For instance, in March 1877 a crowd of 5,000 watched the rugby match at Edinburgh between England and Scotland. By contrast, on 4 March 1878 only 4,000 were attracted to watch the same match at the Oval. In 1877, the annual rugby match between the North and the South drew a crowd of 2,000 to the Oval, just half of the number that attended the same fixture when it was held in Manchester a year later.[40] Towards the end of the decade, certain areas appear to have been rugby crazy. On 19 January 1878, Halifax staged the rugby match between Lancashire and Yorkshire that was watched by a crowd of 14,000.[41] Most dramatic of all, in 1879 it was noted that 12,000 people watched a rugby match in Yorkshire between two fierce local rivals, the commentator continuing 'it will be a great day for the Union if a third of that number can be got together at an International match in London'.[42]

Whereas in the 1860s clubs had shown no interest in using football to generate money, the immense sums earned from admission charges transformed both the rugby and association games. Increasing attention was focused on the financial element and it was almost inevitable that in an effort to bolster the team, talented players were recruited from elsewhere, often drawn by the offer of jobs unrelated to football that were both comparatively easy and well paid. This development first manifested itself in association football, when in 1876 two Glaswegians, P. Andrew and J. Lang, settled in Sheffield, effectively earning their livings by playing football.[43] A number of northern association football clubs, notably Darwen, hired Scottish players in the 1870s, though generally concealing the true nature of the player's employment by providing them with part time or nominal work unrelated to football.[44] Within a few years this development would completely transform association football, especially in the north, where professional and semi-professional players brought a new level of seriousness and expertise to the game. While in the past association football had been largely a recreation that some took very seriously, by the end of the 1870s it was beginning to attain the status of an occupation for some players. Such intensity of focus was simply one manifestation of a new level of efficiency that came to pervade many association football clubs, which showed themselves to be keen on generating revenue.

Some people simply wrung their hands in response to such developments. In 1880 Alcock noted:

> What was, ten or fifteen years ago, the recreation of a few has now become the pursuit of thousands, an athletic exercise carried on under a strict system, and, in many cases, by an enforced term of training almost magnified into a profession. Whether the introduction of so serious and almost business-like an element into the sport is a healthy one or not, this is not the place to enquire, but there are many old fogies who recount with no small satisfaction the days when football had not grown to be so important as to make umpires necessary, and the 'gate' the first subject for conversation.[45]

This concern had become widespread by 1881 and several writers in *The Football Annual* deplored the growing influence of money in association football, especially the unseemly disputes that it generated. Geographically, they were quite clear as to where the problem lay and noted the 'unwholesome prominence the gate occupies in the consideration of football clubs from the North'.[46] This distaste was also felt by some officials from northern clubs, notably Dix of Sheffield. Dix was concerned about the sums paid to players and tried to prevent the introduction of a much larger fixture list, the sole purpose of which, so he thought, was to generate matches and thus enrich semi-professional players. While Dix's stance was principled, it was also futile and he was forced to resign.[47] Unlike the association game, rugby football clubs in the north did not disappear under an avalanche of semi-professional players, but many found the increasing commercialism that was intruding into the game disturbing. In 1881 the Yorkshire Wanderers' official, Hudson, sought to withdraw the Yorkshire Challenge Cup that he had donated because he believed that it was

> doing a vast amount of harm, in converting football clubs into organisations for the collection of very large sums of money (which there was reason to fear was not always disbursed in the best manner), and football grounds into the recognised haunts of betting men.

Amongst the other disturbing developments that Hudson identified was the growth in bad feeling between clubs and the increasing tendency for referees to be hooted and subject to abuse from fans.[48]

The take-over of association football by the professionals

This section of the chapter is devoted to the onset of professionalism in association football and consists of five segments. In the first we consider the attempts of the FA to either prevent or control professionalism. The second examines the drastic decline in the comparative quality of amateur players during the period. The third segment relates to the money that professionals earned and the creation of the Football League, which was the only way that clubs could ensure that such financial demands were met. In the fourth segment we detail the means that the clubs used to control the movement and conditions of professionals, while in the final segment we examine the extent to which professional players profited from football as compared to other groups within the game.

Attempts of the FA to either prevent or control professionalism

In 1881 the FA tried to curb professionalism by restricting the payments that were made to players to legitimate expenses and appointing a commission to examine the account books of clubs that were suspected of making illegal payments. Inevitably, numerous ways were deployed in order to circumvent this and the growth of professional and semi-professional players, especially the influx of those from Scotland into England, did not abate. While the core of the opposition to professionalism was based in the south, some northern associations were no less bitter in their denunciation of such trends and in 1883, the Sheffield FA demanded that players who were suspected of being professionals should be forced to prove that they received only justified expenses.[49] The following year this dispute finally erupted when complaints were made over the payments that Accrington Stanley and Preston made to their players. In October 1884 it was decided to change the rules of the FA Cup so that professionals were excluded from the competition. In response to this, nineteen clubs from Lancashire formed the British Football Association and declared that the FA had no right to interfere in the registration of players.[50]

The more thoughtful officials within British football had seen such a confrontation brewing and in 1884 Alcock had written:

> The recognition of professionalism is, I am fully convinced, an event of the near future, and it seems to me a short sighted policy to attempt to repress a system which would to my mind tend to remove many of the impurities which at present are seriously injuring the game. It is clearly right that the distinction between amateur and professional players should be clearly marked.[51]

Alcock regarded professionalism as inevitable and in certain senses desirable, because it would remove much of the illegality and hypocrisy that pervaded the existing system. As it was, at a meeting in London's Freemasons Tavern on 19 January 1885 that was attended by 21 county and district associations, 120 clubs and 220 players, the pragmatic attitude advocated by Alcock and Sudell, who favoured the legalisation of professionalism, prevailed against those seeking to prevent this, who were represented by Chambers and Crump.[52] The resulting decision meant that football resembled many other sports, the professional element being admitted, though under strict rules. A further meeting in London, on 20 July 1885 laid out the conditions regulating professionalism. These are effectively summed up in the 'Bye laws of the FA for 1886':

> 17: That any member of a club receiving reimbursement or consideration of any sort above his necessary hotel and traveling expenses shall be considered to be a professional. Players receiving any expenses under this rule must give written receipts of the sum.[53]
>
> 20: No professional be allowed to play for more than one club in any one season without special permission of the committee of the FA.[54]

Law 18 specified that professionals must be born or have lived for at least two years within six miles of the headquarters of the club they sign for.

Alcock was very pleased about the formal recognition of professionalism, observing that it clarified football significantly: 'The institution of a clear and distinct line to define unpaid from paid had become an absolute necessity'.[55]

While Alcock was doubtless right, the anxiety created amongst amateurs by such a formal acknowledgement of professionalism can be easily appreciated when one considers the extremely aggressive definition of the term 'amateur' that was provided by the Amateur Athletics Association:

> Law 1: An amateur is one who has never competed for a money prize or staked bet, or with or against a professional for any prize, or who has never taught, pursued, or assisted in the practice of Athletic exercises as a means of obtaining a livelihood.

Interestingly enough, however, some additional clauses detailing those who are exempt stated:

> Exceptions are: Amateur athletes shall not lose their status by competing with or against professional football players in ordinary club matches for which no prizes are given or in cup competitions permitted by the National Football Associations or Rugby Union of England, Ireland, Scotland or Wales, providing that such competitions or matches form no part of, nor have connection with, any athletics meeting.[56]

Thus, hapless amateurs who might have been contaminated by contact with professional footballers were provided with a dispensation. Many amateurs, however, had no desire to have any contact with professionals. In 1886 M'Killop, the president of the Scottish FA, declared that it was necessary to 'have this evil suppressed' and having initiated legislation against professionalism celebrated the fact that

> no fewer than sixty eight Scotchmen playing football in England were prohibited from playing football in Scotland without special permission of the committee. Taken altogether, a good work has begun, a good foundation laid, and if the matter is properly followed up the evil will be kept out of the Association.[57]

Decline in the comparative quality of amateur players

M'Killop's description of professionalism as 'an evil' was endorsed by the Welsh and Irish federations.[58] Many in England felt the same way and in 1888 an article in the major literary review of the age bemoaned the onset of professional football. Football, the reviewer stated, was essentially a game played by public school boys and it was a pity that it had spread from boys to men because such modifications to accommodate older players meant that 'combination and passing has replaced skill and dash'. Still worse, 'the game has reached classes from which the professional element is naturally drawn'. Whereas the reviewer believed that professional cricketers had a valid role, he maintained that professional footballers performed no necessary function. Indeed, he believed that amateurs would soon find themselves being pushed out of the game and replaced by the rough unsporting play of professionals, whose aim was to produce a spectacle for the paying audience rather than for the joy of playing.[59] These sentiments typified the prejudices of many gentlemen within the FA and the acute snobbery that was sometimes displayed. This could manifest itself quite trivially, as with the reasons given by the Hon A. Lyttleton for his failing to pass to Mosforth, 'because I was playing for my own pleasure'.[60] More unpleasantly, the inclusion of the Sheffield amateur, Clegg, in the England team led to his being effectively blacked by the other players, all of whom were from the south and regarded the northern lawyer as their social inferior.[61] At the most fundamental level, until 1886 the England team for international matches against Scotland consisted entirely of amateurs, and when in 1887 this was finally broken, the extent of the change amounted to the inclusion of a single professional![62] Until 1900 there was immense bias involved in the selection of England teams, with amateurs being included despite their obvious inferiority to professionals.[63]

Without exception the English FA had immense sympathy for the amateur game. Indeed, even someone such as Alcock, who in 1888 dismissed many of the fears that had been generated concerning the introduction of professionalism, declaring that there was little evidence that the game's tone had been lowered or that play had become more dangerous, clearly regretted the onset of professionalism. As far as Alcock was concerned the legalisation of professionalism was simply making the best of a bad job.[64] Even commentators who maintained that professionals had done a great deal to improve the calibre of the skill in football, believed that they had removed much of the fun and replaced the blunt, physical side of the game, typified by the shoulder charge, with sly fouls out of view of the referee.[65] To a considerable extent, however, amateurs were responsible for their own decline relative to professionals. Shearman attributed much of the substantial disparity between amateurs and professionals, which was growing ever wider as the latter enjoyed an improvement that was as pronounced as the decline suffered by the former, to the intense conservatism of the public schools.[66] The failure of public schools to practise association football rather than the game peculiar to their foundation inevitably meant that many amateur players lacked experience in the code of the FA. For pragmatic reasons a few schools did accept the association rules but the vital foundations of Eton, Harrow and Winchester resisted change.[67] In the main, association football was practised by the less prestigious public schools, such as Shrewsbury and Lancing College, who from the 1870s used them against similar foundations, namely Rossall, Repton, Malvern, Brighton and Hurstpierpoint.[68] Charterhouse was the only significant public school to adopt the FA rules, doing so in September 1875 'to save the many disputes which occurred in foreign matches under our rules'.[69] At the more major schools association football was left to affiliated bodies that were linked to the foundation, such as the Old Wykehamist Association FC that was formed in 1882, who went on to play against similar bodies at Eton (1892) and Charterhouse (1895).[70] Cumulatively speaking, the failure of the most influential public schools to replace the brand of football peculiar to their foundation with that of the FA meant that a vital source of amateur playing talent was diluted.

High wage-bills of clubs

While the strength and authority of the amateur game was being steadily undermined, professional, or more pedantically semi-professional, football was expanding, particularly in the north and the midlands. The competition to secure players meant that the wage-bill of clubs rocketed. In the 1870s players for the Turton club, who provided the first lesson that Bolton Wanderers had in football, were allowed just 1 shilling expenses.[71] By 1883 Bolton's turnover was over £1,000 but payments to players meant that the club made only eleven pounds profit.[72] While we lack detailed records of the wages paid by most clubs an idea of the progression can be gleaned from teams such as Sheffield Wednesday. In 1887 Wednesday became professional, and in return for receiving wages of nine shillings for home matches and eleven shillings for away games players were required to supply their own equipment. By 1894 the pay of players at Sheffield Wednesday was on an entirely different level, with the club awarding players large bonuses in the FA Cup, £1 for getting through the first round, £2 for overcoming the second round and such like.

In order to afford the considerable expenditure involved in the wage bill, clubs relied on gate money. The cost of admission charges varied depending upon both the match and the ground but on average men were charged between 3d and 6d, boys 1d, and ladies sometimes admitted free.[73] Facilities were often rudimentary and while by the 1880s some clubs had grandstands these were often quite poor and even in the 1890s many grounds left much to be desired.[74] It appears that on occasions much the same could be said for the spectators, particularly those watching the clash between Darwen and Blackburn Rovers in 1880. During the match a fight broke out amongst the players and rapidly spread into the crowd.[75] According to McGregor, the founding figure of the Football League, there was a pronounced improvement in the respectability of those attending football in the early Edwardian period as compared to the 1880s. McGregor wrote that while football was still watched principally by artisans, in the 1880s only one spectator in twenty would have had a clean collar, whereas by 1907 nineteen out of every twenty would have done so.[76]

Ultimately, whether with or without clean collars, from the 1880s spectators were the major components of football clubs, for given the expenditure involved in running a team regular infusions of gate money were a matter of life and death for these organisations. However, for a variety of reasons, not least irregular fixture lists that had been disrupted by local and national cup ties, between 1886 and 1888 many clubs fell into serious financial trouble. In response to this, a number of Midland and Northern clubs created the Football League, which would ensure a regular supply of important, competitive fixtures that would generate the gate money necessary to ensure their survival.[77] While the FA surveyed the new body 'with a jealous eye', in practical terms they made no serious attempt to interfere.[78] On 17 April 1888 a meeting in Manchester formally created the league, enrolling twelve clubs; Accrington Stanley, Aston Villa, Blackburn Rovers, Bolton Wanderers, Burnley, Derby County, Everton, Nottingham County, Stoke City, West Bromwich Albion and Wolverhampton Wanderers. In 1892 the League was expanded to twenty-eight clubs, sixteen in the first division and twelve in the newly created second division.[79] With the creation of the Football League the association game attained a new level of financial viability.

By the late 1880s, association football was a significant commercial sport, the takings from which could be substantial. In January 1888, world records were established in terms of both attendance and receipts in the match between Aston Villa and Preston, with a crowd of 25,827 paying £1,117 to watch the game.[80] In the decade that followed such records were soon smashed and a good insight into the expanding popularity of association football can be gleaned by

Figure 8.3 Newton Heath were soon to disband and reinvent themselves as Manchester United. Match between Newton Heath and Wolverhampton Wanderers.

comparing the average attendance of FA Cup tie crowds. In season 1888–89 the average crowd was 6,000, by 1895–96 this had grown to 12,800.[81] By the 1890s association football clubs were often extremely wealthy, with the income of teams such as Aston Villa exceeding £15,000 in season 1898–99.[82] However, clubs needed to generate large incomes because the legalisation of professionalism in 1885 had been followed by a number of other changes that had driven the wages of players steadily upwards. It is to this topic, the rules regulating professionalism, that we now turn.

How clubs tried to control the movement of professionals

As we have seen, the first generation of paid association football players were effectively semi-professionals, pursuing, with varying degrees, an additional occupation. Evidence indicates that many of these players were drawn from skilled manual occupations.[83] It is likely that these men used their sporting skill to improve their prospects in the wider employment market, sometimes even to the point of obtaining occupations for which they would have been otherwise unqualified.[84] Between 1885 and 1889 the limitations imposed on the employment of professionals were steadily undermined, not least by the creation of the Football League in 1888, whose rules did not insist on players fulfilling the strict residence qualifications that were necessary if they were to be eligible to play for a club.[85] In 1889 these restrictions were also removed by the FA, a decision that prompted Alcock to express great unease, believing that it was likely to 'produce some evil'.[86] Predictably enough, this dramatic increase in the capacity of clubs to recruit players without reference to geography led to a huge infusion of Scottish players. Consequently, two hundred and thirty Scottish players had been imported into England and become registered as professionals by 1890.

While these developments were extremely good news for the players themselves; some of whom received £200 a season and other benefits, instead of the £70 or so that they would have earned for a year's work on the shipyard, many clubs were unhappy about the amount of free movement that the players enjoyed.[87] The immense flexibility of contracts led to a fluidity of movement by players, some of who were lured away by improved offers from other clubs.[88] In 1890 teams pressed to have players contracts extended beyond a season should the club desire it and the product of this lobbying was rule 18, which prevented players joining other clubs without the consent of the owner of the club they had been previously contracted to.[89] The effect of this rule was to enhance the competitive balance within the league by preventing the dominance of a handful of rich clubs who would otherwise have used their wealth to lure players away from their poorer brethren.[90] Naturally, this development impaired the earning capacity of professionals and in the years that followed various rules were introduced, affecting both their wages and their capacity to move clubs.[91] The rules decided upon by the FA in 1892 circumscribed the activities of professionals considerably as the following examples show:

> rule 21: 'Any player registered with the association as a professional, or receiving remunerations or consideration of any sort above his necessary hotel and travelling expenses, shall be considered to be a professional.'[92]
>
> rule 23: 'No professional shall be allowed to play for more than one club.'[93]
>
> rule 32: any club or player competing for money or prizes in any competition the proceeds of which are not devoted to a recognised football club or Football Association, or some charitable institution approved of by this or an affiliated association, should be liable to suspension or penalty as the council may think fit.[94]

At a meeting in Manchester on 18 December 1893 the maximum payment available to a player was restricted to £140 per season. Four years later, Football League clubs agreed that they would not poach one another's players.[95] In December 1899 still more rigid laws were introduced concerning transfers, wages and contracts, with the aim of protecting weaker clubs.[96] Inevitably, these measures were undertaken at the expense of top players, whose movements were significantly impeded, it being forbidden for them to obtain a transfer without the permission of the club they were contracted to.[97] Additionally, in 1900 the maximum wage was restricted to £4. While this was far more than the wage a working man could expect in most other industries, it was certainly less than top professionals would have otherwise commanded.[98]

How much did professional players profit from football

The rules that were set up to regulate professionalism within association football suited the clubs rather than the top players, but given that in the less regulated climate of the early 1890s it was reckoned that large wage bills meant that three quarters of clubs were experiencing significant financial difficulties, the new rules did at least ensure the survival of such teams and were consequently beneficial to the majority of professionals.[99] While this ensured that professionals continued to be employed, the reality was that football was a short and precarious occupation. After a survey of the season 1893–94 Vamplew discovered that only half of the 250 newly signed professionals had their contracts renewed for the following year, and that only 20 per cent had their contracts extended to three years. In total only twelve of the 250 professionals within association football had more than four seasons with a club.[100] Given the possibility of loss of form, injury, and such like, the association game was a precarious occupation in which 'the bulk of professionals could not hope to make a living out of football'.[101] Given all this, except for a fortunate few at the very top of the ability range, association footballers were probably well advised to remain semi-professional, ensuring that they had a trade that could sustain them when their playing days were over. Of course, there was nothing unusual in working-class occupations being precarious, for during the late Victorian and early Edwardian period this was the rule rather than the exception.[102]

While the bulk of professionals do not seem to have fared particularly well from association football, opinion is starkly divided on the reasons why businessmen invested in the game. Predominantly, Mason believes that because dividends from football clubs were limited to 5 per cent they did not represent worthwhile financial investments and consequently believed that businessmen became involved as directors in clubs largely for other, non-commercial factors, such as local prestige.[103] Nonetheless, he does acknowledge that in certain individual cases directors used their position on the management board to secure lucrative contracts but generally believes that such cases were outweighed by examples where directors lost money from financing clubs.[104] Alternatively, Tischler maintains that the 5 per cent limit on dividends could be easily circumvented and that the overriding influence for directors was commercial, with football being run primarily as a profit-making business.[105]

Given the paucity of the information that we have it seems unlikely that definitive conclusions will ever be reached on these matters. From the historical point of view the backgrounds of those involved in the financing of clubs is of interest. After an analysis of the occupations of the directors of twenty-eight clubs between 1888 and 1914, Tischler discovered that 38 per cent could be classified as being either industrialists or merchants, 30 per cent from professional backgrounds, such as solicitors, and 13 per cent from alcohol and tobacco.[106] Mason emphasised the role of the last category, noting the strong relationship between breweries and a number of clubs during the 1880s and 1890s. The most prominent of these were Arsenal and Wolverhampton Wanderers, both of whose grounds were owned by breweries.[107] As we saw in Chapter 3, between 1830 and 1859 publicans were important figures in the promotion of football and the evidence adduced by Tischler and Mason indicated that this continued to be the case, though of course on a scale that was profoundly different! By contrast, with the years between 1830 and 1859, publicans exerted very little influence on the football culture of Sheffield in the 1860s, a period when football clubs did not attempt to use the game to generate money for themselves and on the rare occasions when admission money was charged the proceeds were donated to local charities. In this sense, the association football clubs that grew up from the latter part of the 1870s were a return to an earlier phase of the game – that preceding the creation of the football culture of Sheffield, in which football was often used for financial purposes, either via betting or as an attraction to draw customers. Surveyed in this light, the true descendants of the Sheffield culture of the 1860s were the rugby playing teams that belonged to the RFU. These rugby playing clubs did not see themselves as commercial ventures and donated their gate money to various good causes. Such behaviour was typified by the Yorkshire RFU, which in 1891 handed over a total of £2,120 and 10 shillings to local charities.[108] The question as to how these rugby playing sides responded to the appearance of professionalism forms the subject of the last section of our chapter.

Amateurs, part-timers or professionals? The great split in the rugby game

As we have already seen, by the early 1880s rugby officials such as Hudson had become very disturbed by the increasing presence of commercial elements in their version of football. However, at this stage, unlike association football, the rugby game was far less affected by professionalism and while people were becoming increasingly sensitive towards the question of compensating players for wages they lost while training and playing, it had yet to erupt into a full-blown issue. In 1879 rugby's officials attempted to outlaw professionalism by banning direct payments to players. However, by conceding the right of players to receive compensatory payments for lost wages, 'expenses' as they were called, they had left ample room for difficulties.[109] Naturally, such an ambiguous category was open to abuse and rugby's officials were all too conscious that the legitimisation of professionalism in association football had resulted in the virtual eviction of amateur players from the highest reaches of the game. As Budd wrote,

> only six months after the legitimisation of the bastard we see two professional teams left to fight out the Cup Final tie. Gentlemen who play football once a week for a pastime will find themselves no match for men who give up their whole time and abilities to it.[110]

Rugby determined that it would not end up like association football and in October 1886 banned all expenses for rugby players:

> a man will be a professional and debarred from playing if he receives from his club or any member of it any money payment whatsoever, even for secretarian work or labour for his club, any recompense for loss of time, any training expenses.[111]

The RFU formulated laws against professionalism and the first of these declared that 'professionalism is illegal', while the second defined a professional as: 'Any player who shall receive from his club or any member of it a money consideration whatsoever, actual or prospective, for services rendered to the club of which he is a member'.[112] The RFU had the power to suspend for as long as they saw fit. any players or clubs who contravened these rules.

A number of attempts were made to rationalise the exclusion of professionalism, notably the observation by Vassall that the determined competitiveness of professionals was unsuitable for a game as potentially dangerous as rugby because it could result in violent injuries to others.[113] The writer Shearman was more realistic and noted 'if rugby gates ever prosper professionalism, either open or secret, will assuredly emerge'.[114] By the early 1890s rugby was a very popular sport in some areas, especially in the north, and in order to retain players some clubs wanted the restoration of the law that permitted them to recompense individuals by paying them 'expenses', or 'broken-time payments', as they had come to be called. However, in 1893 the RFU met in London, and having discussed the matter rejected the idea completely. Having done this, the RFU introduced draconian legislation that was designed to ensure that 'broken-time payments' were exterminated and threatened clubs who were suspected of such practices with expulsion.[115]

Inevitably, many northern clubs felt very threatened by this and such behaviour served only to magnify their frustration. As a consequence of this on 29 August 1895 a meeting was convened at Huddersfield and the Northern Rugby Football Union created. The new body opposed professionalism but supported the principle of 'payments for bona-fide broken-time only'.[116] To an extent the situation was not dissimilar to that confronting the FA in late 1884 when a large number of association football clubs from the north and midlands threatened to break away if the FA sought to ban professionalism. Early in 1885 the FA had elected to conciliate with the rebels and introduce a strictly controlled form of professionalism. As we have seen, once out of the bottle the genie of professional association football had a life of its own, and soon trampled over the barriers that the FA had tried to introduce. It is possible that such an experience influenced the attitude of the RFU in 1895, prompting them to adopt a completely different line to that of the FA. The RFU had no interest in conciliation with the rebels and instead became still more militant.

As far as the RFU officials were concerned the issue of 'broken-time payments' was a mere excuse, one observing, 'it is difficult to see why the working man

Figure 8.4 Picture of a match between Everton and Blackburn Rovers from *The Illustrated Sporting and Dramatic News* 21 October 1893, p. 218.

should be made the stalking horse for this innovation'.[117] Additionally, he pointed out that the county that had been keenest on introducing compensation for working men who had lost money through playing the game, Yorkshire, were precisely the same body who were responsible for increasing the number of fixtures. The writer did not accept that working men needed to be compensated for the wages that they lost through playing the game. Indeed, he was inclined to believe that if they could not afford to play they had no business doing so! Practically speaking, he regarded the provisions in the code of October 1886 which allowed clubs to insure players against accident with a 'recognised accidental insurance company' (the maximum payment to the player for injury being 6s a week) as providing all the legitimate financial backing that a player could reasonably expect.[118]

Primarily, the response of the RFU was a vigorous attack on professionalism, which was seen as destroying sportsmanship, and was clearly influenced by the writer's interpretation of the events that had been occurring within association football. As far as he was concerned association football had made a big mistake in mixing the two classes, amateurs and professionals, because professional play gave a 'premium on sharp practice as against straightforwardness'.[119] The writer thought it best that Yorkshire should create a professional rugby association of its own and maintained that 'if professional football is superior to amateur, it will kill the latter on its merits'.[120]

As can be seen, the split was far from amicable, and the RFU introduced draconian legislation against any club or player that was associated with the Northern Rugby Football Union.[121] For their part, the Northern Rugby Football Union endeavoured to occupy a half-way house, admitting the payment of legitimate expenses while continuing to oppose professionalism. Indeed, in a bizarre throw-back to the days of the RFU, they even endeavoured to prevent people from certain occupations, such as billiard markers, from joining clubs.[122] By 1898, the Northern Union gave up their struggle against professionalism and made it legal, though as with the early FA, they endeavoured to regulate it with numerous restrictions.[123]

In terms of popularity, during the first few seasons clubs in the Northern Rugby Football Union did very well financially and this prompted a wide-scale desertion from the RFU by clubs in the north. Ironically, the extent of this defection was such that by 1901 the Yorkshire Cup – the same trophy that Hudson had considered withdrawing in 1881 because of what he saw as the distasteful intrusion of commercialism, the competition that had previously been amongst the most popular of all RFU events, which had once attracted entries from 132 clubs – was reduced to a pale shadow of itself, with just eleven teams competing.[124] However, the actual extent of the transformation elicited by the Northern Rugby Football Union was probably far less than the bulk of its supporters envisaged. While the full recognition of professionalism by the NRFU was surely inevitable and certainly desirable from the point of view of clarification, for the vast bulk of players it probably had no more effect than a lenient application of the rule concerning 'broken-time payments' would have done. While at the highest levels a handful of players in the Northern Rugby Football Union did very well, earning wages that were comparable to those in association football, as Collins observes 'in general players continued the occupations they already had outside football'.[125] The truth was that the careers of professional rugby players were even more precarious than those of their compatriots in the association game and commentators such as Shearman believed that it was more sensible for players to keep a trade because the money gained as a professional simply provided them with an unreal standard of living that they could not hope to sustain.[126] In the wider perspective, the enormous growth in the popularity of association football towards the end of the century undermined the commercial prospects of rugby. This had a drastic effect on clubs within the Northern Rugby Football Union, many of whom suffered significant financial difficulties by the early 1900s.[127]

In the last quarter of the nineteenth century football attained the status of a significant commercial industry employing large numbers of professional and semi-professional players. While it would be mistaken to maintain that amateurs were evicted entirely from the highest reaches of the association game, (for many excellent amateur players and teams would continue to make an impact in the decades that followed), they were very much the exceptions and certainly no longer the rule. By 1900 association football was essentially a game for professionals, with amateurs being increasingly forced to restrict their attention to particular competitions in which the rules protected them from the impact of those who derived their living from the game. The situation in rugby football developed in an entirely different fashion. While amateurs and professionals remained within the rubric of the Football Association, the two groups of players were completely separated within the rugby game. From 1895 the RFU adopted a definition of amateur that was far too extreme for the taste of many northern clubs and this prompted their secession and the creation of a body that would eventually admit full professionalism. Far from being a broad church, rugby came to be administered by two adversarial associations, the Rugby Union and the Rugby League, split by the issue of professionalism.

9 Conclusions

The real history of the creation of modern football?

The established view of football was created in the nineteenth century by a number of writers, mostly former public schoolboys. The picture that they provided was very clear and claimed that there were essentially two varieties of football. One sort of game was very old, almost primeval, and found amongst the general population. This game had few, if any, rules and was essentially barbaric, typifying a society in which there was little order or restraint. The other sort of football was of more recent invention and had been created by those who were from the upper echelons of the social order, generally boys in public schools. These games were quite different to the older varieties, being governed by strict rules that ensured that violence was regulated. Gradually, with the march of economic and social progress, the older forms of football, which had been conducted by the general population, died out, almost to the point of extinction. By contrast, the more restrained forms of football that were conducted in public schools became increasingly sophisticated. By the middle decades of the nineteenth century these sophisticated versions of football were transplanted from the public schools into the wider society and would eventually become the modern sports that we now know as association and rugby football, having been rapidly adopted by the general population.

The big problem with such a convenient theory was that despite its clarity it did not accord with the evidence. As we have seen, the games of football that were conducted in the wider society independent of any public school influence were quite sophisticated, completely transcending the barbaric caricatures with which they were often misrepresented. While, initially speaking, the crucial role that the established model of football gave to the public schools in the creation of the modern game makes it easy to understand why members of these institutions adhered to such an explanation, its adoption by later historians requires other explanations. In the opinions of the author the willingness of later scholars to adopt these notions stemmed essentially from two reasons. The first related to a lack of information on the popularly played football games in the eighteenth and nineteenth centuries. Second, the scholars adhered to underlying developmental theories in which society gradually became more sophisticated. These theories manifested themselves in a variety of ideas, such as the 'taming' of society and the introduction of 'civilising' processes. Such conceptions meant that theorists were happy to accept the stereotyped picture of popularly played football as a rough, wild game governed by few rules. It was for this reason that the standard view of football survived. By contrast, this study argues for an alternative vision of the early history of modern football in Britain, regarding the game as being very much part of the existing sporting culture, emerging from a variety of influences that stemmed from both public schools and the wider society.

From at least the eighteenth century Britain possessed a sporting culture that contained a number of games that were played by professional and semi-professional competitors. These events were watched by large, paying audiences and conducted according to strict rules. As time progressed the number of these games expanded, including such sports as cockfighting, coursing, cricket, foot-racing, horse racing, pedestrianism, pugilism and wrestling, as did the level of the sophistication of the culture. While most of these sports were actively promoted and sometimes practised by the upper and middle ranks, the lower orders were perfectly capable of constructing very detailed rules to regulate their various sporting contests.[1] From the 1840s there is substantial evidence of quite sophisticated rules being used for football games in the wider society, including the use of referees, written codes, and such like. Curiously enough, despite the fact that during this period the middle classes were beginning to create clubs for sports such as wrestling, coursing, pedestrianism, foot-racing and cricket, there is little indication of their endeavouring to do so for football. This is surprising because they surely had an appetite for the game, as was manifest in the period after 1870, when football clubs enjoyed an astonishing growth.

While it seems likely that this receptivity to football had long been present within society, there are two plausible explanations for the failure of the middle classes to create football clubs. In the first place, although those members of the middle classes who had not been to public school did not understand the various codes that these highly prestigious institutions had created to regulate their football games, they were nonetheless aware of their existence and consequently intimidated by feelings of deference from attempting to establish a club that was based upon rules of their own devising. As for members of the middle classes who had attended public schools, the loyalty that these old boys felt for the football game of their particular foundation ensured that they were reluctant to play with members of other schools and this meant that the potential membership of football clubs was significantly restricted. Cumulatively, these two factors fragmented football and impeded its emergence.

The strongest support for this analysis is provided by the origins of the handful of middle-class clubs that did appear in the 1840s and 1850s. These were not independent creations but based upon other existing institutions, including Athenaeums, cricket clubs and such like. More significantly still, the first football culture that appeared in the wider society, Sheffield, contained two very important elements. In the first place, the members of Sheffield Football Club. stemmed from the elite middle class of the area and consequently enjoyed an immense local status which gave their football club significant social sanction. Additionally, there were almost no former public school boys within the team which meant that they were essentially neutral in their selection of rules. The high social status enjoyed by Sheffield FC and their pragmatic attitude towards rules ensured that the other clubs in the area that emerged in their wake adhered to the code that Sheffield had adopted, thus eliminating disputes over rules. As to the rules used by Sheffield, these can plausibly be seen as the product of local rather than public school influences.

While Sheffield demonstrates that a powerful football culture emerged in the provinces that was completely independent of the public schools, parallel developments in London during the early 1860s revealed a football world that was essentially the product of former public schoolboys. By contrast with the homogeneous culture of Sheffield, where the clubs used the same rules, football in London was highly fragmented, reflecting the spectrum of competing ideas from the various public school codes. In 1863 London's culture produced the Football Association, but within a matter of weeks this organisation fragmented into two warring factions, the rugby and association games. Until 1868 the FA was very weak, many of its problems stemming from the indifference and opposition of both the public schools and former public schoolboys. Significantly, but for the support that it received from Sheffield in 1867 the FA might very well have disbanded. In 1868 the FA adopted rules that were close to those used by two public schools, Charterhouse and Westminster, and this helped to bolster membership. However, over the next few years at least twelve aspects of this code proved inadequate and were replaced by rules that were drawn from provincial associations, especially Sheffield. Predominantly, it was the strong co-operation of the Sheffield Association, which was in no sense the product of the public school culture, that enabled the FA to become a significant force in the provinces. Given all this, there is something exceedingly ironic in the way that the public schools have been credited with the creation of modern association football, for their attitude towards the FA was often extremely obstructive.

While the role of the public schools in creating the rugby game might appear altogether more clear-cut, this is not the case. Throughout the 1860s the rugby game was afflicted by disputes over laws, there being no real consensus over issues such as 'hacking', and by 1871 the problem had become so great that the RFU was created to resolve these matters. Interestingly enough, Rugby School refused to involve itself with the RFU, despite the fact that those drawing up the code were old Rugbeians, and the School did not join this body until the 1890s. As for the rules themselves, while the reforms of 1871 prevented some of the disputes, in the years that followed extensive changes were introduced and many aspects of the game were transformed. While these changes enabled the RFU to retain unity, in 1895 the organisation suffered a dramatic split over the issue of payment for players, with a new rival body, the Northern Rugby Football Union, being created. From that time forth, for something like one hundred years, the rugby game was split into two camps, a public school oriented group, and another that adhered to values that the public school rejected entirely – professionalism.

An opposition to professionalism, and more broadly commercialism, was a key tenet of public school football of both varieties. In this, they were fully in accord with their contemporary, the dominant provincial football culture of Sheffield.

In the 1860s footballers in the Sheffield region rejected the commercial element of the game. In this they differed profoundly from the football cultures present in the wider community between 1830 and 1859, which had generally embraced the use of stakes. By the latter half of the 1870s a more sophisticated version of this earlier, more money-based culture would soon supersede that of the public schools and Sheffield. The publicans who had sponsored football matches to attract customers in the 1840s would be replaced by financial interests keen on generating gate money from spectators. Such entrepreneurs would hire the best players they could in order to ensure that large crowds were drawn, and the money that these professionals earned would have dwarfed their share of any stakes they might have won in the earlier period. By the early 1880s this commercial culture had become a major force in football and in 1883, with the victory of Blackburn Olympic over the Old Etonians in the FA Cup final, the supremacy enjoyed by the public school amateurs on the field was ended. Two years later the association game legalised professionalism and from that time onwards the influence of the public schools on association football receded. The impact of professionalism on rugby appears to have been slower and more diluted but by 1895 the only way that the RFU could prevent such an intrusion was to resort to draconian legislation, which split the rugby game in two.

The role of the public schools in the creation of both association and rugby football, particularly in regard to the former brand, was highly ambiguous. While on the one hand the public schools generated ideas for rules, they also nourished division and impeded the creation of national codes. Ultimately, the construction of laws for football that would embrace the whole country involved the neutralising of rivals as much as the assembling of new ideas. In view of this, evidence indicates that both rugby and association football were created by a mixture of influences, stemming from both inside and outside the walls of the public schools. In terms of supremacy, the public schools were predominant in association football from about 1868 to 1883. With regard to rugby, their hold might debatably be extended to 1895, though by then many of the best footballers did not hail from public schools. However, the creation of the Northern Rugby Football Union in 1895 led to the appearance of an altogether more expert game. By then, of course, the amateurs of the RFU did not have to compete against them. Indeed, the rules of the RFU forbade them from doing so and thus preserved a Victorian social framework in aspic.[2]

Appendix

Football as an international game

As we saw in Chapter 3, football was played in a number of countries long before there was any attempt to codify it in Britain. The story of the dissemination of the game outside the shores of Britain generally focuses on the twentieth century, examples being adduced from Asia, Europe and America. In this brief section we are interested in the presence of football outside Britain during the nineteenth century, endeavouring to add new information to the publicly available record.[1] The following list of countries is provided in alphabetical rather than chronological order and the aim is to highlight the fact that even at this early period football was well on its way to becoming an international game. The English were particularly influential on the Continent. For instance, in 1899 five different soccer teams toured Europe: Oxford University visited Vienna and Prague, East Sheen – Paris, Tunbridge Wanderers – Holland, Tunbridge Wells – Belgium, and a team assembled by the FA – called English Wanderers – Germany.[2]

Argentina

The British formed Buenos Aires FC in 1865. In 1891 Argentina commenced their annual soccer championship.

Australia

In 1858 a club was created in Melbourne, the players agreeing to a code that had many similarities with what would later become that of the FA. By 1864 football had become very popular in Australia, there being many clubs.[3]

Austro-Hungarian Empire

A number of clubs were founded in the final decades of the century, notably Ujpesti (1885), MTK (1888) and Ferencvaros (1895) in Hungary, and Slavia Prague (1893) and Sparta Prague (1893) in Czechoslovakia. A large British community lived in Vienna and they introduced association football to the local population. The game enjoyed a substantial boost in Vienna when Southampton FC visited in 1900. The most significant organisational developments in association football occurred in 1896 in Czechoslovakia, with the creation of a league, and in 1901 in Hungary, where a football association was founded.

Belgium

The Royal Antwerp club was founded in 1880 and a football association created in 1895.

Bolivia

The Oruro Royal Club was founded in 1896 by a Chilean.

Brazil

During the 1880s British influence, by way of railway workers or visiting sailors, disseminated association football. However, the major breakthrough came near the end of the nineteenth century when a British resident persuaded the Sao Paulo Athletics Club to commence a football section. In 1895 the Flamengo club was founded.

Canada

Teams of British soldiers from the Grenadier Guards and Fusiliers who were based in Montreal conducted matches using the code of Eton College in both 1862 and 1866.[4] Montreal FC was created in 1868. In the 1870s McGill University Montreal introduced a handling game using an oval ball and went on to conduct an influential match against Harvard in 1874 that led to the creation of a separate game that we now know as American football. Despite this, soccer prospered and in 1880 a team from Canada toured Britain.[5] Indeed, by 1881 there were sixty soccer clubs in Ontario alone.[6] In 1886 there was a soccer match between Canada and the USA.

Central and Eastern Africa

Army influence introduced football into Africa, notably the stimulus given to soccer in Uganda by captain Pulteney.[7]

Chile

Valparaiso FC was founded in 1889 via British influence.

China

From the 1840s football was played by the British in the treaty ports of Shanghai, Canton and Hong Kong.[8] Shanghai was the main centre of activity and in 1863

Figure A.1 By the 1880s teams from the dominions were visiting Britain to play football. Taken from *Pictorial World* 23 October 1888. Canada play Old Carthusians.

a club was created there consisting of players from Aberdeen, Belfast, Cambridge, Dublin, Eton, Glasgow and Harrow. After 'great difficulty' rules were created to unite these players, the code being 'much the same as the Football Association's'.[9] However, many of those who joined the club insisted on using elements of the rugby school code, especially running carrying the ball, and as late as 1868 this was still a matter of contention.[10] The rugby code was particularly popular amongst the Navy and towards the end of the century they instituted an annual cup competition in Kowloon.[11]

Columbia

Football was played in Bogota in 1887, developing via European influence.

Denmark

A great many English footballers visited Denmark during the nineteenth century and inspired by their influence the association variety of the game enjoyed considerable popularity. By 1876 this had reached the point where the first formally organised club were set up, K. B. Copenhagen.

Finland

The English introduced soccer in 1890.[12]

France

In 1863 Bois de Boulogne Athletics and Football Club was created by English businessmen living in Paris. Evidently such a venture was a real novelty in France, requiring the express permission of the authorities, who were 'surprised' at the whole thing. The club was regarded as providing an excellent opportunity for its members to mix with others, especially those who were above them socially. The rules that the club settled on were 'principally those from Rugby School', though the goals that they used did not have a crossbar.[13] This was the earliest football club in France and was followed by another club created by English residents, Le Havre Athletic Club, founded in 1872. Like many of the football teams that were to succeed them, Le Havre was a sports club that included a number of activities. During the last quarter of the nineteenth century three varieties of football were played there, rugby, soccer and combination (a game that fused the other two). The first indigenous football teams in France were Racing-Club de France (1886 – they played rugby) and Le Club Francais (1892 – they played soccer).[14]

Germany

The first major attention that football received in Germany was in 1875, when Oxford University toured. Interest in football gradually grew but it was not until

1887 that the first formally constituted football club, Germania Hamburg, was created. Other sides, such as TSV 1860 Munich, gradually emerged, a football section being established from the general gymnastics organisation. In 1900 the German FA was established.

Greece

In 1863 Piraeus in Greece was the venue for a match between two teams of British naval officers, from the Marlborough and the Trafalgar ships respectively, using the rules of Eton College.[15]

Holland

English sides often toured there and both rugby and association football was played. An association for soccer was founded in 1889 and in 1898 a league championship was created.

India

At Bangalore in 1862 British officers from infantry and cavalry regiments played one another at football under rules that appear to have stemmed from Harrow School.[16] In 1872 a football club was established at Calcutta by British residents.[17] By the 1890s British soldiers stationed at Poona were staging an annual cup competition.[18] Football amongst the indigenous population was often derived from the British-influenced educational system. By the 1880s there were a number of indigenous clubs, notably Mohun Bagan.[19]

Ireland

Ulster FC were founded in Belfast in 1878, they played rugby. The first soccer club in Ireland was Cliftonville, founded in 1879. In 1880 Ireland created an organisation to supervise association football.

Italy

British influence led to the creation of a number of clubs in Italy, notably the Torino club (in 1890), Genoa Cricket and Football club in 1893 and Milan Cricket and Football club in 1899.[20]

Japan

British visitors played football in Yokohama in 1873.[21]

New Zealand

By 1863 football was very popular in New Zealand, clubs being formed at Christchurch and Lyttleton.[22] In 1891 a national organisation for association football was established.

Figure A.2 From 1872, when a club was founded at Calcutta, football, largely of the rugby variety, was very popular in this part of British India. Taken from *The Illustrated Sporting and Dramatic News* 13 November 1875, p. 149.

Figure A.3 In the hill station at Poona an annual cup competition was contested between the various regiments playing association football. It is noticeable that all but one of the team were privates. From *The Illustrated Sporting and Dramatic News* 21 October 1893, p. 211.

Norway

There was a lot of soccer played in Norway during the final portion of the nineteenth century and in 1902 an association was created, Norges Fotbalforbund, to regulate it.

Ottoman Empire

The first football game in Turkey during the nineteenth century was conducted between English and Greek students at Izmir. The activity was regarded as subversive, attracting the attention of the secret police![23] The game was introduced into Bulgaria by a Swiss physical education instructor, who started a class teaching association football at a school in Varna in 1894. British engineers introduced association football into Rumania during the 1880s.[24]

Paraguay

The Dutch brought football to the country in the nineteenth century.

Portugal

In the 1870s British residents introduced football into Lisbon, and in 1875 a club was established there.

Russia

In the 1880s British engineers working in the coal fields introduced association football into Russia. The St Petersburg club was founded in 1897.

South Africa

The first club was Pietermaritzburg County, that was founded in 1879. In 1882 the Natal Association was created and in 1892 the Cape Province Association. In 1892 the Football Association of South Africa was established. The game spread amongst the indigenous population and in 1899 the 'Kaffirs of Orange Free State' toured England.[25]

Spain

In the late nineteenth century British mining engineers introduced football. It was particularly popular in the Basque region and the first club to be created in Spain was Athletic Club de Bilboa in 1898.[26]

Sweden

The first club to be established there was Örgryte IS in 1887. In 1895 a Swedish Football Association was created.

Switzerland

In 1866 there was a match between Lausanne and Geneva with all eleven players on each side being British.[27] In 1869 English students at Le Châteline College Geneva played the game. The earliest club to be established was St Gallen in 1879.

United States

The first American footballer whose name we know is John Greenwood, who in 1846 played the role of 'backgroundsman' in a match in England between two teams from Lancashire, Charlestown and Boston.[28] Judging by press coverage, football soon became popular in America, with books such as *Tom Brown's Schooldays* (1857) enjoying enormous commercial popularity.[29] The Oneida FC was founded in Boston in 1862. The Princeton rules were created by the universities of Yale, Columbia, Rutgers and Princeton in 1873. The North Americans were leaning increasingly towards a rugby-oriented game, and this was significantly amplified by the two matches that Harvard played against Montreal's McGill University in 1874. From then on the most influential football in America was a handling game, using an oval shaped ball, which eventually became what we now know as American football. By the 1880s high quality periodicals in Boston (*New England Magazine*), New York (*Munsey's*, *Nation*, *Outing*) and Philadelphia (*Lippincott's*) were devoting articles to the American version of the game. As for the British, it was not until 1897 that the American football received any attention and then it was the robust nature of the game that caught the eye, especially the fact that players took the field wearing what were portrayed as suits of armour![30] In 1884 an association was formed for soccer and in 1886 a soccer international played against Canada.

Uruguay

The Albion FC was established at Montevideo by an English professor in 1882.

Notes

1 What football was not: the history of Shrove-football

1 S. Tischler, *Footballers and Businessmen. The Origins of Professional Soccer in England* (London: Holmes & Meier, 1981) p. 11.
2 F. Magoun, *History of Football: From the Beginnings to 1871* (Bochum-Langendreer, 1938) p. 57 refers to a game with seven players on each side in 1683.
3 R. Malcolmson, *Popular Recreations in English Society 1700–1850* (Cambridge: Cambridge University Press, 1973) pp. 57, 59, 67, 73–4, 84–5, 88, 100–1, 107, 113, 168.
4 R. Malcolmson, *Popular Recreations in English Society 1700–1850*, p. 171.
5 R. Malcolmson, *Popular Recreations in English Society 1700–1850*, p. 117.
6 B. Harrison, *Drink and the Victorians* (London: Faber and Faber, 1971) p. 331.
7 There is strong evidence that from at least the French wars (1793–1815) organised sport was occurring on a regular basis throughout Britain according to a timetable that was not limited to annually staged events. On the contrary, the bulk of sporting events can be classified as 'weekly', that is they occurred according to a recreational timetable of their own, unrelated to established annual holidays. See A. Harvey, *The Evolution of Modern British Sporting Culture 1793–1850* (DPhil Oxford University, 1995) pp. 43, 49, 71. Contra W. Vamplew, *Pay up and Play the Game: Professional Sport in Britain 1875–1914* (Cambridge: Cambridge University Press, 1988) pp. 43, 316. Vamplew believes that there is no evidence that commercialised sports were organised regularly or available to the bulk of the population until at least the 1830s.
8 Both these issues are examined in H. Cunningham, *Leisure in the Industrial Revolution 1780–1880* (London: Croom Helm) pp. 20–7.
9 See various editions of R. Burn, *Justice of the Peace* (London: H. Miller). As late as 1830, vol. v, p. 20 records bull-baiting as legal. Prize-fighting is not mentioned as illegal until the 1869 edition, vol. v, p. 145, the first cited case being 1831.
10 A. Alison, *Principles of the Criminal Law of Scotland* (Edinburgh: T Cadell, 1832) p. 511.
11 C. Emsley, *Crime and Society in England 1750–1900* (London: Longmans, 1987) pp. 171, 181.
12 J. Golby and A. Purdue, *The Civilisation of the Crowd. Popular Culture in England 1750–1900* (London: Batsford, 1984) pp. 26–7.
13 *Bill to facilitate the formation and establishment of public walks, play grounds, baths and places of healthy recreation and amusement in the open air.* 16 July 1835, p. 5.
14 H. Cunningham, *Leisure in the Industrial Revolution 1780–1880*, pp. 93–6. A rich source of documented evidence on the erosion of recreational areas can be found in J. Hammond and B. Hammond, *The Age of the Chartists 1832–1859* (London: Longmans, 1930) pp. 106, 110–12, 114–15, 119, 121–43.
15 E. Hopkins, 'Working hours and conditions during the industrial revolution. A reappraisal', *Ec HR* 35:1 (1982) pp. 65–6.

16 D. Reid, 'The decline of St Monday 1766–1876', *P&P* 71 (1976) pp. 80–1, 86, 100–1.
17 N. Crafts, 'British economic growth 1700–1831: a review of the evidence'. *Ec HR* 36:2 (1983) pp. 198–9. M. Flinn, 'Comment on Lindert and Williamson' *Ec HR* 37:1 (1984) pp. 88–92. P. Lindert and J. Williamson, 'English workers living standards during the industrial revolution: a new look' *Ec HR* 36:1 (1983) pp. 23–5.
18 The view that during the first half of the nineteenth century popular recreations declined sharply has been criticised by many scholars, notably Cunningham and Holt, the latter declaring that 'there was no vacuum in the history of popular recreations because many traditional sports and recreations survived and often evolved' H. Cunningham, *Leisure in the Industrial Revolution 1780–1880*, p. 22. R. Holt, *Sport and the British: A Modern History* (Oxford: OUP, 1989) p. 349.
19 See E. Dunning and K. Sheard, *Barbarians, Gentlemen and Players* (Oxford: Martin Robertson, 1979) p. 43.
20 F. Magoun, *History of Football: From the Beginnings to 1871*, p. 144.
21 R. Malcolmson, *Popular Recreations in English Society 1700–1850*, pp. 138–41.
22 *Bill to consolidate and amend the laws relating to highways in that part of great Britain called England*, 24 January 1831.
23 *PR 2021*, Lancashire record office.
24 S. Phillips, 'Primitive Methodist confrontation with popular sports: case study of early nineteenth century Staffordshire'. In R. Cashman and M. Mckernan (eds) *Sport, Money, Morality and the Media* (New South Wales: Queensland, 1980) pp. 289–90.
25 *Edinburgh Evening News* 19 February 1910. *Glasgow Herald* 2 January 1897. *Jedburgh Gazette* 2 February, 23 February, 2 March 1834. *Yorkshire Post* 19 February 1896.
26 F. Magoun, *History of Football: From the beginnings to 1871*, pp. 135–6. It is possible that the gulf might have been even wider, for it has been claimed that the earliest mention of football in Britain was in 1175. See *N&Q* 6th series xi (April 1885) p. 436. The first Shrove-game that is mentioned was at Chester in 1533.
27 *Manchester and Salford Advertiser* 25 September 1847.
28 *Manchester and Salford Advertiser* 25 July 1846.
29 *Bell's Life in London* 9 February 1845. J. Thorne, *Handbook of the Environs of London* (1876, reprinted London 1983) p. 401.
30 *Bell's Life in London* 7 March 1830. *Northern Examiner* 3 March 1855.
31 H. Hutchinson, *Blackwoods* vol. 153, p. 758.
32 *Bell's Life in London* 10 April 1825.
33 *The Constitutional* 8 January 1836. *Sporting Magazine* February 1836, p. 308.
34 *N&Q* vol. 160 (1931) p. 849.
35 *Dumfries Weekly Journal* 17 January 1826.
36 *Derby Mercury* 28 February 1827.
37 *Penny Magazine* vol. 8, 6 April 1839, p. 132.
38 *The Sporting Magazine* December 1815, pp. 141–2.
39 *The Sporting Magazine* July 1830, pp. 224, 228.
40 *The Sporting Magazine* July 1830, p. 227.
41 *Derby and Chesterfield Reporter* 16 February 1832; 9 February, 8 March 1844. *Derby Mercury* 28 February, 6 March 1844.
42 *Pioneer* 1 February 1834, pp. 81–2, 22 February 1834, p. 215.
43 A. Delves, 'Popular recreation and social conflict in Derby 1800–50'. In E. Yeo and S. Yeo (eds) *Popular Culture and Class Conflict 1590–1914* (London: Harvester, 1981) p. 106.
44 *Derby and Chesterfield Reporter* 7 February 1845.
45 Ibid.
46 *Derby Advertiser and Journal* 11 February, 25 February 1846.
47 *Manchester Examiner and Times* 20 February 1849.
48 *Derby and Chesterfield Reporter* 16 February 1832; 7 February 1845.
49 *HO45/05 2923*.

50 *Bell's Life in London* 20 April 1845. *Derby and Chesterfield Reporter* 27 February, 6 March 1846.
51 A. Delves, 'Popular recreation and social conflict in Derby 1800–50'. In E. Yeo and S. Yeo (eds) *Popular Culture and Class Conflict 1590–1914*, p. 94.
52 A. Delves, 'Popular recreation and social conflict in Derby 1800–50'. In E. Yeo and S. Yeo (eds) *Popular Culture and Class Conflict 1590–1914*, p. 92.
53 A. Delves, 'Popular recreation and social conflict in Derby 1800–50'. In E. Yeo and S. Yeo (eds) *Popular Culture and Class Conflict 1590–1914*, p. 93.
54 28 February 1846. The paper reprinted, without comment, a report from the *Derby Mercury* that was very hostile to football. Additionally, during the period nowhere in the copious letter columns of the Chartist paper is there a single reference to the threat posed by the suppression of the Shrove-game.
55 *Derby and Chesterfield Reporter* 27 February 1846. See also the mayor's speech *Derby Mercury* 4 March 1846.
56 *Derby and Chesterfield Reporter* 27 February, 6 March 1846, *Derby Mercury* 25 February 1846. *The Derby Advertiser and Journal* 4 March 1846 records that one of the defendants, Samuel Pipes was bailed for £20. Elsewhere in the report it is noted that both his father and his employer gave him a 'good character'. His employer was Mr Pipes, who was a special constable.
57 A. Delves, 'Popular recreation and social conflict in Derby 1800–50'. In E. Yeo and S. Yeo (eds) *Popular Culture and Class Conflict 1590–1914*, pp. 103–4.
58 *Bell's Life in London* 9 February 1845, *Surrey Comet and Kingston Gazette* 9 February 1856, *Surrey Standard* 20 February 1836.
59 *Illustrated Times* 27 February 1858. *Surrey Comet and Kingston Gazette* 7 February 1857; 13 February 1858.
60 Disputes appear to have broken out between inn-keepers over the trade stemming from the game. *Sporting Magazine* April 1830, p. 369, May 1830, pp. 33–4.
61 *Surrey Comet and Kingston Gazette* 2 March 1867.
62 *Surrey Comet and Kingston Gazette* 9 March 1867.
63 *Surrey Comet and Kingston Gazette* 29 February 1868.
64 *Ashbourne News* 4 March 1927. However, the game was occasionally attacked, notably *Derbyshire Advertiser and Journal* 25 February 1846.
65 *Ashbourne News* 4 March 1927. *Derby Mercury* 15, 22, 29 February, 7 March 1860.
66 *Derby Mercury* 6 March 1861. *Sheffield and Rotherham Independent* 9 March 1861.
67 *Derbyshire Advertiser and Journal* 20 February 1863. *Derby Mercury* 6 March 1861; 12 March 1862.
68 *Ashbourne News* 4 March 1927. See, for instance, *Field* 3 March 1888.
69 *Surrey Comet and Kingston, Richmond and Epsom Gazette* 28 February 1857.
70 *Times* 2 March 1840.
71 P. Ditchfield, *Old English Customs Extant at the Present Time* (London: Methuen, 1896) p. 66.
72 *N&Q* vol. 3, 6th series (1881) p. 207.
73 18 February 1888.
74 *Bell's Life in London* 12 March 1854.
75 *Times* 2 March 1840.
76 *HO45/1800*. Letter from mayor dated 6 February 1847.
77 This example contradicts R. Malcolmson, *Popular Recreations in English Society 1700–1850*, p. 143, who maintains that one of the main objections to Shrove-football was the interruption that it caused to 'the normal routines of business'.
78 *Alnwick and County Gazette and Guardian* 25 February 1928.
79 *Field* 13 February 1864.
80 *Derbyshire Times and Chesterfield Herald* 9 February 1856.
81 *Derby Mercury* 28 February 1827.

2 Entertaining the social elite: football in the public schools and universities 1555–1863

1 *Sporting Magazine* May 1802, p. 77.
2 E. Mack, *Public Schools and British Opinion 1780–1860* (London: Methuen, 1938) p. 39.
3 E. Mack, *Public Schools and British Opinion 1780–1860*, p. 223.
4 E. Mack, *Public Schools and British Opinion 1780–1860*, pp. 73, 77.
5 E. Mack, *Public Schools and British opinion 1780–1860*, pp. 79, 80, 83. Throughout the first half of the nineteenth century most of the great schools were beset by at least one rebellion. A good indication of the problems confronting masters can be gleaned from Charterhouse, where there were only seven resident masters and almost five hundred boys. G. Davies, *Charterhouse in London* (London: Murray, 1921) p. 295.
6 T. Chandler, Origins of Athleticism. Games in the English Public School 1800–89 (unpublished PhD Stanford University 1984) p. 76.
7 M. Shearman, *Athletics and Football* (London: Longman, 1889) pp. 46–8. Two of the earliest schools to stage sporting events were Rugby (the crick run) and Shrewsbury School (steeplechase) both in 1837.
8 M. Shearman, *Athletics and Football*, p. 41.
9 M. Shearman, *Athletics and Football*, p. 48.
10 M. Shearman, *Athletics and Football*, p. 49.
11 A. Bain, 'English university education', *Westminster Review* iii (1848) p. 453.
12 G. Davies, *Charterhouse in London*, p. 268.
13 G. Davies, *Charterhouse in London*, p. 295.
14 G. Davies, *Charterhouse in London*, pp. 268–9.
15 *Bell's Life in London* 30 November 1862. *Charterhouse Football Register 1862*, pp. 13–19. 'The Cloister game was almost entirely limited to matches inside the school, e.g. the Sixth v Twenty of the School, or Singers v Non-Singers'. E. Jameson, *Charterhouse* (London and Glasgow: Blackie & Sons, 1937) p. 37.
16 *Charterhouse Football Register 1862*, pp. 13–19.
17 F. Magoun, *History of Football: From the Beginnings to 1871* (Bochum-Langendreer, 1938) p. 79.
18 L. Cust, A *History of Eton College* (London: Spottiswoode & Co, 1899) p. 247. Despite the presence of football at Eton since ancient times the documentary record is 'short and simple'.
19 *Eton College Magazine* vii (November 1832) p. 221.
20 R. A(usten) L(eigh), *Upon St Andrews Day 1841–1901* (Eton, 1902) p. viii.
21 H. Maxwell Lyte, A *History of Eton College* (London: Macmillan, 1911) p. 322.
22 *Eton College Magazine* viii (December 1832) p. 284.
23 M. Shearman, *Athletics and Football*, pp. 284–7.
24 M. Shearman (ed.) *Football* (London: Oakley & Co, 1904) pp. 36–45.
25 L. Cust, A *History of Eton College*, p. 247.
26 *Eton College Magazine* viii (October 1832) p. 140.
27 They were discovered by Graham Curry. E. Dunning, 'Something of a curate's egg', *IJHS* 18: 4 (December 2001) p. 94.
28 H. Maxwell Lyte, A *History of Eton College*, pp. 488, 561.
29 L. Cust, A *History of Eton College*, p. 248.
30 R. A(usten) L(eigh), *Upon St Andrews Day* 1841–1901 (Eton, 1902) p. vii.
31 *Eton College Magazine* viii (December 1832) p. 284.
32 M. Shearman (ed.) *Football*, pp. 49–60.
33 *Eton College Magazine* viii (December 1832) p. 283.
34 An Old Colleger, *Eton of Old, or Eighty Years Since 1811–1822* (London: Hamilton & Adams, 1892) pp. 115–17.

35 *Bell's Life in London*, 16 October 1842; 22 October 1848; 23 November 1856.
36 R. A(usten) L(eigh), *Upon St Andrews Day 1841–1901* (Eton, 1902) p. v.
37 An Old Colleger, *Eton of Old, or Eighty Years Since 1811–22*, pp. 115–16.
38 R. A(usten) L(eigh), *Upon St Andrews Day 1841–1901* (Eton, 1902) pp. vi, vii.
39 R. A(usten) L(eigh), *Upon St Andrews Day 1841–1901* (Eton, 1902) p. viii.
40 R. A(usten) L(eigh), *Upon St Andrews Day 1841–1901* (Eton, 1902) p. v.
41 R. A(usten) L(eigh), *Upon St Andrews Day 1841–1901* (Eton, 1902) p. viii.
42 R. A(usten) L(eigh), *Upon St Andrews Day 1841–1901* (Eton, 1902) p. x.
43 *Bell's Life in London* 16, 30 November 1850.
44 R. A(usten) L(eigh), *Upon St Andrews Day 1841–1901* (Eton, 1902) p. x.
45 From 1856 the positions of players began to appear in reports. *Bell's Life in London* 28 September 1856. Reports in *The Field* commenced 20 November 1858.
46 *Bell's Life in London* 8 October 1848; 2 December 1849; 6 October, 8 December 1850.
47 The first to be recorded was in *Bell's Life in London* 19 October 1851; 3 October 1852.
48 *Bell's Life in London* 29 November 1857.
49 An Old Colleger, *Eton of Old, or Eighty Years Since 1811–22* p. 220. A somewhat more positive emphasis is given to the attitude of masters at Eton by M. Marples, *A History of Football* (London: Secker & Warburg, 1954) p. 120.
50 *Bell's Life in London* 5 December 1841.
51 *Bell's Life in London* 13 November 1842.
52 *Bell's Life in London* 23 November 1850; 18 November 1860.
53 C. Wordsworth *Annals of my Early Life* (London: Longman, 1891) p. 9.
54 *Bell's Life in London* 23 October 1842. The first report in *The Field* was on 27 November 1858.
55 J. Mangan, *Athleticism in the Victorian and Edwardian Public School* (Cambridge: Cambridge University Press, 1981) pp. 32–4.
56 *Bell's Life in London* 31 October 1850.
57 *Bell's Life in London* 12 November 1848; 6 November 1851.
58 J. Fisher Williams, *Harrow* (London: Great Public Schools, 1901) pp. 164–5.
59 *Bell's Life in London* 8 November 1857; 20 November 1859.
60 *Bell's Life in London* 2 December 1860.
61 *Bell's Life in London* 9 March 1862.
62 *Bell's Life in London* 14 November 1863.
63 J. Fisher Williams, *Harrow*, pp. 177–8.
64 J. Fisher Williams, *Harrow*, p. 178.
65 J. Fisher Williams, *Harrow*, p. 178.
66 M. Shearman (ed.) *Football*, pp. 64–71.
67 *Bell's Life in London* 23 November 1851. This was several months earlier than those that Rugby School began to send.
68 *Bell's Life in London* 8 April 1855. Fowler was a good player and was again praised on 9 March 1856.
69 *Bell's Life in London* 2 April 1854.
70 *Bell's Life in London* 30 November 1856.
71 J. Honey, *Tom Brown's Universe* (London: Millington, 1977) p. 105.
72 J. Mangan, *Athleticism in the Victorian and Edwardian Public School*, pp. 24–8.
73 J. Honey, *Tom Brown's Universe*, p. 109.
74 C. Evers, *Rugby* (London and Glasgow: Blackie & Sons, 1939) p. 155.
75 A. J. Lawrence, *The Origins of Rugby Football. Report of the Sub Committee of the Old Rugbeian Society* (Rugby, 1897) p. 7.
76 *The Meteor* 157 (22 December 1880) pp. 155–6.
77 Bloxham's original account in 1876 claimed that Ellis performed the feat in 1824. When Bloxham rewrote his account in 1880 he changed this date to 1823 for the very good reason that Ellis had left Rugby by 1824. Compare *The Meteor* accounts of 10 October 1876 and 22 December 1880.

78 A. J. Lawrence, *The Origins of Rugby Football. Report of the Sub Committee of the Old Rugbeian Society* (Rugby, 1897) pp. 21–2.

79 A. J. Lawrence, *The Origins of Rugby Football. Report of the Sub Committee of the Old Rugbeian Society* (Rugby, 1897) p. 22. The committee that met in 1895 to consider the issue conceded that 'we have been unable to procure any first hand evidence of the occurrence' (p. 11) and the nearest they could get to substantiating evidence was a claim by Harris that 'Ellis was known for taking unfair advantage at football'. Given that in 1823 Harris was aged just ten, and was giving evidence over seventy years later, one is entitled to be sceptical, especially as Harris does not even claim to have heard of the story of Ellis's invention of the game, much less witnessed it. Indeed, Harris was reluctant to make any contribution to the enquiry and requested that the committee 'should not quote him as an authority' (p. 21). Given all this, there is no reason for accepting the supposed invention of the rugby game by Ellis in 1823. There is an interesting and spirited defence of the Webb Ellis story by J. Macrory, *Running with the Ball: The Birth of Rugby Football* (London: Collins Willow, 1991) pp. 29–36. However, there is no sustained attempt to explain the lack of supporting evidence for the theory and the assertion on p. 36 that 'all the evidence supports their (i.e. the committee assembled in 1895) findings' is patently absurd because the committee were unable to find anyone who had even known someone who had witnessed Ellis's exploit.

80 However, despite his efforts, Arnold failed to control such problems as bullying and poaching. E. Mack, *Public Schools and British Opinion 1780–1860*, p. 239.

81 E. Dunning and K. Sheard, *Barbarians, Gentlemen and Players* (Oxford: Martin Robertson, 1979) p. 77.

82 E. Dunning and K. Sheard, *Barbarians, Gentlemen and Players*, p. 78.

83 E. Dunning and K. Sheard, *Barbarians, Gentlemen and Players*, p. 77. They write that Arnold's attack on field sports, was 'connected with his general opposition to the aristocracy'.

84 E. Dunning and K. Sheard, *Barbarians, Gentlemen and Players*, pp. 84–5, 90.

85 E. Dunning and K. Sheard, *Barbarians, Gentlemen and Players*, p. 86.

86 E. Dunning and K. Sheard, *Barbarians, Gentlemen and Players*, p. 89.

87 The extent of Arnold's involvement in sport is probably summed up by Arbuthnot, who writes that 'Arnold encouraged us to play it'. A. Arbuthnot, *Memories of Rugby and India* (London: Allen & Unwin, 1910) p. 31. To the author's knowledge the only piece of evidence that can be offered to support Arnold's adherence to an educational ideology involving team games stems from the following fragment of a biography of Arnold that was composed by Walrond, the head boy at Rugby in 1842: 'his hearty interest in the school games, which he looked upon as an integral part of education'. Given that Walrond's biography was over 4,000 words long and that this is the only reference that it has to sport, it is fairly clear that the topic was extremely minor, even in the opinion of Walrond. *Dictionary of National Biography* ii (London, 1885) p. 587.

88 The author would like to thank Dr Andrew Sanders (then of Birkbeck College) for alerting him to the significance of Arnold's failure to attend the end-of-year cricket match.

89 *Edinburgh Review* (January 1858) p. 190.

90 E. Mack, *Public Schools and British Opinion 1780–1860*, p. 337. J. Mangan, *Athleticism in the Victorian and Edwardian Public School*, pp. 16–18.

91 E. Dunning and K. Sheard, *Barbarians, Gentlemen and Players*, p. 75.

92 E. Dunning and K. Sheard, *Barbarians, Gentlemen and Players*, p. 76.

93 *Bell's Life in London* 5 December 1841.

94 Old Rugbeian, *Recollections of Rugby* (London: Hamilton & Adams, 1848). The Old Rugbeian was C. H. Newmarch. According to *Notes and Queries* (January/June 1909) p. 355, Newmarch was an unreliable source who knew little about the School.

95 T. Hughes, *Tom Brown's School Days* (London, 1857) bk 1 ch 5. For the opinion of others see: M. Marples, A *History of Football*, pp. 114, 116–17, and E. Dunning and K. Sheard, *Barbarians, Gentlemen and Players*, pp. 88–9.

96 A. J. Lawrence, *The Origins of Rugby Football. Report of the Sub Committee of the Old Rugbeian Society* (Rugby, 1897) pp. 12–13.

97 Old Rugbeian, *Recollections of Rugby*, p. 130.

98 Old Rugbeian, *Recollections of Rugby*, pp. 130–1.

99 Old Rugbeian, *Recollections of Rugby*, p. 131. It is quite possible that this passage was the source for the passage in T. Hughes, *Tom Brown's School Days* (London, 1857) bk 1 ch 5, beginning with 'There is none of the colour and tastiness'.

100 T. Hughes, *Tom Brown's School Days* (London, 1857) bk 1 ch 5.

101 W. Rouse, *History of Rugby School* (London: Duckworth, 1898) p. 238. Naturally, Arbuthnot's evidence must be treated with caution because it was composed long after the events that he is endeavouring to describe.

102 J. Macrory, *Running with the Ball: The Birth of Rugby Football*, pp. 80–1.

103 A Rugbeian, *Football: The First Day of the Sixth Match* (Rugby, 1851) pp. 7, 22. Rugbeian was W. D. Arnold's alias.

104 *Bell's Life in London* 23 October 1853. A Rugbeian, *Football: The first day of the sixth match* (Rugby, 1851) p. 22. We are told that the game commenced on 26 September 1846 and finished on 1 October.

105 A Rugbeian, *Football: The First Day of the Sixth Match* (Rugby, 1851) p. 20.

106 A Rugbeian, *Football: The First Day of the Sixth Match* (Rugby, 1851) p. 18.

107 A Rugbeian, *Football: The First Day of the Sixth Match* (Rugby, 1851) p. 19.

108 A Rugbeian, *Football: The First Day of the Sixth Match* (Rugby, 1851) p. 19. Elsewhere it was reported that in 1846, while it was only legal to run with the ball in your hands if you had caught it directly from the foot or on the bounce, in practice it was common for players to pick up a rolling ball and run with it. W. Rouse, *History of Rugby School*, p. 321.

109 E. Dunning and K. Sheard, *Barbarians, Gentlemen and Players*, p. 92. The rules compiled in 1845 can be found in J. Macrory, *Running with the Ball: The Birth of Rugby Football*, pp. 86–90. Unfortunately they do not state the impulse behind their creation.

110 Old Rugbeian, *Recollections of Rugby*, p. 134.

111 A. J. Lawrence, *The Origins of Rugby Football. Report of the Sub Committee of the Old Rugbeian Society* (Rugby, 1897) p. 41.

112 A. J. Lawrence, *The Origins of Rugby Football. Report of the Sub Committee of the Old Rugbeian Society* (Rugby, 1897) p. 41. It is stated that there were no house matches between 1843–45 and 1847–49, though an explanation for this is not provided.

113 A Rugbeian, *Football: The first day of the sixth match* (Rugby, 1851) pp. 10–11. Dunning and Sheard maintain that W. D. Arnold's account was 'imaginary' and 'reflected his father's opinions'. E. Dunning and K. Sheard, *Barbarians, Gentlemen and Players*, p. 90. Throughout their work Dunning and Sheard treat the information that W. D. Arnold provides as dealing with the era when his father was headmaster, pp. 86–7, 90–1. However, as we have seen, W. D. Arnold specifically tells us that his account was of a match that occurred in 1846, that is during a time when Tait was headmaster of Rugby. Marples believes that Hughes derived his account of the football match from that of W. D. Arnold. M. Marples, *A History of Football*, p. 114.

114 A Rugbeian, *Football: The first day of the sixth match* (Rugby, 1851) p. 17.

115 A Rugbeian, *Football: The first day of the sixth match* (Rugby, 1851) p. 14. The first reference to players at Rugby School using coloured jerseys was in a house match from 1861. *Bell's Life in London* 24 November 1861.

116 A Rugbeian, *Football: The First Day of the Sixth Match* (Rugby, 1851) p. 19.

117 Old Rugbeian, *Recollections of Rugby* p. 131. It is not entirely clear whether during Arnold's period boys wore coloured caps, for Newmarch observes that one of the modern improvements is that the boys no longer have mottoes such as '*Cave adsum*' on their caps.

118 *Field* 24 January 1863. The firm exported the balls to Australia and New Zealand.
119 Dunning and Sheard maintain that Arnold's reforms provided the preconditions for the codification that occurred under Tait. However, as we have seen, we know very little about Rugby's football before Arnold and there is no indication of a significant transformation occurring during his period of headship. Consequently, we are entitled to wonder what exactly the contribution of Arnold was to the codification of Rugby's football game. E. Dunning and K. Sheard, *Barbarians, Gentlemen and Players*, p. 91.
120 *Bell's Life in London* 6 November 1853. W. Rouse, *History of Rugby School*, p. 323.
121 *Bell's Life in London* 28 October 1855.
122 *Bell's Life in London* 9 November, 21 December 1856; 10 November 1861.
123 C. Evers, Rugby, pp. 69–70. Temple introduced two important reforms in football. First, he ended the rights of the sixth form to insist that those players who were not selected to play had to attend matches. Second, he abolished 'indiscriminate kicking that was used to get through the mass of players'.
124 The first mention of sport at Rugby School occurs in *Bell's Life in London* 17 April 1842, of a foot race they held. To the author's knowledge the only mention in the press of Rugby's football until the 1850s was an engraving that appeared in *The Illustrated London News* of 20 December 1845. There is no indication that the School was involved in this promotional exercise and there was no follow-up to this coverage. By contrast with the lack of press coverage for Rugby's football, pupils from Eton (*Bell's Life in London* 29 November 1840; 5 December 1941; 16 October 1842; 26 October 1845; 12 December 1847) and Harrow (*Bell's Life in London* 23 October 1842; 5 November 1843; 12 November 1848) submitted accounts of their football, the former enjoying substantial coverage from 1848 (*Bell's Life in London* 8 October, 22 October, 10 December, 12 November 1848; 21 October, 2 December 1849; 6 October, 17 November, 24 November, 8 December 1850).
125 *Bell's Life in London* 10 October 1852.
126 *Bell's Life in London* 17 October 1852.
127 *Bell's Life in London* 19 December 1852.
128 *Bell's Life in London* 10 November 1866; *The Times* 1 October, 12 December 1863.
129 G. Fisher, *Annals of Shrewsbury School* (London: Methuen, 1899) p. 404.
130 T. Chandler, Origins of Athleticism. Games in the English public school 1800–89 (unpublished PhD Stanford University, 1984) pp. 48–9. G. Fisher, *Annals of Shrewsbury School*, pp. 313, 404.
131 G. Fisher, *Annals of Shrewsbury School*, pp. 405–6.
132 G. Fisher, *Annals of Shrewsbury School*, p. 405.
133 *Bell's Life in London* 15 March 1853.
134 *Bell's Life in London* 6 November 1853.
135 G. Fisher, *Annals of Shrewsbury School*, p. 386.
136 G. Fisher, *Annals of Shrewsbury School*, p. 406.
137 *Bell's Life in London* 28 March 1862.
138 *Bell's Life in London* 24 October 1863.
139 *Bell's Life in London* 28 November 1863.
140 G. Fisher, *Annals of Shrewsbury School*, pp. 406–7.
141 J. Basil Oldham, *A History of Shrewsbury College* (Oxford: Oxford University Press, 1952) p. 235.
142 *Field* 5 December 1863.
143 S. Sargeaunt, *Annals of Westminster School* (London: Methuen, 1898) p. 133.
144 F. Forshall, *Westminster School: Past and Present* (London: Shipman & Sons, 1884) pp. 570–1.
145 F. Forshall, *Westminster School: Past and Present*, p. 6. Accidents and injuries occurred in matches at Westminster in the early 1860s. *Bell's Life in London* 3 November 1861; 21 December 1862.
146 F. Markham, *Recollections of a Town boy at Westminster School* (London: Edward Arnold, 1903) pp. 92–5.

147 *Bell's Life in London* 2 November 1851. *Town Boy Ledger 1815–1862*, p. 418. 'Football has met with many supporters. Play has begun between Town Boys and Gown boys, XII a side'. Interestingly enough, reports of football from the school begin to appear in the national press at this time. *Bell's Life in London* 9 November 1851.
148 *Bell's Life in London* 28 December 1856; 12 December 1858.
149 *Bell's Life in London* 11 December 1859.
150 *Bell's Life in London* 12 December 1858; 29 November, 18 December 1859; 16 December 1860; 1, 8 December 1861; 2, 16 February, 23 November, 21 December 1862; 22 February 1863. H. Mckernan and M. Gwyer, *Athletic Records of Westminster School* (London 1898) p. 40.
151 M. Shearman, *Athletics and Football*, pp. 291–2.
152 A. Leach, *History of Winchester College* (London: Duckworth, 1899) p. 446.
153 M. Shearman (ed.) *Football*, pp. 74–84.
154 *Field* 4 January 1862.
155 *Field* 12 December 1863.
156 A. Leach, *History of Winchester College*, p. 449.
157 C. Wordsworth, *Annals of my Early Life*, p. 230.
158 The first report was in *Bell's Life in London* 9 November 1851.
159 A book described a 6 against 6 match at the school. *Bell's Life in London* 11 May 1856.
160 *Bell's Life in London* 14 November 1858.
161 *Bell's Life in London* 30 October 1859.
162 *Bell's Life in London* 27 November, 4 December 1859.
163 *Bell's Life in London* 14 November 1852; 4 December 1858; 4 December 1859; 10 November 1861. *Field* 12 March 1859.
164 T. Chandler, 'Games at Oxbridge and the public schools, 1830–80: The diffusion of an innovation' *IJHS* 8:2 (1991) p. 187.
165 *Bell's Life in London* 21 November 1863.
166 T. Chandler, Origins of Athleticism. Games in the English public school 1800–89 (unpublished PhD Stanford University, 1984) p. 324.
167 A. Arbuthnot *Memories of Rugby and India*, p. 75.
168 J. Lowerson and J. Myerscough, *Time to Spare in Victorian England* (Brighton: Harvester, 1977) pp. 119–20.
169 Whereas house matches were generally used to foster and cement unity, the latter selections were often an attempt to erode established loyalties, that is to break down 'tribes' and were often related to the disciplinary difficulties of the institution.
170 *Bell's Life in London* 4 December 1858. *Field* 12 March 1859.
171 *Bell's Life in London* 29 November 1859.
172 *Bell's Life in London* 2 December 1860.
173 *Bell's Life in London* 12 December 1863.
174 F. Magoun, *A History of football* (Bochum-Langendreer, 1938) pp. 73–4.
175 T. Chandler, Origins of Athleticism. Games in the English Public School 1800–89 (unpublished PhD Stanford University, 1984) p. 137. J. Venn, *Early Collegiate Life at Cambridge* (Cambridge: Cambridge University Press, 1913) p. 280.
176 G. Fisher, *Annals of Shrewsbury School*, pp. 404–5. 'Rugby football in the sixties' *Cornhill Magazine* (1922) p. 572. Judging by Fisher's remarks it appears that the Salopians formed a club of their own at Cambridge in the late 1830s/early 1840s. This is the only reference that the author has uncovered concerning this, and one wonders what relation this body was to the Cambridge University Football Club that Salopians were so influential in creating in 1846.
177 T. Chandler, Origins of Athleticism. Games in the English Public School 1800–89 (unpublished PhD Stanford University, 1984) pp. 140–1. *Field* 14 December 1861.
178 J. Basil Oldham, *A History of Shrewsbury College*, pp. 323–3. E. Dunning and K. Sheard, *Barbarians, Gentlemen and Players*, p. 104. G. Fisher, *Annals of Shrewsbury*

School, pp. 404–5. It would be mistaken to think that members of other public schools did not play matches using the rules of Rugby School, on at least two occasions such matches took place, one being between Old Salopians and Old Rugbeians. It is difficult dating the match but it appears to have occurred at some time between the late 1830s and early 1840s.

179 T. Chandler, Origins of Athleticism. Games in the English Public School 1800–89 (unpublished PhD Stanford University, 1984) pp. 138–9.
180 *Bell's Life in London* 25 November 1855; 30 November 1856; 1 December 1861; 8 December 1861.
181 *Bell's Life in London* 21 February, 12 December 1858; 17 November 1861; 21 November 1863.
182 *Bell's Life in London* 2 December 1860; 24 November 1861; 12 December 1863.
183 *Bell's Life in London* 2 November 1856.
184 *Bell's Life in London* 16 November 1856.
185 *Bell's Life in London* 15 November 1857. Contra C. Marriott's claim in F. Marshall (ed.) *Football: The Rugby Union game* (London: Bassell & Co, 1892) p. 300, in which he states that 'late in 1861 a few old Rugby boys started their favourite game at Cambridge'.
186 *Bell's Life in London* 12 December 1863. *Field* 7 November, 5 December 1863.
187 G. Fisher, *Annals of Shrewsbury School*, pp. 404–6. As earlier mentioned, the Salopians formed a club of their own in the late 1830s/early 1840s but that was presumably absorbed by the Cambridge University Football Club that they were so influential in creating in 1846.
188 *Bell's Life in London* 21 November 1863. *Field* 19 December 1863.
189 *Bell's Life in London* 21 December 1862. *Field* 7 November 1863.
190 F. Magoun, *A History of football* (Bochum-Langendreer, 1938) p. 73.
191 *Bell's Life in London* 26 October 1856.
192 *Bell's Life in London* 22 November, 5, 20 December 1857.
193 *Bell's Life in London* 14 November 1863.
194 *Bell's Life in London* 11 December 1859; 8 December 1861; 28 November 1863.
195 *Bell's Life in London* 26 October, 2 November, 16 November 1851; 13 November 1853.
196 *Bell's Life in London* 23 February, 31 October 1852.
197 *Bell's Life in London* 12 November 1854; 25 November 1855; 23, 30 November, 7 December 1856; 12 December 1858; 13 November, 11 December 1859; 24 November 1861; 23 November 1862; 7, 21 November 1863.
198 *Bell's Life in London* 11 November 1860.
199 *Bell's Life in London* 11 December 1859; 9 December 1860; 18 December 1859.
200 *Bell's Life in London* 12 December 1863.
201 *Bell's Life in London* 31 October 1858.
202 *Bell's Life in London* 18 November 1860, 14 November 1863.
203 *Bell's Life in London* 8 December 1861; 9 March 1862; 5 December 1863.
204 *Bell's Life in London* 14 November, 12 December 1863.
205 *Bell's Life in London* 27 November, 4 December 1859.
206 J. Honey, *Tom Brown's Universe*, pp. 239–40.
207 *Eton College Magazine* vii (5 November 1832) p. 282.
208 *Bell's Life in London* 7 December 1834.
209 G. Fisher, *Annals of Shrewsbury School*, pp. 404–5.
210 *Bell's Life in London* 2 December 1860.
211 *Bell's Life in London* 11 December 1859.
212 *Bell's Life in London* 4 December 1859.
213 P. Young, *A History of British Football* (London: Stanley Paul, 1968) pp. 83–4.
214 *Field* 7 November 1863. It should be remarked that at least one Etonian thought that the rules were dreadful. *Times* 5 October 1863.

215 *Bell's Life in London* 11 December 1859.
216 *Bell's Life in London* 8 December 1861; 9 March 1862.
217 *Bell's Life in London* 8 March, 5 December 1863.
218 *Bell's Life in London* 11 December 1859; 8 December 1861; 28 November 1863.
219 *Bell's Life in London* 7 December 1862. *Field* 5 December 1863. *Times* 2 December 1863.
220 *Bell's Life in London* 26 December 1858.
221 *Bell's Life in London* 10 November 1861.
222 2 November 1861.
223 *Bell's Life in London* 16 January 1859. See for instance the letters in *Bell's Life in London* 19 December 1858; 2 January, 9 January 1859.
224 *Bell's Life in London* 19 December 1858; 2 January 1859. *Field* 22 February 1862. In *Barbarians, Gentlemen and Players*, p. 99, Dunning and Sheard maintain that the period from 1845 until 1863 was one in which Rugby and Eton were involved in a conscious struggle to provide the model for football games, particularly for the new public schools. No evidence is provided in support of this.
225 *Bell's Life in London* 8 October, 22 October 1848; 6 October 1850. In *Barbarians, Gentlemen and Players*, Dunning and Sheard maintain that Rugby's decision to print their rules stimulated other schools, notably Eton, to codify and print the laws of their own football games (pp. 98–9). Additionally, the authors contend that Eton ensured that their rules were 'in crucial respects, diametrically opposite to their Rugby counterparts' (p. 99), which they attribute to the Eton boys becoming 'incensed' at the way 'the fame of Rugby football had begun to spread' and their consequent desire to codify and print a completely alternative set of laws and thus 'assert their leadership of public schools and put the "upstart" Rugbeians in their place' (p. 99). The major problem with this thesis is that it is entirely theoretical, lacking any supporting documentary evidence. During the 1840s there is no evidence of the various public schools taking any cognisance of one another's football games, much less being involved in rivalry over them. It is far more likely, given the long and extensive history of Eton's various football games, some of which had an 'interminable multiplicity of rules' (*Eton College Magazine* vii 1832, p. 284) from early in the century, and included the highly involved wall game (R. Austen Leigh, *Upon St Andrews Day 1841–1901*, Eton, 1902 pp. vii, x), that the College's decision to print their rules was related to internal factors at Eton rather than rivalry with Rugby.
226 *Bell's Life in London* 7 September 1856.
227 *Bell's Life in London* 11 April 1858.
228 *Bell's Life in London* 23 January 1859; 8 December 1861; 19 October 1862.
229 See for instance the remarks on Eton's laws in *Field* 21 December 1863.
230 *Field* 14 December 1861. Cartwright's praise of Rugby's rules is interesting and offers some support, albeit tepid, for Dunning and Sheard's contention in *Barbarians, Gentlemen and Players*, p. 102 that 'the diffusion of rugby was facilitated by its written rules'. It might be noted, however, that schools adopted variants on the Rugby School laws long before the appearance of the comparatively well-developed code that Cartwright was examining, as can be seen from the following list: Cheltenham College (1843), Marlborough (1843), Rossall (1844), Wellington (1853). M. Marples, *A History of Football* (London: Secker & Warding 1954) p. 138.
231 *Bell's Life in London* 26 March 1854. Interestingly enough, at least one noted old Rugbeian footballer, Bullock, played in a club whose code was based on association rather than rugby rules, Wimbledon. See *Bell's Life in London* 7 December 1862 and *Field* 30 November 1862.
232 In 1857 the founders of the Sheffield Football Club did examine various public school codes when attempting to create rules for their game but as we shall see in Chapter 4 they were effectively uninfluenced by them.

3 Football outside the public schools: from American Indians to *The Origin of the Species* – 1600–1859

1 William Wood, *New Englands Prospect* (London, 1634) part 2, ch. 7, p. 74. It appears that other Indians in the area did take precautions to ensure that football did not result in ill-feeling;

> Before they come to this sport they paint themselves, even as when they go to war, in policie to prevent future mischiefe, because no man should know him that moved his patience or accidently hurt his person, taking away the occasion of studying revenge.
>
> (Part 2, ch. 14, p. 86)

I would like to thank Professor Nicholas Canny for making me aware of this text.

2 *The Sporting Magazine* October 1798 p. 44–5.
3 *Sporting Magazine* January 1802 p. 180.
4 E. Tylor, 'The history of games', *Fortnightly Review* xxv (1879) p. 747.
5 F. Magoun, *History of Football: From the Beginnings to 1871* (Bochum-Langendreer, 1938) pp. 50–9, 91–5.
6 F. Magoun, *History of Football: From the Beginnings to 1817*, p. 49.
7 There is a selected list of prohibitions against football in E. Dunning and K. Sheard, *Barbarians, Gentlemen and Players* (Oxford: Martin Robertson, 1979) p. 23.
8 F. Magoun, *History of Football: From the Beginnings to 1871*, p. 95.
9 The rules of Camp can be found in E. Moor, *Suffolk Words and Phrases* (Woodbridge: J. Loder, 1823) pp. 63–4.
10 *The Annals of the Sporting and Fancy Gazette* ii (November 1822) p. 336.
11 *Ipswich Journal* 19 October 1754 (cited in *East Anglian Daily Times* 21 September 1901).
12 *Norwich Mercury* 29 June–6 July 1751. Cited in C. Darkwell, *Studies in the Social History of Sport in Eighteenth Century England* (London: Bexleyheath, 1983).
13 *Badminton Magazine* ix (1899) pp. 91–6. It is not entirely clear when this match occurred, but it appears to have been either at the end of the eighteenth century or the beginning of the nineteenth century.
14 F. Magoun, *History of Football: From the Beginnings to 1871*, pp. 67–8.
15 *Sporting Magazine* August 1795, p. 276.
16 B. Barton, *History of the Borough of Bury and Neighbourhood in the County of Lancaster* (Bury: Wardlewoth, 1874) p. 41. H. Fishwick, *The Parish of Rochdale in the County of Lancaster* (Rochdale: Cheetham Society, 1889) ii, p. 536.
17 John Johnson Collection. *Sports. Box 7* (Bodleian Library, Oxford).
18 *Manchester Mercury* 11 November 1800.
19 F. Magoun, *History of Football: From the Beginnings to 1871*, p. 63. *PR 2021* Lancashire record office.
20 The match at Weatherby was for a stake of twenty guineas and was mentioned in the *Leeds Intelligencer* 2 March 1773. The reference was from A. Collins, *Rugby's Great Split* (London: Frank Cass, 1998) p. 53. The other references are from Magoun.
21 *The World* 16 May 1789.
22 F. Magoun, *History of Football: From the Beginnings to 1871*, pp. 61–8. A picture of football being played in the market place at Barnet can be found in John Johnson Collection. *Sports. Box 7* (Bodleian Library, Oxford).
23 *Bell's Life in London* 7 October 1849.
24 *Sporting Magazine* May 1796, p. 104.
25 *Sporting Magazine* October 1800, p. 33.
26 R. Holt, *Sport and the British: A Modern History* (Oxford: Oxford University Press, 1989) p. 40. F. Magoun, *History of Football: From the Beginnings to 1871*, pp. 70–1, 96. A. Mason, *Association Football and British Society 1863–1915* (Brighton: Harvester, 1980) p. 10.

27 A. Fabian and G. Green (eds) *Association Football*, vol. 1 (London: Caxton, 1960) p. 139. J. Walvin, *The People's Game* (London: Allen Lane, 1975) p. 29.
28 A. Mason, *Association Football in British Society 1863–1915*, p. 14.
29 P. Young, *A History of Football* (London: Stanley Paul, 1968) p. 62.
30 E. Dunning and K. Sheard, *Barbarians, Gentlemen and Players* (Oxford: Martin Robertson, 1979) pp. 98–9.
31 J. Walvin, *The People's Game*, p. 45.
32 R. Holt, *Sport and the British. A Modern History*, pp. 137–9. A. Mason, *Association Football and British Society 1863–1915*, pp. 14–15.
33 *The Sporting Magazine* June 1815, p. 138.
34 *The Sporting Magazine* November 1831, p. 59.
35 B. Barton, *History of the Borough of Bury and its Neighbourhood in the County of Lancaster*, p. 41.
36 Mrs Gaskell, *The Life of Charlotte Bronte* (Malifan: Ryburn, 1857) pp. 15, 17.
37 *Sporting Magazine* February 1816, p. 244.
38 *The Annals of the Sporting and Fancy Gazette* viii (July 1825) p. 57.
39 *Bell's Life in London* 19 February 1826.
40 *Gentleman's Magazine* xxlii (1822) p. 221.
41 W. Litt, *Wrestliana* (Whitehaven: R. Gibson, 1823) pp. 51–2.
42 *Bell's Life in London* 26 March 1826.
43 p. 171.
44 J. Walvin, *The People's Game*, p. 47.
45 A. Mason, *Association Football and British Society 1863–1915*, pp. 26, 30, 33.
46 H. Cunningham, *Leisure in the Industrial Revolution 1780–1880* (London: Croom Helm, 1980) pp. 127–8.
47 R. Holt, 'Football and the urban way of life in Britain'. In J. Mangan (ed.) *Pleasure, Profit and Proselytism. British Culture and Sport at Home and Abroad 1700–1914* (London: Frank Cass, 1988) p. 72.
48 By making extensive use of the newspaper *Bell's Life in London*, the author identified fifty-six teams that were active in Britain between 1830 and 1860, submitting his findings in a dissertation for an MA in Victorian Studies to Birkbeck College, London University, in September 1990. On 6 October 1994 an article by the author entitled 'Football's missing link: the real story of the creation of modern football', in which were listed sixty-eight clubs, was accepted for publication in the *International Journal of the History of Sport* and was supposed to appear in 1995. Unfortunately the manuscript was lost and consequently the piece failed to appear. Upon being alerted to this in 1998 the editor determined to publish it in *The European Sports History Review i* (1999) pp. 92–116. In 1999 a series of communications from the new editor of *IJHS* alerted the author to the fact that John Goulstone had anticipated the existence of the material on football contained in *Bell's Life in London* and had used it in a work entitled *Modern Sport: Its Origins and Development Through Two Centuries* (1974) pp. 39–42, and a number of articles in *Sports Quarterly Magazine* between 1978 and 1982. The author has since examined *Modern Sport* and discovered that the work is without footnotes. Indeed, *Bell's Life in London* is only mentioned once in the text, a reference to 1858, and that consequently the claims that John Goulstone makes in the work are completely unsubstantiated. The author has been unable to trace a copy of *Sports Quarterly Magazine* anywhere (it is not present in the British Library or at any of the colleges affiliated to either London or Oxford Universities) and is consequently unable to comment upon whether the various articles contain substantiating documentation. Despite this lack of footnotes, it is clear to the author from the content of the text of *Modern Sport* that John Goulstone was utilising *Bell's Life in London* and that both he and Mr Goulstone had uncovered the same material independent of one another. In his most recent work, *Football's Secret History* (London: Catford, 2001) John Goulstone has rendered those people who are unable to consult the original newspapers a great service by quoting sources such as *Bell's* verbatim.

49 *Report from the select committee on public walks with the minutes of evidence taken before them* 27 June 1833. Evidence from W. Bolling, p. 393.
50 *Children's Employment Commission. First Report of the Commission on Mines PP 1842* xv, p. 123.
51 *Manchester Examiner and Times* 1 June 1850.
52 *Bell's Life in London* 7 September 1834.
53 *Bell's Life in London* 28 August 1834.
54 *Bell's Life in London* 28 August 1842.
55 *Bell's Life in London* 28 January 1838.
56 *Bell's Life in London* 22 August 1841.
57 *Bell's Life in London* 14 January 1849.
58 J. Walvin, *The People's Game*, p. 28.
59 W. L. Burn, *The Age of Equipoise* (London: Allen & Unwin, 1964) p. 331.
60 *Bell's Life in London* 20 November 1842.
61 *Wheeler's Manchester Chronicle* 28 December 1833.
62 *Bell's Life in London* 12 December 1841; 31 December 1843; 2 February 1845.
63 *Manchester and Salford Advertiser* 24 April 1841.
64 *Bell's Life in London* 20 November 1842.
65 *Report from the select committee on public walks with the minutes of evidence taken before them* 27 June 1833. Evidence from W. Fielden, p. 391.
66 *Bell's Life in London* 4 March 1849.
67 *Bell's Life in London* 26 December 1841.
68 *Bell's Life in London* 12 December 1841; 2 January, 20 November 1842; 26 February, 7 May 1843; 31 March 1844; 4 March 1849. *Manchester and Salford Advertiser* 24 April 1841.
69 *Field* 24 October 1863.
70 *Bell's Life in London* 13 November 1842; 26 February, 7 May 1843; 21 December 1845; 8 February 1846; 4 March 1849; 29 February 1852.
71 *Bell's Life in London* 31 March 1839; 5 December, 26 December 1841; 20 November 1842; 8 February 1846.
72 B. Harrison, *Drink and the Victorians* (London: Faber and Faber, 1971) pp. 51–2.
73 *Bell's Life in London* 26 December 1847.
74 *Bell's Life in London* 27 March 1858.
75 *Bell's Life in London* 26 March 1854.
76 A. Collins, *Rugby's Great Split*, p. 8.
77 *Bell's Life in London* 17 February 1856.
78 N. Tranter, 'The first football club?', *IJHS* x (1993) pp. 104–6.
79 *Bell's Life in London* 24 January 1858.
80 H. Vassall, 'Rugby Union Football', *English Illustrated Magazine* vii (1889–90) p. 430.
81 *Bell's Life in London* 31 January 1858. P. Young, *A History of British Football*, p. 85. There were a number of differences, such as the goals being eight yards long and the ground being marked off by flags. Additionally, the infringement of rules resulted in the player being fined half a crown.
82 *Bell's Life in London* 8 March 1840.
83 *Athenaeum Gazette* 19 October 1849. *Manchester Examiner and Times* 29 December 1849.
84 *Field* 26 February 1859.
85 *Bell's Life in London* 7 October 1849.
86 Information on the early history of Sheffield FC is quite confused and contradictory. One of the contributors to the club histories, Chesterman, claimed that the team started in 1855–65 and appears to have practised athletics and football. *FCR 10* (Sheffield City Archives). However, Chesterman is unreliable. The origins of Hallam FC is even more obscure and their founding date has been given as various years from 1857 to 1860.
87 *Bell's Life in London* 16 February 1851; 23 November 1856; 30 October 1859; *Northern Examiner* 3 March 1855.

88 *Bell's Life in London* 18 October 1857.
89 *Bell's Life in London* 25 March 1838; 13 January 1839; 11 April, 25 April 1841; 15 December 1844; 21 December 1845; *Stirling Journal* 6 November 1835.
90 *Bell's Life in London* 28 March 1852.
91 *Bell's Life in London* 23 October 1842.
92 *Bell's Life in London* 10 March 1844.
93 *Bell's Life in London* 5 December 1841.
94 *Bell's Life in London* 20 December 1846.
95 *Stirling Journal* 6 November 1835.
96 It appears that stakes were rarely used in football matches during the eighteenth century. D. Brailsford, *A Taste for diversions. Sport in Georgian England* (Cambridge: Lutterworth, 1999) p. 213.
97 *Bell's Life in London* 7 May 1843.
98 *Bell's Life in London* 29 February 1852.
99 *Bell's Life in London* 9 March 1851.
100 The various public school registers were the following: R. Arrowsmith *Charterhouse Register 1769–1872* (Godalming: Phillmore, 1974). J. E. Auden, *Shrewsbury School Register* i (Woodhall: Oswestry, 1964). G. F. Russell Barker, *Westminster School Register 1784–1883* (London: Macmillan, 1883). G. Solly, *Rugby School Register Annotated 1675–1857* (Rugby: George Over, 1933). H. Stapylton, *Eton School Lists 1791–1850* (London: E. P. Williams, 1884), H. Stapylton, *Appendix to Eton School Lists* (London: E.P Williams, 1885). J. Wainwright, *Winchester College: A Register 1836–1906* (Winchester: 1907). E. Welch, *The Harrow School Register 1801–1893* (London: Longmans, 1894).
101 *Bell's Life in London* 7 October 1849.
102 We find equal sides, 24-a-side and 10-a-side in two matches from Norfolk somewhat earlier in the century. *The Sporting Magazine* June 1815, p. 138. November 1831, p. 79.
103 *Bell's Life in London* 12 February 1843.
104 *Bell's Life in London* 10 April 1825; 20 December 1846; 22 April, 7 October 1849. 2 February, 6 April 1851.
105 *Bell's Life in London* 20 December 1846.
106 *Bell's Life in London* 9 March 1851. References to the various stipulations concerning the requirements for victory can be found in *Bell's Life in London* 10 April 1825; 20 December 1846; 22 April, 2 October 1849; 2 February, 6 April 1851.
107 Stonehenge, *Manual of British Rural Sports* (London: Routledge, 1856) p. 499.
108 *Chambers Information for the People* lxxxiv (Edinburgh: Chambers, 1842) p. 544. D. Murray, *Memories of the old college of Edinburgh* (Glasgow: Malehurst, Jackson and Co, 1927) p. 445. Samuel Williams, *The Boys Treasury of Sports, Pastimes and Recreations* (London: D. Bogue, 1847) p. 25.
109 *Bell's Life in London* 2 January 1842.
110 *OED* ii (Oxford 1989) p. 591.
111 J. Wright (ed.) *The English Dialect Dictionary* (London: Henry Frowde, 1902) iii, p. 110.
112 *Bell's Life in London* 13 November 1842. J. Strutt, *Sports and Pastimes of the people of England* (London, William Reeve, 1801) p. 92.
113 D. Walker, *Games and Sports* (London: Thomas Hurst, 1837) p. 253. Compare J. Strutt, *Sports and Pastimes of the People of England* XII, p. 92.
114 *Bell's Life in London* 7 October 1849.
115 *Bell's Life in London* 13 January 1839; 13 November 1842. *Field* 13 February 1864.
116 *Bell's Life in London* 13 November 1842.
117 *The Sporting Magazine* June 1815, p. 138. November 1831, p. 79.
118 J. Wright (ed.) *The English Dialect Dictionary* i, p. 474.
119 *Bell's Life in London* 26 January 1845.
120 Stonehenge, *Manual of British Rural Sports*, p. 499. J. Strutt, *Sports and Pastimes of the People of England* XII, p. 92. S. Williams, *The Boy's Treasury of Sports, Pastimes and Recreations*, p. 25.

121 D. Murray, *Memories of the old College of Edinburgh*, p. 444.
122 *Bell's Life in London* 13 January 1839; 2 January 1842; 7 October 1849. *Chambers Journal* 84 (1842) p. 544. E. Moor, *Suffolk Words and Phrases* (Woodbridge: J. Loder, 1823) p. 64. D. Murray, *Memories of the Old College of Glasgow*, p. 445. Stonehenge *Manual of British Rural Sports*, p. 499. J. Strutt, *Sports And Pastimes of the People of England* XII, p. 92.
123 Stonehenge, *Manual of British Rural Sports*, pp. 499–500.
124 *Bell's Life in London* 13 January 1839.
125 *Bell's Life in London* 13 January 1839; 2 January 1842; *Field* 11 January 1862. E. Moor, *Suffolk Words And Phrases* (Woodbridge: J. Loder, 1823) p. 64. *Manual of British Rural Sports*, p. 499.
126 *Chamber's Information for the People*, p. 544.
127 W. Litt, *Wrestliana* (Whitehaven: R. Gibson, 1823) p. 52.
128 Stonehenge, *Manual of British Rural Sports*, pp. 499–500.
129 D. Murray, *Memories of the Old College of Edinburgh*, p. 444.
130 *Bell's Life in London* 13 January 1839.
131 *Chamber's Information for the People*, p. 544.
132 *Bell's Life in London* 2 February 1851.
133 W. Hone, *The Everyday Book, or Everlasting Calendar of Popular Amusements* (London, 1827) ii, p. 374.
134 J. Strutt, *Sports and Pastimes of the people of England*, p. 92. D. Walker, *Games and Sports*, p. 253.
135 *Bell's Life in London* 29 February 1852.
136 *Bell's Life in London* 20 December 1846.
137 P. Young, *A History of British Football*, p. 67.
138 *Bell's Life in London* 12 December 1841; 2 January 1842; 20 December 1846; 9 March 1851.
139 *Bell's Life in London* 20 December 1846.
140 *Bell's Life in London* 9 March 1851.
141 *Bell's Life in London* 9 March 1851.
142 *Bell's Life in London* 12 December 1841.
143 *Bell's Life in London* 2 January 1842.
144 S. Tischler, *Footballers and Businessmen. The Origins of Professional Soccer in England* (London: Holmes & Meier, 1981) p. 7.
145 J. Walvin, *Leisure and Society 1830–1950* (London: Longman, 1978) p. 10. For a contrary view see: R. Holt, 'Working class football and the city', *IJHS* 3:1 (1986) p. 5.
146 E. Dunning and K. Sheard, *Barbarians, Gentlemen and Players*, p. 30.
147 E. Dunning and K. Sheard, *Barbarians, Gentlemen and Players*, pp. 33–4.
148 *Chambers Information for the People*, p. 544.
149 *Bell's Life in London* 4 February 1844.

4 'An epoch in the annals of sport': Britain's first football culture – Sheffield 1857–67

1 B. Bird, *Perambulations of Barney the Irishman* (Sheffield: J. Pearce, 1854) p. 68, records a six-a-side match between Sheffield and Norton in 1793 that ended in a huge brawl which seems to have involved most of the local population. While it is possible that such an event occurred, the first reliable mention to football in the area was in *Bell's Life in London Life in London* 30 January 1831.
2 *Bell's Life in London* 26 March 1852.
3 *Bell's Life in London* 19, 26 March 1854; 17 February 1856.
4 *FCR10* (Sheffield City Archives). There are conflicting accounts as to where Sheffield originally played. Was it W. Ward's East Bank field, a place close to Sheffield Wednesday's ground at Olive Grove, or Strawberry Hall Lane? J. Catton *The Real Football* (London: Sands & Co, 1900) p. 33.

5 *Sheffield Telegraph* 29 September 1954.
6 *FCR10* Manuscript History, p. 1.
7 Sheffield FC probably owed much to existing sporting organisations, notably the local cricket club, from whence three of its key early officials, H. Ellison, N. Creswick and J. Prest, stemmed. *Sheffield Daily Telegraph* 15 November, 24 December 1854.
8 *FCR10* Manuscript History, p. 1 (Sheffield City Archives).
9 *FCR10* Typewritten History, p. 3 (Sheffield City Archives).
10 *Sheffield Daily Telegraph* 5 November 1907.
11 *FCR10* (Sheffield City Archives). According to Chesterman he joined in 1858, replacing Creswick as secretary in 1860. In fact, Chesterman joined the club in 1860 and became secretary in 1862. See *FCR1* and *Sheffield and Rotherham Independent* 8 October, 1 November, 3 November 1862. Chesterman's evidence must be treated with caution.
12 D. Russell, 'Sporadic and curious: The emergence of Rugby and soccer zones in Yorkshire and Lancashire 1860–1914', *IJHS* 5:2 (1988) p. 194. F. Walters, *The History of Sheffield Football Club* (Sheffield: Allen & Unwin, 1957) pp. 4, 7–8.
13 A register of pupils and masters can be found in *The Sheffield Collegiate School* (London, 1852) pp. 13–15.
14 In 1837 two private schools aiming at a higher academic standard than the Grammar School was then attaining were established in Sheffield: the Collegiate School, with a Church of England basis, and the Wesleyan Proprietary Grammar School (Wesley College). In 1885 the Royal Grammar School and the Collegiate School were amalgamated. There are no records of the Collegiate until 1885. One source claims that the Collegiate School started in 1835 not 1837. *Records for King Edward VIII School* (National Register of Archives. South Yorks. Committee). H. Rogers and T. Rogers, *Sheffield and Rotherham Directory* (Sheffield 1841) p. 6. W. White, *General Directory of Sheffield* (Sheffield: Robert Leader, 1849) p. 15.
15 H. Rogers and T. Rogers, *Sheffield and Rotherham Directory*. W. White, *General Directory of the Town and Borough of Sheffield* (Sheffield: Robert Leader, 1845). W. White *General Directory of Sheffield* (Sheffield: Robert Leader, 1849). W. White, *General Directory of Sheffield* (Sheffield: Robert Leader, 1852). Dunning and Curry claim that the headmaster from an earlier era, T. W. Meller (1836–42), might have been the source of the 'minimum handling game that was eventually adopted by Sheffield FC and perhaps beforehand by Sheffield Collegiate'. E. Dunning and G. Curry, 'The curate's egg scrambled again', *IJHS* 19:4 (2002) pp. 200–1. Their argument is entirely speculative and lacks any supporting evidence. First, we know nothing about the football played at Meller's old school, Oakham, while he was a pupil. J. Barber, *The Story of Oakham School* (Wymondham: Sycamore Press, 1984) p. 193. Second, while Dunning and Curry make much of Meller having been at Cambridge Trinity from 1826 to 1831, there is no evidence of football being remotely significant at the college during that period. Most significant of all, there is no indication of Meller expressing any interest or involvement in sport during his entire life!
16 R. Arrowsmith, *Charterhouse Register 1769–1872* (Godalming: Phillmore, 1974). J. E. Auden, *Shrewsbury School Register* i (Oswestry: Woodhall, 1964). G. F. Russell Barker, *Westminster School Register 1784–1883* (London: Macmillan, 1883). G. Solly, *Rugby School Register Annotated 1675–1857* (Rugby: George Over, 1933). H. Stapylton, *Eton School Lists 1791–1850* (London: E. P. Williams, 1884), H. Stapylton *Appendix to Eton School Lists* (London: E. P. Williams, 1885). J. Wainwright, *Winchester College: A Register 1836–1906* (Winchester: Longmans, 1907). E. Welch, *The Harrow School Register 1801–1893* (London: Longmans, 1894).
17 *The Sheffield Collegiate School* (London, 1852) p. 3.
18 The Collegiate School was established in 1837 *National Register of Archives. South York's Committee*. A register of pupils and masters can be found in *The Sheffield*

Collegiate School (London, 1852) pp. 13–15. W. White *General Directory of Sheffield* 1849, p. 15 A list of the members of the Sheffield FC in 1859 can be found in *FCR 1 Sheffield City Archives*.

19 J. Catton, *The Real Football* (London, 1900) p. 32. P. M. Young *Football in Sheffield* (London: Stanley Paul, 1962) pp. 17–18.

20 The Norton match is mentioned in *Sheffield and Rotherham Independent* 14 January 1862.

21 The preamble to the Rugby code of 1846 is typical of the assumption of public schoolboys that the rules were not for outsiders 'The following set of rules is to be regarded rather as a set of decisions on certain disputed points, than on containing all the laws of the game, which are too well known to render any explanation necessary to Rugbeians'.

22 *FCR2. FCR10.*

23 P. M. Young, *Football in Sheffield*, pp. 17–18.

24 Harrow's code does provide the umpire with the power to disallow illegal goals and penalise deliberate fouling by sending the offender off. *Field* 9 February 1867.

25 Stonehenge, *Manual of British Rural Sports* (London: Routledge, 1856) pp. 499–500

26 D. Murray, *Memories of the old College of Edinburgh* (Glasgow: Mailehurst, Jackson and Co, 1927) p. 444.

27 *Bell's Life in London* 9 March 1851.

28 *Bell's Life in London* 2 January 1842.

29 *Bell's Life in London* 7 October 1849.

30 *Bell's Life in London* 11 April 1858. *Field* 10 April 1858. *Sheffield and Rotherham Independent* 10 April 1858.

31 *Sheffield Daily Telegraph* 5 November 1907. In 1907 seven out of the first twelve members were still alive.

32 *FCR1* (Sheffield City Archives) While the club was certainly founded in October 1857, with subscriptions being taken from the players and a Gymnastic Meeting arranged for April 1858, it is curious that the first AGM mentioned in the Club's Minute Book was on 9 October 1858. Indeed, judging by the very elementary propositions that were submitted, such as 1: The club is called the Sheffield Football Club and was established in 1857, the AGM of October 1858 appears to have been the very first AGM of the Club. It has been suggested that earlier Minute Books have been lost but as Young says we have no way of knowing this. P. Young, *Football in Sheffield*, pp. 16–17.

33 *FCR1* (Sheffield City Archives). In the season 1857–58 there were fifty-seven members, with a further twenty-five being elected in 1858 and an additional seven (including one woman) in 1859.

34 F. Walters, *The History of Sheffield Football Club*, p. 51.

35 P. Young, *Football in Sheffield*, p. 17.

36 P. Young, *Football in Sheffield*, pp. 15–16.

37 *Sheffield and Rotherham Independent* 24 December 1858.

38 *The Week* 13 February 1892.

39 *Bell's Life in London* 10 April 1859. *Sheffield Daily Telegraph* 5 April 1859 *Sheffield and Rotherham Independent* 9 April 1859.

40 *Sheffield Daily Telegraph* 2 October 1857.

41 J. Catton *The Real Football*, p. 34.

42 *Sheffield and Rotherham Independent* 29 October, 24 December 1859.

43 *Sheffield Daily Telegraph* 23 December 1959. The main feature was a great hurling match for a stake of £20 between two teams with 42 players on each side. Once this was completed a football match would be held.

44 *Sheffield and Rotherham Independent* 12 May 1860. *The Week* 6 February 1892.

45 *Sheffield and Rotherham Independent* 15 October 1859.

46 Rouges were expansions of four yards on either side of the goal which provided an additional mode of scoring, players being awarded a point for touching the ball down within these areas. Far from being a slavish adherence to a public school model, this was adopted in response to a particular problem, the proliferation of goalless draws due to the fact that Sheffield's goals were only four yards wide.
47 *Bell's Life in London* 23 December 1860. *Sheffield and Rotherham Independent* 29 December 1860.
48 *The Week* 20 February 1892.
49 *Sheffield and Rotherham Independent* 23 March 1863.
50 *Sheffield and Rotherham Independent* 23 March 1863.
51 *Sheffield and Rotherham Independent* 23 March 1861.
52 *Sheffield and Rotherham Independent* 5 December 1861.
53 *Sheffield and Rotherham Independent* 14 January 1862.
54 *Sheffield and Rotherham Independent* 5 October 1861.
55 *Sheffield and Rotherham Independent* 5 October, 21 December, 30 December 1861; 28 February 1862.
56 *Sheffield and Rotherham Independent* 2 April 1862.
57 *Sheffield and Rotherham Independent* 9 March 1863.
58 *FCR3* (Sheffield City Archives).
59 *FCR3* (Sheffield City Archives).
60 *Sheffield and Rotherham Independent* 8 February, 31 October, 14 November 1865. P. Young, *Football in Sheffield* (London, 1962) p. 22.
61 *Sheffield and Rotherham Independent* 5 March 1866.
62 *FCR3* (Sheffield City Archives).
63 A. Mason, *Association Football and English Society 1863–1915*, pp. 23–4. Mason refers to a document from the Sheffield archives dated 13 October 1887. Shaw claimed that when playing Sheffield other clubs in the area would borrow one another's best players. *FCR10* (Sheffield City Archives).
64 *Sportsman* 21 March 1867.
65 *Sheffield and Rotherham Independent* 19 December 1867. Unsurprisingly, Wellington had problems raising a team to play Pitsmoor the following week.
66 *Sheffield and Rotherham Independent* 31 January, 8 February, 18 October 1862.
67 *Sheffield and Rotherham Independent* 5 November 1861.
68 *Sheffield and Rotherham Independent* 16 September 1862; 7 February, 10 October 1863. The vice president of York was also from Sheffield FC, J. Turner. Creswick remained a key figure in the Sheffield club even after 7 February 1862, whence he resigned as secretary and was replaced by Chesterman. J. Catton, *The Real Football*, p. 35.
69 M Huggins, 'Second-class citizens? English middle-class culture and sport 1850–1910: a reconsideration', *IJHS* xvii (2000) p. 14.
70 *Sheffield and Rotherham Independent* 17 January 1863.
71 *FCR3* (Sheffield City Archives).
72 *Sheffield and Rotherham Independent* 31 January, 8 February, 18 October 1862.
73 *Sheffield and Rotherham Independent* 14 March 1863, 6 January, 5 February 1866.
74 *Sheffield and Rotherham Independent* 1 May 1866.
75 *Sheffield and Rotherham Independent* 13 March 1866.
76 *Sheffield and Rotherham Independent* 2 March 1867.
77 *Bell's Life in London* 7 December 1867.
78 *Sheffield and Rotherham Independent* 4 October, 5 November 1861.
79 *Sheffield and Rotherham Independent* 8 October 1862.
80 *Sheffield and Rotherham Independent* 14 February 1866.
81 *Sheffield and Rotherham Independent* 3 October 1865.
82 *FCR3* (Sheffield City Archives).
83 *Sheffield and Rotherham Independent* 4 October, 5, 23, 29 November 1861.
84 F. Walters, *The History of Sheffield Football Club* (Sheffield 1957) p. 26.
85 F. Walters, *The History of Sheffield Football Club* (Sheffield 1957) p. 27.

86 J. Catton, *The Real Football*, p. 37.
87 *Sheffield and Rotherham Independent* 7 October 1865.
88 *Sheffield and Rotherham Independent* 23 November 1861.
89 *Sheffield and Rotherham Independent* 25 October 1862.
90 *FCR3* (Sheffield City Archives).
91 *Sheffield and Rotherham Independent* 2 January, 7 December 1867.
92 *Sheffield and Rotherham Independent* 26 March 1865.
93 *Sheffield and Rotherham Independent* 9 February 1864.
94 *Sheffield and Rotherham Independent* 5 March 1864.
95 *Sheffield and Rotherham Independent* 2 May 1863.
96 *Sheffield and Rotherham Independent* 10 April 1866.
97 *Sheffield and Rotherham Independent* 29 February, 2 April, 4 October 1864.
98 *Sheffield and Rotherham Independent* 14 May 1867.
99 *Sheffield and Rotherham Independent* 2 May 1863.
100 *Sheffield and Rotherham Independent* 4 April, 1 May 1865.
101 *Sheffield and Rotherham Independent* 29 February 1864; 14 February 1866.
102 *Sheffield and Rotherham Independent* 18 March 1865.
103 *Sheffield and Rotherham Independent* 16, 20, 23 April 1866.
104 *Sheffield and Rotherham Independent* 30 March, 3 April 1866.
105 *Sheffield and Rotherham Independent* 8 May 1866.
106 *Sheffield and Rotherham Independent* 22 April, 21 May 1867.
107 *Sheffield and Rotherham Independent* 8 October 1862.
108 Not every club kept the money produced from their athletics meeting to themselves. Both the Mackenzie and Broomhall clubs donated money to local firms which could be used to provide prizes when the firm held its annual sports day. *Sheffield and Rotherham Independent* 2 May 1865.
109 *Sheffield and Rotherham Independent* 24 November 1861.
110 *Sheffield and Rotherham Independent* 5 March 1862.
111 *Sheffield and Rotherham Independent* 1 November 1864.
112 *Sheffield and Rotherham Independent* 13, 20 December 1862.
113 *Sheffield and Rotherham Independent* 6, 17 December 1864.
114 *Sheffield and Rotherham Independent* 30 October 1866. While there is no indication of Sheffield FC ever taking admission money for their football matches against clubs within the region, it seems likely that those wishing to watch their matches against teams from outside the area were charged. For instance, an advertisement for the match between Sheffield and Nottingham at Bramall Lane in 1865 stated that tickets were only available to members of Sheffield FC and their friends and were to be obtained from Loxley Brothers. *Sheffield and Rotherham Independent* 24 January 1865. As Loxley Brothers were a commercial firm who dealt with the tickets of many of the athletics meetings that were staged throughout the area it is reasonable to assume that money did change hands. Quite what happened to this money is unclear but it is possible that the Club reaped a profit from such undertakings.
115 *Sheffield and Rotherham Independent* 11, 16 March, 20, 25 April 1867. The cost of the cups is not given and it is possible that the trophy awarded as a second prize was valued at £2 10 shillings. The competition was run by a committee comprising of two delegates from each competing club.
116 *Sheffield and Rotherham Independent* 1, 31 March, 17, 18 September 1866.
117 *Sheffield and Rotherham Independent* 12 November 1862.
118 *Sheffield and Rotherham Independent* 8 December 1865.
119 Amongst the popular sports in the Sheffield area was an event at Hyde Park which involved measuring the time it took a dog to kill one hundred rats. This was a sport that appears to have been invented in London during the early 1820s and was presumably illegal by 1863. Despite this, the Sheffield display is mentioned in *Bell's Life in London* 28 November 1863.

120 *Sheffield and Rotherham Independent* 25 November 1865. The Hallam club were the first to insert such an advertisement.
121 *The Week* 6 February 1892. Contains a contrary view, asserting that Sheffield adopted Eton's rules.
122 *Sheffield and Rotherham Independent* 23 March, 23 November 1861.
123 *Sheffield and Rotherham Independent* 25 January 1862; 10 October 1862.
124 *FCR12*.
125 *Field* 9 February 1867.
126 There was an extensive correspondence on this matter in *Sheffield and Rotherham Independent* 3, 6, 7, 8, 9, 10 January and finally 12 January 1863, whence the editor brought the dispute to a close. It is difficult reconstructing events, especially as some of the correspondents appear less than neutral, denouncing statements as being the 'usual Hallam excuse'. It appears likely that the tension between Sheffield and Hallam was further stoked by an incident between two athletes belonging to the respective clubs that occurred during a foot race at York a couple of months earlier. The dispute is described in *Sheffield and Rotherham Independent* 8, 9, 10 October 1862.
127 *Field* 26 December 1863.
128 In a letter from H. Chambers in 1867 it was recorded that the offside law, with its definition of the goalkeeper, was adopted at the beginning of 1863 season. *Field* 9 February 1867.
129 P. Young, *Football in Sheffield*, pp. 20–1. Young details the ideas that Chesterman proposed. The only one that appears particularly strange was Chesterman's advocacy of spiked shoes, which he did not believe to be dangerous.
130 *Sheffield and Rotherham Independent* 3 October 1863.
131 *FCR3* (Sheffield City Archives).
132 *Field* 9 February 1867. *Sheffield and Rotherham Independent* 4, 18 November 1865. It appears that previous to the 1865–66 season Sheffield FC were the only team in the region who used an offside law. See remarks at Sheffield FC AGM September 1865 *FCR3* (Sheffield City Archives).
133 *Bell's Life in London* 24 February 1866. *Sheffield and Rotherham Independent* 13, 22 November 1866. Sheffield rules dictated that ends should be changed at halftime.
134 *Sheffield and Rotherham Independent* 23, 24, 25 January 1866. Heeley retorted that both umpires were from the Norfolk club, though Norfolk insisted that Heeley had made no protest when the officials were selected.
135 *Sheffield and Rotherham Independent* 23 February 1867.
136 *Sheffield and Rotherham Independent* 16, 20 February, 2 March 1867.
137 *Sheffield and Rotherham Independent* 16 February, 2 March 1867. Despite such efforts to improve supervision matches could be over-physical. A report complained that there was 'too much playing the man not the ball' in the Hallam–Mackenzie match. *Sheffield and Rotherham Independent* 4 March 1867.
138 *Sheffield and Rotherham Independent* 11 March 1867. *Sportsman* 14 March 1867.
139 *Sheffield and Rotherham Independent* 22 October 1867.
140 *Sheffield Daily Telegraph* 10 October 1867.
141 *Sheffield Daily Telegraph* 22 October 1867.
142 *Sheffield and Rotherham Independent* 7 January 1865 claim that Sheffield won 1–0. *Bell's Life in London* 7 January 1865 state that play was later stopped and the game agreed drawn.
143 *Bell's Life in London* 8 April 1865.
144 *FCR3* (Sheffield City Archives).
145 *Bell's Life in London* 27 January 1866.
146 *Sheffield and Rotherham Independent* 16 March 1866.
147 *Sheffield and Rotherham Independent* 15, 16 March 1867.
148 *Sheffield and Rotherham Independent* 28 February 1865.

149 *Bell's Life in London* 8 April 1865. *Sheffield and Rotherham Independent* 11 March, 11 April 1865.
150 *Bell's Life in London* 27 January 1866. *Sheffield and Rotherham Independent* 16 January 1866.
151 *Bell's Life in London* 24 February 1866. *Sheffield and Rotherham Independent* 17 February 1866.
152 *Bell's Life in London* 22 December 1866.
153 *FCR3* (Sheffield City Archives) *Sportsman* 14 February 1867.
154 *Sportsman* 14 November 1867.
155 *Sheffield and Rotherham Independent* 6 December 1866.
156 *Sheffield and Rotherham Independent* 25 November, 30 December 1865.
157 *Bell's Life in London* 25 November 1865.
158 *Sheffield and Rotherham Independent* 14, 26, 31 December 1867.
159 *Sheffield and Rotherham Independent* 11, 16 March 1867. P. Young, *Football in Sheffield* pp. 20–1.
160 *The Field* 31 March 1866.
161 J. Catton, *The Real Football*, p. 17.
162 A. Fabian and G. Green, *Association Football* (London: Caxton, 1960) i, p. 151.
163 *FCR3* (Sheffield City Archives).
164 *Sheffield and Rotherham Independent* 24 March 1866.
165 *Bell's Life in London* 7 April 1866.
166 *Field* 26 January 1867.
167 *Field* 7 April 1866.
168 *Sheffield and Rotherham Independent* 24 October 1867. *Sportsman* 14 March 1867.
169 P. Young, *Football in Sheffield*, p. 24.
170 P. Young, *Football in Sheffield*, p. 175.
171 *Field* 9 March 1867. *Sheffield and Rotherham Independent* 28 February 1867.
172 *Sheffield and Rotherham Independent* 19, 20 February, 16 March 1867.
173 *Sheffield and Rotherham Independent* 16 March 1867.
174 *Bell's Life in London* 7 December 1867.
175 *Sheffield Daily Telegraph* 26 November 1867. *Sheffield and Rotherham Independent* 23, 30 November 1867.
176 *Sheffield and Rotherham Independent* 2 March 1867.

5 Footballing backwaters?: London, the FA and the rest 1860–67

1 *Bell's Life in London* 17 November 1861. J. Catton, *The Real Football* (London, 1900) p. 17. *Lincolnshire Chronicle* 20 November 1863. H. Vassall, 'Rugby Union football', *English Illustrated Magazine* vii (1889–90) p. 430.
2 C. Alcock, 'Association football' *English Illustrated Magazine* viii (1890–91) 282–3. There is a photo of Forest FC from 1863 in B. Butler, *The Official Illustrated History of the F.A. Cup* (London: Headline, 1998) p. 35.
3 *Bell's Life in London* 23 March, 13 April 1862; 14, 21, 28 November, 26 December 1863.
4 *Bell's Life in London* 19 December 1863.
5 *Bell's Life in London* 28 February 1863. Of course, playing areas were often less than ideal. Even in the early 1870s the Royal Engineers team often played on a ground with a large tree in the middle and on one occasion had to help their hosts drive the occupying sheep from the turf and remove the animals 'leavings'. R. M. Ruck, 'Football in the early seventies', *Royal Engineers Journal* xlii ns (December 1928) p. 639.
6 *Bell's Life in London* 8 February, 8 March 1863.
7 *Bell's Life in London* 31 October 1863.
8 *Field* 23 February 1862.

9 *Bell's Life in London* 9 March 1862. *Field* 15 March 1862.
10 *Bell's Life in London* 23 February 1862. *Field* 15 March 1862.
11 *Bell's Life in London* 7 December 1862. P. Young, *A History of Football* (London: Stanley Paul, 1968) p. 90.
12 *Bell's Life in London* 21 December 1862. *Field* 7 December 1862.
13 P. Young, *Football on Merseyside* (London: Stanley Paul, 1963) p. 14. The club of 1862 had fifty or so players, many of who were socially distinguished. The author is unclear as to exactly what relation this club was to the Liverpool FC who were formed by old Rugbeians in 1858. It appears that the same personnel were involved, notably Mather. *Bell's Life in London* 31 January 1858.
14 *Lincolnshire Chronicle* 30 October 1863.
15 *Bell's Life in London* 25 March 1860.
16 *Bell's Life in London* 7 December 1862.
17 *Bell's Life in London* 5 December 1863.
18 *Bell's Life in London* 1 December 1861.
19 *Bell's Life in London* 2 January 1864.
20 On at least one occasion it seems likely that the occupation of players was influential in creating a team. For instance, the War Office club, who used Eton rules, was made up of civil servants. *Bell's Life in London* 17 November 1861.
21 Of course, as we have seen, Sheffield had published codes of rules in 1857 and 1862, but as these lacked the prestige of the elite institutions they did not attract notice beyond the Sheffield area.
22 *Bell's Life in London* 7 September 1862.
23 In Hampshire the rugby game was played by Romsey and Queenswood College but we have no clue concerning the rules that were used or whether the players involved were old Rugbeians. *Field* 30 November 1861.
24 *Bell's Life in London* 4 December 1860. The Merchiston–Edinburgh Academy matches became important annual fixtures in Scotland, involving a great deal of coaching and preparation by both sides. The fixture was supposed to be limited to boys rather than adults but Merchiston included at least one player who should have been excluded because of his age, which they justified by pointing out that their school had only one hundred students to choose from, Edinburgh having five times that. *Field* 17 December 1865; 21 January 1865.
25 *Bell's Life in London* 21 November 1863. *Field* 21 November 1863.
26 *Bell's Life in London* 23 November 1862.
27 *Bell's Life in London* 19 December 1863.
28 *Bell's Life in London* 9 September, 4 November 1860. *Swindon Advertiser* 10 September 1860.
29 *Lincolnshire Chronicle* 7 March 1862.
30 *Field* 26 December 1863.
31 *Bell's Life in London* 21 November 1863.
32 *Bell's Life in London* 28 November, 12 December 1863.
33 *Bell's Life in London* 5 December 1863.
34 *Lincolnshire Chronicle* 2 October 1863.
35 *Field* 18 January 1862; 24 January 1863.
36 *Field* 4 January 1862.
37 *Field* 15 March 1862.
38 *Bell's Life in London* 7 November 1863.
39 *Bell's Life in London* 14 November 1863.
40 *Bell's Life in London* 7 November 1863.
41 *Times* 9 October 1863.
42 *Times* 5 October 1863.
43 *Bell's Life in London* 31 October 1863.

44 *Bell's Life in London* 5 October, 16 November 1862. *Field* 31 October 1863. Instructively enough, Thring's book was advertised as being for 'Army, Volunteer and Village clubs'. The book was reissued in 1864. *Field* 20 January 1864.
45 *Field* 22 February 1862.
46 *Times* 5, 6, 7, 9, 10 October 1863.
47 *Times* continued to report on the FA's progress, 27 October, 6 November 1863.
48 *Bell's Life in London* 31 October 1863. F.A. *Minute Books 1863–1874* 26 October 1863.
49 27 October 1863.
50 *Bell's Life in London* 14 November 1863. It appears that the only club who communicated in a positive manner that week were Aldereshott (sic) who sent the rules that were used for officer's football in the club that had been established in the camp.
51 F.A. *Minute Books 1863–1874* 10 November 1863.
52 *Bell's Life in London* 21 November 1863
53 F.A. *Minute Books 1863–1874* 17 November 1863.
54 F.A. *Minute Books 1863–1874* 24 November 1863.
55 *Bell's Life in London* 28 November 1863. F.A. *Minute Books 1863–1874* 24 November 1863.
56 *Field* 5 December 1863.
57 Scholars will observe that only fifteen delegates were listed as attending the meeting of the FA on 1 December 1863. Consequently, the author is at a loss to explain how the vote against Campbell's motion is recorded as being 13–4. The likelihood appears to be that the teller made a mistake and the result was probably 11–4 against Blackheath. Interestingly, members of the press who were opposed to Campbell were keen on emphasising the fact that the meeting was 'well attended'. *Bell's Life in London* 5 December 1863. Of course, the previous meeting was attended by four more delegates and was consequently more representative.
58 While it might appear strange that Wimbledon and Kensington schools are included amongst those who were sympathetic towards rugby, it should be remembered that they played at least two matches under rules that bore similarities to that code. See *Bell's Life in London* 17 November 1861, *Field* 30 November 1861.
59 *Bell's Life in London* 5 December 1863. *F.A. Minute Books 1863–1874* 1 December 1863. This episode has often been misunderstood by historians. P. M. Young, *A History of British Football* (London: Stanley Paul, 1968) p. 91 maintains that at its very inception it was decided to 'civiliz{e} the game by banning one of its most objectionable features'. Young is referring to hacking and he then asserts 'the majority of F.A. delegates determined at the first meeting to follow this body of opinion', and declares that 'The Blackheath group were for retention {of hacking}, the rest of the delegates for excision'. However, as we have seen, the first embryonic code of laws included hacking. A detailed examination of the minute books and reports of the early meetings of the FA reveals that it was the opponents of hacking who were undemocratic. The Blackheath group were the majority but because the bulk of their supporters was absent from the meeting their views were not represented. It is interesting that Bryon Butler in *The Official History of the Football Association* (London: Headline, 1991) p. 6 ignores the case of Blackheath and their supporters and states that when confronted with the banning of hacking they 'moodily withdrew'.
60 It is, of course, debatable how sincere Campbell's excuse was. It is quite possible that by this juncture he had set his face against all compromise.
61 *Bell's Life in London* 12 December 1863.
62 Opponents of hacking often pointed out that the practice rendered football too dangerous for adults and the practice's removal was vital if the game was to cease being restricted to the activity of school boys. *Bell's Life in London* 12 December 1863.
63 *Bell's Life in London* 12 December 1863.

64 In an unpublished research paper Neil Rhind has established that Blackheath's chief delegate, Francis Maule Campbell was educated at Blackheath Proprietary School between the ages of 6 and 15 (1850–59) and then entered the family business as a wine merchant.

65 *Field* 19 December 1863.

66 *Bell's Life in London* 12 December 1863.

67 E. Ereaut *Richmond Football Club* (London: Howlett & son, 1926) pp. 10–11.

68 E. J. Ereaut *Football club*, pp. 9–11. I am grateful to Piers Morgan for drawing my attention to this. In the match using the FA rules Barnes had six tries at goal but failed to score.

69 So far as the author can see the only real stumbling block to the FA establishing two sets of rules was the idea that the meeting should create the definitive laws of football.

70 *Field* 9 January 1864.

71 *Field* 5, 12 December 1863; 9 January 1864.

72 *Bell's Life in London* 2 January 1864.

73 *Bell's Life in London* 2 January 1864. The old boy ridiculed the pretensions of the FA, observing that the removal of hacking had prompted six clubs to withdraw, leaving the FA with just nine members.

74 F.A. *Minute Book 1863–1874* 23 September 1864.

75 *Field* 8 October 1864.

76 *Bell's Life in London* 5 November 1864.

77 F.A. *Minute Book 1863–1874* 28 October 1864.

78 *Bell's Life in London* 9 April 1864.

79 *Bell's Life in London* 10 December 1864; 16 December 1865.

80 *Bell's Life in London* 12 December 1863. *Field* 28 November 1863. Two matches were arranged between Eton and Winchester at Vincent Square, Westminster, one with each team's code. For some reason they were postponed. The author has not uncovered an external match by Winchester, though old Wykehamists did play a match at New College, Oxford in 1863 and against Radley in 1863. *Bell's Life in London* 14 November 1863; 2 January 1864.

81 *Field* 9, 30 November 1867.

82 *Field* 23 December 1865.

83 *Bell's Life in London* 5 March 1864; 7 January 1865. *Field* 6 February 1864; 23 December 1865.

84 *Bell's Life in London* 2 December 1865. *Field* 23 November 1867.

85 *Bell's Life in London* 3 February 1866. *Field* 9 February 1867.

86 *Bell's Life in London* 27 February, 5 March, 12 November, 24 December 1864 24 February 1866; 23 December 1867. *Field* 10 November, 15 December 1866.

87 24 November 1866; Further matches between the schools are noted in *Field* 11, 25 November, 23 December 1865.

88 *Bell's Life in London* 28 December 1867. *Field* 27 February, 19 November 1864; 4 February 1865.

89 *Field* 27 October, 8 December 1866.

90 *Bell's* 21 December 1867. *Field* 30 November 1867.

91 *Bell's Life in London* 24 December 1867. P. Young *A History of Football*, p. 94.

92 H. Vassall 'Rugby Union football' *English Illustrated Magazine* vii (1889–90) p. 432.

93 *Bell's Life in London* 2 January, 3 February 1864, 23 March 1867. *Field* 3, 17 November 1866; 16 February, 2, 16, 23 November, 7 December 1867. In F. Marshall (ed.) *Football: The Rugby Union Game* (London: Cassell & Co, 1892) p. 266. H. Vassall claims erroneously that previous to 2 November 1869, when a meeting of old Rugbeians at Balliol College established a Rugby at Oxford there had been no organised version of the game there.

94 *Bell's Life in London* 9 February, 23 *November* 1867.

95 *Bell's Life in London* 10 December 1864; 2 March 1867. *Field* 10 December 1864; 18 November 1865; 2, 20 November 1867.
96 *Bell's Life in London* 24 December 1864. *Field* 2, 9 November 1867.
97 *Bell's Life in London* 24 November 1866. *Field* 23 February, 30 November 1867.
98 *Field* 9 December 1865. 2 March, 16 December 1867. It is possible that they might have been used in some matches, such as Jesus v Emmanuel College Cambridge.
99 *Bell's Life in London* 5 November 1864. *Field* 30 November 1867.
100 *Field* 23 December 1865. *Sportsman* 3 January 1867.
101 *Bell's Life in London* 14 January 1865.
102 N. Jackson *Sporting Days and Sporting Ways* (London: Hurst & Blackett, 1932) pp. 21–2.
103 *Field* 1 April 1865. 10 March 1866.
104 *Field* 17 September 1864.
105 *Bell's Life in London* 7 October 1865.
106 *Bell's Life in London* 6 October 1866.
107 *Field* 3 March 1866. The word 'amateur' almost certainly meant gentleman and designated the middle and upper classes.
108 *Bell's Life in London* 7 January, 25 November 1865. *Sheffield and Rotherham Independent* 15 March 1867.
109 *Bell's Life in London* 7 January 1865.
110 *Field* 13 October 1866.
111 *Bell's Life in London* 31 March 1866.
112 *Field* 6 February 1864.
113 *Field* 21 January 1865.
114 C. Alcock, 'Association football', *English Illustrated Magazine* viii (1890–91) pp. 282–3. P. Young, *A History of Football*, pp. 85, 90. The No Names club were swallowed up by the Wanderers.
115 *Field* 6 February 1864.
116 *Sportsman* 3 January 1867. The Louth FC had taken over a hall that had once been a Baptist Church and having removed the fitments converted it into a gymnasium. *Bell's Life in London* 22 October 1864.
117 *Field* 27 February 1864; 25 March 1865.
118 *Bell's Life in London* 29 October 1864. They suggested giving prizes in an effort to generate excitement. *Field* 15 October 1864. The author has been unable to find any reference to the Louth club after October 1864 and it is therefore possible that the club disbanded. If this were the case one wonders if their adoption of the FA code was related to this?
119 *Field* 16 December 1865. Lincoln often tried the code of the FA but found it unappealing. *Bell's Life in London* 24 February 1866.
120 *Sportsman* 3 January 1867.
121 *Sportsman* 31 January 1867. A couple of weeks later the Lincoln players were kicking around a block of wood on a thick sheet of ice that lay on the ground in order to get some practice. *Sportsman* 12 January 1867.
122 *Sportsman* 8 October 1867. Lincoln were defiantly supportive of their rules and in 1866 an official wrote to *Bell's Life in London* stating that in six seasons no one has ever broken his head playing football and insisting that their code forbade hacking and throttling (3 March 1866). The reformed version of their football 'only permitted tripping if a player was running holding the ball'. *Sportsman* 2 November 1867.
123 *Field* 27 January 1866.
124 *Field* 24 February 1866.
125 *Field* 10 February 1866.
126 *Field* 19 November 1864.

127 *Field* 23 December 1865; 26 January 1867.
128 *Field* 27 February 1864.
129 *Field* 26 December 1863.
130 *Bell's Life in London* 14 January 1865.
131 *Field* 17 March 1866.
132 *Field* 1 December 1866. The teams even used eleven men on each side.
133 *Field* 8 December 1866.
134 *Field* 26 January 1867.
135 *Field* 1 April 1865; 10 March 1866.
136 N. Jackson, *Sporting Days and Sporting Ways*, pp. 21–2. The code was created by a doctor who lived in the village and had played football while training at a London hospital.
137 *Bell's Life in London* 29 December 1866.
138 *Field* 11 November 1865.
139 F. Marshall (ed.) *Football: The Rugby Union Game*, p. 418.
140 *Field* 26 March 1864.
141 Reports and letters relating to this match can be found in *Bell's Life in London* 7, 14, 21, January, 28 January, 4 February 1864. It is interesting to note that the letter that Blackheath produced from A. H. Turner, the secretary of CCC, in which he stated that his club's rules were the same as Blackheath's, was from 22 November 1864, a time when Turner was secretary of the Royal Military Academy team, having not yet joined CCC
142 *Field* 12 March, 26 March 1866.
143 *Field* 15 December 1866. These accusations were not new and had been made in *Bell's Life in London* on 9 December 1865 where attention was drawn to Brighton College's use of 'throat seizing' and 'shinning'. Brighton were angry about this and responded by writing to *Bell's Life in London* that they were fully capable of playing association-based codes and did so against Lancing College, it being their practice to play matches on the home and away system, with the visitors adopting the home side's code. *Bell's Life in London* 23 December 1865.
144 *Field* 17 December 1865; 21 January 1865.
145 *Field* 24 December 1864. For further examples of the disputes that occurred between Rugby teams over rules during the 1860s see E. Dunning and K. Sheard in *Barbarians, Gentlemen and Players* (Oxford: Martin Robertson, 1979) p. 113.
146 *Field* 24 November 1866.
147 *Field* 1 December 1866.
148 In terms of scoring, Blackheath counted touch-downs as 'tries', whereas Rugby did not. Players at Rugby did not throw or knock the ball on, unlike the Blackheath club. *Field* 8 December 1866.
149 *Field* 8 December 1866.
150 *Bell's Life in London* 17 November 1866.
151 *Field* 26 March 1864; 22 December 1866.
152 R. G. Graham, 'The early history of the Football Association', *Badminton Magazine* viii (1899), pp. 81–2.
153 Although the FA's creation inspired contact from other provincial clubs, such as Louth and Lincoln, both of whose games were more akin to that of Rugby School, it appears to have been journalists, rather than the FA, who persuaded Lincoln to adopt the FA's rules and forbid hacking. *Bell's Life in London* 28 November 1863. *Field* 26 December 1863.
154 F. A. *Minute Books 1863–1874* 1 December 1863.
155 It is characteristic of the passive nature of the FA that the meeting opened with letters being read from P. Shipley (Lincoln) and Chesterman (Sheffield), who were arranging a match between their sides. It was the teams who were taking the initiative and organising matters, the FA appear to have been the last people to find out! F. A. *Minute Book* 22 February 1866.
156 *Bell's Life in London* 24 February 1866.

157 *Bell's Life in London* 29 October 1864. *Field* 25 March 1865.
158 *Bell's Life in London* 24 February 1866.
159 F.A. *Minute Books 1863–1874* 1 December 1863.
160 *Bell's Life in London* 24 February 1866. F.A. *Minute Books 1863–1874* 22 February 1866.
161 *Bell's Life in London* 3 March 1866.
162 F. A. *Minute Book* 22 February 1866.
163 J. Catton *The Real Football*, p. 19. P. Young, *Football in Sheffield*, p. 20.
164 F. A. *Minute Books 1863–1874* 28 February, 13, 24 March 1866. *FCR* 3 (Sheffield City Archives).
165 The return at Sheffield was planned for March 1867 *Sheffield and Rotherham Independent* 16 March 1867.
166 J. Catton *The Real Football*, p. 16.
167 *Sportsman* 14 March 1867 detailed a meeting of Sheffield FC at the Adelphi Hotel and discussed the differences in the rules of the Sheffield Association and those of the FA. There were three principle areas of divergence (1) Sheffield has no offside law (2) Sheffield penalises handling (3) rouges count if goals are equal.
168 *Bell's* 2 March 1867.
169 *Field* 2 March 1867. J. Catton, *The Real Football*, p. 21.
170 F. A. *Minute Books 1863–1874* 12 February 1867. *Field* 2 March 1867. Sheffield suggested three amendments to the rules, all of which were rejected. While the first, which related to the introduction of rouges, was not taken up in later years, the other two did become part of the Football Association's code within a few years. They were

> 7: any player between an opponent's goal and the goal keeper, unless he has followed the ball there, is off his side and out of play. The goal keeper is that player in the defending side who for the time being is nearest to his own goal.
>
> 11: Holding the ball or knocking or passing it on with the hands or arms is altogether disallowed and the side breaking this rule forfeits a free kick to the opponents' side.

171 *Bell's* 2 March 1867.
172 The rules of the FA as selected in February 1867 were as follows:

> 1 The maximum length of ground shall not exceed two hundred yards, and the maximum breadth shall be one hundred yards. Flags will mark out the length and width. The goals shall be upright posts, eight yards apart, with a tape across them eight feet high.
> 2 Teams will toss for choice of goals. The team which loses shall kick off. It will be a place kick from the centre, and until the ball is kicked the other side must not approach within ten yards.
> 3 Every time a goal is scored ends must be changed. The side losing the goal shall kick off.
> 4 A goal shall be won when the ball passes between the goal posts and under the tape, not being thrown, knocked on or carried.
> 5 When the ball is in touch, the first side to touch it shall throw it from the boundary line at the pace where it went off. It must be thrown straight, at right angles, and the man throwing it cannot touch it twice.
> 6 When a player has kicked the ball anyone of the same side who is nearer the opponents goal line is out of play and may not touch the ball himself nor in any way whatsoever prevent any other player from doing so until the ball has been

played unless there are at least three of his opponents between him and their own goal; but no player to be out of play when the ball is kicked.

7 When the ball is kicked behind the goal line the defenders must kick it out from the limit of their goal (within six yards of). It must be kicked off by the side behind whose goal it went within six yards of the limit of their goal. The side who thus kick the ball are entitled to a fair kick off in whatever way they please without any obstruction, the opposite side not being able to approach within six yards of the ball.

8 No player shall carry or knock the ball on.

9 No tripping or hacking, no holding or pushing with hands.

10 Players shall not throw the ball, nor pass it to one another.

11 Whilst the ball is in play, players cannot pick the ball up.

12 No projecting nails, or gutta percha plates, on soles or heels of boots.

Definition of terms:

A place kick is when ball is on the ground in any position where the player may chooses to place it.
Hacking is tripping adversary intentionally.
Tripping is throwing adversary by the use of the legs.
Knocking on is when a player strikes or propels the ball with the hands or arms.
Holding is obstructing with the hand any part of your opponent's below the elbow.
Touch is the dead ball area.

173 An entry in the F.A. *Minute Books 1863–1874* for 12 February 1867 reveals the change in the association's attitude. For the first time since 1863 the code of the association, all twelve rules, is written in by hand. The FA became a far more aggressive body after this, as the *Minute Books* show. For instance, on 30 September 1867 the FA announced to the press that a county match was being organised to promote the rules and 'resolved to waive the £1 10s subscription in the event of any club being prevented from joining the association by that subscription'. They also appear to have circulated letters to clubs and on 14 October 1867 and received responses to some of these. By 17 January 1868 a circular letter had been sent to all members inviting them to propose alterations to the laws. This flurry of activity represents a substantial contrast to the apathy of earlier years.

174 J. Catton, *The Real Football*, pp. 20–1. R. G. Graham, 'The early history of the Football Association', *Badminton Magazine* viii (1899) pp. 79–82. M. Shearman *Athletics and Football* (London: Longman, 1889) p. 336.

175 *Field* 9 March, 20 April 1867.

176 R. G. Graham, 'The early history of the Football Association', *Badminton Magazine* viii (1899) pp. 81–2. Graham replied by stating that the FA did not have sufficient time for such an undertaking.

177 Naturally, one wonders how sincere Rugby's representative, Ellis, was in this. It is significant, however, that Ellis replied as he did. In the past Rugby had ignored communications from the FA and there was certainly no reason why Ellis should send such a specific and detailed reply unless he was serious.

178 R. G. Graham, 'The early history of the Football Association', *Badminton Magazine* viii (1899) pp. 79–82.

6 Football splits up but goes national: the creation of a national football culture (1868–73)

1 F.A. *Minute Book 1863–1874* (Lancaster Gate). The list of the teams responding to the circular is on a letter dated 1 January 1868.

2 J. Lillywhite, *The Football Annual 1870–71*, p. 37. This inclusive behaviour towards the provinces does not appear to have lasted. The following year, 1871, the FA's officials were: D. Allport (Crystal Palace), A. J. Baker (Wanderers), M. Betts (West Kent), J. Cockerell (Brixton), J. Giffard (Civil Service), A. Kinnaird (Eton), J. Kirkpatrick (Civil Service), Captain Marindin (Royal Engineers), C. Stephenson (Westminster), R. Willis (Barnes).
3 J. Lillywhite, *The Football Annual 1867–8*, p. 1.
4 J. Lillywhite, *The Football Annual 1869–70*, p. 36.
5 J. Lillywhite, *The Football Annual 1867–8*, p. 1.
6 J. Lillywhite, *The Football Annual 1869–70*, p. 37.
7 The FA's rules appear to have established themselves as the accepted code for the game in the popular consciousness by 1869. See *The Gentleman's Journal* Supplement 1 November 1869, pp. 17–18.
8 J. Lillywhite, *Football Annual 1873–4*, p. 55.
9 O. I. Owen, *The History of the Rugby Football Union* (London: Playfair, 1955) pp. 59–60.
10 J. Lillywhite, *The Football Annual 1870–71*, p. 4.
11 *Rugby Football Union Minute Book* 22 June 1871. (Held at Museum of Rugby, Twickenham.)
12 *Rugby Football Union Minute Book* 22 June 1871. The laws were largely drawn up by L. Maton, though one of the committee members, I. H. Ewart , evidently made a number of suggestions that Maton responded to in the margins of the minute book. I would like to thank Rex King of the RFU library for his assistance.
13 B. Butler, *The Official Illustrated History of the F.A. Cup* (London: Headline, 1998) p. 19. A photo of the original entry in the FA minute book is on p. 23.
14 B. Butler, *The Official Illustrated History of the F.A. Cup*, p. 33. Butler gives a very helpful biography of Alcock, drawing out his many achievements. A. Mason, *Association Football and English Society 1863–1915*, p. 16. While Charles Alcock was a towering figure in the history of the Football Association and an important figure in cricket, who Butler describes as 'the inventor of modern sport', it is scarcely correct to say that he invented the concept of the sudden death knock-out competition, for the Youdan Cup had substantially anticipated this.
15 B. Butler, *The Official Illustrated History of the F.A. Cup*, p. 20.
16 J. Catton, *The Real Football* (London, 1900) pp. 25–6.
17 B. Butler, *The Official Illustrated History of the F.A. Cup*, p. 21.
18 A. Mason, *Association Football and English Society 1863–1915*, p. 208. Mason provides an interesting account of the type of game that would have been played in the final of 1872.
19 Though, of course, the spectators at the Youdan final only paid 3d admission. One shilling was the minimum charge to watch the FA Cup final.
20 J. Catton, *The Real Football*, pp. 37–8.
21 N. Jackson, *Association Football* (London: George Newnes, 1899) p. 41.
22 P. Young, *Football in Sheffield*, p. 27.
23 J. Catton, *The Real Football*, pp. 21–2.
24 P. Young, *Football in Sheffield*, p. 24. It is rather strange that by 1894 Alcock was to overlook the contribution of Sheffield to the creation of football, for he described the Forest FC as 'the progenitor of all the now numerous clubs playing football of any kind throughout the kingdom'. B. Butler, *The Official Illustrated History of the F.A. Cup*, p. 35.
25 P. Young, *Bolton Wanderers* (London: Stanley Paul, 1961) p. 15.
26 T. Arnold, 'The president of the Football League. A talk with J.J. Bentley', *Windsor Magazine* xv (1901–02) p. 666. P. Young *Bolton Wanderers*, pp. 14, 159. In 1873 the club produced its first printed rule book.
27 N. Gannaway, *Association Football in Hampshire until 1914* (Hampshire Papers ix 1996) p. 4. The Southampton vs Romsey match in February 1868 provides further examples

of clubs who were outside the influence of the FA. The match was beset by disputes over rules.

28 J. Catton, *The Real Football*, p. 21.
29 J. Catton, *The Real Football*, p. 41.
30 J. Lillywhite, *The Football Annual 1871–2*, pp. 41–2.
31 J. Lillywhite, *The Football Annual 1873–74*, pp. 45–6.
32 J. Catton, *The Real Football*, pp. 30–1.
33 J. Lillywhite, *The Football Annual 1872–3*, pp. 45–6.
34 J. Honey, *Tom Brown's Universe* (London: Millington, 1977) p. 106. King's School Canterbury nearly had a rebellion in 1873.
35 J. Honey, *Tom Brown's Universe*, p. 228.
36 J. Lillywhite, *Football Annual 1867–8*, p. 19.
37 N. Gannaway, *Association Football in Hampshire until 1914* (Hampshire Papers ix 1996) pp. 2–3.

7 Kicking and carrying: the geographical distribution of sporting rules 1860–73

1 John Lillywhite, *Football Annual 1867–8*, pp. 73–5.
2 J. Lillywhite *The Football Annual 1868–69*, p. 63. It is highly likely that a large number of football clubs within Britain between 1868 and 1873 were not mentioned in the book by Lillywhite. For instance, an examination of N. Gannaway, *Association Football in Hampshire until 1914* (Hampshire Papers ix 1996) pp. 4–5, reveals clubs at Southampton (1868), Romsey (1868), Portswood (1870), Ryde (1870) and the Fordingbridge Turks (1868). While it appears that these clubs did use the rules of the FA, this is far less certain than the very specific data given by Lillywhite. For this reason the author elected to exclude such clubs because it was felt that they might compromise the very exact data provided by Lillywhite.

8 Cups, leagues and professionals: rugby and association football 1874–1901

1 A. Mason, *Association Football and English Society 1863–1915* (Brighton: Harvester, 1980) p. 24.
2 H. Cunningham, *Leisure in the Industrial Revolution 1780–1880* (London: Groom Helm, 1980) p. 128.
3 P. Young, *Bolton Wanderers* (London: Stanley Paul, 1961) p. 18.
4 P. Young, *Bolton Wanderers*, pp. 19, 163.
5 A. Collins, *Rugby's Great Split* (London: Frank Cass, 1998) pp. 29–33.
6 A. Collins, *Rugby's Great Split*, p. 114.
7 K. Sandiford, 'Cricket and Victorian society', *Journal of Social History* 17:2 (1983) p. 308.
8 J. Catton, *The Real Football* (London: Sands & Co, 1900) p. 39.
9 N. Fishwick, *From Clegg to Clegg House* (Sheffield: Clegg House, 1986) p. 4.
10 C. Alcock, *Football Annual* 1875/76 (London, 1876) p. 87.
11 J. Catton, *The Real Football*, p. 45.
12 C. Alcock, *Football Annual* 1879/80 (London, 1880) p. 104.
13 J. Catton, *The Real Football*, p. 200.
14 C. Alcock, *Football Annual* 1878/79 (London, 1879) p. 41.
15 J. Lowerson and J. Myerscough, *Time to Spare in Victorian England* (Brighton: Harvester, 1977) pp. 120–2.
16 A. Metcalfe, 'Football in the mining communities of East Northumberland 1882–1914', *IJHS* 5:3 (1988) p. 270.
17 B Trescatheric, *Sport and Leisure in Victorian Barrow* (Barrow: Hongenai, 1983) pp. 20–1, 23.

18 G. Wests, *Football Calendar 1875–6*, p. 32. Wests stated that the only major differences between the SFA rules and the FA rules were that a player can kick the ball in from touch in any direction, not straight as in the FA rules. Wests believed that Sheffield's rule was better because he thought that the FA stipulation penalised the side playing the ball in.
19 C. Alcock, *Football Annual* 1874–75 (London, 1875) p. 37.
20 J. Catton, *The Real Football*, p. 19.
21 N. Gannaway, *Association Football in Hampshire until 1914* (Hampshire Papers ix, 1996) p. 6.
22 N. Gannaway, *Association Football in Hampshire until 1914* (Hampshire Papers ix, 1996) p. 6.
23 C. Alcock, *Football Annual* 1874–1875 (London, 1875) p. 24. An examination of the *Rugby Football Union Minute Book* of 22 June 1871 reveals that although the laws were largely drawn up by L. Maton, one of the committee members, I. H. Ewart , suggested that law 7, which decreed that 'A match shall be decided only by a majority of goals' was too restrictive. It seems likely that Ewart believed that 'tries at goal' should decide the result in the event of the number of goals being equal at the end. This was adopted in November 1875.
24 P. Young, *Football in Sheffield* (London: Stanley Paul, 1962) p. 20.
25 C. Alcock, *Football Annual* 1883/84 (London, 1884) p. 65.
26 C. Alcock, *Football Annual* 1883/84 (London, 1884) p. 83.
27 *RFU Handbook 1894–5* (London, 1895) p. 10.
28 N. Jackson, *Association football*, p. 81. Peculiarly enough, until 1912 goalkeepers were able to use their hands outside the penalty area. A. Mason, *Association Football and English Society 1863–1915*, p. 211.
29 K. Macklin, *The History of Rugby League Football* (London: Stanley Paul, 1962) p. 18.
30 M. Shearman, *Football* (London: Oakley & Co, 1904) p. 98.
31 C. Alcock, *Football Annual* 1875/76 (London, 1876) p. 17. M. Shearman, *Football*, pp. 97–8.
32 C. Alcock, *Football Annual* 1875/76 (London, 1876) p. 17.
33 M. Shearman, *Football*, pp. 98–9.
34 C. Alcock, 'Association football', *English Illustrated Magazine* viii (1890–91) p. 287. M. Shearman, *Football*, pp. 99–100. The first 'combination' team appear to have been The Royal Engineers, who were a formidable force in the early 1870s. R. M. Ruck, 'Football in the early seventies', *Royal Engineers Journal* xlii ns (December 1928) p. 637.
35 C. Andrews, 'The 1883 Cup Final: Patricians v Plebeians', *History Today* (May 1983).
36 C. Alcock, *Football Annual* 1874–75 (London, 1875) p. 38. C. Alcock, *Football Annual* 1875/76 (London, 1876) p. 86.
37 C. Alcock, *Football Annual* 1877/78 (London, 1879) p. 46.
38 C. Alcock, *Football Annual* 1878/79 (London, 1879) p. 104.
39 J. Catton, *The Real Football*, p. 56. Presumably they meant in England, for as we have seen Queen's Park had long exceeded this in Scotland.
40 C. Alcock, *Football Annual* 1876/77 (London, 1877) pp. 26–7. C. Alcock, *Football Annual* 1877/78 (London, 1878) p. 35.
41 C. Alcock, *Football Annual* 1877/78 (London, 1879) p. 39.
42 C. Alcock, *Football Annual* 1878/79 (London, 1879) p. 31.
43 J. Catton, *The Real Football* (London, 1900) p. 53.
44 J. Catton, *The Real Football* (London, 1900) pp. 54–5. A. Mason, *Association Football and English Society 1863–1915*, pp. 69–70.
45 C. Alcock, *Football Annual* 1879/80 (London, 1880) pp. 9–10.
46 C. Alcock, *The Football Annual* 1880/81 (London, 1881) p. 81.
47 *The Football Annual* 1881, pp. 81–2.
48 *The Football Annual* 1881, pp. 8, 108.

49 A. Mason, *Association Football and English Society 1863–1915*, pp. 2, 75, 241. Mason regards attitudes towards professionalism as being largely related to regions, with the northern clubs fighting to preserve their professionals while middle- and upper-class southerners were inclined to deprecate professionalism.
50 J. Catton, *The Real Football*, pp. 56–59.
51 C. Alcock, *Football Annual* 1884/85 (London, 1885) p. 97.
52 J. Catton, *The Real Football*, p. 61.
53 C. Alcock, *Football Annual* 1885/86 (London, 1886) p. 185.
54 C. Alcock, *Football Annual* 1885/86 (London, 1886) p. 185.
55 C. Alcock, *Football Annual* 1885/86 (London, 1886) p. 134.
56 *Amateur Athletics Association Laws* (London, 1887). These rules were published periodically from the very inception of the organisation in 1866. Interestingly enough, the rules for 1887 appear to have been influenced by events in early 1885, precisely the period when professional football becomes legalised by the FA.
57 C. Alcock, *Football Annual* 1885/86 (London, 1886) p. 214.
58 While the Scottish federation fought a long, and according to some, very hypocritical campaign against professionalism, in May 1893 the Scottish Football Association was forced to recognise professionalism. J. Catton, *The Real Football*, pp. 64–5, 194.
59 'Professionals in English sport', *Saturday Review* 14 April 1888, pp. 437–8.
60 A. Mason, *Association Football and English Society 1863–1915*, p. 213.
61 A. Mason, *Association football and English society 1863–1915*, p. 80, n32.
62 C. Alcock, Football Annual 1886–87 (London, 1887) p. 66.
63 A. Mason, *Association Football and English Society 1863–1915*, p. 76.
64 C. Alcock, *Football Annual* 1887/88 (London, 1888) p. 96. The English FA sought to assist the Scottish FA by endeavouring to prevent Scottish players from being imported into England where they would be hired as professionals.
65 M. Shearman, *Football*, pp. 146–7.
66 M. Shearman, *Football*, pp. 181–2.
67 M. Shearman, *Athletics and Football* (London: Longman, 1889) p. 279.
68 G. Fisher, *Annals of Shrewsbury School* (London: Methuen, 1899) p. 406. Change in public school football was usually a ponderous business. In 1875 it was decided to reduce the School team at Rugby from twenty players to fifteen but this was not officially sanctioned until 1881. C. Evers, *Rugby* (London and Glasgow: Blackie & Sons, 1939) p. 157.
69 *The Carthusian* March 1981, p. 5.
70 N. Gannaway, *Association Football in Hampshire until 1914* (Hampshire Papers ix, 1996) pp. 2–3.
71 T. Arnold, 'The president of the Football League. A talk with J. J. Bentley', *Windsor Magazine* xv (1901–1902) p. 666.
72 A. Mason, *Association Football and English Society 1863–1915*, p. 72. In 1886 Bolton's wage bill was £15 11s a week in season, £4 in summer, by 1899 it was £80 and £60. J. Catton, *The Real Football*, p. 185.
73 A. Mason, *Association Football and English Society 1863–1915*, p. 149. In 1890 the Football League implemented a minimum admission charge of 6d to league games. S. Tischler, *Footballers and Businessmen. The Origins of Professional Soccer in England* (London: Holmes & Meier, 1981) p. 133.
74 A. Mason, *Association Football and English Society 1863–1915*, p. 140.
75 C. Alcock, *Football Annual* 1879/1880 (London, 1880) p. 104.
76 B. Corbett, *Football* (London: Longmans, 1907) p. 20.
77 S. Tischler, *Footballers and Businessmen. The Origins of Professional Soccer in England*, pp. 58–60.
78 J. Catton, *The Real Football*, p. 77.
79 J. Catton, *The Real Football*, pp. 69–77, p. 87.
80 J. Catton, *The Real Football*, p. 140.
81 A. Mason, *Association Football and English Society 1863–1915*, p. 143.

82 J. Catton, *The Real Football*, p. 142.
83 A. Mason, *Association Football and English Society 1863–1915*, p. 92.
84 A. Mason, *Association Football and English Society 1863–1915*, p. 95.
85 W. Vamplew, 'Playing for pay: the earnings of professional sportsmen in England 1870–1914'. In R. Cashman and M. Mckernan (eds) *Sport, Money, Morality and the Media* (New South Wales: Queensland, 1980) p. 119.
86 C. Alcock, *Football Annual* 1888/89 (London, 1889) p. 128.
87 J. Catton, *The Real Football*, p. 67.
88 As Tischler observes 'teams engaged in what came to be known as "poaching" – an ironic referring to the securing of labour in an open market'. The removal of restrictions meant that players such as Roston (Blackburn Rovers) were offered money by rival clubs not to play against them! S. Tischler, *Footballers and Businessmen. The Origins of Professional Soccer in England*, pp. 54–5.
89 S. Tischler, *Footballers and Businessmen. The Origins of Professional Soccer in England*, p. 61.
90 S. Tischler, *Footballers and Businessmen. The Origins of Professional Soccer in England*, p. 63.
91 A. Mason, *Association Football and English Society 1863–1915*, p. 97. W. Vamplew, 'Playing for pay: the earnings of professional sportsmen in England 1870–1914'. In R. Cashman and M. Mckernan (eds) *Sport, Money, Morality and the Media*, pp. 119–120.
92 C. Alcock, *The Football Annual* 1891/92 (London, 1892) p. 105.
93 C. Alcock, *The Football Annual* 1891/92 (London, 1892) p. 105.
94 C. Alcock, *The Football Annual* 1891/92 (London, 1892) p. 107.
95 J. Catton, *The Real Football*, p. 95.
96 J. Catton, *The Real Football*, p. 101.
97 J. Catton, *The Real Football*, p. 86.
98 S. Tischler, *Footballers and Businessmen. The Origins of Professional Soccer in England*, p. 95.
99 J. Catton, *The Real Football*, p. 92.
100 W. Vamplew, 'Playing for pay: the earnings of professional sportsmen in England 1870–1914'. In R. Cashman and M. Mckernan (eds) *Sport, Money, Morality and the Media*, p. 126.
101 W. Vamplew, 'Playing for pay: the earnings of professional sportsmen in England 1870–1914'. In R. Cashman and M. Mckernan (eds) *Sport, Money, Morality and the Media*, p. 124.
102 It would be interesting to know how the life expectancy of professional association footballers compared to other groups. The author was able to identify the life span of thirty-four of the thirty-seven professional chess players who were based in Britain during the period between 1830 and 1901. These appear to have enjoyed an unusual longevity, with life spans averaging sixty-five and a half years, at a time when the average male life expectancy was forty-six! A Harvey, 'Wie man kunst zu geld macht: Schach, profitum und der Viktorianer' *Kaissiber* xiv (2,000) p. 45.
103 A. Mason, *Association Football and English Society 1863–1915*, p. 42.
104 A. Mason, *Association Football and English Society 1863–1915*, pp. 46–7, 257.
105 S. Tischler, *Footballers and Businessmen. The Origins of Professional Soccer in England*, pp. 69–70.
106 S. Tischler, *Footballers and Businessmen. The Origins of Professional Soccer in England*, pp. 72–3.
107 S. Tischler, *Footballers and Businessmen. The Origins of Professional Soccer in England*, p. 78.
108 C. Alcock, *Football Annual* 1891–92 (London, 1892) pp. 1–2.
109 A. Collins, *Rugby's Great Split*, pp. 51, 55.
110 C. Alcock, *Football Annual* 1886–87 (London, 1887) pp. 51–2.
111 C. Alcock, *Football Annual* 1886–87 (London, 1887) p. 52.
112 C. Alcock, *Football Annual* 1886–87 (London, 1887) p. 160.

113 H. Vassall, 'Rugby Union Football', *English Illustrated Magazine* vii (1889–90) p. 435.
114 M. Shearman, *Athletics and Football*, p. 368.
115 A. Collins, *Rugby's Great Split*, pp. 140–4.
116 A. Collins, *Rugby's Great Split*, p. 148.
117 *RFU Handbook 1894–5* (London, 1895) p. 6.
118 *RFU Handbook 1894–5* (London, 1895) pp. 45, 69.
119 *RFU Handbook 1894–5* (London, 1895) p. 5.
120 *RFU Handbook 1894–5* (London, 1895) pp. 6–7.
121 A. Collins, *Rugby's Great Split*, pp. 162–5.
122 A. Mason, *Sport in Britain* (London: Faber, 1988) p. 39.
123 A. Collins, *Rugby's Great Split*, pp. 168–9.
124 A. Collins, *Rugby's Great Split*, p. 162.
125 A. Collins, *Rugby's Great Split*, pp. 171, 175.
126 M. Shearman, *Football*, p. 275.
127 A. Collins, *Rugby's Great Split*, p. 176.

9 Conclusions: the real history of the creation of modern football?

1 A. Harvey, *The Evolution of British Sporting Culture 1793–1850* (unpublished DPhil Oxford University 1995) pp. 224–90, see particularly the rules of wrestling on pp. 228–9.
2 The public schools had considerable influence on the varieties of football that evolved up in certain foreign countries as is shown in the appendix.

Appendix: football as an international game

1 Unless otherwise stated the information is drawn from G. Oliver, *The Guinness Record of World Soccer* (Enfield, Guinness, 1988).
2 J. Catton (London, Sands 1900) p. 207.
3 *Field* 13 August 1864. These were what would be formally constituted as the 'Melbourne Rules' in May 1859 and eventually became 'Australian Rules football'. I am grateful to Dr Gary Magee for this information. The author is very puzzled about the relationship between football in Britain and the code of the game that became Australian football. Australian football had no offside rule, a fact that made it profoundly different to every football code that appeared in Britain during the 1860s. The following codes made it illegal to play a ball that was passed from behind you: Eton, Harrow, Marlborough, Rugby, Shrewsbury, Winchester. It was legal to play a ball that had been passed from behind you providing that there were at least three opposing players between you and their goal: Charterhouse, FA, Westminster. There was only one code, Sheffield, that made it legal to play a ball that had been passed from behind you providing there was at least one opponent between you and their goal. A discussion of the role of the British in creating Australian rules football can be found in G. Hibbins, 'The Cambridge connection: The English origin of Australian rules football'. In J. Mangan (ed.) *The Cultural Bond: Sport, Empire, Society* (London: Frank Cass, 1992) pp. 108–127.
4 *Bell's Life in London*: 16 November 1862; 1 December 1866.
5 See Figure A.1.
6 J. Catton (London: Sands, 1900) p. 204.
7 J. Catton (London: Sands, 1900) p. 208.
8 D. Twydell, *The Little Red Book of Chinese Football* (Harefield: Yore, 1994) pp. 29–30. Strictly speaking, records of football play in China exist from 32 BC.
9 *Field* 13 August 1864.

10 *North China Herald* 22 December 1868, p. 626. A match was played between Tea and Silk vs The World.
11 J. Catton, p. 209.
12 D. Signy, *A Pictorial History of Football* (London: Hamlyn, 1969) p. 36.
13 *Field* 19 December 1863; 16 January 1864; 23 January 1864.
14 G. Hare, *Football in France: A Cultural History* (London: Berg Publishers, 2003) pp. 16–19.
15 *Bell's Life in London* 7 November 1863. Of course, this was not the first ball game played in Greece. The ancient Greeks called their game *episkyres*. D. Signy, *A Pictorial History of Football* (London: Hamlyn, 1969) p. 12.
16 *Bell's Life in London* 9 February 1862.
17 *Illustrated Sporting and Dramatic News* 13 November 1875 (see Figure A.2).
18 *Illustrated Sporting and Dramatic News* 21 October 1893 (see Figure A.3). The army assisted the dissemination of football throughout Africa and Asia.
19 B. Majumdar, 'Sport in Asia: Soccer in South Asia – Review Essay', *IJHS* 19:4 (2002) pp. 204–10.
20 The ancient Romans had a ball game called *harpustum*. D. Signy, *A Pictorial History of Football*, p. 12. Naturally, the clubs established in the nineteenth century were unrelated to this.
21 D. Signy, *A Pictorial History of Football*, p. 21.
22 *Field* 28 November 1863.
23 A very amusing account of this is provided by G. Oliver, *The Guinness Record of World Soccer* (Enfield: Guinness, 1988) p. 546.
24 D. Signy, *A Pictorial History of Football*, p. 34.
25 J. Catton (London: Sands, 1900) p. 206.
26 D. Signy, *A Pictorial History of Football*, p. 34.
27 *Field* 22 December 1866.
28 *Bell's Life in London* 20 December 1846.
29 J. Mangan and R. Park (eds) *From Fair Sex to Feminism* (London: Frank Cass, 1987) p. 60.
30 *Strand Magazine* 13 (1897) p. 285.

Bibliography

Manuscript sources

(A) Bodleian Library, Oxford
  (1) John Johnson Collection
    Sports (Boxes 1–16) and Large Folders (1–2)
  (2) Harding Collection
    Harding Murder Sheets II–III B 9 (262–83)
  (3) *Police Reports* (*Proctors Records*) (1829–31, 1835–37, 1844)

(B) Football Association (25 Soho Sq, London, W1D 4FA)
  FA Minute Books 1863–74

(C) Rugby Football Union (Twickenham)
  RFU Minute Books 1871

(D) Lancashire County Record Office (Preston)
  Letter prohibiting quoits on the Black Swans premises 1840 (DDPr 130/21)
  Orders of JP's to constables and overseers concerning playing at leaping, football and quoits on the Sabbath 1727–1851 (DDNw 9/12)
  Order of suppression of games on Sundays, Fulwood, Preston 1801 (PR 2021)

(E) Public Record Office
  HO 41
  HO 45
  HO 52

(F) Sheffield City Archives (52 Shoreham Street, Sheffield, S1 4SP)
  Football Club Records (FCR 1–5, 10–11)

(G) Westminster School (London)
  Town Boy Ledger 1815–62

Printed sources

Primary sources

Government papers

A Bill to prevent bear baiting and other cruel practices 4 March 1825.

Act to prevent the malicious wounding and wanton cruelty to animals 9 June 1809 (651).

An Act for the more effectual prevention of cruelty to animals 19 July 1848.

Bill for preventing the practice of bull-baiting and bull-running (1801–02, (70) I. 251).

Bill to alter applications of penalties for offenses against Highway Laws (1818).
Bill to consolidate and amend the several laws relating to cruel and improper treatment of Animals, and so on (1835, II [93] 27 March). Amended by Committee 5 June 1835 (107). Amended on recommitment 11 August 1835 (123).
Bills to amend Acts for the preservation of Public Highways as rules to notices of appeals against diverting public highways (1814–15).
Bills to amend Acts for preservation of Highways in England by authorising appointment of special surveyors (1816).
Bills to consolidate and amend laws relating to highways in England (1830–1) (1831).
Bill to consolidate and amend several laws relating to the cruel and improper treatment of animals and mischiefs arising from the driving of cattle, and to make other provisions in regard hereto 18 April 1832.
Bill to prevent cruel and improper treatment of cattle 6 May 1825.
Children's Employment Commission on Mines (pp. 1842).
Cruelty to Animals Prevention Bill 9 May 1849.
Hansard Parliamentary Debates:
xxix (1835) July 14.
cvi (1849) June 13.
Report from the Select Committee on Gaming (pp. vi, 1844).
Report of the Select Committee on Newspaper Stamps (pp. xvii [1] 1851, [558]).
Report of the Select Committee on Public Walks and Places of Exercise (1833).

Newspapers and periodicals

The Annals of the Sporting and Fancy Gazette (1822–28).
An Historical List of All Horse-Matches Run (1729, 1749).
Bell's Life in London (1822–50).
Bell's Weekly Messenger (1796–1822).
Cobbett's Annual Register (1802).
The Exchange Herald (Manchester) (1820–26).
The Era (1838–50).
The Football Annual (1867–1901).
The Illustrated London News (1843, 1850).
Jackson's Oxford Journal (1793–1850).
Manchester and Salford Advertiser (1840–48).
Manchester Examiner and Times (1848–50).
The Manchester Mercury and Harrop's General Advertiser (1793–1811, 1815–19).
The Meteor (Rugby) (1876, 1880).
The New Rugbean (1860–61).
New Sporting Magazine (1831–45).
News of the World (1843, 1845).
Notes And Queries (1880–81, 1885, 1891, 1900, 1904, 1909, 1931). The periodical has an excellent index.
Penny Magazine (1833, 1839).
Pierce Egan's Life in London (1824).
Poor Man's Guardian (1831–32).
The Racing Calendar (1793–1850).
Reynold's Weekly Newspaper (1850).
The Sporting Kalendar (1751–57).
The Sporting Magazine (1792–1850).

Sporting Review (1840)
Sportsman and Veterinary Journal (1835–37).
Sunday Times (1830, 1840).
Thacker's Courser's Annual (1842–50).
The Times (1793–1816, 1825, 1835, 1845, 1850).
Tom Spring's Life In London (1840–42). The paper was nothing to do with the boxer Tom Spring.
The Weekly Dispatch (1801–04, 1814, 1817–22).
Wheeler's Manchester Chronicle (1812–14, 1826–39).
The World (1787–91).

Books

C. Alcock, *Football: our Winter Game* (London: Field, 1874).
A. Alison, *Principles of the Common Law of Scotland* (Edinburgh: Cadell, 1832).
W. Andrews, *Old Church Lore* (Hull: Andrews & Co, 1891).
An Old Colleger, *Eton of Old* (London: Griffith, 1892).
A. Arbuthnot, *Memories of Rugby and India* (London: Allen and Unwin, 1910).
W. D. Arnold, *The 1st Day of the 6th Match* (Rugby: Crossley and Billington, 1851). (The book appeared anonymously simply being credited to a Rugbeian.)
G. Russell-Barker, *Westminster School Register* (London: Macmillan, 1883).
D. Barton, *History of the Borough of Bury and Neighbourhood* (Bury: Wardleworth, 1874).
B. Bird, *Barney the Irishman* (Sheffield: J. Pearce, 1854).
J. Brand, *Observations on Popular Antiquities* (Newcastle: J. Johnson, 1810).
R. Burn, *Justice of the Peace* (London: H. Miller, 1869).
R. Chambers, *Book of Days* (Edinburgh: Chambers, 1888).
L. Cust, *History of Eton College* (Glasgow and London: Spottiswode and Co, 1899).
G. Fisher, *Annals of Shrewsbury School* (London: Methuen, 1899).
H. Fishwick, *The History of the Parish of Kirkham in the County of Lancaster* (Lancaster: Cheetham Society, 1874).
H. Fishwick, *History of the Parish of Rochdale in the County of Lancaster* (Rochdale: Cheetham Society, 1889).
Mrs Gaskell, *Mary Barton* (Halifax: Ryburn, 1847).
Mrs Gaskell, *The Life of Charlotte Bronte* (Halifax: Ryburn, 1857).
W. Hone, *The Everyday Book* (London: Tegg and Co, 1827).
W. Hone, *The Table Book* (London: Tegg and Co, 1827).
W. Hone, *The Year Book* (London: Tegg and Co, 1832).
N. L. Jackson, *Association Football* (London: George Newnes, 1899).
A. J. Lawrence, *Rugby School Register 1675–1849* (London: J. S. Crossley, 1889).
A. J. Lawrence, *The Origins of Rugby Football* (Rugby: J. S. Crossley, 1897).
A. Leach, *History of Winchester College* (London: Duckworth, 1899).
W. Litt, *Wrestliana* (Whitehaven: R. Gibson, 1823).
F. Marshall, *Football: the Rugby Union Game* (London: Cassell & Co, 1892).
E. Moor, *Suffolk Words and Phrases* (Woodbridge: J. Loder, 1823).
The New Statistical Account of Scotland (Edinburgh: Blackwoods, 1845).
Old Rugbaen, *Recollections of Rugby* (London: Hamilton & Adams, 1848). This was actually written by C. H. Newmarch; see, *Notes And Queries* (Jan/June 1909) p. 355.
W. Rouse, *History of Rugby School* (London: Duckworth, 1898).
C. Sharp, Sir, *Diary of Jacob Bee of Durham* (Durham: Surttees Soc, vol. 118, 1910).

S. Sergeaunt, Annals of Westminster School (London: Methuen, 1898).
M. Shearman, *Athletics and Football* (London: Longmans, 1889).
H. Stapylton, *Eton School Lists* (London and Edinburgh: E. P. Williams, 1885).
Statistical Account of Scotland (1973), East Ardsley.
F. Stokes (ed.) (1765) *The Bletchley Diary of Reverent William Cole* 1931 edition (London: Constable and Co).
Stonehenge, *Manual of British Sports* (London: Routledge & Co, 1856).
J. Strutt, *The Sports and Pastimes of the People of England* (London: William Reeves, 1801).
J. Thorne, *Handbook for the Environs of London* (London: J. Murray, 1876).
D. Walker, *Defence Exercises* (London: Thomas Harris, 1837).
D. Walker, *Games and Sports* (London: Thomas Hurst, 1836).
E. Welch, *The Harrow School Register* (London: Harrow on the Hill, 1894).
W. White, *General Directory of Sheffield* (Sheffield: Robert Leader, 1849, 1852).
J. M. Wilson, *Imperial Gazetteer of England and Wales* (Edinburgh: Chambers, 1869).
S. Williams, *The Boys' Treasury of Sports, Pastimes and Recreations* (London: D. Bogue, 1847).
W. Wood, *New England's Prospects* (London: John Bellamie, 1634).
C. Wordsworth, *Annals of my Early Life* (London: Longmans, 1891).

Articles

A. G. G., 'A big side at Rugby', *London Society* 12 (1867).
C. Alcock, 'Association football', *English Illustrated Magazine* 8 (1890).
'A football match', *All the Year Round* 66 (Jan/June 1890).
'Are we an athletic people?', *New Review* 16 (1897).
J. D. C (artwright) 'Football at Rugby, Eton and Harrow', *London Society* 5 (1864).
Chambers Information for the People 84 (1842) p. 544.
W. Lucas Collins, 'School and college life: its romance and reality', *Blackwoods* 89 (1861).
J. Doxey, 'Wirksworth football play', *The Reliquary* 9 (1868).
M. Dutt, 'The last camping match', *Badminton Magazine* 9 (1899).
M. Ensor, 'The football madness', *Contemporary Review* (1898).
Eton College Magazine 7 (1832).
'Football', *Chambers Journal* (1864).
T. Ford, 'Tom Brown's schooldays', *Quarterly Review* 102 (1857).
'Games', *Chambers Journal* (1864).
R. Graham, 'The early history of the FA', *Badminton Magazine of Sports and Pastimes* 8 (1899).
H. Hutchinson, 'Evolution of games at ball', *Blackwoods* 153 (1893).
R. Macgregor, 'Old football gossip', *Belgravia* 34 (1878).
H. Maxwell, 'Games', *Blackwoods* 152 (1892).
'Popular customs and superstitions in Herefordshire', *Gentleman's Magazine* 92 (1822).
'Professionals in English sport', *Saturday Review* 14 April (1888).
'Review of Tom Brown's Schooldays', *Saturday Review* 3 October (1857).
F. Stephens, 'Review of Tom Brown's Schooldays', 107, *Edinburgh Review* (1858).
'The wall game', *Saturday Review* 56:1 December (1883).

Secondary sources

Books

R. Arrowsmith, *Charterhouse Register 1769–1872* (Godalming: Philmore, 1974).
J. Auden, *Shrewsbury School Register* (Oswestry: Marshall & Co, 1964).

P. Bailey, *Leisure and Class in Victorian England* (London: Routledge, 1978).
J. Barber, *The Story of Oakham School* (Wymondham: Sycamore Press, 1984).
G. Best, *Mid-Victorian Britain 1851–1875* (London: Weidenfeld, 1971).
P. Borsay, *The English Urban Renaissance* (Oxford: Clarendon, 1989).
D. Brailsford, *A Taste for Diversions. Sport in Georgian England* (Cambridge: Lutterworth, 1999).
A. Briggs, *Victorian People 1851–1867* (Chicago: Chicago University Press, 1972).
W. Burn, *The Age of Equipoise* (London: Allen and Unwin, 1964).
B. Butler, *The Illustrated History of the F.A. Cup* (London: Headline, 1998).
R. Cashman and M. McKernan (eds) *Sport in History* (Queensland: New South Wales University Press, 1979).
R. Cashman and M. Mckernan (eds) *Sport, Money, Morality and the Media* (Queensland: New South Wales University Press, 1980).
J. Catton, *The Real Football* (London: Sands and Co, 1900).
A. Collins, *Rugby's Great Split* (London: Frank Cass, 1998).
H. Cunningham, *Leisure in the Industrial Revolution 1780–1880* (London: Croom Helm, 1980).
G. Davies, *Charterhouse in London* (London: Murray, 1921).
B. Delves, 'Popular recreation and social conflict in Derby 1800–1850'. In E. Yeo and S. Yeo (eds) *Popular Culture and Class Conflict 1790–1914* (London: Harvester, 1981).
E. Dunning and K. Sheard, *Barbarians, Gentlemen and Players* (Oxford: Martin Robertson, 1979).
E. Ereaut, *Richmond F.C.* (London: Howlett & Sons, 1926).
C. Evers, *Rugby* (London and Glasgow: Blackie & Sons, 1939).
N. Fishwick, *From Clegg to Clegg House* (Sheffield: Clegg House, 1986).
J. Golby and A. Purdue, *The Civilization of the Crowd. Popular Culture in England 1750–1900* (London: Batsford, 1984).
J. Goulstone, *Football's Secret History* (London: Catford, 2001).
G. Hare, *Football in France. A Cultural History* (London: Berg Publishers, 2003).
B. Harrison, *Drink and the Victorians* (London: Faber and Faber, 1971).
A. Harvey, *The Beginnings of a Commercial Sporting Culture in Britain 1793–1850* (Aldershot: Ashgate, 2004).
G. Hibbins, 'The Cambridge connection: The English origin of Australian rules football'. In J. Mangan (ed.) *The Cultural Bond: Sport, Empire, Society* (London: Frank Cass, 1992) pp. 108–27.
R. Hine, *The History of Hitchin* (London: Allen & Unwin, 1929).
R. Holt, *Sport and the British: A Modern History* (Oxford: Clarendon, 1989).
R. Holt, *Sport and the Working Class in Britain* (Manchester: Manchester University Press, 1990).
J. Honey, *Tom Brown's Universe* (London: Millington, 1977).
N. Jackson, *Sporting Days and Sporting Ways* (London: Hurst & Blackett, 1932).
G. Jarvie and G. Walker (eds) *Scottish Sport in the Making of the Nation. Ninety Minute Patriots* (Leicester: Leicester University, 1994).
M. Judd, 'Popular culture and the London fairs'. In J. Walton and J. Walvin (eds) *Leisure in Britain* (Manchester: Manchester University Press, 1983).
R. A(usten) L(eigh), *Upon St Andrews Day 1841–1901* (Eton, 1902).
J. Lowerson and J. Myerscough, *Time to Spare in Victorian England* (London: Harvester, 1977).
H. C. Maxwell Lyte, *A History of Eton College* (London: Macmillan, 1911).
E. Mack, *Public Schools and British Opinion 1780–1860* (London: Methuen, 1938).

K. Macklin, *History of Rugby League Football* (London: Stanley Paul, 1962).
J. Macrory, *Running with the Ball* (London: Collins Willow, 1991).
F. Markham, *Recollections of a Town Boy at Westminster School* (London: Edward Arnold, 1903).
F. Magoun, *History of Football* (Bochum-Langendreer, 1938).
R. Malcolmson, *Popular Recreations in English Society 1700–1850* (Cambridge: Cambridge University Press, 1973).
J. Mangan, *Athleticism in the Victorian and Edwardian Public School* (Cambridge: Cambridge University Press, 1981).
J. Mangan and R. Park (eds) *From 'Fair sex' to Feminism* (London: Frank Cass, 1987).
J. Mangan (ed.) *Pleasure, Profit and Proselytism: British Culture and Sport at Home and Abroad 1700–1914* (London: Frank Cass, 1988).
J. Mangan, 'Social Darwinism and English upper class education'. In *Aspects of the Social History of Sport. Proceedings of British Society of Sport History* (Liverpool: University of Liverpool, 1982).
J. Mangan (ed.) *The Cultural Bond: Sport, Empire, Society* (London: Frank Cass, 1992).
M. Marples, *A History of Football* (London: Secker & Warburg, 1954).
A. Mason, *Association Football and English Society 1863–1915* (London: Harvester, 1980).
A. Mason, *Sport in Britain* (London: Faber, 1988).
A. Mason, 'Sport'. In J. Dan Vann and R. T. Van Ardsel (eds) *Victorian Periodicals and Victorian Society* (Toronto: Modern Languages Association, 1994).
A. Metcalfe, 'Potshare bowling in the mining communities of East Northumberland 1800–1914'. In R. Holt (ed.) *Sport and the Working Class in Britain* (Manchester: Manchester University Press, 1990).
B. Mitchell, *British Historical Statistics* (Cambridge: Cambridge University Press, 1988).
R. Mitchison, 'Scotland'. In F. M. L. Thompson (ed.) *The Cambridge Social History of Britain*, i (Cambridge: Cambridge University Press, 1990).
D. Murray, *Memories of the Old College of Glasgow* (Glasgow: Malehouse, Jackson & Co, 1927).
J. B. Oldham, *A History of Shrewsbury School* (Oxford: Wilding & Son, 1952).
G. Oliver, *The Guinness Record of World Soccer* (Enfield: Guinness, 1988).
O. I. Owen, *History of the Rugby Football Union* (London: Playfair, 1955).
R. Phillips, *The Story of Scottish Rugby* (Edinburgh: Foulis, 1925).
S. Kendall Phillips, 'Primitive methodist confrontation with popular sports'. In R. Cashman and M. Mckernan (eds) *Sport, Money, Morality and the Media* (Queensland: University press, 1980).
R. Poole, 'Oldham wakes'. In J. Walton and J. Walvin (eds) *Leisure in Britain* (Manchester: Manchester University press, 1983).
R. Poole and J. Walton, 'The Lancashire wakes in the nineteenth century'. In R. Storch (ed.) *Popular Culture and Custom in Nineteenth Century England* (Manchester: Manchester University press, 1982).
D. A. Reid, 'Interpreting the festival calendar: wakes and fairs as carnivals'. In R. Storch (ed.) *Popular Culture and Custom in Nineteenth Century England* (London: Croom Helm, 1982).
J. Rule, 'Methodism, popular beliefs and village culture in Cornwall 1800–1850'. In R. Storch (ed.) *Popular Culture and Custom in Nineteenth Century England* (London: Croom Helm, 1982).
J. Sambrook, *The Eighteenth Century. The Intellectual and Cultural Context of English Literature 1700–1789* (London: Longman, 1986).
M. Shearman (ed.) *Football* (London: Oakley & Co, 1904).
D. Signy, *A Pictorial History of Football* (London: Hutchinson, 1969).

G. Solly, *The Rugby School Register* (Rugby: George Over, 1933).

M. Speak, 'Social stratification and participation in sport'. In J. Mangan (ed.) *Pleasure, Profit and Proselytism. British Culture and Sport at Home and Abroad 1700–1914* (London: Frank Cass, 1988).

R. Storch, 'The problem of working-class leisure. Some roots of middle-class moral reform in the industrial north; 1825–1850'. In A. Donajgrodzki (ed.) *Social Control in Nineteenth Century Britain* (London: Croom Helm, 1977).

R. Storch, ' "Please to remember the 5th of November". Conflict, solidarity and public order in southern England 1815–1900'. In R. Storch (ed.) *Popular Culture and Custom in Nineteenth Century England* (London: Croom Helm, 1980).

R. Storch, 'Persistence and change in nineteenth century popular culture'. In R. Storch (ed.) *Popular Culture and Custom in Nineteenth Century England* (London: Croom Helm, 1982).

R. Storch (ed.) *Popular Culture and Custom in Nineteenth Century England* (London: Croom Helm, 1982).

F. M. L. Thompson (ed.) *The Cambridge Social History of Britain 1750–1950* (Cambridge: Cambridge University Press, 1990).

S. Tischler, *Footballers and Businessmen. The Origins of Professional Football in England* (London: Holmes & Meier, 1981).

B. Trescatheric, *Sport and Leisure in Victorian Barrow* (Barrow: Mongenai, 1983).

D. Twydell, *The Little Red Book of Chinese Football* (Harefield: Yore, 1974).

W. Vamplew, *Pay up and Play the Game. Professional Sport in Britain 1875–1914* (Cambridge: Cambridge University Press, 1988).

W. Vamplew, 'Playing for pay: the earnings of professional sportsmen in England 1870–1914'. In R. Cashman and M. McKernan (eds) *Sport, money, Morality and the Media* (Queensland: New South Wales University Press, 1980).

W. Vamplew, 'Sport and industrialisation: an economic interpretation of the changes in popular sport in nineteenth century England'. In J. Mangan (ed.) *Pleasure, Profit and Proselytism. British Culture and Sport at Home and Abroad 1700–1914* (London: Frank Cass, 1988).

J. Vann Dan and R. T. Van Ardsel, *Victorian Periodicals: A Guide to Researchers* (New York: Heffer & Sons, 1978).

J. Wainwright, *Winchester College: A Register 1836–1907* (Winchester: Longmans, 1907).

F. Walters, History of Sheffield Football Club (Sheffield: Allen & Unwin, 1957).

J. Walton and R. Poole, 'The Lancashire Wakes in the nineteenth century'. In R. Storch (ed.) *Culture and Custom in Nineteenth Century England* (London: Croom Helm, 1982).

J. Walvin, *The People's Game* (London: Allen Lane, 1975).

J. Fisher Williams, *Harrow* (London: Great Public Schools, 1901).

A. R. Wright, *British Calendar Customs in England* (London: William Glasher, 1940).

J. Wright (ed.) *The English Dialect Dictionary* (London: Henry Frowde, 1902).

E. Wrigley and R. Schofield, *The Population History of England 1541–1871* (Cambridge: Cambridge University Press, 1981).

E. Wrigley (ed.) *Nineteenth Century Society* (Cambridge: Cambridge University Press, 1972).

E. Yeo and S. Yeo, *Popular Culture and Class Conflict* (London: Harvester, 1981).

G. M. Young, *Early Victorian England* (Oxford: Oxford University Press, 1934).

P. M. Young, *Bolton Wanderers* (London: Stanley Paul, 1961).

P. M. Young, *Football in Sheffield* (London: Stanley Paul, 1962).

P. M. Young, *A History of British Football* (London: Stanley Paul, 1968).

Articles

R. Anderson, 'Sport in the Scottish universities', *IJHS* 4:2 (1987).

T. Arnold, 'A talk with J. J. Bentley', *Windsor Magazine* 15 (Dec 1901/May 1902).

W. Baker, 'The making of a working class football culture in Victorian England', *JSH* 13:2 (1979).

T. Bamford, 'Public Schools and social class, 1801–1850', *British Journal of Sociology* xii (1961).

D. Brailsford, 'Religion and sport in eighteenth century England', *IJHS* 1:2 (1984).

D. Brailsford, 'Sporting days in eighteenth century England', *Journal of Sports History* 9:3 (1982).

T. Chandler, 'Emergent athleticism: games in the English Public Schools 1800–1860', *IJHS* 5:3 (1988).

T. Chandler, 'Games at Oxbridge and the Public Schools, 1830–1880: the diffusion of an innovation', *IJHS* 8:2 (1991).

N. Crafts, 'British economic growth, 1700–1831. A review of the evidence', *EcHR* 36:2 (1983).

Devon and Cornwall Notes and Queries 10 (1918–19) 113–14.

E. Dunning, 'Something of a curate's egg: comments on Adrian Harvey's "An Epoch in the Annals of National Sport"', *IJHS* 18:4 (2001).

E. Dunning and G. Curry, 'The curate's egg scrambled again: comments of the Curate's Egg Put Back Together', *IJHS* 18:4 (2002).

A. Harvey, 'An epoch in the annals of national sport: football in Sheffield and the creation of modern soccer and rugby', *IJHS* 18:4 (2001).

A. Harvey, 'Curate's egg pursued by red herrings: a reply to Eric Dunning and Graham Curry', *IJHS* 21:1 (2004).

A. Harvey, 'Football's missing link: the real story of the evolution of modern football', *The European Sports History Review* 1 (1999).

A. Harvey, 'Schach, profitum und die viktorianer', *Kaissiber* 14 (2000). This work was translated from English into German by Stefan Bücker.

A. Harvey, 'The curate's egg put back together: comments on Eric Dunning's response to "An Epoch in the Annals of National Sport"', IJHS 19:4 (2002).

E. Hopkins, 'Working hours and conditions during the industrial revolution: a reappraisal', *EcHR* 35:1 (1982).

P. Lindert and J. Williamson, 'English workers' living standards during the industrial revolution: a new look', *EcHR* 36:1 (1983). This was replied to by M. Flinn, *EcHR* 37:1 (1984) accompanied by a rejoinder from Lindert and Williamson.

J. Maguire, 'Images of manliness and competing ways of living in late Victorian and Edwardian Britain', *IJHS* 3:3 (1986).

W. Mandle, 'Games people played – cricket and football in England and Victoria in the late nineteenth century', *Historical Studies* 15 (1973).

A. Mason, 'Football and the historians', *IJHS* 5:1 (1988).

B. Majumdar, 'Sport in Asia: soccer in South Asia: review essay', *IJHS* 19:4 (2002).

D. Reid, 'Folk football, the aristocracy and cultural change. A critique of Dunning and Sheard', *IJHS* 5:2 (1988).

D. A. Reid, 'The decline of Saint Monday 1766–1876', *Past and Present* 71 (1976).

R. M. Ruck, 'Football in the early "seventies"', *Royal Engineers Journal* 42 (December 1928).

'Rugby football in the sixties', *Cornhill Magazine* (November 1922).

D. Russell, 'Sporadic and curious: the emergence of rugby and soccer zones in Yorkshire and Lancashire 1860–1914', *IJHS* 5:2 (1988).

K. Sandiford, 'Amateurs and professionals in Victorian county cricket', *Albion* 15:1 (1983).

R. Storch, 'A plague of blue locusts', *International Review of Social History* 20 (1975).

R. Storch, 'The policeman as domestic missionary: urban discipline and popular culture in northern England 1850–1880', *JSH* 9:4 (1976).

R. Sturdee, 'The ethics of football', *WR* 159 (1903).

N. Tranter, 'Popular culture and the industrial revolution in Scotland: the evidence of the Statistical Accounts', *IJHS* 4:1 (1987).

N. Tranter, 'The social and occupational structure of sport in central Scotland during the nineteenth century', *IJHS* 4:3 (1987).

W. Vamplew, 'Not playing the game: unionism and British professional sport 1870–1914', *IJHS* 2:3 (1985).

W. Vamplew, see also K. Sandiford.

G. Watson, 'Shrove-tide football', *Border Magazine* 25 (Feb 1920).

C. Wright, 'Before Tom Brown: education and the sporting ethos in early nineteenth century', *Journal of Educational Administration and History* 9:1 (1977).

Unpublished works

K. Allan, 'Recreations and amusements of the industrial working class in the second quarter of the nineteenth century, with special reference to Lancashire' (University of Manchester MA Dissertation, 1947).

T. Chandler, 'Origins of athletic games in the English public school 1800–1880' (Stanford University, PhD, 1984).

J. Goulstone, 'Historical reality vs Academic myth: the social origins of modern football'. (This work was a typescript that was deposited in the British Library. The work bears the imprint 1998.)

J. Goulstone, 'Modern sport: its origins and development through two centuries'. (This was a typescript that was deposited in the British Library. The work bears the imprint 1974.)

A. Harvey, 'Leisure in the bleak age' (Birkbeck College, London University, MA Dissertation 1990).

N. Rhind. Francis Maule Campbell. (This was a typescript that bears the date 1995. I am grateful to Piers Morgan for making me aware of this and Neil Rhind for giving me permission to quote from it.)

M. B. Smith, 'The growth and development of popular entertainment's and pastimes in Lancashire cotton towns 1830–1870' (Lancaster University, MLitt, 1970).

Index